Francis Beatty Thurber

Coffee: From plantation to cup

A brief history of coffee production and consumption

Francis Beatty Thurber

Coffee: From plantation to cup
A brief history of coffee production and consumption

ISBN/EAN: 9783337146962

Printed in Europe, USA, Canada, Australia, Japan

Cover: Foto ©Andreas Hilbeck / pixelio.de

More available books at **www.hansebooks.com**

COFFEE:

FROM

PLANTATION TO CUP.

A BRIEF HISTORY OF

COFFEE PRODUCTION AND CONSUMPTION.

WITH AN

APPENDIX

CONTAINING LETTERS WRITTEN DURING A TRIP TO THE COFFEE PLANTATIONS OF THE EAST, AND THROUGH THE COFFEE CONSUMING COUNTRIES OF EUROPE.

BY

FRANCIS B. THURBER.

AMERICAN GROCER PUBLISHING ASSOCIATION,
28 AND 30 WEST BROADWAY, NEW YORK.
1881.

Trow's
Printing and Bookbinding Company,
201-213 *East 12th Street*,
NEW YORK.

TO THE MAN AT POUGHKEEPSIE,

WHO KEEPS THE RAILROAD REFRESHMENT ROOMS,

THIS BOOK IS RESPECTFULLY

Dedicated.

I DO NOT KNOW HIS NAME, BUT YEAR IN AND YEAR OUT HE GIVES THE PUBLIC AN IDEAL CUP OF COFFEE, AND, ON THE PRINCIPLE OF "ACT WELL YOUR PART, THERE ALL THE HONOR LIES," HE IS ENTITLED TO THE PUBLIC'S BEST THANKS. PERHAPS IN THE FAR DISTANT FUTURE SOME OTHER RAILROAD BUFFET PROPRIETOR MAY FIND THAT A GOOD CUP OF COFFEE ADDS TO, RATHER THAN DIMINISHES, THE CHANCES FOR GATHERING IN A GOODLY NUMBER OF SHEKELS, AND BE PROMPTED TO GO AND DO LIKEWISE. THERE IS EVEN A POSSIBILITY THAT THE ENGLISH STEAMSHIP LINES, WHICH NOW ENJOY A PRE-EMINENCE FOR BAD COFFEE, MAY LEARN THAT SOMETHING BESIDES GOOD SEAMANSHIP WILL ATTRACT BUSINESS, AND WHEN "THAT NEW ZEALANDER" APPEARS UPON THE SCENE THERE MAY NO LONGER BE EXTANT ANY SUCH REPROACH AS "SON OF A SEA COOK." I KNOW OF NO PERSON SO WELL ENTITLED TO THE HONOR OF THIS DEDICATION, AND SO THIS WORK IS ADMIRINGLY AND RESPECTFULLY INSCRIBED

TO THE MAN AT POUGHKEEPSIE,

ONE OF THE CHOSEN FEW WHO KNOW HOW TO MAKE

A GOOD CUP OF COFFEE.

PREFACE.

I HAVE endeavored to tell the story of coffee in a practical way, so as to make the information valuable alike to consumers and dealers. I have been induced to add to the innumerable company of books from the fact that there seemed to be a want for a work which, besides furnishing statistical and historical matter relative to the coffee-plant, should give the reader a thorough knowledge of the characteristics of the world's coffee supply, and the mode of preserving and preparing the coffee-bean so as to best secure all those qualities which make coffee the favorite beverage with most of the civilized nations of the earth. My reliance has been chiefly upon twenty years' experience as a dealer, and such information as was to be gathered from a trip around the world. I have to acknowledge my indebtedness to many books for facts regarding coffee culture, and historical matter relating thereto, and also to a large circle of business acquaintances for valuable statistical information. To mention them specifically is hardly possible, and would be of little interest to the general reader. It is, however, but just that I should here recognize the many courtesies and favors rendered me by General Joseph Nimmo, Jr., Chief of

is more than likely that some defects will be noticed, and many infelicities of style or expression; and were it not for my confidence in the good nature and generosity of those who are likely to read the following pages, I scarcely could have summoned courage to send them forth. At least I have the satisfaction of having made an honest effort in the direction of making the breakfast tables of the land the source of greater enjoyment, notwithstanding that I may have brushed aside some fond fancies or revealed trade secrets that others would have jealously guarded.

CONTENTS.

CHAPTER VIII.

CHAPTER IX.

CHAPTER X.

CHAPTER XI.

CHAPTER XII.

CHAPTER XIII.

CHAPTER XIV.

CHAPTER XV.

CHAPTER XVI.

CHAPTER XVII.

APPENDIX.

"NOTES BY THE WAY."

ILLUSTRATIONS.

COFFEE:

FROM

PLANTATION TO CUP.

CHAPTER I.

INTRODUCTORY.

COFFEE, a most important item in our domestic economy, is entitled to more attention than it generally receives. At a majority of breakfast tables, "if the coffee is good everything is good," a fact so significant in itself that no other argument is needed to prove the all-importance of uniform success in the preparation of this one article.

Books innumerable have been written about this famous berry. It has been made the subject of investigation by savants; government commissions have made voluminous reports upon the soil, climate, and varieties of the plant desirable for production; yet little attention seems to have been given to what is really the most important branch of the subject, viz., the selection and treatment of the bean subsequent to production, so as to ensure with a proper degree of certainty, the development of its admirable qualities in that much-to-be-desired article, a good cup of coffee. In issuing this work, therefore, while including some facts of general interest relative to production, I have given greater prominence to those which relate to consumption, and are likely to prove of immediate interest and benefit to dealers in coffee as well as coffee-drinkers.

The present undertaking originated in my love for a good cup of coffee, and a curiosity to know why there existed such a wide range in the quality of the article at my own table, as well as at others. I began by investigating the mysteries of the kitchen; and this led to an examination into the different ways of making the beverage, including the use of many patent coffee-pots; the degree of fineness to which the coffee should be ground; the method and extent of roasting; the deterioration in quality after roasting; the best receptacle for the preservation of the aroma; and finally, in connection with my own business, a study of the varieties and qualities producing the best results. This, as may be inferred, extended over a period of several years, and through many hundreds of experiments, and since then I have had an opportunity to verify impressions then formed by observations made in some of the principal coffee producing and consuming countries.

Grown in different and widely separated parts of the world, it is natural that there should be a considerable difference in the appearance, quality, and flavor of coffee. It is not, therefore, strange that individual tastes, accustomed to the use of a particular variety, should prefer it to other kinds which possess, possibly, even greater intrinsic value. It is this difference in tastes and opinions which renders it a difficult task for even an expert to point out an infallible way of suiting every consumer. There are, however, conditions both in the selection and preparation of the bean which apply equally to all varieties, and which, if observed, will add greatly to the satisfaction of lovers of coffee. It is not within the scope of this little volume to treat of matters that chiefly concern the producer, except to take a cursory glance at such items as may have a direct bearing upon supply; such, for instance, as the ravages of leaf-disease in Ceylon, or the labor problem in the empire of Brazil.

In the start I recognize that prejudice, the result of habit, is met with at every turn. There are honest differences of opinion as to what constitutes a good cup of coffee, and therefore it is not my design to attempt to convince the lover of black coffee that a weaker beverage is the more palatable, or to argue with those who are best pleased with an infusion made by grinding the fragrant bean with some foreign substance. Experience has demonstrated that the beverage is one that speedily wins friends. I incline to the belief, as often expressed, that coffee was designed for man's sustenance and happiness as much as the golden grain, or the delicious fruits of mother earth. Somewhere I have read of the great surprise and delight manifested by the Indians on the Western plains when first made acquainted with the beverage. Usually indifferent to new objects, they fail to restrain their delight over the comforting draught. It is a matter of record that they have travelled several hundred miles in order to gratify their taste for coffee. The story has been told of an Indian chief who, dressed in a robe of great beauty, came in contact with a trader, who tried every means to secure the coveted garment. At last the meeting terminated with the accustomed treat of coffee. The chief was one of the first to gratify his palate with the beverage. It seemed as if his spirits had been roused by some unseen power. He pressed eagerly for more, and, delighted at receiving a second supply, he threw upon the trader, as an expression of his joy, the magnificent robe that money could not purchase. Similar experiences attended the introduction of coffee into all the countries where it is consumed, and if to-day thousands fail to find pleasure in lingering over a cup of delicious coffee, it is due, probably, to a lack of knowledge how to select and prepare the bean. My experience at home and abroad leads me to the belief that two-thirds of the lovers of coffee are, from lack of knowledge, daily cheated out of the solid enjoyment of an ideal cup of coffee. Especially is this true on lines of travel and at places of refreshment. The sort of coffee served in the average American restaurant or hotel is not calculated to command the homage of either savage or civilized creatures. It is, then, my design to try and point out how dealers may select and furnish, and how consumers may prepare coffee which will satisfy the critical palate.

CHAPTER II.

THE PLANT AND ITS CULTURE.

The range of coffee-culture extends over almost the whole of the tropical belt of the globe, the isothermal lines between the twenty-fifth degree north and the thirtieth degree south of the equator comprising the principal regions adapted to the growth of the plant. The plant seems to bear greater climatic extremes than most members of the vegetable kingdom, and thrives in localities differing as much as twenty to thirty degrees in average temperature.

It is a fact well worthy of notice that in many of the countries where the Coffœa Arabica—the coffee of commerce—has been introduced, indigenous varieties of the coffee-plant have been discovered, as in Mauritius, Southern India, Liberia, Costa Rica and Mexico, Peru, Guiana and Brazil. In the last-named country no fewer than sixteen species are distinguished, growing in a wild state.

The coffee-plant, although of hardy growth, is not without enemies, among which the principal are the borer, the bug, and the leaf fungus. Drought, damp, and rot also affect and injure the plant. In some countries shade-trees are necessary in order to protect it from excessive heat. In Ceylon coffee-trees under shade do not produce as liberally as trees planted in open ground, and, except in very low districts, shade is rarely provided. In Venezuela the long dry season makes it necessary to give the plants the shelter of large overhanging trees. In Brazil coffee is grown in the open. Monkeys, squirrels, and jackals are fond of the ripe berries, and make no scruple to plunder the plantations. A species of rat is also addicted to making inroads upon the coffee-fields and biting off the leaves and tender shoots.

The limit of average productiveness is about thirty years. After that time the trees may continue to live and grow, but they yield little or no fruit. In Java, coffee-trees planted nearly a hundred years ago are said to be yet in existence, being now some forty feet high, with trunks of the thickness of a man's thigh; but they grow entirely wild and produce no berries. On an average, the trees are replaced on the plantations every twenty years. This process of replanting goes on constantly. On the whole, the cultivation requires great care and unceasing attention, together with considerable capital to await the coming into bearing of the trees and to meet the heavy current expenses.

Coffee grows best on the uplands—usually on mountain sides at an elevation of from 1,500 to 4,500 feet above the level of the sea. In dry districts it is grown at an elevation of 5,500 and even 6,000 feet. The following directions are given by an experienced planter in the East: "As a general rule, the best zone of latitude for coffee is 150° on each side of the equator; of altitude from 3,000 to 4,500 feet. The deeper, freer, and richer the soil is the better. It should be specially tested for phosphoric acid and potash. The latter will be in abundance if a large forest is felled, and burned grass-land must be very good to grow coffee. An eastern or southeastern exposure is good, but not always essential. Shelter from tearing wind, however, is of the utmost importance, and in windy situations should be secured by leaving belts of timber, or planting fast-growing Australian trees. A mean temperature between 65° and 70° or 73° is desirable, and a rainfall of from 70 to 150 inches of rain, well distributed, about 100 inches being the best." The trees are raised from the seeds in nurseries, and transferred to their final positions when about a year or eighteen months old. Plants raised from seeds are much better than those obtained from cuttings. A costly system of raising plants in pots has been commenced in Brazil, the planter claiming a gain of one year for those thus raised over such as are obtained by the ordinary method, as there is no set back to the plant in the process of transplanting, the roots remaining undisturbed.

The plants are usually set at intervals of eight or ten feet, although in some plantations they are placed a little closer, the rows, however, being about this distance apart. They begin bearing at the age of three to four years, their product annually increasing, and at six years they may be said to be in full bearing. The yield varies greatly, however, in different countries, being influenced by modes of culture and changes in the character of the seasons; taking one year with another a tree in full bearing produces from two to three pounds per annum. Careful pruning is required to develop and maintain the productive capacity of the trees. Left to themselves they would grow to a considerable height; but when about eight feet high the tops are cut off, which causes them to spread instead of growing taller, and afterward they are kept pruned down to about eight feet, and in some countries, notably Ceylon, even lower. Within recent years pruning in Ceylon has been lighter than was formerly the custom. A heavily pruned tree is regarded as most liable to be attacked with leaf disease. Regarding the Coffœa Liberica, a planter in the low country of Ceylon says: "Topping the Liberian coffee-tree is a very objectionable operation. The Arabian coffee-plant can be forced into an artificial form without the sacrifice of any of its crop, because there is a period, longer or shorter, between the crop and the blossom, in which old wood can be eliminated, but I cannot very clearly see how the artificial form is to be advantageously imposed on a tree that carries its full crop all the year round, and on which pruning can only be carried out at a sacrifice of crop. One of the objects of forcing Arabian coffee into the artificial form is to get the whole growth under hand, so as to facilitate and cheapen the gathering of the crop; but the average Liberian tree puts out its first branches at a height of stem little short of that at which the Arabian plant is usually topped, so that this end cannot be answered by topping at six or seven feet. I do not insist on these objections as the result of experimental study of the tree, but so far as I have gone they seem to me to be well founded." The average diameter of the trunk in full-bearing trees is about the size of a man's wrist. They bear a profusion of dark green, glossy leaves, and the fruit or berry forms on the woody stems, usually at the base of these leaves.

A dissection of the fruit or berry, which, when ripe, is red in color and much resembles a large cranberry, or medium-sized

cherry, shows that it consists of five different parts, covering the two beans, which lie within, face to face. First, we find the outer skin, very similar to that which surrounds the cranberry or cherry. Second, we have a soft pulp enclosed by and adhering to the outside covering. The removal of the two first reveals a third coating, which consists of a soft glutinous substance, strongly saccharine in its character. The fourth part is a sort of envelope, called by some the parchment. It is rather tough and somewhat thicker than the husk of wheat. It is of a yellowish-white color, and is easily removed by friction. Next to the parchment there is found a thin gossamer film, designated in Ceylon "silver-skin" and in Brazil the *pergaminho*, and in appearance resembling the thin skin which covers the white onion designated "silver-skin."

Picking begins in Java in January and lasts three or four months. The chief part of the Ceylon crop is gathered from April to July. A small crop, chiefly young coffee, is picked from September to December. In Brazil they commence gathering the crop in April or May, the work continuing until September. Women and children are largely employed in gathering the fruit, carrying it from the field in baskets to the mill house or terrace, where the preparation of the berry for market commences.

CHAPTER III.

PREPARATION OF COFFEE FOR MARKET.

After the berries have been harvested the first operation to which they are treated is designated pulping. This is accomplished in either of two ways: one fashion is to pulp the berries or "cherry," as they are termed in the East, in the soft state, which mode is favored in Ceylon; the other seeks to dry the berry first, and then remove the dried skin and pulp by a machine called a huller. The latter is the old way, while the former is known in the East as the West India method. Where the latter way is chosen the berries are spread upon terraces or drying grounds of stone, mortar, or cement, somewhat elevated in the centre, and there kept until complete desiccation takes place, care being taken to cover them over if it should rain when they are wholly or partially dried. Coffee prepared in this way is designated THICK HULL OR SUN DRIED.

The first process is adopted when the fruit is fully ripe. If, however, the berries have been allowed to remain too long upon the branch, or have been gathered before arriving at maturity, the pulper is not brought into use, and the second method comes into favor, which takes the berries, after being properly dried, and runs them through a machine called a huller, which in Brazil is generally of American make. These machines are worked either by hand or steam-power. Some hullers, that will hull 10 arrobas (323 pounds) of coffee when worked by hand, will hull 800 arrobas (26,824 pounds) in the same length of time when run by steam, another instance of the power of machinery to compensate for a deficiency in the labor supply.

In Ceylon the natives remove the dry pulp by pounding, using a common pounder, such as is used for removing the hull from

PULPING COFFEE IN BRAZIL

rice. From want of care in the harvesting of the fruit, and the use of somewhat primitive methods of preparation, the native coffee lacks "style," and contains more or less damaged beans. In consequence of this the new method of preparation is rapidly growing in favor, although there are many coffee-drinkers who maintain that coffee produced by the old method is superior in flavor.

The new method, sometimes termed the "West India preparation," seeks the removal of the skin and pulp by maceration in water. On large Brazilian plantations the berries are carried to a large vat, from the bottom of which the heavier berries are drawn off by a pipe to the pulping-machine (despolpador), the lighter or worthless berries being carried off by the retreating water. This is also the plan adopted on the best plantations in Venezuela and Ceylon.

The pulping process is best accomplished as soon after the berries are gathered as is possible. On the opposite page will be found an illustration showing the working of a pulping-machine upon a plantation in Brazil. It is a simple contrivance, consisting of an iron cylinder, set with teeth, and covered on one side by a curved sheet of metal, which it strikes as it revolves. A stream of water carries the berries to the cylinder, where they are crushed between it and the cover, the operation loosening the pulp. The macerated berries are then conveyed to a vat some distance off, the water being kept agitated by a revolving wheel, and serving to remove the loosened pulp, which is carried away by the waste water, the seeds sinking to the bottom of the vat, from which they are taken to a strainer, which drains off the water, leaving them ready for the next operation.

A variety of machines are used, and the process of conveying the berries to and from the pulper is more or less elaborate. In Ceylon the pulpers are of two kinds, the pulping surface of one being a cylinder, and that of the other a disk. The former are large, and the most expensive, the latter small, cheap, and portable, thus bringing them into favor upon estates lying far in the interior. The disk pulpers are largely used in Java and on the coast of India.

Messrs. Walker Brothers, of London, who are large manufacturers of pulpers, say:

"In pulping three things are aimed at—to pulp rapidly, cleanly, and without damaging the beans. By clean pulping we mean separating entirely and thoroughly the bean from the pulp, so that as little as possible of the pulp should pass to the cisterns with the parchment. It is of great importance, too, that the beans be not pricked or scratched. If the inner skin of the bean be broken, it will generally run to powder when dried, and so be lost to the planter. The point, therefore, is to find a surface that will be rough enough to take off the pulp, and yet have no sharp points or edges to injure the bean. The surface of both cylinder and disk is a thin sheet of copper or brass—generally copper. For the disks the copper is punched or knobbed by what is called a 'blind' punch; it merely raises the surface of the copper into rows of oval knobs, but does not pierce through the sheet, and hence leaves no sharp edges. The cylinders have a patent 'half-moon' punch, which pierces the copper and throws up the broken edge into almost a half-circle, and it is found that this form of punch does extremely little injury to the beans.

"Some of the cylinder-pulpers used in the East are very large, having a capacity to readily pulp 100 bushels of berries per hour, and when pushed can be made to pulp 150 to 160 bushels per hour.

"The 'gearless' pulper has two pulping cylinders, two pairs chops, hopper and feed-boxes of galvanized iron, a large sieve with circular motion, and a set of elevator buckets for the purpose of raising unpulped or imperfectly pulped cherry thrown out by the sieve, and re-delivering it to the pulping cylinders. No wheels are used in driving the cylinders, and otherwise it is simple in its construction, less liable to accident than most pulpers, and all its working parts are easily reached. It can be driven at a very effective speed by a sixteen-feet water-wheel, or a three-horse-power engine. In this pulper the cherry is dropped into a central hopper, and from thence passes into two side hoppers. From these it drops on to the sides of the cylinders, and the pulping is effected at the chops, where the cherry is pressed between the cylinders and the upper chop, which loosens the beans. The pulp is drawn down between the cylinder and the edge of the lower chop, while the beans pass out between the chops. The pulp and beans are thus separated, the former being floated away to the pulp-pit, to be afterward used as manure. The beans, along with which there is always a quantity of unpulped cherry and pulp, fall into a sieve, which allows the beans to pass through it nearly clear of any of the unpulped cherry and pulp, and to be carried off by means of spouts to the cisterns. The unpulped cherry and pulp are delivered into a well, from which they are returned by an elevator into the central hopper, to be again passed through the pulper along with fresh cherry. This work goes on continuously till all the cherry picked the same day is pulped. One man is generally placed to see that the supply of cherry is kept up, and another to attend to the pulping. All our experience goes to show that regular feeding of the cherry at the hopper is of the utmost importance in pulping.

"The berry, after being divested of its pulp, is called parchment-coffee, it being within a cover resembling thin parchment, to which adheres a glutinous substance, slightly saccharine, and the inner bean is again surrounded by a thin gossamer filament known as the silver-skin. The Ceylon process allows the parchment to remain in a cistern for forty-eight hours, or until the glutinous matter is removed. After this it is subjected to repeated washings with water, and then dried in the sun. It is dried sufficiently on the estate to enable it to be conveyed to Colombo, the port of shipment, and at Colombo it is more thoroughly dried, and during the operation it is subjected to careful examination, and all foreign substances—bits of stick, stones, mud, etc.—are picked out by hand; and then the two husks—the parchment and silver-skin—are removed by a machine called a peeler. After the peeler, it has still to pass through the winnower and the sizing machine, the latter being a machine for the purpose of separating the beans into different sizes; and when these processes are complete the parchment has become clean coffee, and is ready for shipment.

"Cisterns for fermenting and washing operations are usually made of solid masonry, covered either with asphalt or cement. The arrangements made by different planters are not all alike. Some have cisterns (generally two) into which the pulped coffee is received from the pulper and kept till it is fit for washing. These are called fermenting cisterns, and alongside of them there are other cisterns for washing only. The latter are so arranged that the coffee can be run into them from the fermenting cisterns.

"Other planters prefer to do their fermenting and washing in the same cisterns. The pulped coffee is received into the cisterns; it is allowed to remain there till fit for washing, and then washed without change of cistern. Under both arrangements a tail cistern, generally long and narrow, is formed at the lower end of the washing cisterns, at a lower level, and with a perforated iron bottom. There is a door-frame at the lower end of each washing cistern, and this frame is fitted with two doors. One is of perforated iron, the perforations being such as to allow water freely to escape, but not coffee. The other is usually made of movable little boards placed on edge, the edges fitted exactly to each other, so that one, or two, or more boards may be put in to retain as much water as may be wanted during washing operations.

"Three fermenting and washing cisterns, each about 20 ft. × 10 ft. × 2 ft. will be found sufficient for an estate taking in 400 bushels cherry per day.

"If more coffee be expected daily, the cisterns may be deepened up to three feet, and for very large estates they may be made longer and wider.

"A rule for the size of fermenting cisterns might be stated thus: One cubic foot for each bushel of cherry expected each day. This would be ample, and would apply to large and small estates.

"On low estates with a high temperature—say from 68° to 80° Fahrenheit—coffee is ready for washing in about thirty-six or forty hours after pulping; but in some of the higher and colder districts, where fermenting progresses less rapidly, it may require as much as sixty hours. During this time no water should be allowed to flow in among the coffee which has been drained after being pulped; it would hinder fermentation. But after the proper time has elapsed, and fermentation has taken place, the mucilage which, after pulping, adheres to the parchment skin, may be easily washed from it. This is done by admitting a free flow of water into the cistern and stirring the coffee with a wooden implement, similar to that used by natives in their rice fields.

DRYING COFFEE BY STEAM IN BRAZIL.

It consists of a thin board, about twenty inches by five, with a handle about five feet long. It is worked like a rake, and in the washing and stirring the light coffee and skins are separated from the heavy and good beans, and floated into the tail cistern. Clever coolies soon get very expert at this separating process, retaining only good parchment coffee in the washing cistern, and floating off the light beans and skins.

"Another kind of cistern is used on some estates that are subject to much wet weather, and it may be referred to here. It is found that parchment coffee, after being washed and before being exposed to the sun, will remain perfectly sound and good if kept in water. A large cistern is therefore made for this purpose, and a stream of water is allowed to flow in, sufficient to keep the coffee covered, and in this way it may be kept for many days, or until good drying weather comes.

"Parchment coffee should be dried with the least possible delay, and it ought not to be exposed to rain. Large barbecues, or smooth open spaces, are necessary for this purpose, so that it may be thinly spread over a large surface, and so exposed to the sun. The surface of these barbecues has in many cases been formed of small stones plastered over with mortar, and coated with a mixture of tar and resin. But latterly the more economical practice has been only to make the ground smooth and hard, and over the barbecue thus easily formed to lay down coir matting, on which the coffee is spread out. It is a recommendation of this plan that the coir matting can be turned into a temporary covering for the coffee in the event of rain suddenly coming on. A large store is also necessary, so that the coffee may not be stored too deep on one floor. If, from want of space, too much is heaped together, it must be frequently turned over in order to prevent it from heating."

In Brazil and Central America the drying is effected in different ways. By the old process the berries are spread out upon a stone or mortar floor and exposed to the sun until dry, care being taken to rake over the seeds during the day and to protect them from rain or sudden showers.

A newer method employs steam. Beneath large zinc covered tables, with raised edges, steam pipes are run. Negroes are engaged in constantly stirring the seeds and taking them away when dried. By this process only a few hours are occupied in thoroughly drying the berries. It is also claimed that the coffee thus dried shows better quality than that which is sun dried on the terraces, as there is no chance of its being rain damaged.

Different kinds of machines are used to remove the coffee-grains from their dry coverings. Some resemble a fanning mill, and others are immense structures specially built for the purpose. In all of them the one object is sought—the securing of bright, hard, and thoroughly clean beans. The following diagram and

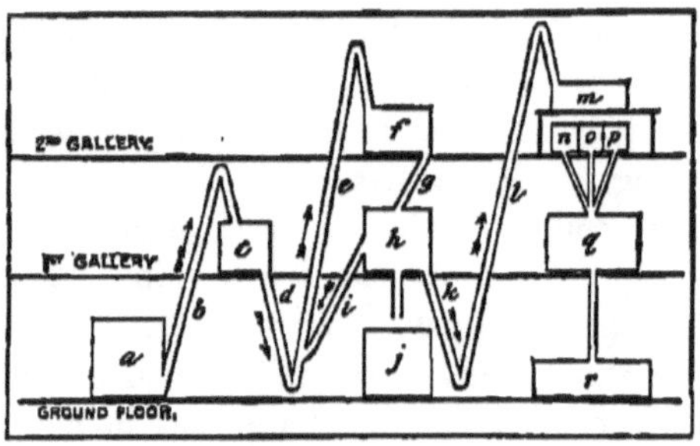

description from Herbert H. Smith's work on Brazil make clear the cleaning operation as carried on upon extensive plantations in Brazil:—

"The dried berries are placed in the bin *a*. A band elevator, *b*, carries them to the ventilator *c*, where sticks and rubbish are removed and the dust fanned away. It then passes through the tube *d* to another elevator, *e*, which carries it to the sheller *f*, where the outer and inner shells are crushed by revolving toothed cylinders. The grains and broken shells pass through a pipe, *g*, to the ventilator *h*, where the shells are sifted and fanned away; the unbroken nuts are separated on a sieve and passed by the pipe *i* back to the elevator *e*, and so again to the sheller; the shells and rubbish fall into a bin, *j*, from which they are removed for manure; the coffee-grains fall into the pipe *k*, and are carried by the elevator *l* to the separator *m*. This separator is composed of a pair of hollow revolving copper cylinders pierced with holes of different sizes and shapes; the coffee-grains, dropped into the cylinders, fall through these holes and are assorted by them into large and small, flat and round grains, which pass into different bins, *n*, *o*, *p*. There still remains a portion of the fine inner covering of the grains, which is removed in the box *q*, with constant shaking, trituration, and fanning. Falling into the bin *r*, the cleaned coffee is removed and carefully picked over by hand before it is finally consigned to the sacks. The picking is generally done by women, and in the manner depicted in the illustration."

Picking over Coffee.

In countries where the most primitive methods are still in vogue, the coffee is very imperfectly cleaned, and the fine inner covering adheres more or less to the bean, largely reducing its commercial value.

While in Java I for the first time found a seemingly plausible method of accounting for what is termed in commerce the "male berry" coffee. This, as is well known by all dealers in the article, is a bean of a roundish, oval shape, and its merits have been highly extolled by some who claim that it is much better than the ordinarily shaped coffee. Mr. J. W. E. de Sturler, the owner of a large coffee plantation in the Preanger district, assured me that his observations had led him to believe that the so-called male berries are simply those berries which do not develop and attain the full size of the average bean; in short, that they are imperfect berries; that, while all the trees bear more or less of them, the older plants, which are less thrifty and vigorous, bear by far the larger percentage, and that, perhaps, a fair estimate of the average quantity of this style produced by his plantation was five per cent., or one-twentieth. Owing to the demand, however, which has been created for the "male berry" coffee, it often sells for ten to twenty per cent. more than the ordinary coffee. He thought it possible that there was something in the popular belief that this style possessed a higher flavor than the ordinary coffee; but it was more probable that the higher price was due to fashion in trade, which often exhibits such strange vagaries. I was confirmed in this view of the matter by a conversation which I had subsequently, in Ceylon, on the same subject, with the experienced manager of the Cotchicaddy Mills, at Colombo.

Having briefly considered the preparation of the bean for the market, I now pass to a consideration of special matters connected with its production in the coffee-growing countries, describing the peculiarities of the different varieties of bean and how they reach consuming markets, together with special features of interest to dealers.

Each country furnishes a coffee different in some respects from that coming from any other; and again the product of each often differs according to the climate, soil, temperature, and cultivation received in the various districts of the country in which it is grown. It may therefore readily be seen that it requires no small degree of skill to enable a purchaser to judge of the quality and value of the different kinds. With a view to render assistance in this direction, I shall in succeeding chapters consider the product of each important producing country separately.

In the following table are enumerated the countries contributing to the supply of the United States, and the quantities furnished by each during the years 1878, 1879, and 1880.

Order.	COUNTRIES.	Quantities. Year ending June 30, 1878. Pounds.	Value.	Per cent. Total.	Quantities. Year ending June 30, 1879. Pounds.	Value.	Per cent. Total.	Quantities. Year ending June 30, 1880. Pounds.	Value.	Per cent. Total.
1	Brazil	211,654,160	$38,367,992	68.30	273,837,142	$31,795,101	72.46	296,731,718	$37,865,578	66.41
2	Venezuela	38,623,291	6,228,297	12.46	29,138,035	4,069,213	7.71	35,518,910	4,956,068	7.95
3	Dutch East Indies	14,678,766	2,799,592	4.70	18,492,343	3,224,874	4.89	28,033,006	4,839,854	6.27
4	Central America	13,868,955	2,473,178	4.48	11,463,136	1,698,231	3.03	19,254,218	2,567,768	4.31
5	Hayti	12,813,113	1,891,207	4.13	16,660,030	1,946,706	4.41	22,669,285	2,926,544	5.07
6	Mexico	6,337,063	1,082,272	2.04	8,307,040	1,371,979	2.19	9,818,625	1,523,658	2.19
7	United States of Colombia	5,931,709	1,022,216	1.91	8,938,044	1,254,938	2.36	12,687,423	2,018,471	2.84
8	British West Indies and Honduras	2,340,187	364,679	0.76	1,963,611	238,697	0.62	2,049,577	279,553	0.46
9	England*	1,309,785	273,507	0.42	2,976,592	632,640	0.78	6,617,103	991,928	1.24
10	British East Indies	1,269,667	196,925	0.41	2,179,583	336,126	0.57	4,647,062	707,909	1.04
11	China and Hong Kong and other countries in Asia	331,893	63,096	0.11	590,453	107,087	0.15	1,043,535	189,716	0.23
12	Netherlands*	156,034	32,712	0.05	1,688,158	321,347	0.44	3,083,840	550,366	0.69
13	Hawaiian Islands	160,194	26,577	0.05	72,794	11,935		77,923	12,834	0.01
14	Liberia	107,600	22,746	0.04	109,024	22,352		143,781	25,873	0.03
15	Chili	106,356	21,179	0.04	....	....		....	....	......
16	Porto Rico	105,856	13,083	0.04	120,309	19,701		2,937,053	502,090	0.66
17	Dutch West Indies and Dutch Guiana	44,939	6,896	0.01	576,044	87,442		1,204,363	169,323	0.27
18	British Possessions in Africa and adjacent islands and all others	36,794	5,177	0.01	8,761	1,944		894,051	129,168	
19	Africa—Ports not specified	33,452	7,112	0.01	856	172		1,220	192	
20	Spanish Possessions, all others	82,125	4,737	0.01	139,141	29,159		9,733	1,407	
21	Italy*	22,400	6,180		....	....		....	....	
22	French Possessions, all others	9,050	1,431		495	103		60,091	4,974	
23	Danish West Indies	6,870	1,318		58,842	8,461		239,902	34,205	
24	Peru	4,694	942		....	....		840	136	
25	French Possessions in Africa and adjacent islands	3,526	722		....	....	0.49	1,442	266	
26	Germany*	2,888	353		27,864	4,068		238,495	24,996	
27	Cuba	2,044	438	0.02	2,215	353		29,538	4,644	
28	Belgium*	1,593	444		61,245	11,856		79,492	8,867	0.33
29	Nova Scotia, New Brunswick, Prince Edward Island*	1,298	257		....	....		....	....	
30	Azores, Madeira, Cape Verde Islands	674	137		7,000	1,181		1,286	224	
31	Turkey in Africa	622	162		....	....		10,300	2,013	
32	British Guiana	365	45		170	24		170	26	
33	Provinces of Quebec, Ontario, Manitoba, etc.*	336	86		1,602	299		329	48	
34	British Columbia*	80	20		....	....		....	....	
35	France and French West Indies	....	....	......	276,235	....		33,905	7,746	
36	Portugal (1879) and Spain (1880)*	....	....	......	12,681	1,076		1,870	235	
37	Portuguese Possessions in Africa	....	....	......	46,058	6,320	......	....	....	
38	San Domingo	....	....	......	94,040	14,265	......	150,709	24,073	
		309,882,540	$51,914,605	100.	377,848,473	$47,356,819	100.	446,850,727	$60,360,769	100.

* Non-producing countries.

(The per cent. 0.02 for 1878 is bracketed for Nos. 21–34; 0.49 for 1879 for Nos. 13–36; 0.33 for 1880 for Nos. 18–38.)

CHAPTER IV.

THE SELECTION OF THE BEAN.

How to determine quality from the appearance of the bean is a question of great importance to every interested party, from the export merchant at the place of production to the buyer for consumption.

Between these two parties usually come the import merchant, the wholesale grocer, and the retail merchant, on whose parts respectively, care and knowledge are necessary, yet often wanting, to insure to the consumer a satisfactory result.

Coffee is frequently damaged on the voyage of importation by dampness, which soon renders it musty; and when the coffee-bean once becomes musty its delicate flavor is much injured, and no amount of attempted renovation can fully restore it. A greater or less portion of nearly every cargo is thus damaged. The renovating process consists of opening the bags, emptying the contents out upon the floor of the warehouse, and skimming off, as well as may be, the mouldy and musty beans, which usually are those next the bag; these are kept separate. If wet, they are dried, and afterward are often run through a polishing machine to remove the mould and give them a more sightly appearance. They are then put upon the market and generally sold for within one or two cents per pound of the price of sound coffee, although the intrinsic value is much diminished. The portion which remains after the skimming, is called "sound," and is put up in new bags and sold as such, although it is far from being as good as that which has never been damaged; for the skimming process is not perfect, and some of the musty beans remain, imparting their flavor, to some extent, to the sound beans. This fact is lost sight of by many merchants, who only look for samples which show handsomely in the hand, thus neglecting the far more important quality of flavor.

There is no item which enters into the supply of our tables, with which I am acquainted, unless it be butter, which is so easily injured in flavor as coffee, or which exhibits such a tendency to absorb surrounding odors. Vessels from Central and South America often arrive with mixed cargoes of coffee and hides, in which the former has been almost ruined by absorbing the smell of the latter. Roasting the coffee dissipates to some degree the "hidey" smell, yet to an expert it is very perceptible, enough remaining to destroy the delicate flavor of the volatile oil or caffeone. The same effect is produced by the foul bilge-water of vessels, and the extreme sensitiveness of coffee to surrounding odors is further demonstrated by the readiness with which roasted coffee absorbs the flavor of the wood when put in a pine box or bin. Roasted coffee should never be long kept in anything except a tightly closed tin box, or better yet, an air-tight glass or earthen jar.

Different varieties of coffee show a great diversity of flavor, and even the same variety from different parts of one district will show like divergencies. Different seasons produce different qualities; indeed, there are as many kinds, qualities, and shades of flavor of coffee as there are of tea, and in the latter these variations, as is well known, are almost numberless.

In the review of coffee production I have indicated the variety of kinds, qualities, and flavors which exists, and also, to some extent, the vicissitudes to which even the best coffee is exposed during the voyage of importation. From this it will be seen how necessary it is for dealers to exercise great caution in selecting their stocks. It is impossible to judge accurately of the quality and strength of coffee without roasting and making an infusion with boiling water, in a manner similar to that practised in drawing tea, and yet, strange as it may seem, it is not customary, even with the largest dealers, to judge of quality except by the general appearance of the berry.

Before buying a large lot, wholesale dealers sometimes roast a small quantity to see how it looks when roasted, but this is the exception rather than the rule, and by far the larger portion of all varieties of coffee are sold simply upon their appearance in the hand. This oftentimes is exceedingly deceptive, for a bright, large-beaned, handsome looking sample will sometimes turn out to be woody and comparatively flavorless; while another that, according to the usual standard by which coffee is judged, would be rated considerably lower in price, will, when roasted, prove to be of very superior quality, greatly increasing in size during the roasting process, and developing that delicious fragrance which occasionally surprises and delights all lovers of a perfect cup of coffee.

It is quite within the power of wholesale dealers to greatly improve the quality of the coffee sold by them if they will carefully roast and try a portion of every considerable lot before buying it, refusing such as do not come up to a proper standard of strength and fragrance, and especially avoiding lots which show the least trace of any musty or foreign flavor.

To some extent in producing countries, and also at the large distributing points, an artificial appearance is given to the bean by "sweating," "polishing," or by the use of coloring matter. By the first-named process Savanilla and other sorts (sometimes Santos) are made to imitate Padang Java. Laguayra is polished and sold for Rio. Very dangerous powders or mixtures are used to color the beans, the practice being resorted to in order to meet the prejudices of consumers in certain sections for a bright yellow, black, or olive-green colored bean. These colors are obtained by the use of poisonous compounds. The composition of these mixtures respectively, as proved by chemical analyses, is as follows (Report Department Agriculture, 1879, p. 79):

Orange Powder.—Chromate of lead ("chrome yellow"), 1 part; sulphate of barium ("heavy spar"), 2 parts.

Black Powder.—Consisted wholly of burnt bones ("crude bone-black").

Olive-Green Powder.—Chromate of lead ("chrome yellow"), 1 part; bone-black, 3 parts; sulphate of barium ("heavy spar"), 3 parts.

Both the natural and the faced berries were examined, with the result that every sample of the "improved" berries was found to have been treated with some powder containing the same substances as those in the above olive-green powder.

The amounts of foreign adulterants were—

	Per cent.		Per cent.
No. 1	0.68	No. 4	0.64
No. 2	0.19	No. 5	0.63
No. 3	0.08	No. 6	0.58

The "uncolored" berries were what was claimed for them, viz., free from any adulteration.

The Government chemist, in referring to the above, said:

"The foolish demands of the people are the direct cause for the manipulation of coffee. Yet this is no reason why the national legislature should not enact laws, and have them rigidly enforced, preventing the use of poisonous compounds."

There can be but little doubt that these added coloring matters must prove injurious, and, probably, directly poisonous to the consumer. Especially is chromate of lead liable to be changed by roasting, so that its lead may be soluble in the acids of the stomach; and it is well known that soluble lead salts have a decidedly poisonous action.

CHAPTER V.

ROASTING THE BEAN.

The most important of all the conditions necessary to be observed in the production of a cup of good coffee is the process of roasting the bean. The finest quality of coffee unskilfully roasted will give a less satisfactory result in the cup than a poor quality roasted in the best manner. It is no easy matter to acquire the skill in manipulation and accuracy of judgment necessary to roast coffee successfully. Among professional coffee roasters some are bunglers, although their lives have been spent in the occupation, while others seem to be peculiarly adapted to the business, and with much less experience uniformly turn out good work. As in a competitive trial of firemen for steam engines, a boy of sixteen obtained more revolutions of the engine with a given amount of fuel than the most experienced engineers, so will special adaptability for a certain work sometimes be developed where least expected. The skilful roaster can tell when the bean has been roasted to the desired degree by the aroma which is carried away in the smoke that arises during the process of roasting.

The revolution which has taken place in the coffee-trade of the United States during the last twenty years, is a striking confirmation of the principle that work can be done in the best and cheapest manner on a large scale, where machinery is employed that is controlled by the best available skill. It may safely be said that twenty years ago there was not one pound of roasted coffee sold in this country, where now there are twenty. Then retail grocers bought and sold coffee green, and consumers roasted it in an iron pot or skillet over an ordinary fire. While this method had its advantages so far as having coffee freshly roasted was concerned, these advantages were heavily counterbalanced by the impossibility of obtaining uniform work from the crude appliances used, and a still greater obstacle was encountered in the lack of experience and the occasional stupidity on the part of persons intrusted with the work. At that time there were a few so-called "coffee and spice mills," whose proprietors roasted coffee for their own trade, in large cylinders turned by machinery. The results obtained were so satisfactory that wholesale grocers, in order to hold their trade, began to employ these "mills" to roast coffee for them, and this business has steadily increased until now there are coffee-roasting establishments, using steam-power, in every city of considerable size in this country, and the demand for coffee thus roasted has so increased that some of the larger wholesale grocery houses have found it expedient to erect mills especially for their own accommodation.

The first complete apparatus for roasting and grinding coffee, was set up in Wooster street, New York, opposite the present Washington square. It was brought over from England by James Wilde, in 1833 or 1834, and consisted of two cylinders, with an engine of sufficient power to run the roasters and a mill for the grinding. Prior to this time, a Mr. Ward roasted coffee for the grocers, by hand, making this his special business. Mr. Withington, in Dutch street, about the same time, used horse-power for running his roasters. In 1835, the once famous Hope Mills were started in Elizabeth street, near Bleecker street. Coffee-roasting was undertaken by the proprietors on a large scale, four cylinders being run. These mills were burnt in 1845, after which the business was transferred to 71 Fulton street, near to the present establishment of Mr. John Bynner, who, I believe, is the oldest living representative of the coffee trade in New York. In subsequent years numerous smaller machines have been designed for the use of families and retail dealers. Almost without exception, however, those designed for the use of families have failed to give satisfaction, owing to the great difficulty of roasting the beans with any degree of uniformity in small quantities.

The largest sized portable machines for the use of retail grocers have yielded somewhat better results; still it is only now and then that the experience of those using them is entirely satisfactory. It is with difficulty that uniformly good work can be obtained, and then it is only after repeated failures, necessarily costly to the retailer, because, in addition to losing the coffee, his trade is imperilled. Oftentimes a customer, whom it has taken years to secure, has been lost during the experimental effort to acquire sufficient skill to properly roast coffee in a portable roaster. Sometimes there will be too much, and then, again, too little fire; the attention of the same person cannot always be conveniently given; the turning is not usually as steady and continuous by hand as when done by steam-power, while it is manifestly impossible for a person only roasting occasionally to attain the same degree of skill and experience that is acquired by a fit person who makes it a business.

These considerations, together with the occasional spoiling of a roast through carelessness or by a novice; losses in weight by roasting more than is necessary; the expense of a machine, and fuel, time and trouble, altogether make it doubtful whether it will pay the average retail grocer to undertake this service himself. It must also be borne in mind that the result of his work is liable to come into competition with that of adepts in the art. There may be cases where grocers are so far from any available market that they cannot obtain regular and frequent supplies of roasted coffee from the wholesale dealer, and in such cases they will, undoubtedly, find it better to undertake the roasting of coffee sold by them, than to trust to the care and attention of the average consumer, to whom it is an impossibility, with the facilities at command, to roast properly, and who, nevertheless, is very apt, when the result is unsatisfactory, to attribute the failure to the poor quality of the coffee furnished. Where parties attempt to roast their own coffee, their object should be to produce a rich chestnut-brown; for making "black" or French coffee, the bean should be roasted higher than usual, but the first mentioned color will best suit the majority of palates. As a rule, it will not pay consumers to roast their own coffee where they are so situated that they can procure frequent supplies of the roasted article from the retail dealer; and it will be found that retail dealers, as a rule, will in turn find it to their interest to have their supplies roasted by professional roasters, whose constant practice enables them, on the whole, to turn out the best article. We believe that this policy is the most economical for retailers, as the use of machinery and the division of labor into specialties in this, as in many other branches of trade, effects a far greater saving than is possible by individual effort when not thus organized.

Dealers should buy their roasted coffee in small quantities, and this, with our extended modern facilities of communication and transportation, is quite feasible. A supply sufficient to last a week or ten days is enough to buy at a time, and if the dealer is situated close to the "mill" or wholesale grocer, let him purchase but half that quantity. Roasted coffee loses in quality and aroma from the moment it leaves the roaster; hence it should be kept in tightly closed receptacles (never in a wooden box or bin possessing any odor, for, as remarked elsewhere, it is peculiarly susceptible to surrounding odors); if exposed to the air its delicate fragrance is rapidly dissipated. The above remarks also apply to consumers, who will find that small and frequent purchases of freshly roasted coffee give better satisfaction than larger quantities purchased less frequently, and whatever quantity is purchased, it should be kept in a glass or earthen jar, or a tightly closed tin canister. Recently, roasted coffee packed in one-pound papers, has come into favor with consumers, the reason for this doubtless being that large dealers in coffee, possessing a thorough knowledge of the characteristics of coffee produced in the various countries, and the flavors which harmonize in blending, have succeeded in producing grades adapted to the tastes of different sections where coffee is largely consumed, and, doing business on a large scale, have been able to secure the greatest uniformity of result, and consequently, the utmost satisfaction to the consumer. Through being tightly sealed in wrappers while fresh from the roaster, the aroma is the more effectually preserved, while, in some instances, a preservative gloss is added with this object in view. Dealers prefer this package coffee because there is no loss in weight, and the time and labor of weighing and putting up are saved; a child can hand out a package of coffee where a man would otherwise have to be employed, and the consumer also has that guarantee of correct weight and uniformity of quality afforded by the transaction of business on a large scale, where everything is reduced to an exact system.

The illustration upon the opposite page exhibits the interior of a large roasting establishment, and shows the manner of filling and emptying the cylinders, and the process of cooling the coffee. The perforated iron cylinders are built large enough to hold three hundred pounds of coffee, but not more than two hundred pounds are placed at one time in each. It will be seen from the engraving that the cylinder may be removed from over the fire upon the shaft upon which it revolves, which shaft is made to extend from the brick frame-work which protects the fire, far enough to permit of the cylinder being readily filled and emptied. In some roasting establishments the cylinders are so arranged that they cannot be removed from over the fire, which feature is deemed objectionable by the best roasters, as, in case of any accident to the machinery the coffee could not be quickly enough removed. This arrangement also subjects the empty cylinder to the influence of a strong heat after the coffee is removed and before a new lot can take its place, the effect of which is to "speck" the coffee unless great care is exercised.

Upon an average, about forty-five minutes are required to roast the berry, which, in addition to the time taken to fill and empty the cylinder and to cool and re-sack the coffee—makes the time occupied by the entire process about one hour.

The Mocha and other small bean coffees will roast in a little less time than Java and other large varieties. The phrase "little less time" is full of significance to the professional roaster, for the keeping of the coffee over the fire from thirty to sixty seconds longer than is necessary will sometimes ruin the roast. For the New England trade a light roast is required, and for Western, a dark, or pretty full roast. What are termed white, dead, sour, or black beans injure the roast, in fact a very small quantity of sour beans present in a lot of coffee will greatly damage it. A well seasoned berry that is solid and oily, and from one to two years old, makes the finest roast. The white beans which are so often seen in roasted coffee are from imperfect or immature berries, analagous to the miniature kernel of corn which is often found at one end of the cob. White beans being destitute of caffeone containing the aroma are but little changed in color during the process of roasting, and are comparatively destitute of flavor.

COFFEE-ROASTING.

Shrivelled coffee, or that having a shrunken appearance, will not, as a rule, roast nicely, although some such lots will occasionally turn out a bright, handsome roast. When the berry has been sufficiently roasted and the cylinder withdrawn from the fire, the operator throws in a small quantity of cold water. The rapid vaporizing of the water carries off the heat, and the changes wrought during this part of the process cause the berry to swell, thus giving it a much more sightly and attractive appearance. The addition of water does not, as might be supposed, add to the weight of the coffee, for the heat is so intense as to immediately convert the water into steam, which readily escapes. The coffee, after being removed to the cylinder, is placed in the cooler, a large box having a heavy wire bottom through which currents of air are forced, soon reducing the temperature so that it can be handled. When cooled it is re-sacked, or put into other packages, and is then ready for shipment.

The average loss of weight in the process of roasting coffee is reckoned at sixteen per cent., or sixteen pounds upon every one hundred pounds, which accounts for the higher price of roasted coffee as compared with green. This loss sometimes runs as low as fourteen and one-half per cent., and again as high as seventeen per cent., and in exceptional cases where coffee has been roasted that was very green, and grown in places not far distant, it has reached twenty to twenty-two per cent. The temperature and season of the year exert some influence, but the difference in loss depends more upon the age and consequent dryness of the coffee than on anything else. The difference in loss made between a light and a dark roast will not usually average over one per cent. It is the custom not to roast as high during the summer as in the winter, because the higher the roast the greater is the tendency to sweat, the high temperature of the summer months causing the oil to exude; this soon becomes sour or rancid, and injures the flavor of the coffee.

We present a table of losses made in roasting, compiled from the record of one establishment in New York. During one month a total of 173,056 pounds of all kinds of green coffee roasted showed a loss of 27,385 pounds, or .1582 per cent.

	Java best.	Java medium.	Maracaibo best.	Maracaibo good.	Maracaibo fair.	Rio best.	Rio good.	Rio fair.	Mocha.
January	$.16^{59}$	$.16^{66}$	$.16^{89}$	$.15$	$.14^{1}$	$.14^{19}$	$.14^{10}$	$.13^{38}$	$.14^{19}$
February	$.16^{3}$	$.16^{98}$	$.16^{9}$	$.15^{15}$	$.14^{10}$	$.14^{39}$	$.14^{60}$	$.12^{60}$	$.14^{47}$
March	$.16^{35}$	$.16^{16}$	$.16^{8}$	$.16^{5}$	$.14^{4}$	$.14^{80}$	$.13^{46}$	$.11^{76}$	$.14^{77}$
April	$.15^{75}$	$.17^{6}$	$.15^{46}$	$.14^{99}$	$.14^{86}$	$.13^{91}$	$.14^{14}$	$.13^{69}$	$.15^{1}$
May	$.16^{50}$	$.17^{29}$	$.15^{88}$	$.15^{83}$	$.15^{71}$	$.13^{65}$	$.13^{80}$	$.13^{99}$	$.15^{66}$
June	$.15^{96}$	$.17^{32}$	$.15^{19}$	$.14^{69}$	$.15^{33}$	$.13^{65}$	$.13^{41}$	$.13^{09}$	$.14^{78}$

It will be noted that Rio loses about one per cent. less than Java or Maracaibo, which we believe can be accounted for upon the ground that the Rio bean is more solid than the Sumatra or Java berry, or even the Maracaibo bean, the latter sorts being larger and more spongy than the Brazilian product. It will be noted also that an allowance of sixteen per cent. will, as a rule, cover all the loss in roasting. The usual charge for roasting coffee for the trade is from one-half to three-fourths of a cent per pound. Since means of communication from coffee-growing countries have grown more rapid, coffee has arrived in our markets much greener than formerly, and lacking in that mellowness which is so highly prized by connoisseurs.

As confirmatory of the preceding remarks, based upon a long experience gained in preparing and distributing roasted coffee, the following extract from a report of the late celebrated chemist, Baron Von Liebig, will be found interesting:—

"The chief operation is the roasting. On this depends the good quality of the coffee. In reality the berries should only be roasted until they have lost their horny condition, so that they may be ground, or, as it is done in the East, pounded to a fine powder.

"Coffee contains a crystalline substance named caffeine or theine, because it is also a component part of tea. This matter is volatile, and every care must be taken to retain it in the coffee. For this purpose the berries should be roasted till they are of a pale brown color; in those which are too dark, there is no caffeine; if they are black, the essential parts of the berries are entirely destroyed, and the beverage prepared from these does not deserve the name of coffee.

"The berries of coffee once roasted lose every hour somewhat of their aroma, in consequence of the influence of the oxygen of the air, which, owing to the porosity of the roasted berries, can easily penetrate. This pernicious change may best be avoided by strewing over the berries when the roasting is completed, and while the vessel in which it has been done is still hot, some powdered white or brown sugar (half-an-ounce to one pound of coffee is sufficient). The sugar melts immediately, and by well shaking or turning the roaster quickly, it spreads over all the berries, and gives each one a fine glaze, impervious to the atmosphere. They have then a shining appearance, as though covered with a varnish, and they in consequence lose their smell entirely, which, however, returns in a high degree as soon as they are ground. After this operation they are to be shaken out rapidly from the roaster and spread on a cold plate of iron, so that they may cool as soon as possible. If the hot berries are allowed to remain heaped together, they begin to sweat, and when the quantity is large, the heating process, by the influence of air, increases to such a degree that at last they take fire spontaneously. The roasted and glazed berries should be kept in a dry place, because the covering of sugar attracts moisture.

"If the raw berries are boiled in water, from twenty-three to twenty-four per cent. of soluble matter is extracted. On being roasted till they assume a pale chestnut color, they lose from fifteen to sixteen per cent., and the extract obtained from these by means of boiling water is twenty to twenty-one per cent. of the weight of the unroasted berries. The loss in weight of the extract is much larger when the roasting process is carried on till the color of the berries is dark brown or black. At the same time that the berries lose in weight by roasting, they gain in volume by swelling; one hundred volumes of green berries give, after roasting, a volume of one hundred and fifty to one hundred and sixty; or two pint measures of unroasted berries give three pints when roasted."

CHAPTER VI.

GRINDING THE COFFEE, OR GRINDING, BLENDING AND MIXING COFFEE.

SIMPLE as it may seem, the process of grinding the roasted bean is one that requires considerable attention. If ground too coarsely, the coffee requires protracted boiling to extract its strength, and much boiling is fatal to a good cup of coffee. While one may grind too finely, the mistake of grinding too coarsely is that most frequently made. Just to what degree of fineness it should be ground depends somewhat upon the manner of making the coffee. If any of the filtering coffee-pots are used the grinding should be very fine, in order that the strength may more readily be exhausted by the water simply passing through; but where boiled for ten or fifteen minutes, as is most frequently the case, the coffee should be ground so that the larger particles are about the size of pin-heads.

Every family should own a small coffee-mill and grind their own coffee, grinding it just as required for each meal, and the less time that elapses after grinding until the coffee is in the pot the better. The aroma of coffee passes off rapidly enough after being roasted, but still more quickly after being ground, hence the necessity for grinding it only for immediate use. If during wet weather the beans become damp and tough, so that they do not rattle when stirred, warm them up in a clean pot or skillet before grinding, stirring them meanwhile—so as not to scorch them—and thus drive off the moisture, develop their flavor and make them grind better. Most retail grocers keep a large coffee-mill and when requested will grind coffee for those customers who do not find it convenient to grind it at home; the latter method, however, is the best, as it gives the customer fresher ground coffee and a closer control as regards fine or coarse grinding. When dependent upon the store for ground coffee it is best not to buy at one time more than a supply adequate for two or three days' consumption. Another consideration in favor of consumers buying coffee in the bean is that there can be no suspicion of adulteration with chicory, ground peas or other substances, with which grocers are sometimes unjustly charged, and the satisfaction is thus greater on all sides.

As individual tastes differ, it frequently occurs that no single variety of coffee exactly suits certain consumers, and therefore they seek to gratify their palate by either blending two sorts or mixing with one variety some vegetable substance. While some kinds of coffee possess a rich aroma they do not give to the infusion that "body" which is requisite to make the perfect cup of coffee. It is a very common practice to blend Java and Maracaibo in the proportion of eighty pounds of the former to twenty pounds of the latter, selling the mixture for straight Java. The addition of fifteen to twenty per cent. of Marcaibo to Padang coffee undoubtedly improves the latter for the majority of those who are fond of Old Government Java, as it lends to the Java the essential quality which is lacking.

Another popular blend is to take one-third Mocha and mix with two-thirds of fine old Mandheling Java, taking care that the two kinds have been roasted separately. Others dislike either of the above blends, and choose a mixture of Java and Rio. No definite rule can be given for combining two kinds of coffee together. The dealer should study the requirements of his trade, observing its peculiarities, and experiment until he is certain that he has found a combination that exactly meets certain wants, and once found he should adhere to the formula, being careful always to select as nearly as possible the same grade of coffee in the primary market. If conscientious in this, low prices and bargains will never be an inducement to take hold of some other variety which some anxious seller is sure possesses drinking qualities fully equal to that which he has been using. For mixed or adulterated coffee I have no liking. It has always been a mystery to me how persons who profess to be lovers of good coffee can satisfy their appetite with a decoction made of coffee and chicory, or coffee and various known and unknown compounds which have neither the flavor nor the nutritious and stimulating properties of pure coffee. I recognize, however, the fact that the best of the mixtures do meet the taste of thousands. At the same time I am glad to record that the practice of requiring the grocer to grind coffee in the presence of the purchaser has very largely reduced the sale of mixed or adulterated coffee.

It may be that a time will again come similar to that of our civil war, when the scarcity and high price of coffee will make it desirable to use substitutes for coffee, and therefore I give here several formulas for mixing coffee that have stood the test of years:—

No. 1.—40 pounds O. G. Java, 20 pounds Maracaibo, 25 pounds of roasted rye mixture, 15 pounds chicory.

No. 2.—50 pounds of Maracaibo, 30 pounds of roasted rye mixture, 20 pounds of chicory.

No. 3.—60 pounds of Rio, 20 pounds of roasted rye mixture, 20 pounds of chicory.

No. 4.—40 pounds of Rio, 40 pounds of roasted rye mixture, 20 pounds of chicory.

The above formulas are sufficient to show how to mix ground coffee in a manner that will furnish a good-flavored infusion. The proportions may be altered at pleasure, always taking care to have the rye mixture in excess of the chicory. During the war and since, mixtures have found ready sale that had not over five to ten pounds of pure coffee to every one hundred. The ingredients should be thoroughly mixed and ground together, the dry and dusty rye mixture absorbing the moisture of the chicory, and thus preventing the mill from becoming clogged.

CHAPTER VII.

MAKING THE COFFEE.

For this there are many recipes, and farther on will be found formulas for making Turkish coffee as made at Constantinople, French coffee as made in Paris, and the celebrated coffee of the Vienna cafés; also various methods in vogue in different coffee-producing countries, for all of which there are a certain number of admirers. The first consideration has been to provide a recipe adapted to the tastes of the great mass of the American people, and also to the facilities usually at command, while economizing material. With these conditions in mind I have ignored many so-called "improved" or "patent" coffee-pots, which, within my own knowledge, have yielded good results, but the expense of which, together with the fact that, as a rule, they do not utilize the full strength of the bean, makes them undesirable for many persons. The following recipe will be found plain, convenient, good, and economical, with the additional good feature that it may be slightly varied in regard to the quantity of coffee used, so that those who prefer a greater or less strength may be suited: I present it as

THE THURBER RECIPE.

Grind moderately fine a large cup or small bowl of coffee; break into it one egg with shell; mix well, adding enough cold water to thoroughly wet the grounds; upon this pour one pint of boiling water: let it boil slowly for ten to fifteen minutes, according to the variety of coffee used and the fineness to which it is ground. Let it stand three minutes to settle, then pour through a fine wire-sieve into a warm coffee-pot; this will make enough for four persons. At table, first put the sugar into the cup, then fill half-full of boiling milk, add your coffee, and you have a delicious beverage that will be a revelation to many poor mortals who have an indistinct remembrance of, and an intense longing for, an ideal cup of coffee. If cream can be procured so much the better, and in that case boiling water can be added either in the pot or cup to make up for the space occupied by the milk as above; or condensed milk will be found a good substitute for cream.

In order to emphasize some of the important points previously mentioned, as well as those in the above recipe, I shall recall points before noticed. Endeavor to have fresh roasted coffee, and, where practicable, grind it yourself. Never use cold milk, as coffee to be good must be hot; cream or condensed milk, however, may be used cold, owing to the much smaller quantity required, and by most persons one or the other will be preferred to milk. In cold weather rinse out the coffee-cups with hot water just before pouring out the coffee.

Coffee should be served as soon as made, for it rapidly deteriorates if left stewing upon the stove. This is one of the principal reasons why the coffee served at hotels and restaurants is so often of poor quality. It is not made often enough, and is usually kept simmering in a copper-boiler, which alone is sufficient to spoil the best coffee ever grown. If the coffee lacks clearness, and when milk is added turns dark, it is an indication that it is stale or the milk sour. Freshly made coffee ought to have a clear, amber-brown color, which milk will render lighter instead of darker. When coffee is served immediately after making it does not greatly matter in what kind of vessel it is boiled; a common tin coffee-pot will do, although one made of block tin is to be preferred. It should be served in an earthenware or porcelain coffee-pot, either being much better than nickel or silver-plated, and, in order that no heat may be lost, the vessel should be rinsed with hot water before the coffee is turned into it from that in which it is made. Some connoisseurs prefer an earthen pot in which to prepare it, and advocate placing the coffee in a fine linen bag, allowing it to simmer, not boil, for ten or fifteen minutes.

I now pass to the consideration of modes of making and serving coffee in foreign countries. Many of the recipes and much of the information is the result of my own personal investigation during a trip around the world, in the course of which particular attention was given to the subject of coffee, both in producing and consuming countries. Other data have been received from reliable correspondents or occasionally borrowed from trustworthy sources.

TURKISH COFFEE.

Everybody has heard of Turkish coffee. While in Constantinople I investigated the mysteries of that far-famed luxury. In the numerous coffee-houses of the Moslem capital, when a person calls for a cup of coffee it is specially made for him. Every coffee-house has a number of long-handled little brass coffee-pots, made to hold one, two, or more cups, as the case may be. They are smaller at the top than at the bottom and are fitted with a little grooved spout, but have no cover.

When a cup of coffee is wanted, the requisite amount of finely powdered coffee is measured into one of these little coffee-pots; water enough to fill the pot is poured in, and it is then set upon live coals, until it heats up to just the boiling point. It is then, without straining or otherwise settling the grounds, poured out into a tiny cup, and this is Turkish coffee. As may be supposed, it is thick, muddy, and the lower half of the cup composed principally of grounds; but the flavor is good, and I noticed that most Turks swallowed the grounds with the same relish that they showed for the thinner part of the beverage. The Turks never use milk with their coffee; to them the mixture would be an abomination. In Constantinople the coffee is generally ground in a mill, but in many places it is powdered with a mortar and pestle; in either case, it is almost as fine as flour—a condition which, I suppose, is necessary to get the strength of the coffee with the little boiling which they give it. The coffee used is mostly from India and Ceylon, although a considerable quantity of Arabian coffee is consumed. I am convinced that the reputation of Turkish coffee is chiefly due to the fact that great care is exercised in roasting the coffee, and not more than twenty-four hours' supply is roasted or purchased at one time.

Coffee is consumed by all classes, at all hours, and on all sorts of occasions. The little berry is indeed a very important factor in Turkish society. Nothing is done without it; no business discussed, no contract made, no visits and civilities exchanged without the aromatic cup and the accompanying chibouque or narghileh. If a purchaser enters a bazaar to price a shawl or a carpet, coffee is brought to him. If a person calls at another's house, coffee with the inseparable tobacco must greet the newcomer. There can be no welcome without it, and none but words and forms of general etiquette take place until this article has been served all round. At parting, coffee must still be present and speed the guest on his way. We are told of beggars clamoring for money to buy, not bread, as with our mendicants, but coffee.

To minister to this universal demand, coffee-houses abound in all Turkish cities. In Smyrna and in Constantinople, they are as numerous as the bar-rooms in American cities. They are generally small, often consisting of but one room, opening to the street or the bazaar, with a divan around three sides and carpets on the floor, where grave Turks sit cross-legged and may be seen from morn till eve alternately sipping the favorite liquid and puffing at the flexible-stemmed narghileh, or the long chibouque. I am inclined to think that the Turkish coffee-house, as it looms up in the mind's eye of many who have not had ocular evidence of the reality, is a rather overdrawn picture; and, as we must go to London or Paris to enjoy the luxuries of a perfect Turkish bath, so it is not unlikely that only in the descriptions by imaginative writers shall we readily find the genuine, original, old Turkish coffee-house with its "tesselated pavement," "sparkling fountains," "dark and shady cypress," and the general dazzle of decorations some of us have read about.

Coffee is made and consumed in essentially the same way in Egypt and Arabia as in Turkey. Cairo is proverbial for the number of its coffee-houses, mostly establishments of small size, and of rather uninviting appearance to the foreigner.

The traveller who puts up at the large European hotels in Constantinople, Cairo, and Alexandria, is given coffee made *à la Turque,* with the grounds in the cup, but sweetened to accommodate his heretical Christian notions. The sugar is placed in the coffee-pot with the coffee, and they are boiled together.

In Greece, also, I noticed that the coffee one found at the cafés, especially in the eastern islands, was prepared Turkish fashion, and the narghileh stood ever ready-filled, awaiting the bidding of the customer. The Greek coffee-house, however, has chairs and tables, and by its size, appearance, and general stage of evolution, approaches much nearer the cafés of Western Europe than the Mohammedan establishments. A peculiar and picturesque feature of the Greek cafés is their frequent outdoor development, in the shape of numerous small tables, which sometimes cover an entire public square. There the modern Hellene seeks the cool of evening in summer, or suns himself in winter, while taking his coffee and enjoying the light of his brilliant skies, of which he is still so proud.

"Eternal summer gilds them yet,
But all except their sun is set."

There the stranger, on pulling out his purse to pay for the cup he has consumed, may find, as it happened to me once, that it is already settled for, Greek hospitality having preceded him in this.

From the coffee-houses of Stamboul to the cafés of Paris is a great leap. We are here altogether in a new school of coffee-making and coffee-drinking. If the cup of coffee which is handed to you on the shores of the Bosphorus may be considered the general type of the beverage in Eastern lands, it is perhaps equally true that the manner in which coffee is used in the French capital prevails more or less over the rest of the Western world. The *café au lait* and the *café noir* are to be found everywhere among the Christian nations of both hemispheres. There are, of course, different methods for their preparation, which I shall notice in the course of my investigations.

The reader may perhaps remember the famous axioms which Brillat Savarin lays down in his "Physiologie du Gout:"

"A beast gorges itself.

"Man eats.

"The man of taste alone knows how to eat."

Another French writer, a lover of coffee, formulates the following paraphrase:

"The common run of mankind take coffee.

"A few amateurs know how to take coffee.

"The man of taste alone knows how to take coffee and appreciate its poetic aroma."

As might be expected from the spirit which has prompted these wise and witty sayings, the art of coffee-making, as well as that of general cookery, has received profound attention in France, that classical land of good things for the inner man. While there, I elicited from a "cordon-bleu" of Paris, the following recipes, with which I am happy to favor my readers.

FRENCH RECIPES.

First, to make black coffee—"café noir:"

For one cup, grind two tablespoonfuls of coffee, which pack solidly in the coffee-pot (the regular French filtering pattern); then pour boiling water, passing it twice or thrice through the coffee-pot.

The same recipe applies to the preparation of *café au lait*, which is merely black coffee to which milk is added in quantity to suit the individual taste, the proportion being generally three parts of milk to one of coffee.

The French, as is well known, often mix chicory with their coffee, mostly when taken in the form of *café au lait*. The recipe is then as follows:

For one cup, grind coffee enough to make two tablespoonfuls, mix half a tablespoonful of chicory, *en semoule* (in powder). After thoroughly mixing, pour boiling water and pass twice through coffee-pot.

In many French families the grounds that remain in the coffee-pot are utilized, for economy's sake. Hot water is poured over them, and, after passing through, is stored in a bottle, and used the next time instead of simply water. This is said to be the manner of making the best French coffee.

Some French coffee artists maintain that the roasting is best done at home, as no doubt it well may be in such knowing hands. Sometimes a simple iron pan is used for the purpose, but great care must then be taken to keep constantly agitating the berries with a wooden knife or spatula, bringing the operation to an end as soon as the berries have assumed a light brown color. A single burnt berry would impair the aroma. Use no butter nor lard during the process.

Before grinding, the roasted berries are put on a metallic plate, which is placed on the stove and heated until the aroma of the coffee, developed by the operation, perfumes the room. Then grind in the ordinary mill and make according to the above recipe.

In some of the most renowned of French cafés a mixture of different varieties of the berry is often resorted to—Mocha, Java, Martinique, Guadaloupe, or East India being generally used together in carefully ascertained proportions. The result is a cup which, for its felicitous combination of strength, aroma, roundness, and delicacy, is prized by the French epicure as a product of the highest art.

There is, perhaps, no more characteristic feature of Paris than its cafés. They line all the boulevards and abound in all the principal streets, with their rows of chairs and tables on the sidewalk, and their large plate-glass windows brilliantly lighted at night, through which extends the vista of the great *salon* (or main room), with its crowd of customers, its ornamented walls, large mirrors, and general gilding and decoration in the gay but seldom gaudy French style. Through the maze of chairs and tables waiters with the inevitable whiskers and long white aprons glide about, tray in hand, attending to the groups of well-behaved *habitués*, while the *dame de comptoir*, sitting on a raised platform in a sort of compromise between a box and a throne, presides majestically over the scene, computes *l'addition*, gives *change*, and receives and returns the courteous salutation of every one who enters or who leaves.

Coffee, in the vocabulary of the place, may be called for in the shape of a "demi-tasse," a "capucin," or a "mazagran." The "demi-tasse" is merely a small cup of black coffee, to which the customer occasionally adds "cognac," "kirsch," or some other liqueur. When the "demi-tasse" is taken with a "petit verre" (meaning a little glass of liqueur), it is sometimes denominated a "gloria." The "capucin," which, however, is a term seldom used, is merely another name for "café au lait," but served in a glass; while a "mazagran" is coffee taken with water instead of milk. The coffee, which is exactly the same as that of the "demi-tasse," is served in a tall, narrow glass, and a decanter of cold water is brought along with it; the customer does the mixing himself. It is said that, after some glorious achievement or other in Africa, near the city of Mazagran, neither milk nor brandy being forthcoming, the French soldiers were compelled to use water with their coffee—hence the drink and its name. The "demi-tasse" costs generally from thirty-five to forty-five centimes (from seven to nine cents), with a "pourboire" of ten centimes (two cents) to the waiter.

It is a curious and endless study for a foreigner to observe the life at the cafés—either at the Grand Café and the Café de la Paix, under the Grand Hotel, on the Boulevard des Capucines, the chief rendezvous of the fashionable floating population; or at the Café de Madrid, on the Boulevard Montmartre, where lawyers, journalists, and Bohemians most do congregate; or at the Café du Helder, chiefly patronized by artists, students of the military schools, officers, etc.; or at the Cafés Riche and Grétry, where he will hear no end of talk about the Bourse and the "cours des valeurs;" or at the Grand Café Parisien, near the Chateau d'Eau, the largest of all these establishments, although not the finest; or, indeed, at any of the thousand and one cafés scattered all over the gay metropolis, and which go so far towards giving it its peculiar physiognomy. It has been well remarked that Paris without cafés would be a landscape without water, a bride without a veil, a thing incomplete and disfigured. The café is indispensable to the Frenchman, and especially to the Parisian. He may submit to having some of his liberties curtailed, even to seeing his favorite newspaper suppressed by the authorities; but if government should lay hand on the Arch of his most cherished associations and affections, he would die fighting in its defence. Life without the café would be a mockery to him. It is there that, in the morning, he often takes his first breakfast, consisting of a large cup of "café au lait" with a crisp rusk of bread, and perhaps a little butter. There he may possibly return for his second breakfast, the mid-day meal. To the café he will certainly apply again for an appetizer before dinner, or, it may be after the repast, for his demi-tasse of black coffee to assist his digestion, clear the fumes of the claret, and give additional zest to the enjoyment of his cigar. And the café may see him once more, after the performance is over at the theatre, if his stomach hints at a little cold meat, or beer, etc. At any time during the day the slightest inducement will cause him to take a seat at one of the tempting little tables; if he meets a friend, it is the best place to converse; if the weather is fine and people crowd the boulevards, it is the very best point of observation. If it rains, no better refuge than the cheerful hall. If he has no friend, does not care to look at the promenaders, knows not precisely what to do, whither could he go, indeed, but to the café, where he will find newspapers, and life, and comfort. Such at least were the reasonings with which I could not help crediting the crowds of customers at whom I marvelled, as I passed café after café in full bloom and activity at almost any hour of the day or night.

The café does not confine itself to the serving of coffee. It represents, in reality, a compound idea, a happy combination of the coffee-house properly so-called, the restaurant, the confectionery or ice-cream saloon, and the drinking saloon, or wine-room. You may always obtain there breakfast and other light meals. Besides the extract of the tropical berry, liquors, wines, beer, and drinks of all sorts are also dispensed. None, however, of the more or less disreputable and vulgar associations which the "saloon" calls up in our minds, attach to the café. It is, in every sense, proper, respectable. Perfect order, urbanity, and good manners prevail generally. Everybody goes to the café; ladies will be seen there. True, they may avoid some of the establishments on the boulevard, where the "demi-monde" may, perhaps, be too fond of airing extraordinary toilettes; but none will disdain to stop for a *tutti-frutti* at the Café Neapolitain, or at Tortoni's for one of the famous ices which that renowned café furnishes. In the interior of most of the first-class cafés smoking is only allowed in the evening. On the whole, the café is a genial and not unhealthy factor in French life, for it has civilized drinking, and relegated intemperance to the "brasseries," the wine-shops, and the "guinguettes" frequented by the workingmen in the poorer quarters of the city.

The correspondent of an American periodical thus comments on the general character of the Paris cafés:

"Alimentary, and not literary, is the modern café. Times are so changed since Voltaire, Diderot, and the rest sang and shouted in the Café Procope—jested, reasoned, and made themselves immortal there—there are so many people who have the means to frequent cafés, and there is such an immense floating population, eager, curious, and bent on sight-seeing, that no clique can live. Its precincts, no matter how hallowed, are invaded by the leering mob and His many-headed Majesty the Crowd. Still, certain cafés are able to boast a clientèle, with the military, journalistic, artistic, or commercial element in preponderating force—cafés where the stockbrokers, students, or officers go—but the old historic café, the café of tradition, where you were sure to find some celebrity on exhibition—a first-class poet, or a philosopher—may be said to be defunct."

If the café of tradition has been transformed in France, it has disappeared altogether in England. Of the old coffee-houses, of which we have read so much, with which the names of Pope, Addison, Steele, Dryden, Johnson, and so many other poets, writers, and public men, stand indissolubly connected in our minds, and which were all in full stir and activity in the time of Queen Anne, nothing remains at the present day; for who would venture to recognize them in the solemnly magnificent clubs of Pall-Mall? The English, from the point of view of coffee, have rather fallen into bad ways, and tea has far outstripped the Arabian berry in their affections. The term "coffee-house" in England has become hardly more than nominal, the restaurant being the principal feature, and one hears orders given for "a pint of bitter" or "'arf and 'arf" much more frequently than for a cup of coffee.

Still, that guiding-star of gastronomic England, M. Soyer, in his all comprehensive solicitude for the human stomach, could not overlook coffee. I respectfully transcribe into these pages the directions of the master:

M. SOYER'S METHOD.

"Put two ounces of ground coffee in a stewpan, which set upon the fire, stirring the coffee round with a spoon until quite hot; then pour over a pint of boiling water; cover over closely for five minutes: pass it through a cloth, warm again, and serve."

With the sanction of such a name, the above may be looked upon as embodying the most approved English recipe, although I believe M. Soyer was French by birth and education. Of its general observance, however, I have strong doubts, for England is certainly not the country where the ideal cup of coffee is found. Indeed, I give it as my experience that, as a rule, the English do not know how to make coffee; and even in the very best hotels and restaurants, a sloppy mixture is served which compares very unfavorably with that to be obtained in establishments of the same grade in Paris, Vienna, or New York.

Of all the outrageous travesties upon good coffee, however, the slops dignified by that name on the English steam lines plying between New York and Liverpool are the worst. I have crossed on the Cunard, White Star and Inman boats, and all of these noble lines, which vie with each other in speed, safety and seamanship seem to compete as strongly in the badness of their coffee. When one is wrestling with the pangs of sea-sickness the memory of the fragrant, refreshing and grateful beverage which cheers the home breakfast-table comes strongly to mind, but oh! what a disappointment to the palate, stomach and brain is the reality which is forced upon the passenger. Repeated investigations and experiments as to the cause of this have led to the conclusion that it is almost wholly the result of either ignorance or indolence, or both. As stated elsewhere the great central truths in producing good coffee are *fresh roasted*, *fresh ground*, *fresh made*. As regards the first requisite it is not usually convenient to roast coffee on shipboard, nor is it necessary if supplies are purchased at each end of the voyage and kept in a tightly closed tin receptacle. The second requisite is important; the coffee should be ground in a hand-mill just before it is required for use, and if the roasted beans have become damp and tough they should be warmed or toasted in the oven of the galley until crisp and fragrant so that they will grind easily. The third requisite, however, is the most important of all. Coffee should always be served as soon as made, and should never be more than fifteen minutes old. It is useless for the steward to say this is too much trouble. It is never too much trouble to trim the sails or adjust the ventilators, and it ought not to be too much trouble to make coffee every fifteen minutes during the hours when coffee is served. They understand this on French steamers, and there are fortunes in store for the steamship company that has the enterprise to combine English seamanship with a French cuisine. They have introduced the French system into English hotels; why should it not be done upon English steamers?

In colonial times and in the early days of the Republic, New York had its coffee-houses. The names of Burn's Coffee-house, the Merchants' Coffee-house, and later the Tontine Coffee-house are familiar to all who are acquainted with the history of the City. They differed somewhat, however, from the European cafés in being chiefly business or political headquarters. Valentine's Manual of the City of New York gives an interesting account of these coffee-houses, accompanied with illustrations, showing them to have been quite stately affairs. Among other interesting matter relating to these famous old resorts we find newspaper advertisements of sales to take place there—among others "a parcel of likely negroes to be sold at publick vendue, to-morrow at ten o'clock, at the Merchants' Coffee-house." I must add for the honor of our metropolis that this occurred in 1750. The Merchants' Coffee-house stood on the southeast corner of Wall and Water streets. The "Tontine," on the northwest corner of Wall and Water streets, succeeded to its popularity and fame; in 1795 it was in full operation. The Merchants' Exchange was then located in the building, but subsequently moved further up Wall street. The name of "Tontine" is found as late as 1832, and to this day the buildings on this site now occupied for commercial purposes are known as the Tontine buildings. Browne's Coffee-house, on Water street, between Pine and Wall, obtained considerable notoriety, in 1832, as a favorite resort of those who believed in pure coffee as an antidote to the cholera epidemic.

The coffee-house, however, no longer exists among us. Americans are the greatest coffee consumers in the world, but take the beverage mostly at meals, either at home or at the restaurant. There are, indeed, in New York, a number of coffee-rooms, or cafés, as they sometimes call themselves, attached to some of the principal hotels; but they are expensive and rather exclusive establishments and cannot be said to realize the cheerful ideas and associations called up by the word coffee-house. We are perhaps too busy a people to support cafés like those of Europe, which one sees crowded from morning to night with customers disposing apparently of endless leisure.

A NEW ORLEANS RECIPE.

Some of my Southern readers, no doubt, remember the cup of coffee they have drunk at the coffee-stands of the French Market in New Orleans, on the broad "levee." Famous resorts they were formerly! There the early riser sought for the cheer of the aromatic cup; there the keeper of late hours called for the grateful stimulant after the theatre or the ball. The coffee to be had at the French Market was proverbial for its excellence; and the old "auntie" who presided over one of those stands loomed up forever after as a prophet and lawgiver in all that pertained to coffee! From one of these venerable authorities I hold the following recipe, warranted to give the best "Creole coffee," as she termed it:

"Roast the coffee carefully until it assumes a uniform brown color. Then cover it up and allow it to cool. Then grind and cover it up again carefully, until placed in the coffee-pot (generally of the French pattern), where it must be pressed as compactly as possible. Pour a little boiling water over it and let it filter into the coffee, then pour again a tablespoonful of boiling water, repeating this every five minutes."

The result is a very strong extract, not more than a tablespoonful or two of water being measured in for each ordinary-sized cup of café au lait desired.

If the fact of the above being *in toto* a Southern recipe could induce the average eating-house keeper at the stations along many of the Southern railways to adopt it in exchange for the one, whatever it be, which they now follow, I think I should be laying claim by this publicity to the deepest gratitude of my Southern friends and of travellers generally. My past personal experience warrants me in crediting the following entry in the diary of a traveller, a Southerner, who had been around the world with me, and who returned to New York *via* New Orleans and the Southern States:

"GRENADA STATION, MISSISSIPPI.

"Stopped for breakfast: tried tea, but was not equal to it; tried coffee, same result. I denominate this the champion establishment, of all places I have been at around the world, for the utter depravity of its tea and coffee."

The coffee-house flourishes both in Italy and in Spain, as any one can vouch who has seen the large and crowded cafés in the principal Italian and Spanish cities. These establishments, by their general character and by the mode of serving the beverage, belong essentially to the French school. You find them along the Corso in Rome, the Toledo in Naples, in the Galleria Vittorio Emanuele, and around the Piazza del Duomo in Milan; along the Riva degli Schiavoni and the arcades which surround the Piazza di San Marco in Venice, etc.—seemingly ever full, but ever decent and orderly. They are, indeed, institutions, landmarks, important features of every city. The guide-book invariably gives you a list of them, and frequently, not without reason, advises you to take at least breakfast there. Ask a direction of a passer-by in the streets and he will, not improbably, answer: You know the Café di Roma, on the Corso, or the Café d'Italia; well, walk right on to it, then turn to your left, etc. And that in a country where monuments mark almost every spot. But the chances are that your informant is returning from the café or intending to go there sometime during the day, and naturally enough, in any given direction, the café is the first thing that looms up in his mind's eye.

In Madrid the Puerto del Sol is the great café centre. They abound all around this noted spot, and in the principal adjoining streets. As a rule, they do not compare in splendor of appointments with the Paris cafés. One of them, however, was to me a never-failing source of wonder and interest—the great café under the Hotel de Paris, in the angle formed by the Carrera de San Geronimo and the Calle de Alcalá, as they run into the Puerto del Sol. The immense hall, thus reaching from street to street, had its floor a few feet below the level of the square; and, glancing through one of the large windows facing on the Puerto del Sol, one commanded a view of its entire extent. And a sight it was! We were there in winter. The sensitive Madrileños avoided the open air and crowded into the café. Every one of the, perhaps, one hundred tables was surrounded by customers, four, six at a time; some reading the newspapers; others conversing and gesticulating; some taking chocolate or coffee; others playing at dominoes, or at cards; men, women, even children in the throng; here, a uniform resplendent with brass buttons and gold lace; there, a "mantilla" with a bright smile not far under it; near by, the dark gown of a priest; and over and around all, a sort of haze or mist of tobacco smoke. Customers came in, and customers went out; but look in at any time, and the same general picture greeted your eyes—busy and idle, unintelligible to an American.

Besides coffee and chocolate, the national beverages, one finds in the coffee-houses of Spain, as in those of France and Italy, wines, liquors, and a great variety of refreshing drinks. These form a very important department of a Spanish café. There is the "orchata," a drink made of a sort of milk of sweet almonds; the "bebida de naranja" (of orange), "de limon" (of lemon), "de fresa" (of strawberry), "de guindas" (of cherry), etc.; "sorbetes," or ices, of all kinds; "espumas de chocolate, or de café"—light, frothy creams made of these substances, and the "panales," or "azucarias," a little loaf of white blown sugar, in the shape of a French roll, very light and very porous, which is allowed to dissolve in a glass of water, and with the addition of a little lemon-juice or liquor constitutes a favorite beverage. Cigars and cigarettes, of course, are essentials.

VIENNA COFFEE.

In making coffee at the large cafés and hotels on the Karthner Ring, in Vienna, the coffee is prepared as follows: To make six quarts, one pound six ounces of coffee are used. Within a very heavy cylinder or urn that is securely pinned to the floor or table, there is fitted a coarse sieve, a piece of cord or rope surrounding the sieve making it fit tightly. Over the sieve there is placed a piece of Canton flannel, fastened down by means of an iron ring that fits into the rim which holds the sieve. Attached to the sieve is an iron frame with a hook at the top.

The sieve is pressed to the bottom of the cylinder, the coffee placed upon the flannel, and boiling-hot water poured upon it. This receptacle is then closed and covered, and allowed to stand six minutes. A screw fitted into an iron frame is then hooked on to the frame holding the sieve, which is then forced toward the mouth of the urn, the pressure forcing the infusion through the Canton flannel. The coffee is then ready to be served with hot milk and whipped cream. For the use of families a coffee-pot of a somewhat novel character is employed. This is more complicated than the simple contrivance described above. The water is boiled by means of an alcohol lamp underneath the pot. When the water boils the steam passes through a tube, and through the finely-ground coffee which has been placed loose in the top, and protected by several strainers. A glass top enables the operator to see when the coffee is ready for use, and when finished the glass cover is removed and a metallic one put in its place. This process secures a perfect infusion of the coffee without loss of aroma, and it has made Vienna coffee deservedly popular.

THE BEVERAGE IN BRAZIL.

Brazil is not only the largest coffee-producing, but also, essentially, a coffee-drinking country. Coffee constitutes almost the exclusive beverage of the people, by whom it is consumed very largely, especially in the regions where it is grown. They almost universally take it "black," as we term it—that is, without milk.

The coffee is roasted as with us, sometimes in closed roasters, but more frequently in open pans. As a rule, it is more roasted than with us, and a larger quantity used, the beverage being taken very strong. It is made by grinding the coffee very fine, almost to a powder, placing it in a woollen bag, upon which boiling water is poured and the strength thus extracted.

Coffee-houses abound in Rio Janeiro. They are generally of smaller size than their European or North American namesakes, but provide for three cents, a cup of coffee which is said to equal any to be found in Paris or New York. It seems to be a matter of indifference to the great mass of Brazilian coffee-drinkers whether new or old coffee is used; but there are epicures among the rich planters of Brazil who keep the coffee destined for their own table five or six years in the hull. It is claimed by good judges that there is no coffee in the world superior to old Rio preserved in the hull until mellowed by age; it develops thus a richness, and at the same time a delicacy of flavor not found in any other variety of the bean, but for this I cannot personally vouch.

COFFEE IN JAVA.

In Java and Sumatra the natives roast the leaves of the coffee-tree, and make with them an infusion which they prefer to the beverage extracted from the bean. The preparation is said to possess a delicate flavor, not unlike that of tea—a resemblance accounted for by the presence in both plants of the same chemical principle, caffeine or theine. The coffee leaves appear to be rich in caffeine.

The use of this coffee-leaf tea, however, is confined to the aborigines. The following recipe, which I procured from an old resident when in Batavia, describes the process of coffee-making as practised by the Dutch settlers in Java:

"Take a coffee-pot composed of two detached parts, the lower one a reservoir, and the upper one a sort of top-story filter, the bottom of which is pierced with very fine holes. Over the bottom of this filter a double piece of flannel cloth is placed so as to cover it entirely, fitting well all round. A sufficient quantity of well-ground coffee being then filled in and firmly tamped or rammed down, cold water is slowly poured over it, after which the whole is allowed to stand still until the water has passed through the coffee into the reservoir underneath. The passing of the water through the coffee should occupy at least four to five hours, in order to extract the full strength and flavor of the substance. For that reason, care must be exercised to press the coffee very tightly into the filter—an operation facilitated by this part of the coffee-pot being separable from the other. The filter should also be high and narrow to retard the passage of the liquid, and large enough to contain the required quantity of both coffee and water; to pour in a subsequent supply of water is not to be recommended."

It will be observed that this filter is very similar to the familiar French filtering coffee-pot. The extract thus obtained should be of such strength that, mixed with three or four parts of hot milk, it will give a splendid cup of *café au lait à la Hollandaise.*

Coffee, being exceedingly cheap, is used in profusion in Java, but the form of coffee-making as there in use is probably too expensive for any but a coffee-producing country.

I may remark here that the coffee which a traveller ordinarily finds at the hotels in Java, and in Ceylon as well, is not such as he might anticipate. At many of the stations along the lines of the New York Central, or New York and New Haven railroads, one can get a cup of coffee which is perfection itself, compared with that which is offered the traveller in Java or Ceylon.

BARON VON LIEBIG'S METHOD.

Baron Von Liebig, some years since, commented upon the different methods of making coffee, and also furnished the world with the manner in which he prepared it for his own use:

"The usual methods of preparing coffee are, 1st, by filtration; 2d, by infusion; 3d, by boiling.

"Filtration gives often, but not always, a cup of coffee. When the pouring of the boiling water over the ground coffee is done slowly, the drops in passing come in contact with too much air, whose oxygen works a change in the aromatic particles, and often destroys them entirely. The extraction, moreover, is incomplete. Instead of 20 to 21 per cent. the water dissolves only 11 to 15 per cent., and 7 to 10 per cent. is lost.

"Infusion is accomplished by making the water boil, and then putting in the ground coffee, the vessel being immediately taken off the fire and allowed to stand quietly for about ten minutes. The coffee is ready for use when the powder swimming on the surface falls to the bottom on slightly stirring it. This method gives a very aromatic coffee, but one containing little extract.

"Boiling, as is the custom in the East, yields excellent coffee. The powder is put on the fire in cold water, which is allowed merely to boil up a few seconds. The fine particles of coffee are drunk with the beverage. If boiled long the aromatic parts are volatilized, and the coffee is then rich in extract, but poor in aroma.

"As the best method I adopt the following, which is a union of the second and third: The usual quantities both of coffee and water are to be retained; a tin measure containing half an ounce of green berries, when filled with roasted ones, is generally sufficient for two small cups of coffee of moderate strength, or one so-called large breakfast-cup (one pound of green berries, equal to sixteen ounces, yielding, after roasting, twenty-four tin measures) of one-half ounce, for forty-eight small cups of coffee. With three-fourths of the coffee to be employed after being ground, the water is made to boil ten or fifteen minutes. The one-quarter of the coffee which has been kept back is then thrown in, and the vessel immediately withdrawn from the fire, covered over, and allowed to stand for five or six minutes. In order that the powder on the surface may fall to the bottom it is stirred round; the deposit takes place, and the coffee poured off is ready for use. In order to separate the dregs more completely the coffee may be passed through a clear cloth, but generally this is not necessary, and often prejudicial to the pure flavor of the beverage. The first boiling gives the strength, the second addition to the flavor. The water does not dissolve of the aromatic substance more than the fourth part contained in the roasted coffee.

"The beverage, when ready, ought to be of a brown black color; untransparent it always is, somewhat like chocolate thinned with water; and this want of clearness in coffee so prepared does not come from the fine grounds, but from a peculiar fat resembling butter, about twelve per cent. of which the berries contain, and which, if over-roasted, is partly destroyed. In the other methods of making coffee more than half the valuable part of the berries remains in the 'grounds' and is lost.

"To judge as favorably of my coffee as I do myself, its taste is not compared with that of the ordinary beverage, but rather the good effects might be taken into consideration which my coffee has on the organism Many persons, too, who connect the idea of strength or concentration with a dark or black color, fancy my coffee to be thin and weak, but these were at once inclined more favorably directly I gave it a dark color by means of burnt sugar or by adding some substitute. The real flavor of coffee is so little known to most persons, that many who drank my coffee for the first time doubted of its goodness, because it tasted of the berries. A coffee, however, which has not the flavor of the berry is no coffee, but an artificial beverage, for which many other things may be substituted at pleasure. Hence it comes that if to the decoction made from roasted chicory, carrots, or beetroot, the slightest quantity of coffee be added, few persons detect the difference. This accounts for the great diffusion of each such substitute. A dark mixture, with an empyreumatical taste, most people fancy to be coffee. For tea there are no substitutes, as everybody knows what real tea is like."

The charm of many breakfast-tables is taken away by the effects of an unclean coffee-pot. The vessel should be thoroughly cleansed before using, especially the bottom of the receiver and the spout, and under no circumstances should the grounds or stale coffee be allowed, after using, to remain in the pot for any length of time. Economy in the use of ground coffee is fatal to securing a delicious beverage. To sum up, the essentials required to secure a cup of coffee suited to any table are:

First.—The very best quality of freshly roasted and ground coffee.

Second.—Thoroughly clean utensils.

Third.—Enough coffee, and prepared with sufficient care in the manner most according with the taste of the consumer, either as café noir, café au lait, Vienna style, or in the Arabian, Turkish, or Brazilian method.

CHAPTER VIII.

EARLY HISTORY OF COFFEE.

In Abyssinia and Ethiopia, where the coffee-plant is found both wild and in a cultivated state, coffee seems to have been used as a beverage from time immemorial. In those remote regions the Arabs are said to have first tasted the fragrant draught, and, wondering much and approving greatly, to have brought over, toward the beginning of the fifteenth century, some of the precious beans into their own country, where the use of the beverage spread rapidly. Different accounts, however, are given by the Arabs of the way in which this favorite drink of theirs first gained introduction into Arabia. In an Arab manuscript, preserved in one of the public libraries of Paris, it is stated that the Mufti of Aden, travelling in Persia, became acquainted there with the use of coffee, which had for long years been known in that country and in Africa, and introduced it into Arabia. The date of this important event is also laid down, in the above-mentioned work, at about the beginning of the fifteenth century. This makes the introduction of coffee into Arabia a comparatively recent occurrence—dating not much more than half a century before the discovery of America, and about eight hundred years after the time of Mahomet. According to another version, a mollah, rejoicing in the name of Chadeby, was the first Arab to take coffee, and this he did to conquer a perpetual sleepiness which sadly interfered with his evening prayers. Still another legend ascribes to the vigilant superior of an Arabian monastery the first experiment in coffee-drinking. This worthy man, it seems, had endless trouble with his dervishes, from their invariable tendency to sleep during evening service. Having heard of the peculiar effects of coffee upon the goats which browsed upon the plant, he bethought himself of trying the virtue of the berry upon his monks. The experiment proved a complete success; the dervishes took eagerly to the new beverage, to the sacrifice of their formerly cherished slumbers. Laymen followed the example—even those who did not need to be kept awake, and coffee became the national drink of Arabia. The Mahometan pilgrims who flocked annually to Mecca were initiated into this new fragment of the Faith, and carried back coffee-beans in their saddle-bags to all parts of the globe professing the faith of Islam. Coffee overran Egypt. It reached Constantinople. In that city there was a great rush to the coffee-houses as soon as these establishments were opened.

But for some reason or other coffee excited the animosity of the priests. Perhaps it was jealousy of the new shrines in the land! According to one account, the Arabs having called coffee *kahwah*, which was an old word in their language for wine, the result was a confusion of ideas; hence the ire of the bigoted. Others state that the gatherings at the coffee-houses furnished such opportunities for discussions as to alarm the government, which, under Amurat III., ordered the closing of all these public places, and allowed the use of the beverage only in the privacy of the family.

But coffee was already enthroned in the Turkish heart. It triumphed over all. The edict could not be maintained. Similar discomfiture attended another attempt, at the time of the Candian war, during the minority of Mahomet IV., to suppress the coffee-houses. Nor were the opponents of coffee more successful in Cairo. We read that, in the year 1523, a certain Abdalla Ibrahim, the chief priest of the Koran in Cairo, began, from the pulpit of his great mosque, a violent campaign against coffee-drinking. Thereupon the Cheik el Belek, or governor of the city, assembled all the doctors of the law, and after listening with patience to a long discussion, he simply had coffee served all round; and then he rose and left, without saying a single word. There never was heard in Cairo any more preaching against coffee.

The first coffee-house in Europe was established in 1554, in Constantinople. It was not, however, till the middle of the following century, nearly two centuries after its first introduction into

Arabia, that coffee stepped over the boundaries of Mohammedanism, and was introduced among the Christian nations. The first coffee-house in London was opened in Newman's Court, Cornhill, in 1652, by a Greek named Pasqua Rossie. This Greek, says a writer on the subject, "was the servant of an English merchant named Edwards, who brought some coffee with him from Smyrna, and whose house, when the fact became known, was so thronged with friends and visitors to taste the new beverage, that, to relieve himself from annoyance, Edwards established his servant in a coffee-house."

As early as 1658 the use of coffee had been revealed to the inhabitants of Marseilles by merchants and travellers. About that year, Thévenot, a citizen, on his return from his Eastern travels, is said to have "regaled his guests with coffee after dinner."

"This, however," says Le Grand d'Aussy in his "Vie Privée des Français," "was but the eccentricity of a traveller, which would not come into fashion among such people as the Parisians. To bring coffee into credit, some extraordinary and striking circumstance was necessary. This circumstance occurred on the arrival, in 1669, of an embassy from the Grand Seigneur Mahomet IV. to Louis XIV. Soliman Aga, chief of the mission, having passed six months in the capital, and during his stay having acquired the friendship of the Parisians by some traits of wit and gallantry, several persons of distinction, chiefly women, had the curiosity to visit him at his house. The manner in which he received them not only inspired a wish to renew the visit, but induced others to follow the example. He caused coffee to be served to his guests, according to the custom of his country; for since fashion had introduced the custom of serving this beverage among the Turks, civility demanded that it should be offered to visitors, as well as that these should not decline partaking of it. If a Frenchman, in a similar case, to please the ladies, had presented to them this black and bitter liquor, he would have been rendered forever ridiculous. But the beverage was served by a Turk—a gallant Turk—and this was sufficient to give it inestimable value. Besides, before the palate could judge, the eyes were seduced by the display of elegance and neatness which accompanied it; by those brilliant porcelain cups into which it was poured; by napkins with gold fringes, on which it was served to the ladies. Add to this the furniture, the dresses, and the foreign customs, the strangeness of addressing the host through the interpreter, being seated on the ground, on tiles, etc., and you will allow that there was more than enough to turn the heads of his visitors. Leaving the hotel of the ambassador with an enthusiasm easily imagined, they hastened to their acquaintances, to speak of the coffee of which they had partaken; and Heaven only knows to what a degree they were excited."

Marseilles lays claim to the first coffee-house in France, 1671. In the following year, an Armenian, named Pascal, opened a shop at the Fair of Saint-Germain, near Paris, in which he dispensed the exotic beverage to the sightseers. This success encouraged him to establish a coffee-house in the capital, on the Quai de l'Ecole. It was small in proportions and modest in appointments, chiefly frequented by travellers, knights of Malta, and officers of the army and navy; but it soon achieved with these considerable reputation, sold its coffee very high, and proved a most profitable venture. Pascal is said to have subsequently gone to London, to engage there in the coffee trade. Is it not barely possible that this person is identical with the Greek, Rossie, previously mentioned? At last, an enterprising spirit, Etienne d'Alep, built what was for the time a magnificent hall, with mirrors, divans, marble tables, etc., in the Oriental taste. He soon had several competitors. The celebrated Procope, after having long sold coffee at the Fair of Saint-Germain, founded in 1689, in the rue des Fossés Saint-Germain, in Paris, near the theatre of the Comédie Française, the establishment which has since been immortalized by its association with the names of Boileau, Lafontaine, Molière, and later, Voltaire, the Encyclopedists, etc. Later on, under Louis XV., the famous Café de la Régence was established, which became the Mecca of chess-players. The café had definitively struck root in Paris, and no breeze of political change or popular fickleness was ever to destroy it.

In London the growth of coffee in popular favor had been still more rapid. "Three years after the first introduction of coffee upon the statute books," says Mr. Simmonds, "the increase of houses for its sale had become so great that by the Act passed in 1663, 'For the better ordering and collecting the duty of excise, and preventing the abuses therein' (15 Chas. II., Cap. II., Sect. 15), express provision is made for the licensing of all coffee-houses at the quarter sessions, under a penalty of £5 for every month during which any person should retail coffee, chocolate, or tea, without having first procured such license from the magistrates. From that time to the Revolution, coffee-houses multiplied so rapidly that, when Ray published his 'History of Plants,' in 1688, he estimated that the coffee-houses in London were at that time as numerous as in Cairo itself; while similar places of accommodation were to be met with in all the principal cities and towns in England."

Indeed, such favorite meeting-places had the coffee-houses become with the politicians and wits of London, "for discussing, theorizing, and general wagging of tongue," under the exhilaration of coffee, that in 1675 the government of Charles II. came to look upon them as public nuisances, and endeavored to have them prohibited by the courts of law as "hot-beds of seditious talk and slanderous attacks upon persons in high stations." A decision was, in fact, rendered to that effect; but, in England as in Turkey, coffee rose superior to its foes. The English coffee-houses could not be stifled; they grew daily in popularity and attained the height of activity and splendor in the first half of the eighteenth century.

It is curious to contrast this immediate and enthusiastic adoption of coffee-drinking in England with its rather slow beginnings in France—a country which has since become as devoted to coffee as England has grown indifferent to it. A French writer suggests that one of the reasons why the English took so quickly to coffee was that Great Britain, neither at home nor in her colonies, had any cheap and good wines. By the use of the new stimulant not only the British stomach, but British pride was gratified; for England, ever disliking dependence, political or commercial, had not to borrow coffee from her continental neighbors, with whom she was on doubtful terms. France, on the contrary, raised an abundance of wines. Coffee found the grape in full possession of the popular heart. The "cabarets," or wine-shops, were resorted to openly and generally by the young nobility, the celebrated authors of the time, the military, etc. In fact, wine-drinking was a national trait, and, besides the extreme cheapness of wine, many Frenchmen were inclined to look with disdain upon the new "drug." Even when coffee had come into general use, says one author, some pig-headed old patriots, who had sworn never to forsake the bottle, persisted in frequenting the wine-shops out of a sheer spirit of nationality. It is also well known that Louis XIV. did not like coffee, which is as much as to say that the court did not, nor fashionable society. The ladies of the "grand monde," with Madame de Sévigné at their head, had declared themselves decidedly against coffee. "Racine and coffee will pass," predicted the amiable letter-writer. But all this opposition gradually fell; even then, as we have seen, independent spirits did not follow these prejudices. The next king, Louis XV., to please his mistress, Madame du Barry, began to take coffee; immediately all the court went wild over the beverage, which already had hosts of fervent worshippers in the outside public.

At the beginning of the eighteenth century, the consumption of coffee was probably general among the fashionable and upper classes in England and on the Continent. With new sources of supply in the following years, the use of the beverage extended downward among the people generally. The Germans, who had long been preceded in the practice by the Netherlanders, began drinking coffee during the seven years' war (1756–1763). Several of the smaller German states at this time, says a Dutch writer, considered the use of coffee a very dangerous innovation, and proclamations were issued prohibiting its use, with the view thereby to prevent an outflow of money from the country. These ridiculous measures only stimulated the consumption, and, at the commencement of the present century, coffee was known all over the western part of Europe, and considered one of the most important staple articles. Nothing less than the hand of Napoleon clutching Europe by the throat sufficed to check for a while the drinking of coffee. The "Continental Blockade" and the enormous prices consequent thereupon restricted coffee drinking for many years to the wealthier classes on the Continent. But Napoleon fell, and a few years later, after the readjustment of the supply and demand, coffee steadily resumed the course of its popular conquests, which are still extending.

For more than fifty years after the introduction of the beverage into Europe, Arabia still furnished the entire coffee-supply of the world—a necessarily very limited quantity. Then the Hollanders, in the second decade of the eighteenth century, made their appearance in the markets of Europe with the product of Java. In a few years the culture extended to the West Indies, where it spread with wonderful rapidity. Those islands had become, in the beginning of the present century, the chief source of supply, the industry in Java having in the meantime progressed at a comparatively slow pace. Another revolution worked itself out toward the middle of the century. There was witnessed the gradual decline and almost abandonment of coffee-production in the West Indies, brought about by low prices, the scarcity of labor, political disturbances, the adoption of more remunerative cultures, etc. But Java, in the East, had already developed to vast proportions her coffee-industry, while an immense coffee-producing power was growing up in South America—Brazil not only soon overtook Java, but continued to advance, until, at the present day, more than one-half of the coffee consumed in the world issues from her fields. Java now holds the second rank in the list of coffee-producers, while Ceylon follows close on the heels of the Dutch Island, and, of late, Southern India and Central America have assumed a very decided importance as coffee-producing countries. Thus Brazil, in the Western Hemisphere, and Java and Sumatra, Ceylon and India, in the Eastern, constitute at this time the great centres of coffee-production, with minor areas of culture scattered in the West Indies, Mexico, South and Central America, Arabia, the Eastern Archipelago, and the western and eastern coasts of Africa.

CHAPTER IX.

THE MOCHA BERRY.

In popular estimation Arabian coffee, known as Mocha, ranks as the finest. For more than four centuries coffee-culture has been carried on in Arabia, and for two centuries that country furnished the world with its supply, which was, however, limited. As stated elsewhere, while Abyssinia claims the honor of giving the coffee-tree to the world, Arabia furnished to Java the first plants grown in the East Indies, and Java, in turn, transmitted the tree to Europe, whence the West Indies and Brazil obtained it, so that virtually Arabia gave to the world the far-famed plant.

The coffee-production of Arabia, however, cannot be said to have, at the present day, any real importance in the world's supply. The quantities of genuine Arabian coffee which reach Europe and America are very small, and it is estimated that only about four thousand tons of coffee are now annually exported from Arabia, although thirty years ago the exports reached 10,000 tons. East India coffee is now freely imported into Arabia, and even the product of Brazil finds its way to the Arabian coffee-pot.

The plant is mostly cultivated on terraces in the hills of Yemen, toward the districts of Aden and Mocha. The excessively hot, dry, and sandy character of the region renders irrigation and shade indispensable, and these peculiarities of soil and climate are said to account for the smallness and the acrid flavor of the Mocha bean. Certain it is that Mocha seeds planted in Brazil produce trees which in a short time give Brazil, and not Mocha coffee. In Arabia the berries are dried in the pulp, and the processes employed in preparing the bean for market are most primitive. The product, especially in the lower grades, remains very imperfectly cured, and generally mixed with fragments of hull, small stones,

ARABIAN COFFEE PLANT.

and other extraneous substances. A portion of that destined for export finds its way to Aden, whence it is reshipped on passing steamers. Captain Hunter, author of a monograph on Aden, gives the following interesting account of coffee-cultivation in Arabia:

"There are three distinct states in its culture: 1st, the preparation of the seed; 2d, the sowing; and 3d, the bedding out of the plant. The seed is prepared by removing the shell or pericarp; it is then mingled with wood-ashes and dried in the shade. Seed thus prepared is frequently purchased by planters who seek to avoid the trouble of preparation. The seed is planted in prepared beds of rich soil, mingled with manure consisting of cattle and sheep dung. The beds are covered with the branches of trees to protect the young plants from the heat of the sun during October, November, and December. They are watered every six or seven days. After about six or seven weeks the plants are carefully removed from the ground in the early morning, placed in mat-bags, and carried to the field or gardens, which are always in the vicinity of springs of water. The plants are placed in rows, at a distance of from two to three feet from each other, and are watered every fortnight; if necessary, the soil is manured. After about two, or sometimes three, or even four years, the tree begins to yield. The quantity of coffee brought to Aden, chiefly on the backs of what Madame Rachel used to advertise as 'swift dromedaries,' now amounts to about eighty thousand hundred-weight a year. About seven thousand camel-loads passed the barrier in the year 1875–76. The value of coffee now exported is something over £300,000 a year, and of the fifty-seven thousand hundred-weight exported in 1875–76 one-half went to France."

The bulk of the supply is sent to London and Marseilles; but two or three of the leading importing houses in this country have agents in Aden and Alexandria, who select and ship to Boston and New York the genuine Mocha, in addition to which there is received a good deal that is only Mocha in name. Generally, the coffee arrives here in large bales containing smaller packages, styled eighth (forty pounds) and quarter bales (eighty pounds), peculiar in shape and constructed of a coarse material, sewed with a vegetable substance that becomes hard and excessively tough by age. The tare allowed varies somewhat—from two and a half to three and a half pounds on eighths, and from four to four and a half pounds on quarter bales. The infusion made from the roasted beans possesses a heavier body than that from Java, and has a somewhat pungent or acrid flavor. When fresh roasted, Mocha gives forth a rich aroma, regarded by many as superior to that of other sorts; but some connoisseurs regard Mocha as inferior to the finest Java and the choice kinds produced in other countries. The high repute in which it is held is undoubtedly due more to its scarcity, its former reputation, and the fact that Arabia was the starting-point from which the nations using coffee obtained their supply, than to its being superior to choice selections of other varieties. As in all other kinds of coffee, however, we find good and poor qualities. At Aden and Alexandria the coffee is carefully picked over and assorted in compliance with the singular fashion in trade, which creates a demand in Europe for the larger beans, while the United States will have none but the smaller ones. In point of fact, the larger beans are the best, being fully developed and more perfect, both in appearance and flavor; but fashion in food is all-powerful in this as in other branches of trade. A striking illustration of this is found in the item of pepper: in public estimation white pepper is superior to black, and I had always supposed that they were two distinct varieties, but when visiting a pepper-plantation at Singapore, a few years since, I found that white pepper was simply black pepper which had been soaked in water during the process of preparation until the black outside skin could be rubbed off, leaving the white inside kernel. The most desirable aromatic properties are contained in the skin and a thin layer of matter next it, and both of these are sacrificed to a mistaken notion of consumers that white pepper is more pleasing to the eye. When to this fact is added another, that the process of preparing white pepper is long, tedious, and costly, making it necessary to charge, perhaps, fifty per cent. more for the white than for the black article; and further, that chemicals are sometimes used to bleach the white kernels still whiter, injuring the flavor still more, and making it positively bitter—the absurdity of this fashion is evident. But to resume the consideration of Arabian coffee: up the Red Sea, about one hundred and twenty miles from Aden, is the little port of Mocha, which furnishes the trade-name for the Arabian coffee, and from whence, until the construction of the Suez Canal, when Aden was made the port of call for the Eastern steam lines, most of it was exported. Now it goes either to Aden by native trading vessels or to Alexandria by the Khedive's Red Sea line of steamers. Considerable quantities of African coffee from the north coast also find their way, through the Berber and other native traders, to the same destination and go into consumption as "Mocha." The imports received into the United States under the name of Mocha amounted in 1878 to 12,788 bales, in 1879 to 16,346 bales, and in 1880 to 14,172 bales—only about one-half of which were probably of Arabian growth.

CHAPTER X.

THE JAVA BERRY.

THE coffee that occupies the highest place in the estimation of the American public, and, with the single exception of Mocha, commands the highest price, is *Java*, deriving its name from the island where it is produced, although, as with many other articles of commerce, the name has, to a considerable extent, become a generic one, applying to all coffee of similar character produced in the same part of the world. In point of fact, almost the entire portion of the "Java" coffee consumed in the United States is produced on the Island of Sumatra. It is none the worse for this, however, and indeed the Sumatra coffee is generally preferred by American connoisseurs to that of Java growth.

In the early history of the industry the propagation of the coffee-plant progressed slowly in Java. It began in 1696 by the introduction of plants from Malabar; but it was not until 1712 that the first invoice of Java coffee apeared in the Amsterdam market, consisting of 974 pounds, of which more than one-half was mountain coffee. It was sold for $23\frac{5}{8}$ stuivers per Amsterdam pound, equivalent to $43\frac{3}{8}$ cents per United States pound. It brought, however, such a high price as to induce strict orders to push its cultivation on a larger scale. Twelve years later, 1,396,486 pounds of this coffee were sold in Amsterdam, and coffee henceforth held undisputed priority among the staples of Java. After a period of comparative inactivity under the management of the Dutch East India Company, the government of the Netherlands established the system of cultivation which is still in existence, and which by degrees has developed the production of Java to its present magnitude. This system is, in brief, a monopoly of the Dutch government. The coffee is raised by the natives under the supervision of the government, which buys the entire product at a low fixed price, and disposes of it through the "Maatschappy," or Netherlands Trading Company, by sales at public auction, either in Batavia, Padang, or Amsterdam. There are also plantations owned and worked by individual proprietors, but the aggregate production of these estates amounts to only about one-sixth of the entire yield of the island. These plantations were mostly in existence before the adoption of the government monopoly system, or are worked on lands of inland princes who have retained that part of their native sovereign rights.

A visit to Java, made in 1876, afforded me an opportunity of inspecting the Java coffee-fields and the methods of culture. One of the finest estates visited was that owned by Mr. J. W. E. de Sturler, situated in the Preanger district. It comprises upwards of 20,000 acres, upon which, at various elevations, are grown rice, coffee, tea, cloves, and nutmegs. The coffee-plantation covers over 800 acres, upon which I found more than half a million trees in all the various stages of growth and bearing, producing in average years 3,000 piculs (408,000 lbs.), which would be equivalent to 3,000 government bags, or 6,000 half-picul mats. The trees are here raised from the seed, which is the regular coffee-bean of commerce, and begin bearing at the age of two years, their product annually increasing thereafter for many years. The yield varies greatly, however, with different trees and different years, a tree in full bearing producing from one to two pounds of beans per year. The trees are set at regular intervals of about ten feet, although in some plantations they are set in rows somewhat closer than this, the rows, however, being about that distance apart. The trees are kept pruned down to a height of about ten feet, the top being cut off, thus causing the tree to spread. The diameter of the trunk, of course, varies with age, but the average size of trees in full bearing may be said to be about that of a man's wrist. In Java the picking begins in January, and lasts for three or four months. In this work men, women, and children are employed, and as the fruit is brought in from the field in baskets it is thrown into large heaps, where it is allowed to ferment for about three days. It is then spread out in the sun to dry, which usually takes two weeks or more, according to the weather, and when dry it is put into a hulling-machine as described in a previous chapter. After the beans are carefully picked over and assorted they are packed for transportation to the shipping ports. There the coffee is "dumped," and the planter's bags returned to him, and when sold it is understood to be "in bulk," the purchaser having to provide his own bags for shipment. The coffee is also prepared by the other and newer method, commonly designated the "washed" or "West India preparation." The advocates of the old method claim, however, that it retains the caffeone, in which is embodied the flavor of the coffee, in a much greater degree, and that it is therefore superior to the washed coffee. In this, after repeated trials, I am inclined to concur, although many professionals claim that the "dried hulled" coffee is inferior to the washed. Mr. de Sturler sells his coffee by sending a circular-note to the principal firms in Batavia, informing them that he has so many thousands of piculs for sale and inviting proposals. These proposals are opened on a certain day, and the entire lot is disposed of to the highest bidder. While this is not exactly the same as the government method of marketing the crops, it is the same in principle and accomplishes the same object—that of obtaining a free competition.

The scenery upon the islands of Java and Sumatra is of the most diversified and beautiful character. Lofty mountains, ranging in height from four thousand to ten thousand feet and covered with luxuriant foliage, abound in both islands. Deep gorges, rushing streams, fertile valleys, fine plateaus, jungles and forests, lowlands and highlands, hills and volcanoes, lakes and rivers, all contribute to make these islands the most attractive spots in the world. Certainly one of the most delightful pictures lingering in my memory is that of the hill slopes of Preanger, near Buitenzorg, with their thousands of shapely and luxuriant coffee trees in all stages of bearing, and in the background the high volcanic cone of *Salac*, towering far above the entire range. Another pleasant picture which lingers in memory is that of a Javan tea plantation in the Buitenzorg district. The residence is situated nearly in the centre of the large estate, upon high ground, surrounded with a mass of tropical foliage. In front is a grove of banyan and other magnificent shade trees; in the rear, a grove of handsome cocoanut palms, while the garden, both in front and rear, is filled with an endless variety of gaudy flowers, and with nutmeg, clove, coffee, cocoa, plantain (banana), and many other fruit-bearing trees and shrubs. The house is built in the "bungalow" or one-storied style, common in tropical countries, the centre of it being occupied by a large square room or hall, which constitutes the chief sitting-room. While sitting there, enjoying a cup of tea, a peculiar cry uttered by the planter brought down a parrot of gorgeous hue from the top of one of the tall trees near the house, which perched upon his shoulder and proceeded to share his tea with him. The tinkling upon a teacup with a spoon was the signal for a flock of beautiful tame pigeons to come; these were rewarded with a little rice and sent away. Another signal filled the room with dogs of many sizes and kinds. In a short time we were again surprised at seeing a number of beautiful horses brought around to eat their rice from off the stone veranda. Upon enquiring the reason for this we found that it was because the attendants were in the habit of appropriating a part of the quantity allotted to the horses, and could not be trusted to give them the requisite supply of this article unless under the immediate eye of the owner. Here were the choicest breeds of English and Arab racing stocks, and upon expressing admiration for them I was shown the stables, where there were about thirty horses of all sorts and sizes, which are used only for racing and saddle purposes.

Hunting is one of the amusements of a planter's life—the tigers, leopard, rhinoceros, and wild boar being the principal kinds of game pursued in Java, deer also abounding. In a small enclosure in the rear of the house were various specimens of the last named beautiful animals, including one species, which, when full grown, was not over eight inches high, looking more like a delicate rabbit with pipe-stem legs than like a deer. At a little distance from the house was a small park, within which there was a herd of still another variety, larger in size than those in the small enclosure at the house, being fully as large as our American deer, but destitute of as fine horns, nor are they so pretty.

One feature of plantation life in Java would jar upon the sensibilities of most persons educated in American ideas and in the principles which lie at the foundation of government in the United States, viz., the contempt and want of consideration with which the natives are treated. As the natives approach the planter, bearing some written message or report from the superintendents, they uncover their heads, and, bowing to the ground, they creep upon their hands and knees in order to hand the message to their "master." While the movement added wonderfully to the oriental aspect of the scene, it did not dispel the thought that "oriental" has come to be entirely associated with the idea of despotism and cruelty, the day for which has gone by. The natives, however, are better than slaves in the following respects: they cannot be punished by whipping, and are free to come and go when they please. They are, however, miserably poor, ignorant, and degraded, and whether this is the effect of the climate, or not, is hard to determine. The old residents of the island represent that they do not seem to display much energy or to make much effort to elevate themselves. This is, doubtless, owing in a great measure to the fact that the Dutch government has adopted the plan of maintaining the authority of the native chiefs over them, the Dutch, in turn, subsidizing and controlling the chiefs, who, for hundreds of years, have maintained a most grinding despotism over their miserable subjects, levying forced loans and otherwise despoiling those who, by exceptional industry and prudence, have accumulated anything beyond their daily subsistence. The Dutch first conquered the island by force of arms, thereby establishing a claim to ownership of all the land, and then kept the native chiefs friendly by giving them a larger income than they formerly enjoyed, but requiring the chiefs in turn to make their people work systematically in cultivating the soil, and to sell their entire product to the Dutch government at a price so low that it barely gave them a subsistence. By this system the Dutch have derived an enormous revenue from their East India possessions, and in turn have given the natives greater security for life than they before enjoyed; but this has been the only improvement, the despotism of the native chiefs being perpetuated indefinitely, and most of the people kept so poor that there is but little chance for them to better their condition. As the population increased, a greater supply of labor became available than could be profitably employed under government supervision; and as there was an abundance of land, portions of it were from time to time leased to individuals with the privilege of planting, until now there are a considerable number of private planters in Java, from whose enterprise the government derives a large revenue, not only in the sums received for leases but also for export and import duties on the articles produced and consumed by them. Dutch rule in the East has not been very beneficent to the governed, but, on the other hand, it may probably be said with truth that the people of these countries are no worse off now than they were before, while Holland has been greatly benefited.

The soil in the island of Java is rich, never seems to be exhausted, and when apparently used up on the surface, the planter has only to go deeper and secure a richer soil at once. For coffee-growing, plantations formed on forest clearings, one thousand five hundred to four thousand feet above sea-level, are the best; although the lowlands are also used for coffee culture, but the tree in that case is not as productive or as long-lived.

Under the system of government monopoly, each family of natives is required to raise and take care of about six hundred and fifty trees, and to pick, dry, and deliver at the government stores the product thereof. The price received by the natives from the government is placed at a figure low enough to leave an enormous margin of profit to the government, which deducts from the gross price paid to the growers a duty of ten florins ($4) per picul. It may well be doubted, however, whether the plan of compulsory culture by natives, whose eagerness to be rid of the task induces them to hastily perform it, with great waste of product, and the exclusion of foreign capital and enterprise from the vast stretches of unimproved lands are calculated to develop the full resources of the country, and to compete successfully with the unfettered and scientific industry of the wealthy and energetic Anglo-Saxon cultivators.

The first of the Java crop, as previously stated, was sold in Amsterdam, in 1712, by the Dutch East India Company, which monopoly, or its successors, has controlled the sale of the coffee-product of Java ever since. It exists to-day under the name of the Netherland Handel Maatschappy, with headquarters in Amsterdam, and branches in all parts of the world, including New York, at which point an agency was established in January, 1879.

In the fifteenth century the nations of Europe contended for the trade of the East Indies. Prince John of Portugal led the way, and securing a foothold in India, monopolized the trade for nearly a century. Toward the close of the sixteenth century a war between Spain, which had annexed Portugal, and England forced the latter country to draw its Indian produce from the Dutch. Lisbon, at that time, was the chief port of entry for the rich merchandise of the Indies, but the revolt of the Netherlands closed Lisbon to the Dutch, and forced them to find a direct passage to India. Between 1590 and 1600, as the result of that move, those twin monopolies known as the East India Companies of England and Holland were formed.

On April 2, 1595, an Amsterdam corporation, known as a "Company for Remote Parts," despatched four small vessels, via the Cape of Good Hope, to the East Indies. Other companies started at the same time, and finally, in 1602, the interests of the different organizations were merged into one association, chartered by the States General, with the privilege granted of exclusive control of trade to the East Indies for twenty-one years, with the addition of all necessary civil and military power. Within twenty years the enormous amount of 30,000,000 guilders ($12,000,000) was divided among the stockholders, who originally paid in 6,500,000 guilders ($2,600,000) as capital. The company also had great possessions in land, vessels, and war material. In 1623 the charter was renewed for a second term of twenty-one years, and again in 1644, after which the company colonized the Cape of Good Hope, and gained control of Ceylon and Formosa, and other settlements of the Portuguese. In 1665 the payment of a heavy sum secured a new lease of power until 1700. From that date the monopoly occupied the chief centres of trade, and virtually controlled the wealth of the Indies. A renewal of the charter was secured in 1735, 1741, and in 1776 for a period of thirty years. In 1781 pecuniary aid was required, as the resources of the company had been depleted by wars and expenses incident to maintaining its vast extent of territory and extended commerce.

Upon the formation of the republic of Batavia, on September 15, 1795, the existence of the company ceased, and its affairs passed under government control. In 1824 King William I. established a new trading company, with a capital of over £3,000,000, the king guaranteeing an interest of four per cent. on the paid-up capital. In its early history the king was compelled to make good his guarantee, but after 1830 the affairs of the company prospered. Large quantities of merchandise, suited for the different markets of the world, are purchased at the various branches of the trading company. The East Indian products are generally sold at the periodical sales held in Amsterdam, Rotterdam, etc. Some idea of the extent of these sales may be formed, when it is stated that the business of one year (1872) reached nearly $28,000,000, representing the sum obtained for the coffee, sugar, tin, dyes, rattans, tobacco, cotton, nutmegs, cassia, camphor, fine woods, etc., sent from the East by the company's agents. The present capital of the company is $14,400,000, with its affairs in a flourishing condition, the American branch contributing largely to swell its income.

The following record gives the quantity of Java coffee sold in the Netherlands by the East India Company from 1751 to 1794:

Year.	U. S. lbs.	Year.	U. S. lbs.
1711	—	1721	127,212
1712	974	1722	13,208
1713	2,933	1723	79,808
1714	2,782	1724	1,462,685
1715	1,734	1725	2,786,930
1716	4,464	1726	4,729,912
1717	10,066	1727	4,578,464
1718	14,464	1728	4,456,632
1719	30,818	1729	3,649,435
1720	42,661	1730	3,148,349
1711–1720	110,896	1721–1730	25,032,635
Piculs (136 lbs.)	815	Piculs (136 lbs.)	184,063

Year.	U. S. lbs.	Year.	U. S. lbs.
1731	3,220,909	1741	1,554,567
1732	4,669,546	1742	1,470,827
1733	1,779,644	1743	4,739,173
1734	3,753,319	1744	4,779,039
1735	4,374,210	1745	3,266,358
1736	4,466,197	1746	3,310,766
1737	4,949,091	1747	4,413,980
1738	4,558,842	1748	2,434,288
1739	3,908,422	1749	1,982,940
1740	1,051,528	1750	1,999,907
1731–1740	36,821,708	1741–1750	29,951,845
Piculs (136 lbs.)	270,747	Piculs (136 lbs.)	220,234

Year.	U. S. lbs.	Year.	U. S. lbs.
1751	4,395,098	1761	4,340,588
1752	3,119,552	1762	4,593,033
1753	3,032,883	1763	3,258,368
1754	3,430,505	1764	2,848,520
1755	3,831,885	1765	4,163,849
1756	3,259,731	1766	4,220,492
1757	3,093,340	1767	3,087,621
1758	4,155,952	1768	1,947,124
1759	396,614	1769	5,039,919
1760	4,786,056	1770	4,786,384
1751–1760	33,502,216	1761–1770	38,285,898
Piculs (136 lbs.)	246,339	Piculs (136 lbs.)	281,514

Year.	U. S. lbs.	Year.	U. S. lbs.
1771	6,045,615	1781	—
1772	5,413,821	1782	—
1773	789,743	1783	2,891,680
1774	6,286,243	1784	3,271,120
1775	6,726,428	1785	9,486,921
1776	6,015,932	1786	8,577,440
1777	6,317,940	1787	4,992,534
1778	4,575,060	1788	—
1779	4,493,243	1789	3,610,734
1780	4,673,097	1790	4,371,674
1771–1780	51,287,122	1781–1790	37,202,103
Piculs (136 lbs.)	377,111	Piculs (136 lbs.)	273,545

Year.	U. S. lbs.
1791	5,499,478
1792	9,444,798
1793	8,704,383
1794	1,436,568
	25,085,227
Piculs (136 lbs.)	184,450

In 1840–41 the total production was about equal to the entire amount raised from 1711 to 1794 inclusive. Between 1794 and 1808 an unsettled state of affairs brought the export to the Netherlands to a stop, yet the cultivation continued, the government receiving 123,532 piculs (16,800,352 pounds) in 1808; 117,832 piculs (16,025,152 pounds) in 1809, and 120,963 piculs (16,450,968 pounds) in 1810. From 1811 to 1816 the cultivation was under British control. The result of the industry from 1817 to 1826 was as follows:

Year.	Piculs.	Pounds.	Year.	Piculs.	Pounds.
1817	98,900	13,450,400	1822......	91,600	12,457,600
1818	86,100	11,709,600	1823......	67,900	9,234,400
1819	65,400	8,894,400	1824......	70,900	9,642,400
1820	52,600	7,153,600	1825......	115,900	15,762,400
1821	98,000	13,328,000			

The following statement exhibits the production in the island of Java. It was prepared and published in 1880 by N. P. Van Den Berg, LL.D., President of the Java Bank, in a pamphlet entitled: "Historical and Statistical Notes on the Production and Consumption of Coffee." The exports from the island, for the years mentioned, exceeded the production, as they included imports into Java from neighboring islands:

Java produced in the year	In thousands of Piculs.	Production reduced to thousands of lbs. U. S. standard.	Java produced in the year	In thousands of Piculs.	Production reduced to thousands of lbs. U. S. standard.
1825...........	268	36,448	1850..........	769	104,584
1826...........	333	45,288	1851..........	1,130	153,680
1827...........	394	53,584	1852..........	930	126,480
1828...........	414	56,304	1853..........	949	129,064
1829...........	277	37,672	1854..........	954	129,744
1830...........	280	38,080	1855..........	1,234	167,824
1831...........	290	39,440	1856..........	1,160	157,760
1832...........	293	39,848	1857..........	938	127,568
1833...........	337	45,832	1858..........	1,060	144,160
1834...........	438	59,568	1859..........	933	126,888
1835...........	437	59,432	1860..........	887	120,632
1836...........	453	61,608	1861..........	1,004	136,544
1837...........	634	86,224	1862..........	968	131,648
1838...........	563	76,568	1863..........	924	125,664
1839...........	721	98,056	1864..........	1,040	141,440
1840...........	1,085	147,560	1865..........	793	107,848
1841...........	924	125,664	1866..........	991	134,776
1842...........	973	132,328	1867..........	1,124	152,864
1843...........	929	126,344	1868..........	834	113,424
1844...........	1,158	157,488	1869..........	855	116,280
1845...........	949	129,064	1870..........	1,176	159,936
1846...........	867	117,912	1871..........	880	119,680
1847...........	993	135,048	1872..........	980	133,280
1848...........	758	103,088	1873..........	1,075	146,200
1849...........	857	116,552			

A change in the manner of keeping trade statistics since 1873 renders it impossible to present the production by years after that date, as the quantity imported into Java cannot be ascertained.

A glance over the preceding table shows that from 1833 there was a very rapid increase in production, due to measures, calculated to push the industry, that were carried out under the able administration of Governor General Van Den Bosch. The largest crop on record is that of 1855, which reached nearly 168,000,000 pounds. Twelve times within a period of forty years the crop has exceeded one million piculs, dropping as low as 758,000 piculs in 1848; averaging 1,002,600 piculs in 1840–50; 1,057,900 piculs in 1850–60, and 1,081,700 piculs in 1860–70. The quantity delivered to the government, added to the private production of Java made available an average supply of 1,500,000 piculs annually from 1870 to 1880. The following detailed statement of the quantity delivered to the government from 1833 to 1880 is taken from the official returns, giving the amount in thousands of piculs:

Year.	Government account. In thousands of Piculs.	Private account. In thousands of Piculs (136 lbs.).	Total, in thousands of Piculs.	Total, in thousands of U. S. lbs.
1833............	336	—	—	45,696
1834............	432	—	—	58,752
1835............	358	—	—	48,688
1836............	576	—	—	78,336
1837............	589	—	—	80,104
1838............	539	—	—	73,304
1839............	905	—	—	123,080
1840............	706	—	—	96,016
1841............	877	—	—	119,272
1842............	975	—	—	132,600
1843............	1,048	—	—	142,528
1844............	956	—	—	130,016
1845............	637	—	—	86,632
1846............	880	—	—	119,680
1847............	772	—	—	104,992
1848............	860	—	—	116,960
1849............	461	67	528	71,808
1850............	977	125	1,102	149,872
1851............	1,069	82	1,151	156,536
1852............	880	112	992	134,912
1853............	686	98	784	106,624
1854............	1,084	119	1,203	163,608
1855............	1,165	108	1,273	173,128
1856............	747	61	808	109,888

Year.	Government account. In thousands of Piculs.	Private account. In thousands of Piculs (136 lbs.).	Total, in thousands of Piculs.	Total, in thousands of U. S. lbs.
1857	901	135	1,036	140,896
1858	908	95	1,003	136,408
1859	735	83	818	111,248
1860	928	120	1,048	142,528
1861	896	110	1,006	136,816
1862	659	89	748	101,728
1863	1,113	138	1,251	170,136
1864	434	101	535	72,760
1865	941	123	1,064	144,704
1866	1,087	93	1,180	160,480
1867	920	139	1,059	144,024
1868	558	131	689	93,704
1869	962	144	1,106	150,416
1870	986	153	1,139	154,904
1871	446	121	567	77,112
1872	984	185	1,169	158,984
1873	774	152	926	125,936
1874	1,032	180	1,212	164,832
1875	494	122	616	83,776
1876	1,266	203	1,469	199,784
1877	875	185	1,060	144,160
1878	857	116	973	132,328
1879	1,250	394	1,644	203,584
Total yield, 1833 to 1880				5,774,280

The estimate of the government crop of 1880 is 618,055 piculs. That of private coffee cannot be given in figures, but it is thought that it will equal or possibly exceed that of 1879. The amount of private coffee given for 1879 includes Palembang and Bali coffee exported from Java, but to what extent cannot be shown. From the above statement, it appears that from 1833 to 1880 inclusive, not far from six thousand million pounds, or 2,678,571 tons of government and private coffee were furnished to the world by the island of Java, the bulk of which passed through the hands of the Maatschappy and was consumed in Western Europe.

Thus far the story of Java coffee has been partially told, and therefore we will pass in the next chapter to an account of the rise and progress of the industry upon the island of Sumatra and other portions of the Dutch East Indies, first stopping to consider the imports of Java coffee into the United States.

Importation of Java and Singapore Coffee into the United States (Atlantic Coast), 1866 *to* 1881.

Year.	Pockets.	Tons.	Java from Holland.	
			Bags.	Tons.
1866	121,669	2,262	21,727	1,306
1867	140,277	3,821	1,291	78
1868	237,617	5,375	17,549	1,141
1869	230,726	6,066	4,123	236
1870	266,510	7,846	1,306	78
1871	441,452	11,330	16,538	960
1872	410,158	10,069	8,066	486
1873	167,906	5,084	1,456	91
1874	277,920	8,210	7,078	310
1875	355,952	10,783	1,927	112
1876	289,103	8,502	—	—
1877	297,732	8,639	797	48
1878	251,243	7,291	4,066	236
1879	302,586	8,781	22,311	1,295
1880	559,992	16,251	6,714	195
Average for 15 years, 1866–1881	290,056	8,021	7,663	438
Average for 10 years, 1871–1880	335,404	9,494	6,895	373

The Java crop of 1880 fell largely short of that of previous years, but the enormous Brazil crop and the large crops in Central America will tend to prevent a return to what must be considered the artificially high prices of 1875 to 1880.

CHAPTER XI.

SUMATRA, AND OTHER JAVA SORTS.

The island of Sumatra lies directly under the equator, stretching from northeast to southwest, with an area of 168,000 square miles. It is 1,040 miles in length, and measures from 60 to 266 miles in breadth, being the second largest of the Malayan group. A chain of mountains runs from one extremity of the island to the other, reaching an altitude of from 1,550 feet to 6,000 feet, often dividing into double and treble ranges. A score of lofty volcanic cones rear their heads 6,000 to 12,000 feet above the sea-level. Between the ranges are vast plateaux which are thickly populated, owing to the fine climate. Between the sea-shore and the mountains on the west coast there are narrow stretches of low land interspersed with spurs, which reach the shore in the form of bold, overhanging cliffs. Slow-running rivers wind their way through broad alluvial plains, which are covered with jungle and forest. Lakes of great beauty lie hid away amidst the mountains. In 1666 Padang came under the rule of the Netherlands, and so continued until 1795, when the British gained control, holding it until 1819, when it again passed under Dutch rule.

A small quantity of coffee was produced on the west coast of Sumatra in the eighteenth century, but owing to careless cultivation the product was of poor quality.

From the only available authorities, which are not over reliable, we learn that, in the year 1800, there were exported 2,000 piculs (272,000 pounds), but from that date until 1820 the exports were of small account. From 1820 to 1830 an average of about 4,000,000 pounds were exported annually, rising to between 11,000,000 and 12,000,000 pounds annually from 1836 to 1845.

In 1847 the Dutch government decreed that all coffee grown

in Sumatra should be delivered to the government at a fixed price, and further, "that all coffee delivered to government shall be sold at Padang, by public auction, to the highest bidder." Within the last thirty-five years the cultivation of coffee has been fostered by the government, which leased land to private planters. Prior to 1878 the quantity of free coffee exported was comparatively small, while since that time it has rapidly increased, as new plantations came into bearing. The colonial report of 1878 placed the crop raised on private plantations in Sumatra, in 1877, at 1,001 piculs (151,376 pounds). For the last three years the quantity raised on private account in Java and Sumatra is about one-fifth to one-sixth the government crop, the average for the past three years being in Java 168,000 piculs (22,848,000 pounds), free, against 999,000 piculs (135,864,000 pounds), government; and in Sumatra 20,000 piculs (2,720,000 pounds), free, against 127,000 piculs (17,272,000 pounds), government coffee. These figures indicate a rapid growth in the development of private plantations. The Sumatra crop, like that of all coffee-producing countries, shows a great variation, ranging, within the past eight years, from 12,500,000 pounds to 24,000,000 pounds. The Java crop also varies greatly; that of 1880 is estimated to fall 500,000 piculs below that of the previous year.

The leaf disease which has largely reduced the Ceylon crop, made its appearance in Sumatra in the summer of 1876. Its progress has been described as follows by M. Scheffer:

"Ordinarily it is not noticed except when the parasitic plant is in fructification. The lower surface of the leaves is then covered with a yellow-orange dust, which can be easily removed with the hand. This dust is formed by the spores, which afterward germinate and produce a large quantity of filaments (mycelium), which penetrate the stomata, and which develop and ramify speedily in the intercellular ducts. Some of these filaments again leave the interior of the leaf and produce new fruit. The mycelium soon extends not only over the entire surface of the leaf, but over the stem. In the latter case it is very difficult to identify the disease, but it appears that a plant once infected can never be cured. Mr. Thwaites, when in 1874 the planters of Ceylon believed they had got rid of the evil, could not find a single tree uninfected. During a certain period, however, the mycelium appears not to do much injury to the trees, until periodically, at different places and different seasons, under the influences of circumstances entirely unknown, it begins to fructify abundantly. The spores produce innumerable new filaments, which, by their rapid growth, require abundant nourishment, which they draw from the shrub. The consequence is that the leaves, the young berries, and the extremities of the stems wither and finally die. The tree usually produces fresh shoots, but the disease immediately renews its attacks; the young leaves again die. The second attack is very dangerous, and few plants, without a long enough respite, survive the third. The general public do not believe in the attack except when the spores are visible, but the presence of the fungus can be recognized at other times also, and with the naked eye. It may then be noticed on the leaves in almost transparent spots, which are caused by the destruction of the cellular tissues of the leaves, on which the filaments of the mycelium feed. Naturally, the tree then feels the influence of the parasite, but not to such an extent as to reduce perceptibly the yield. The case is very different when the spores appear.

"One consolatory fact, which has been more and more confirmed, is that by high cultivation the trees can offer more resistance to the disease. At first it was asserted that manuring favored the progress of the disease, but this has not been proved, and *a priori* it would be difficult to admit it. There is no remedy known for this disease, and one cannot be discovered. The preservatives will be to uproot and burn the infected trees, and to prohibit the introduction of coffee from places where the disease exists. But after all, high cultivation is the best preservative. In what manner and at what period the disease appeared in Sumatra, or indeed whether it was introduced, it is impossible to say, and probably sooner or later it will make its appearance in Java also. Some of the natives asserted that long ago they noticed it in Sumatra, bnt very rarely, and especially when a very long drought succeeded to constant and superabundant rains. Hitherto it seems to have restricted itself to the Pandangsche Bovenlanden residency, and the Ayer Bangies district. In that residency it has now been recognized in the districts of the Limapoeloe Kotas, Pangkalan, Agam, 2 and 13 Kotas (sub-district Soepajang), Tanah Datar, Batipoe, and X Kotas. In some localities the young leaves, which came out after the first attack, were again affected. In other places, however, they remained healthy. There has been no case known of a third attack in Sumatra. It seems that the disease has not as yet done much damage to the crop. This is probably because the berries were scarcely ripe when the disease appeared for the first time. In Sumatra also it has been proved that high cultivation, manure, etc., have a salutary influence on the course of the disease. The news which is now received from all parts is very reassuring. However, it is possible that the fungus still exists in the coffee-trees, and that at some future time it may develop again from some causes as yet unknown to us."

Mr. Scheffer also calls attention to another disease, called the coffee-root disease, which appears on the roots, and is apparently the work of an insect. Its work has assumed a serious character in the Mandheling and Ankola districts, and also in central Java. It is fatal to the trees.

In the year 1852 the government inaugurated quarterly auctions, which have been regularly held since that date. The following is the government statement of the Sumatra crop from 1852 to 1879.

Year.	Piculs.	U. S. pounds.	Year.	Piculs.	U. S. pounds.
1852......	122,900	16,714,400	1866......	134,000	18,224,000
1853......	119,400	16,238,400	1867......	158,400	21,542,400
1854......	131,500	17,884,000	1868......	142,800	19,420,800
1855......	127,500	17,340,000	1869......	141,900	19,298,400
1856......	128,300	17,448,800	1870......	163,800	22,276,800
1857......	190,900	25,962,400	1871......	156,500	21,284,000
1858......	129,100	17,557,600	1872......	90,800	12,348,800
1859......	140,600	19,121,600	1873......	108,500	14,756,000
1860......	157,600	21,433,600	1874......	131,500	17,884,000
1861......	123,800	16,836,800	1875......	145,000	19,720,000
1862......	159,100	21,637,600	1876......	102,900	13,994,400
1863......	125,600	17,081,600	1877......	175,000	23,800,000
1864......	187,500	25,500,000	1878......	104,000	14,144,000
1865......	123,700	16,813,200	1879......	121,860	16,572,960

The exports of Padang coffee from 1858 to 1880, as reported by Messrs. Dummler & Co., were as follows:

Year.	Piculs.	Pounds.	Year.	Piculs.	Pounds.
1858......	192,347	26,159,192	1872......	110,838	15,073,968
1859......	119,777	16,289,672	1873......	97,805	13,301,480
1860......	124,199	16,891,064	1874......	128,557	17,483,752
1861......	169,928	23,110,208	1875......	160,844	21,874,784
1862......	149,634	20,350,224	1876......	141,780	19,282,080
1863......	129,357	17,592,552	1877......	141,854	19,292,144
1864......	161,058	21,903,888	1878......	124,175	16,887,800
1865......	154,170	20,967,120	1879......	104,504	14,212,544
1866......	146,574	19,934,064	1880......	134,633	18,310,088
1867......	112,609	15,314,824			
1868......	189,891	25,825,176			
1869......	168,320	22,891,520	Total...	3,286,931	447,022,616
1870......	121,099	16,469,464	Average, per year.	142,910	19,435,766
1871......	202,978	27,605,008			

The average export per annum for the five years, 1876 to 1880, was 129,389 piculs, equivalent to 17,596,904 pounds, or 7,856 tons. The distribution of this quantity was as follows:

	1880. Piculs.	1879. Piculs.	1878. Piculs.	1877. Piculs.	1876. Piculs.
America (Atlantic Coast)....	126,279	99,385	94,964	106,205	98,823
California................	2,916	2,164	3,775	——	——
Holland..................	3,971	2,244	20,418	24,876	33,593
France..................	——	——	1,000	——	——
Java.....................	1,464	711	4,018	10,773	9,364
Coromandel Coast..........	3	——	——	——	——
Total	134,633	104,504	124,175	141,854	141,780

CELEBES.

In 1822, according to a book of travel published in 1856 by P. Bleeker, the Island of Celebes delivered to the government 80 piculs (10,880 pounds) of coffee. From 1826 to 1833, inclusive, the crop averaged 3,860 piculs (524,960 pounds). In 1833 it had reached 6,000 piculs (816,000 pounds); in 1834, 10,000 piculs (1,360,000 pounds), dropping to 4,000 piculs (544,000 pounds) in 1835. From that date until 1852 the crop varied from 2,500 piculs (340,000 pounds) to 13,000 piculs (1,768,000 pounds). The colonial reports state that the deliveries to the government from 1852 were as follows:

Year.	Piculs.	Pounds, U. S.	Year.	Piculs.	Pounds, U. S.
1852......	7,700	1,047,200	1866......	16,000	2,176,000
1853......	16,000	2,176,000	1867......	13,000	1,768,000
1854......	23,000	3,128,000	1868......	7,000	952,000
1855......	25,000	3,400,000	1869......	38,000	5,088,000
1856......	27,000	3,672,000	1870......	13,000	1,768,000
1857......	15,000	2,040,000	1871......	8,000	1,088,000
1858......	23,000	3,128,000	1872......	6,500	884,000
1859......	22,000	2,992,000	1873......	11,000	1,496,000
1860......	15,000	2,040,000	1874......	16,000	2,176,000
1861......	15,000	2,040,000	1875......	10,600	1,441,600
1862......	7,600	1,033,600	1876......	8,000	1,088,000
1863......	14,000	1,904,000	1877......	14,000	1,904,000
1864......	13,000	1,768,000	1878......	36,000	4,896,000
1865......	37,000	5,032,000	1879......	13,100	1,781,600

The product of the province of Menado, in the northern part of Celebes, is in high favor in the Holland market, where it commands a high price, selling for more money than any other kind of Java coffee. Macassar is the shipping port for the southern part of the island, and may be called the main point of shipment for the products of the small adjacent islands. The export from this port has increased rapidly, as will be seen by the following figures, which will be used in obtaining a statement of the average amount of coffee available as Java coffee.

Year.	In thousands of piculs.	In thousands of U. S. pounds.	Year.	In thousands of piculs.	In thousands of U. S. pounds.
1857.........	27	3,672	1769.........	53	7,208
1858.........	21	2,856	1870.........	67	9,112
1859.........	43	5,848	1871.........	50	6,800
1860.........	24	3,264	1872.........	62	8,432
1861.........	21	2,856	1873.........	84	11,424
1862.........	38	5,168	1874.........	61	8,296
1863.........	23	3,128	1875.........	110	14,960
1864.........	24	3,264	1876.........	112	15,232
1865.........	29	3,944	1877.........	115	15,640
1866.........	50	6,800	1878.........	124	16,864
1867.........	47	6,392	1879.........	125	17,000
1868.........	45	6,120			

Dr. Van Den Berg, President of the Java Bank, Batavia, estimates the entire production in the Dutch East Indies, on an average of the three years, 1876–1878, as follows:

	Piculs.	In thousands of U. S. pounds.
Java, for government....	999,000	135,864
Java, for private account..................	168,000	22,848
Sumatra, for government..................	127,000	17,272
Sumatra, for private account...............	20,000	2,720
Celebes, for government..................	20,000	2,720
Celebes, for private account...............	95,000	12,920
Bali, and other small islands...............	50,000	6,800
Average total.......................	1,479,000	201,144

From the above it will be seen that there were placed at the disposal of the government in each of the three years an average of 1,146,000 piculs (155,856,000 pounds), of which 333,000 piculs (45,288,000 pounds) were produced on private plantations. The average in 1866–68, ten years previous, was 1,012,000 piculs (137,632,000 pounds) government; 201,000 piculs (27,336,000 pounds) private account, or a total of 1,213,000 piculs (164,968,000 pounds), showing an increase in the crop, during the ten years, of 266,000 piculs (36,176,000 pounds), or 21½ per cent.

The term "Old Government Java" arises from the fact that the Dutch government formerly held considerable quantities for a long time before selling it, and as this was usually of very good quality, "Old Government Java" soon became a trade term denoting the highest quality. Of late years, however, this term has been used somewhat indiscriminately to designate all brown Java, whether packed in the old style of government bag containing about one hundred and thirty-six pounds, or in the smaller grass mat holding one-half picul (65 to 68 pounds), the latter style being preferred in the American market. No other coffee acquires, except by artificial means, the dark yellowish brown shade that marks the Java and Sumatra bean, which color governs, in a great measure, its commercial value. Another very good indication of genuineness is the size of the bean, which is considerably larger than that of other kinds of coffee, excepting Liberian. There is, however, some coffee produced in the other islands of the Malay Archipelago which does not differ materially in size of bean or general appearance, but which, as a rule, is inferior in flavor; this is packed in grass mats of the same weight and style as the genuine Java and Sumatra coffee. Importers generally sell these various kinds, and also the inferior kinds grown on the islands of Java and Sumatra, for what they really are and at prices considerably below those obtained for the finest kinds. The wholesale and retail dealers, however, through whose hands such kinds afterwards pass may not care to remember the place of production, or the fact that the price which they paid was below the market price for fine goods; so, under the pressure of excessive competition, and the necessity of in some way carving out a profit, the article is finally represented to be what it is not, and the consumer is swindled.

In the producing islands the coffee is transported by contract to the warehouses, where, at stated periods, it is sold at auction by the Maatschappy, generally in lots of two hundred piculs. The two islands are divided into districts, Java having twenty-three, with Batavia as the principal shipping port; Sumatra is divided into "residences," which are subdivided into districts. Padang is the chief port from which the United States receives its supplies; Benkoelen is the principal shipping port for Holland. The coffee takes its name from the district in which it is grown, and varies greatly in quality. Upon the mats there is branded the initial letter of the importing house, and also a letter or letters designating the district where grown, as Æ for Ayer Bangies. The peculiar, slightly musty smell that marks Padang Java is acquired on the voyage. The passage through the tropics and the sweating the coffee undergoes is believed to improve the quality. The true Java bean is not, on an average, quite as large and in color not as brown as the Sumatra, although both become darker and more mellow with age. At the time of shipment all Java coffee is of a light green shade, but during the long voyage through the tropics this gradually changes to a yellowish brown, and the deeper this color the higher the price it commands. For most consumers age improves the drinking qualities, and as color is popularly regarded as an indication of age, that coffee which is the brownest in color is generally regarded as the best. Some of the best judges, however, regard the drinking qualities of the light Javas as fully equal to those of the very dark brown.

As the Java crop varies in quality from year to year, it is impossible to ascribe to any one sort the virtue of being preëminently the best. Two years ago Preanger was regarded as the best of the Java crop that comes into the port of New York, but this year it ranks below several others in point of merit. The following list, with an estimate of the quantity of coffee raised in each district on the Island of Java, gives some of the names of the different varieties that are from time to time sold on the New York market, together with the estimated crop of each district for 1879:

Name.	Crop of piculs.	Name.	Crop of piculs.
1. Bantam	10,000	12. Bekoeki	36,000
2. Krawang	1,430	13. Banjoewangie	4,400
3. Preanger Rogent-schappen	320,000	14. Banjoemas	19,650
4. Cheribon	37,240	15. Bageten	36,000
5. Tagal	83,000	16. Kadoe	80,210
6. Pekalongan	28,500	17. Sarakarta	50,000
7. Samarang	60,000	18. Djokdjakarta	4,000
8. Japara	2,610	19. Madioen	72,200
9. Soerbaya	7,500	20. Kediri	19,400
10. Passoeroean	300,000	Total piculs	1,207,140
11. Probolingo	35,000		

In Holland, to which country the bulk of the Java crop is exported, the grades are recognized as follows:

West India preparation:
- Extra green.
- Fine green.
- Good green.
- Green.

Java coffee:
- Brown.
- Light brown.
- High yellow.
- Yellow.
- Yellowish.

Java coffee:
- Light yellowish.
- Fine blue.
- Blue.
- Bluish.

Passoeroean:
- Green.
- Good greenish.
- Greenish.
- Pale greenish.

Triage: Ordinary broken with much black.
Ordinary broken with little black.

Menado is considered to be one of the finest, if not the finest coffee, but the quality varies more or less every year. The crop of 1880–81 was 12,500 piculs, against 25,000 piculs in 1879–80.

The product of the Island of Sumatra runs more uniform as to quality, and the following list gives the product of the different districts in the order in which it has ranked in quality in the New York market for many years:

1. Mandheling.
2. Ayer Bangies.
3. Ankola.
4. Painan.
5. Interior.
6. Triage.

The triage or trash rarely comes to the United States, being sent generally to the China market.

SINGAPORE JAVA

is coffee shipped from the English free port of that name. Singapore is situated on a small island, eight or ten miles square, and not of itself particularly fertile; yet this place is the great emporium for the productions of the whole Malayan Peninsula and Archipelago, comprising hundreds of islands, many of them of large size, and upon which many valuable and important articles are produced. The coffee exported from Singapore is raised in the small islands of Netherlands India, and the Philippine Islands. It does not possess the fine flavor and intrinsic value of Padang and Batavia Java, and some years it is of decidedly inferior quality. All Java coffee received here, and which was produced free from the restrictions imposed by the government, is known as "free coffee."

The exports from Singapore were, according to the Singapore market report as follows:

To Great Britain.			To United States.		
Year.	Piculs.	Pounds.	Year.	Piculs.	Pounds.
1875......	16,827	2,288,472	1875......	16,588	2,255,968
1876......	20,292	2,759,712	1876......	13,947	1,896,792
1877......	16.115	2,191,640	1877......	5.452	741,472
1878......	8,379	1,139,544	1878......	9,248	1,257,728
1879......	16.462	2,238,832	1879......	22,324	3,036,064
1880......	19,948	2,712,928	1880......	6,277	853,672

There were exported from Penang to the Continent of Europe the following quantities:

Year.	Piculs.	Pounds.	Year.	Piculs.	Pounds.
1875......	13,134	1,786,224	1878......	11,958	1,626,288
1876......	9,448	1,284,928	1879......	22,795	3,100.120
1877......	31,691	4,309,976	1880......	15,583	2,119,288

As before stated, the coffee exported from Singapore is grown on the neighboring islands, and the deficiency of statistics makes any estimate of the production in the Philippine islands more or less liable to question. Dr. Van Den Berg makes the average production of the Philippines as follows, in piculs of 125 Amsterdam pounds (U. S. pounds 136).

PHILIPPINES.

1856 to 1858.		1866 to 1868.		1876 to 1878.	
Piculs.	Pounds.	Piculs.	Pounds.	Piculs.	Pounds.
22,000.....	2,992,000	35,000......	4,760,000	55,000......	7,480,000

The Philippine Islands are said to be peculiarly adapted to the raising of coffee, producing, with proper cultivation and preparation, a berry which is equal, if not superior, in flavor and aroma, to the Java berry. Public attention was for a time turned with great earnestness to the development of this industry, and rewards were offered by the Economical Society of the Island of Luzon for the best and largest plantations. But, after a prize of $10,000 had been awarded, the plantations were suffered to run to waste, and their aggregate yield does not now exceed 3,300 tons per annum.

From various sources we gather the following figures, showing the exports from Manila, 1870–1880 inclusive, omitting 1872, the figures for which year are not obtainable:

Year.	Pounds.	Tons.	Year.	Pounds.	Tons.
1870	4,786,600	2,137	1876........	8,024,380	3,582
1871	7,471.800	3,336	1877........	8,553,580	3,819
1873	7,868,700	3,513	1878........	5,359,480	2,393
1874	6,428,800	2,870	1879........	9,014,740	4,025
1875	9,326,800	4,164	1880........	11,759,360	5,250

The exports from Manila, Cebu, and Iloilo in 1879 were 64,391 piculs, and in 1880, 83,999 piculs (140 lbs.) distributed as follows: to the United States, 645 piculs; to Great Britain, 7,747 piculs; to the Continent of Europe, 68,942 piculs; to Singapore, 3,639 piculs; to China, 3,026 piculs. Coffee pays an export duty of 28½ cents per picul.

Importation of Manila Coffee into the United States (Atlantic Coast), 1866 to 1881.

Year.	Packages.	Tons.	Year.	Packages.	Tons.
1866	7,084	220	1874	1,336	84
1867	354	14	1875	3,609	172
1868	5,054	240	1876	—	—
1869	2,267	128	1877	—	—
1870	1,010	32	1878	—	—
1871	1,605	87	1879	70	4
1872	813	48	1880	299	8
1873	62	4			

Average for fifteen years, 1866-1881..........1,571 packages, 69 tons.
Average for ten years, 1871-1880..............779 " 41 "

The direct receipts of Java and Sumatra coffee in New York have been as follows:

Year.	Bags.	Pockets, mats, etc.	Pounds.	Year.	Bags.	Pockets, mats, etc.	Pounds.
1857	—	38,261	1,965,518	1871	1,239	319,507	18,445,036
1858	2,159	70,342	3,483,152	1872	629	324,025	17,923,979
1859	39	71,715	4,140,468	1873	1,000	145,238	9,938,833
1860	166	27,512	1,533,942	1874	780	250,812	16,951,347
1861	—	40,472	2,013,024	1875*	12,079	290,665	20,924,071
1862	3	44,201	2,303,920	1876	551	276,811	18,232,393
1863	—	10,150	839,405	1877	—	224,379	15,161,930
1864	—	104,075	6,384,908		Macassar.	32,514	2,283,610
1865	875	689	178,000	1878	—	247,665	16,329,740
1866	—	70,754	2,665,837		Macassar.	341	50,012
1867	302	75,816	5,102,660	1879	—	220,286	13,098,586
1868	185	135,881	6,854,475		Macassar.	44,070	2,709,077
1869	—	139,357	8,118,808	1880	—	468,836	28,757,832
1870	53	108,085	6,952,443		Macassar.	51,736	3,207,632

* Including Macassar.

The receipts of Java at New York from Rotterdam and Amsterdam have been as follows:

Year.	Bags.	Pounds.	Year.	Bags.	Pounds.
1857............	3,183	451,599	1869............	805	108,742
1858............	51.211	7,144,590	1870............	600	80,670
1859............	2,933	408,755	1871............	1,415	190,754
1860............	4,401	594,530	1872............	8,066	1,089,306
1861............	9,215	1,244,550	1873............	1,456	203,226
1862............	5,508	746,046	1874, 3,485 mats..	3,643	696,505
1863............	3,210	435,291	1875............	1,927	259,162
1864............	2,845	383,220	1876............	3,447	452,862
1865............	5,708	770,580	1877............	797	100,212
1866............	20,351	2,745,840	1878............	4,413	594,606
1867, 3 casks....	1,288	175,680	1879............	28,494	3,987,214
1868............	5,348	711,641	1880............	8,381	1,162,607

In this connection, it will be of interest to note what proportion the importations of all kinds of Java coffee bear to the total imports of coffee into the United States. According to Moring's tables, such receipts constituted, in 1876, 7.13 per cent. of the total; 1877, 5.75; 1878, 5.16; 1879, 5.10; 1880, 9.31—the average for five years being 6.48 per cent.; and yet the fragrant Java is the favorite berry throughout a large part of the United States, and every storekeeper in sections where it is in favor believes he has the genuine article. If we deduct the low grades of Java imported, we discover that a very small quantity of fine brown old Government Java is consumed in the United States.

CHAPTER XII.

CULTIVATION IN CEYLON.

The great rival of Java in the East is Ceylon. The Dutch appear to have introduced the plant into the island, then one of their colonies, late in the seventeenth century. In the year 1721 about sixteen pounds of the Ceylon product were sold in the Amsterdam market, commanding a higher price than either Mocha or Java. The quantity exported was small until 1741, when 370,192 (U. S.) pounds were sold in Holland. The low prices ruling at this period, taken in connection with full supplies from Java, discouraged planting in Ceylon. Between 1751 and 1794 there were 1,600,806 (U. S.) pounds disposed of in Amsterdam. In 1795 the island passed under British control, but the culture did not make any notable progress until 1824, when coffee-planting on a large scale was commenced by Sir Edward Barnes and Sir George Bird. The great development of the industry dates from 1832 to 1836. Coffee estates sprung up on all sides, and, with the exception of a short pause from 1849 to 1850, owing to commercial depression, they have continued to increase ever since. There were, in 1877, in Ceylon, 1,357 coffee plantations owned by Europeans, and the area of coffee lands actually under cultivation is stated to have been 272,243 acres, to which must be added an estimated area of 50,000 to 70,000 acres worked by the natives.

As far back as 1806 we find the record of the export of 846 cwts. (94,752 lbs.). The author of a work published in 1817, entitled, "A View of the Agricultural, Commercial, and Financial Interests of Ceylon," reported the export in 1810 to be 217,500 lbs.; 1813, 216,500 lbs. According to Martin's "History of the Colonies of the British Empire," the yield from 1830 to 1836 inclusive was as follows:

Year.	Bushels.	Pounds. (60 lbs. to bushel.)	Year.	Bushels.	Pounds. (60 lbs. to bushel.)
1830.....	28,938	1,536,280	1834....	138,800	8,328,000
1831.....	32,756	1,965,360	1835....	161,975	9,736,500
1832.....	61,110	3,666,600	1836....	190,161	11,409,660
1833.....	88,318	5,299,080			

The exports from 1840 to 1857, according to "M'Culloch's Commercial Dictionary," were as given below:

Year.	Cwts.	U. S. lbs.	Year.	Cwts.	U. S. lbs.
1840.....	41,863	4,688,656	1849....	280,010	31,361,120
1841.....	68,206	7,639,072	1850....	373,593	41,842,416
1842.....	80,584	9,025,408	1851....	278,473	31,188,976
1843.....	119,805	13,418,160	1852....	349,957	39,195,184
1844.....	94,847	10,622,864	1853....	372,379	41,706,448
1845.....	133,957	15,003,184	1854....	328,971	36,844,752
1846.....	178,603	20,003,536	1855....	506,540	56,732,480
1847.....	173,892	19,475,904	1856....	440,819	49,371,728
1848.....	293,221	32,840,752			

The further progress of coffee raising is shown by the following table, taken from the "Ceylon Directory and Almanac" for 1878, showing the development of the industry:

Year.		Total acres planted or opened for coffee.	Plantation coffee exported for season ending 10th October.		Estimate of coffee area in bearing.	Average production of coffee per acre.	Lowest and highest quotations per cwt. of middling plantation coffee in London.
		Acres.	Cwts.	Lbs.	Acres.	Cwts.	s. d. s. d.
1856.....		80,950	325,438	36,449,056	64,000	5.08	60 0 to 80 0
1862.....	Doubtful estimates.	150,000	476,824	53,404,288	130,000	3.66	75 6 to 93 0
1863.....		152,000	649,194	72,709,728	136,000	4.77	75 0 to 117 0
1864.....		155,500	574,476	64,341,312	140,000	4.10	76 0 to 114 0
1865....		160,000	714,259	79,997,008	146,000	4.89	80 0 to 88 0
1866.....		160,000	676,448	75,762,176	150,000	4.50	71 0 to 89 0
1867.....		168,000	720,174	80,659,498	152,000	4.73	72 0 to 86 0
1868.....		176,000	788,737	88,338,544	155,500	5.07	66 0 to 82 0
1869.....		176,467	835,686	93,596,832	160,000	5.22	68 0 to 84 0
1870.....	Es.	185,000	885,728	99,201,536	160,000	5.53	60 0 to 82 0
1871.....		195,627	814,710	91,247,520	168,000	4.84	60 0 to 84 0
1872.....		206,000	576,878	64,610,336	176,000	3.27	74 0 to 87 0
1873.....		219,974	860,360	96,360,320	177,000	4.85	86 0 to 119 0
1874.....		237,345	509,329	57,044,848	185,000	2.75	100 0 to 135 0
1875.....		249,604	873,654	97,849,248	195,000	4.48	90 0 to 115 6
1876.....		260,000	603,929	67,642,048	203,000	2.97	99 0 to 118 0
1877.....		272,243	850,911	95,302,032	212,000	4.01	99 0 to 121 0

The largest export of plantation coffee and the maximum average rate of production, 5½ cwts. (616 lbs.) per acre for the country, were obtained in 1870. The effects of leaf disease, which had that season made its appearance all over the coffee districts, were at once manifested in the falling off in the succeeding year, and the alternate bad and average crops since realized, notwithstanding the greatly increased area in cultivation.

In the year 1878 the crop fell behind that of the previous year nearly thirty-four per cent.; in 1879 it rose above the average for eight years, but again fell 125,313 cwts. behind in 1880. The exports from Ceylon for the past eight years have been as follows:

Year.	Coffee.—Cwts.			Tons.	Pounds.
	Plantation.	Native.	Total.		
1880............	622,306	47,308	669,614	33,481	74,996,768
1879............	767,293	57,216	824,509	41,225	92,345,008
1878............	551,046	69,246	620,292	31,015	69,472.704
1877............	851,201	91,846	943.047	47,152	105,621,264
1876............	626,636	93,791	720,427	36,021	80,687,824
1875............	855.661	113,033	968,694	48,435	108,493,728
1874............	521,193	96,149	617,342	30,867	69,142,304
1873......... ..	861,575	133,918	995,493	49,775	111,495,216
Total.	5,656,911	702,507	6,359,418	317,971	712,254,816
Average.......	707,113	87,813	794,927	39,746	89,081,824

It will be observed that while the out-turn of plantation coffee varies greatly, one season falling and another rising, and the past season giving a return considerably below the average, in native kinds, on the other hand, the export has gone steadily down almost year by year, until now Ceylon does not ship much more than one-third the quantity of native coffee despatched eight years ago. There can be no doubt that the native gardens have suffered greatly from leaf disease, more in proportion than well-cultivated plantations.

The value and magnitude of the coffee enterprise in and to Ceylon is shown by the following extract from the "Ceylon Directory and Almanac:"

"From the year which is usually taken to represent the commencement of the coffee enterprise in Ceylon, namely 1837, to the end of 1877, we calculate that more than thirty million pounds sterling ($150,000,000) have been paid in wages to immigrant coolies from Southern India, apart from the very considerable amount given to Kandyan woodcutters, Sinhalese laborers in certain districts, carpenters, artisans, cartmen, etc., and indirectly to the coffee-store employés in Colombo, the women and children who pick, and the men who prepare and pack, as well as those who transport and ship our staple. We are probably on the safe side in saying that from fifty to sixty million pounds sterling ($250,000,000 to $300,000,000) may be taken as an approximation to the total amount of British capital introduced into Ceylon in connection with coffee, while our returns show an export of 'Plantation coffee' in the same period of about seventeen million hundredweights, valued by the Customs at forty-eight million pounds sterling ($240,000,000), but really worth a good deal more.

"Our calculation is that from each acre of coffee land opened here, five native men, women, and children (of Ceylon or Southern India) directly or indirectly derive their means of subsistence."

According to the same authority, the total valuation of investment in the coffee industry of the island (including factories, stores, and offices in town) approached, in 1877, the sum of fourteen millions of pounds sterling ($70,000,000).

"In the young districts, between Great Western and Adam's Peak, over 7,000 acres have been added to the cultivated area since last year, averaging sixty new coffee plantations annually since 1869, equalling 114 square miles, and costing in the conversion at least one and a-half million pounds sterling. There is a large extent of young coffee not yet yielding a first good crop, estimated at 54,000 acres under four years of age, or very nearly equal to the total in bearing in 1856."

Between June, 1875, and November, 1877, there was an addition of 22,639 acres to the extent of land opened and cultivated in coffee.

The large and improved estates are almost all situated in the hill region of the island, coffee prospering best in Ceylon, as well as in other countries, at an elevation of from 2,000 to 4,000 feet.

The cultivation may be carried on, however, at much lower levels, and, with a proper system of irrigation and shade, successful plantations are worked as low as 1,500 feet. The small gardens of the natives are found everywhere, almost to the water's edge. The coffee trees are raised from the seed in nurseries, as in Java, and transplanted when about a year old; the distances usually observed in the rows being six feet by six, or six feet by five. It is claimed that close planting is serviceable in hindering the growth of weeds and in enabling the plants to shelter each other from the effects of high winds. They are kept pruned much lower than in the Dutch island, the average height they are allowed to attain being only four feet; and where the soil is poor, or the situation not well sheltered, the cutting of the trees to a still lower point is advocated. Weeding, manuring, and all the details of scientific cultivation are carefully observed. The value of the manures imported in 1876, almost entirely for coffee plantations, amounted to £140,809, or about $704,045.

There is, however, a dark spot on the coffee industry in Ceylon. In the year 1869 the Ceylon planters were disturbed by the appearance of a fungus, which two or three years later had become and has ever since remained a source of serious injury to the crops. It is known as the *Hemileia vastatrix*, or leaf disease, and is the same pest that annoys the planters in Java and other producing points. How to stamp out this coffee-leaf fungus has been a leading question in Ceylon for the past ten or twelve years. Recently several reports have been made by Government and other authorities, but as yet no positive remedy has been found that will cause it to disappear. The deficiencies in the crop are attributed to this evil, as the disease destroys the leaves, and their continued renewal so draws upon the vitality of the tree that its power to mature a crop is largely reduced.

Last year a number of experiments were made by Mr. Schrotty, a chemist, who publishes the result in the following opinion:

"I have all along been of opinion that the relative intensity with which coffee-leaf disease develops and spreads on certain trees, while on others in close proximity the attack is confined to a few of the oldest leaves only, and is easily shaken off, can only be due to the sap of one tree being in a certain condition more favorable to the germination and development of the fungus, while this same condition of the sap in another tree is almost or entirely absent. Neither chemical nor microscopical analysis of the sap of the coffee-tree can, I am of opinion, reveal this difference of condition, no more than a chemical or microscopical analysis could find any difference between the blood of a healthy man and of one who suffers from malarious fever, due also, as you will remember, to the action of a minute fungus, according to recent discoveries. But I hold that differences of condition of the sap could be artificially created by the diffusion through the system of the trees of different chemicals suited for the purpose. Repeated trials had conclusively proved that this could not be done through the medium of the rootlets, the peculiar food-selective properties of which completely defeated the attempt to physic the trees through the soil, and I adopted, therefore, a novel plan of inducing absorption of different substances into the sap of the plant through the cambium of the stem, and, being satisfied that a certain absorption did take place in all but very thickly barked trees, I have adopted this method in my experiments on coffee-trees."

Mr. Schrotty's investigations did not result in finding a remedy, but it was found that some of the materials injected by him into the plant checked the progress of the fungus, and thus encouraged further experiments. Opinions vary, as evidenced by the following extract from a letter which appeared in the Ceylon *Observer*, of December 15, 1880:

"Depend upon it the leaf disease is not *the* 'disease,' but an effect arising upon and from a *diseased* condition already contracted by the coffee trees. Fungus, blight, mouldiness, appear only upon already diseased subjects! Wherefore surely we are less concerned as to inquiring into how the evil operates in its development, propagation, and continuity, than in ascertaining *the cause* of it. There exists a cause, producing an enfeebled constitution of the coffee tree, upon which the *Hemileia* fixes with avidity. See how invigorating manures and treatment sets up the tree, and enables it to cast off *the disease* (as we say, but *not* 'the disease'—*that* we have not yet discovered—but cast off the attack) and hold on the better under it."

Mr. Schrotty, in a later communication, says:

"I think it would be utterly futile to hope that any endeavors to eradicate leaf disease could succeed so far as to enable Ceylon coffee-planters to sweep the fungus out of the island, to be seen no more. We have evidence to show that the fungus was in existence and feeding on coffee-leaves long before it was first brought to prominent public notice in 1869, and probably this same fungus, though perhaps not quite in the same form, could have been found in the island centuries before the first coffee-plant was introduced. But what reasonably can be expected is, that the ravages of this pest can be reduced by man to such an extent as to enable him to cultivate coffee with profit.

"A careful investigation of the subject, taking into consideration what has been done in the case of other blights, has led me, and can, in my opinion, only lead to one conclusion, and that is: that, though an attack of coffee-leaf disease leaves behind its mark upon the tree, increasing in effect with every successive attack, and though a peculiar condition of the sap seems to be necessary to its establishing a firm hold over the tree, it is essentially an external and easily accessible enemy, and can be successfully battled with. And to the question, why it has not been successfully battled with as yet, there can only be one answer, and that is: We have not tried enough."

In June, 1880, a report was made to the Hon. the Colonial Secretary, Director of the Royal Botanic Gardens, by Mr. H. Marshal Ward, the government cryptogamist, from which we extract the conclusions which were the result of this gentleman's investigations:

"In conclusion, I feel justified in drawing these inferences from what has been seen so far. Derived from some source purely external, a fungoid organism finds its way into the passages between the cells of the leaf; here it has a term of existence shown to the observer by the origin and spread of the yellow 'disease spots,' caused by the changes in consistence and color of the leaf contents at those places.

"The outbreak of the yellow 'rust' from the leaf-passages, through the stomata, takes place when the leaf begins to fail in supplying sap. Such an explanation is in accordance with all the facts yet known to me, and also with the present state of physiology. In seedlings, the cotyledons especially become yellow, and in older plants the lower leaves usually suffer first; on wind-blown ridges, quartz patches, and dry soil generally, bad attacks of rust are conspicuous when more sheltered and moist portions of the estate do not appear to be suffering; in sudden dry weather 'an attack' commonly comes over an estate, while during the last stages of crop 'leaf disease' is often very bad.

"Now, if the mycelium, ramifying among the loose cells of the leaf, is absorbing its food from those cells, as is well known to be the habit of such parasites, we can see how so much more work is thrown upon the plant. Whereas, a leaf normally supplies a certain quantity of elaborated food for the tree in a given time, we have here the same leaf compelled to provide food for tree *and fungus*—its cells must work the harder and its life be the shorter.

"Until we fail to account for the ravages of leaf disease according to known principles we have no right to seek an explanation elsewhere. Many, and in some cases elaborate, experiments are being planned to establish the important point as to what actually occurs between the fall of the leaf, with its 'rust' and mycelium, and the reappearance of the yellow 'pin-spots'; I have already indicated the direction in which these are leading, and it only remains to patiently carry on research. When it is remembered that these germinating spores have to be kept under observation during the night as well as day, that all kinds of minute organisms have to be guarded against, and hence that out of many attempts few succeed, I hope that the importance of this plan will be admitted."

While the Ceylon planter is fighting his enemy with sulphur and lime, or trying other remedies, the Ceylon *Observer* takes rather a hopeful view of the coffee industry, as the following, from its columns, will show:

"If we refer to the past history of the staple exports of the colony, we shall find much reason to congratulate ourselves on a record of steady progress. Even in the case of coffee, although there has been a check, there is no reason to anticipate more than temporary depression. Our largest shipment of plantation coffee appears to have been in the year 1869–70—the date of the appearance of coffee-leaf disease—but this export, 886,000 cwts., was nearly equalled in 1874–75 with 874,000 cwts. In 1878–79 it was 775,000 cwts. The falling off in quantity has, however, been more than made up in value, the customs return showing 41,060,000 rupees worth exported last year against only 23,910,000 rupees in 1870, though perhaps the valuation in the latter year was too low. The great decline has been in native coffee, from 218,000 cwts., valued at 4,371,000 rupees, in 1868, to 49,284 cwts., worth 1,675,565 rupees, in 1879. If value as well as quantity is taken into account, there can be no doubt that 1877 was the culminating year so far in the coffee trade of Ceylon, for the 974,330 cwts. (we now speak of the calendar year) shipped then was valued at close on fifty millions of rupees. If any one wishes to understand the cause of present depression in business throughout the island, they have only to remember that the deficiency in hard cash to coffee planters as indicated by the shipments of 1878 and 1879 cannot be less than twenty-six millions of rupees, which would make an average of ten thousand rupees per annum loss for every plantation in the country. No wonder that new products are required to turn the scale. Nevertheless the progress of the coffee-planting industry in Ceylon in forty-three years is little less than marvellous: the export in 1837 being valued at a million of rupees; that of 1879 at over forty millions. The quinquennial record is as follows, showing a progressive increase up to 1871 when the *Hemileia vastatrix* began to tell; after which year the average fell twenty per cent. to 1876, and it has continued to fall at this rate for the last three years:

For five years	ending	1841	the average	annual	export was	54,872 cwts.
"	"	1846	"	"	"	140,220 "
"	"	1851	"	"	"	315,049 "
"	"	1856	"	"	"	411,264 "
"	"	1861	"	"	"	600,942 "
"	"	1866	"	"	"	785,998 "
"	"	1871	"	"	"	973,975 "
"	"	1876	"	"	"	799,115 "
For four years	ending	1880	"	"	"	761,365 "

COFFEE-HULLING MACHINE.

"Unless 1881 gives a really good coffee crop all over the country, the average for the next quinquennial period ending with that year must show a further marked decrease."

In Ceylon the principal crop is picked from April to July; but there is also a small crop, chiefly from the young plants, gathered from September to December. The yield varies from 2 cwts. to 12 cwts. per acre. Some estates show an average yield of from 9½ cwts. to 11½ cwts. per acre for a term of years. It requires fully 3 cwts. of coffee per acre annually to cover the cost of cultivation.

Of the different processes necessary to prepare the bean for market, that of removing the outer rind, or of "pulping," as it is called, is the only one performed on the plantation. The "West-India process" is the method employed in Ceylon. A description of this method will be found in Chapter IV.

The berries pass from the pulper into a cistern filled with water. There they are allowed to soak for about twelve hours, a slight fermentation setting in and decomposing the sticky fluid, or mucilage, which adheres to the parchment skin. The berries are then washed clean and spread on large drying-grounds, called barbecues, to dry. When this is accomplished, the planter has done his part, and the coffee is sent "in parchment"—that is to say, in the dry, tough skin enveloping the bean—to the shipping ports, where the subsequent operations of "peeling," "garbling," "sizing," and packing for export, a more detailed description of which is given further on, are completed. The reason for this is that each plantation could not well afford the expensive machinery used for these processes; and also that labor is much cheaper on the coast than in the interior, the laborers being nearly all "Tamils" imported from the Coromandel Coast of India. The Sinhalese, as a rule, will have nothing to do with the work.

Colombo, as is well known, is the chief port of export, and a railroad, eighty miles long, has been opened to the interior, almost solely for the purpose of transporting coffee and the fertilizers which its cultivation requires. On the arrival of the coffee in Colombo, it is taken to the coffee "mills," as they are there called, spread out on the drying-grounds in the sun, and thoroughly dried; it is then put into the "peeler" (for illustration, see p. 99), a large circular machine in which heavy rollers are constantly revolved on a bed of coffee, giving sufficient pressure to break and detach the "parchment," or thin outer covering, without crushing the bean. It is then run through "fanning-mills," which separate the bean from the parchment, dust, and trash; and the beans are separated into different sizes by running them through a series of screens, the first of which allows the pea-berry and the smaller and more imperfect kernels to drop through, the second separating the next larger size, while the third receives the larger and more perfect beans, known as "No. 1." The next smaller size is known as "No. 2," and the black, trashy, and imperfect berries as "triage." After the different kinds have been thus approximately separated by machinery, they are sent to the "picking-room," where a vast number of women and children are employed in carefully picking and sorting the different grades; indeed it may be said that each individual coffee-bean passes through the fingers of these pickers. Of course this care in manipulation results in clean, perfect grades of coffee, and the grades "No. 1" and "No. 2 Plantation Ceylon" are as well defined in the trade as the terms "granulated" and "A" sugars are among grocers in the United States. The pea-berry, or male berry, is here also made into a separate grade, as in Java, and usually commands a slightly higher price than the No. 1, although this depends much upon the demand, and at times it sells for the same price.

The prospects of Ceylon, as a coffee-producing country, may perhaps be well summed up in the words of Mr. Simmonds in his book on "Tropical Agriculture:"

"It would seem that, if the problem is solved of sufficiently maintaining, by manure and proper cultivation, the bulk of the present estates, so as to continue an average yield, there are resources in Ceylon which ought to carry the crop eventually to nearly double the present export of coffee. It will, however, be a long time before that result can be realized, if it ever comes, but in 1880, there ought to be crops averaging 1,500,000 cwts. of coffee, plantation and native, to deal with."

The export in 1880, was 669,614 cwts., showing that the enemies of the plant, and more especially the ravages of leaf disease have seriously affected the production, so that the average export for the past eight years was little over half of what Mr. Simmonds stated should result.

The following gives the prices of native Ceylon coffee known as good ordinary in the London market:

End of 1873	118s. per cwt.	End of 1876	89s. per cwt.
" 1874	82s. "	" 1877	85s. "
" 1875	92s. "	" 1878	67s. "

The following shows the range of prices as to quality:

1879.		1880.	
Native Bold	75s. to 80s. per cwt.	Native bold	64s. to 66s. per cwt.
Good & fine ordin'y.	70s. to 74s. "	Good & fine ordin'y.	60s. to 61s. "
Small and ordinary.	62s. to 69s. "	Small and ordinary.	50s. to 59s. 6d. "

The comparative prices of Plantation Ceylon on January 1, 1880 and 1881, in London, together with the prices of West India and Central American coffee, were, per hundredweight, in bond (duty, 1½d. per pound and one-fourth per cent.), as follows:

	1880.				1881.			
	s.	d.	s.	d.	s.	d.	s.	d.
Ceylon, Native, good and fine	61	0 @	66	0	71	0 @	80	0
Small to good ordinary	50	0 @	60	0	60	0 @	70	0
Plantation, fine	98	0 @	110	0	112	0 @	120	0
Fine middling	87	0 @	95	0	107	0 @	110	0
Good middling	81	0 @	86	0	103	0 @	106	0
Low and middling	60	0 @	80	0	81	0 @	102	0
Triage and inferior	50	0 @	58	0	70	0 @	80	0
Jamaica, finest	93	0 @	105	0	102	0 @	110	0
Middling to good	80	0 @	90	0	92	0 @	100	0
Inferior and triage	50	0 @	74	0	60	0 @	88	0
Costa Rica, middling to fine	70	0 @	86	0	85	0 @	100	0
Low to f. f. ordinary	52	0 @	65	0	61	0 @	82	0
Guatemala, good to fine	76	0 @	84	0	90	0 @	97	0
Ordinary to middling	53	0 @	73	0	60	0 @	84	0

The imports of Ceylon coffee into the United Kingdom were as follows:

Year.	In Thousands, U. S. Lbs.	Total Cwts.	Year.	In Thousands, U. S. Lbs.	Total Cwts.
1869.........	95,200	850,000	1875.........	84,000	750,000
1870.........	98,000	875,000	1876.........	56,560	505,000
1871.........	96,656	863,000	1877.........	87,360	780,000
1872.........	80,976	723,000	1878.........	57,008	509,000
1873.........	95,200	850,000	1879.........	71,792	641,000
1874.........	60,592	541,000	1880.........	55,664	497,000

The distribution of the crop of 1879–80, was as follows:

Distribution from October 1, 1879, *to September* 30, 1880.

Shipped to.	Plantation.	Native.	Total.
	Cwts.	Cwts.	Cwts.
London................................	530,907	17,612	548,519
Southampton	43	—	43
Marseilles..............................	3,545	4,025	7,570
Havre....................................	1,001	1,700	2,701
Trieste	63,678	3,079	66,757
Venice	2,475	11,261	13,736
Ancona................................	100	—	100
Leghorn................................	308	—	308
Genoa..................................	61	475	536
Port Said..............................	—	400	400
Suez	16	—	16
Aden....................................	457	100	557
Mauritius..............................	947	—	947
New York	619	3,131	3,750
Calcutta	5	—	5
Pondicherry..........................	6	—	6
Madras	—	296	296
Bombay	6,708	3,670	10,386
Kurrachee	2	—	2
Tellicherry	—	75	75
Singapore..............................	10	—	10
Hongkong	13	—	13
Shanghai	7	—	7
Australia	4,992	201	5,193
Melbourne	347	—	347
Sydney	3,799	512	4,311
Hebson's Bay	1,923	763	2,686
Glenelg................................	337	—	337
Total........................	622,306	47,308	669,614

The great bulk of the crop, as will be seen from the foregoing, finds a market in England, where it commands a higher price than most other growths. The imports into the United States (Atlantic Coast), were as follows from 1866 to 1881:

Importation of Ceylon Coffee into the United States (Atlantic Coast), 1866 *to* 1881.

Year.	Packages.	Tons.	Year.	Packages.	Tons.
1866	32,055	2,074	1874............	7,118	763
1867	9,110	590	1875............	10,141	732
1868	18,405	1,212	1876............	14,359	962
1869	22,347	1,483	1877............	3,232	197
1870	35,181	3,947	1878............	348	22
1871	18,404	1,306	1879............	9,184	615
1872	18,906	1,638	1880............	5,722	383
1873	7,823	542			

Average for fifteen years, 1866–81 ....14,160 packages, 1,098 tons.
Average for ten years, 1871–80........... 9,530 " 716 "

The Plantation Ceylon usually comes in casks and tierces, containing 1,000 pounds in the former and 400 to 600 pounds in the latter. It is known as Pea-berry, No. 1, 2, 3, and Triage. The bean is very heavy or solid, rather more so than the best Rio, and about the same in size and appearance as fine Blue Mountain Jamaica. The beans in the different grades are all of a size, and scrupulously clean. No. 1 is the largest. Native Ceylon is a light, spongy coffee, that loses two per cent. more in roasting than the Plantation. It is usually packed in bags, weighing either 112, 140, or 168 pounds. The bean varies in color from a white to yellow, and in size is sometimes quite as large as Java, and again as small as Mocha.

The same quantity in weight of roasted Plantation Ceylon will make a heavier bodied liquor than a similar amount of Java. In flavor it ranks with the finest of mild coffee.

In the year 1882 we look for a considerable export of Liberian coffee from Ceylon. Quite an area is under cultivation; the plants have thriven, and promise well. This matter has more than a passing interest to Americans, for it is due to the industry of the liberated slaves of America upon the plantations of Liberia in cultivating a species of coffee indigenous to the forests of Liberia, and known as Coffœa Liberica, that Ceylon, Brazil, and other coffee-growing countries are enabled to utilize land for coffee production that is not suitable for growing Coffœa Arabica.

In the spring of 1873 the first Liberian coffee plants were set out in Ceylon by Mr. L. St. George Carey. The honor of planting the first seed is claimed by a Mr. Massey, who as early as 1866 made an unsuccessful attempt to raise plants from native seed. One of the parchment beans he had at that time measured one and one-eighth inch in length.

In 1876 there were thirteen estates in Ceylon cultivating Liberian coffee, with two hundred and forty-one acres planted. It seems specially adapted to the low lands, but will not flourish at as high an elevation as Coffœa Arabica, which thrives from five thousand to six thousand feet above sea level; while its competitor flourishes from sea level to five hundred feet higher in Liberia. It is hoped that a hybrid will be secured which will do well between one thousand and three thousand feet above sea-level.

CHAPTER XIII.

CULTIVATION IN INDIA.

British India is also making great strides in the production of coffee, the first plantations of which were, it is said, opened in Bengal by some French or Spanish refugees from the Philippines in 1820. Legend says that the first plant was brought by Baba Buden, a pilgrim, from Arabia, ten to twenty generations back. It was planted in Mysore, and from this parent stock probably came the coffee trees that were found in Wynaad, Coòrg, and other parts of the peninsula by travellers, these trees bearing evidence of being thirty to forty years old. The culture is now principally carried on in the Madras Presidency, and in the native states of Mysore, Travancore, and Coorg. It has been largely taken up by the natives as well as by Europeans. The province of Coorg has about seventy thousand acres under cultivation, from which from seven thousand to ten thousand tons of coffee are produced annually. The mountain-grown coffee of Mysore commands a high price at home, owing to its fine quality. It is grown some four thousand feet above sea level. In Neilgherry the tree flourishes at an altitude of six thousand feet, and trees thirty years of age are found as productive as the young trees.

From an official "Statement of the Material Progress of India" we learn that: "The extension of coffee cultivation commenced experimentally in the Wynaad in 1840, and in 1862 there were 9,932 acres under cultivation in the Wynaad alone. In 1865, Wynaad coffee cultivation had increased to 200 estates, covering 14,613 acres. The exports in 1860–61 amounted to 19,119,209 pounds, and coffee cultivation became a very important and increasing source of wealth. In 1873 the total number of acres under coffee were 29,595, in 6,913 holdings, of which 195 belong to Europeans and 6,718 to natives." At present there are some 35,000 acres under cultivation, on which $5,000,000 has been expended by British capitalists. The unemployed area in Wynaad fit for coffee growing is placed at 200,000 acres. The shipping ports of this promising district are Madras, Tellicherry, and Calicut.

At the Vienna Exhibition the first prize for coffee was secured by coffee grown in the hill tracts of the Chittagong district, Bengal, where from 1,000 to 1,350 pounds of coffee are secured per acre. Active work on these plantations is carried on from October to February.

The similarity of the seasons and the general physical character of Southern India, give rise to the same routine of cultivation as in Ceylon. The abundant supply of labor offers, however, peculiar advantages in India.

The exports, according to the "Government Statistical Reporter," were as follows, and they exhibit the great progress made during the period from 1856 to 1872. The severe drought of 1876, together with leaf disease and the ravages of the borer, reduced subsequent crops.

Exports from British India, 1856–57 *to* 1878–79.

Year.	Quantity. Lbs.	Tons.	Year.	Quantity. Lbs.	Tons.
1856–57.....	5,205,400	2,324	1868–69....	47,788,773	21,334
1857–58.....	6,123,807	2,734	1869–70....	36,081,003	16,108
1858–59.....	11,695,195	5,221	1870–71....	33,459,426	14,937
1859–60.....	14,345,809	6,404	1871–72....	56,363,838	25,162
1860–61. ...	19,119,041	8,535	1872–73....	41,462,705	18,510
1861–62.....	21,505,676	9,601	1873–74....	40,715,638	18,177
1862–63.....	21,045,733	9,395	1874–75....	36,653,008	16,363
1863–64.....	26,752,961	11,943	1875–76....	42,691,712	19,059
1864–65.....	32,387,889	14,459	1876–77....	36,165,920	16,147
1865–66.....	34,700,197	15,491	1877–78....	33,399,352	14,910
1866–67.....	17,636,375	7,873	1878–79....	38,467,408	17,173
1867–68.....	33,189,134	14,817			

The home consumption is quite large in Southern India, it being estimated at from 16,000,000 to 18,000,000 pounds. About one-half the quantity exported goes to the United Kingdom; one-third to France; the balance is distributed to Turkey, Arabia, and Mediterranean ports, scarcely any reaching the United States.

LIBERIAN COFFEE PLANT.

CHAPTER XIV.

LIBERIAN AND OTHER AFRICAN GROWTHS OF COFFEE.

THE product of the African Republic, although limited in amount, has, during the last few years, attracted considerable notice. The plant differs somewhat from the tree known as C. Arabica, and botanically is known as C. Liberica. It is cultivated very successfully in the hot and moist lowlands or on hills of no great altitude. The tree grows wild in various parts of Liberia, but by transplanting to points near the coast, and careful cultivation, the bean has been improved.

The C. Liberica is more prolific, its berries, of varying size, being frequently much larger than those obtained from C. Arabica, which rarely exceed one-half inch in length, while Liberian coffee has been shown from an inch to one and one-eighth inch in length. The Liberian plant has been taken to Java, Ceylon, Brazil, and other points, and subjected to experiments with a view of testing its merits as compared with C. Arabica. The fruit, when ripe, lacks the bright red color characteristic of C. Arabica, and its covering is hard, fibrous, and rather rough, containing little pulpy matter; it does not drop from the tree when ripe, as in the case of Coffœa Arabica. The flavor is good, and if the culture and preparation were systematized and pursued upon a larger scale, it would undoubtedly become a favorite variety.

The plantations in Liberia are scattered, poorly cultivated plots of ground, lying along the banks of the river. It is stated that a single tree has produced from twenty to twenty-four pounds of beans. While peculiarly adapted to growing in low countries, the plant is being successfully cultivated in Ceylon at an elevation of 3,000 feet, and upon one estate 1,500 feet above sea-level a crop was gathered of two tons per acre. As the future of C. Liberica is full of promise and the plant likely to gain a permanent foothold in countries where C. Arabica is cultivated, I make quite a full extract from notes prepared by Mr. Morris, of Ceylon, for a work on Liberian coffee, more especially as our dealers and consumers will be called upon to test its merits and fix for it a place with other kinds of coffee now in popular favor.

"Taking the description given in a former paragraph as an enumeration of the characters of a typical tree of C. Liberica, it is necessary to remark that there are varieties within certain limits which require to be noticed. Among the trees cultivated in the Botanical Gardens at Peradeniya there are some which have characters so distinct as to be easily recognized even by a casual observer. For instance, one variety is distinguished by having rather small concave leaves, by developing a more vigorous growth of primaries and secondaries, and by constantly producing globose berries with very large flower scars: these are among the largest trees, and bear the best crops. Another variety appears to have flatter and narrower leaves, the berries are distinctly ellipsoidal, and the seeds are very characteristically pointed at both ends. Other trees are marked by less distinguishing characters, but in trees where the number of petals varies between six and nine, it is to be expected that variation would take place in other organs. The instances given above are the most distinct varieties which have come under notice. It may be added that plants raised from these varieties retain their characters, and are easily recognized. If there are several well-marked varieties of C. Liberica, it would be well to propagate and distribute those only which exhibit a vigorous and healthy growth of wood and produce the largest crops. The variation in the number of petals is not constant in the same tree, but the petals are never fewer than six, nor more than nine. The berries, when ripe, are of a dull red color, not so bright as those of C. Arabica. Hiern, in his description, probably from dry specimens, speaks of the berries as black. At Peradeniya they have never become black; indeed they are not always completely red. If C. Liberica is the original of Cape Coast coffee, we shall have to add another variety to those indicated above. Dr. Roberts, who has had many opportunities for observing the trees on the West Coast of Africa, considers C.

Liberica and Cape Coast coffee to be distinct. There are three trees received as Cape Coast coffee now in the Botanic Gardens, about eighteen months old. They are more robust in habit even than C. Liberica; their leaves are thick and leathery, and more than fifteen inches in length. No trace whatever of leaf disease has appeared upon them, though young plants of C. Liberica, under similar conditions, have suffered more or less from it. When these plants have flowered and produced berries, it will be easier to notice any further points of difference which exist between them and typical plants of C. Liberica. With regard to liability to attack from leaf-disease, it appears that plants of Mocha coffee suffer more severely from it than any others—so severely, indeed, as to kill a large number of very fine young plants in a few weeks. The ordinary coffee comes next, followed by C. Liberica, and with Cape Coast coffee, so far as our present experience goes, at the head of the list.

"It is well known that young plants of C. Liberica suffer severely in nurseries from attacks of the *Hemileia*, but if the soil is good and a little liquid manure is applied, they soon recover, and after eighteen months or two years they seem to be strong enough to withstand the disease and become healthy and productive trees.

LIBERIAN COFFEE BERRIES AND SEEDS.

"As may be supposed, from the habit and size of the trees, the berries of Liberian coffee are larger and finer than those of the ordinary coffee. The average length of the berry of C. Arabica seldom exceeds half an inch, while the average length of the berry of C. Liberica is nearly one inch. The pulp or outer covering of the Liberian coffee berries is thick, rather fibrous, and more or less fleshy, but never succulent, as in the ordinary coffee. The shell just under the pulp, the indurated endocarp, is hard and brittle, seldom looks clean, and is generally of a dull brown color. The "silver skin," which comes next, is strong and tough, dipping into the deep furrow on the face of the seed and carefully investing the substance of the coffee bean. In descriptive notes on Liberian coffee berries and seeds, it may not be out of place to describe their character and structure with some detail, and place before those interested in the subject facts which may prove of value in dealing with the propagation and distribution of this promising plant. The seeds of Liberian coffee enclosed within their investing coats are generally two in number; when one seed, as is sometimes the case, becomes abortive, the other seed receiving all the nourishment of the berry, becomes large and rounded, and is termed a "pea bean." When the pulp is removed, the seed covered by the hard brittle shell, the indurated endocarp, is technically termed a "pyrene;" there are, therefore, two "pyrenes" in each perfect berry. The "pyrene" is convex on the back, flat, with a narrow, usually deep longitudinal furrow on the face. If the hard shell investing the pyrene, the "parchment," be removed, we expose what is generally called "rice coffee." Carefully examined, the structures which make up the rice coffee or *seeds* are resolved into a membranous testa or coat of the seed, the "silver skin," a horny folded mass termed the albumen, and embedded in the substance of the latter, near its base, a small body called the embryo, the miniature Liberian coffee tree, not more than one-third inch in length. Botanists classify the different parts of a fruit like the coffee berry as follows: (1) the outer skin of the berry is termed the *epicarp;* (2) the pulpy mass between the skin and the parchment is the *mesocarp;* (3) the indurated shell called the "parchment" is botanically the *endocarp;* (4) the "silver skin," which comes next to the parchment, is the *testa* or integument of the seed; (5) the mass of the coffee bean under the "silver skin" is the *albumen;* (6) and contained in the albumen, embedded near its base, is the minute *embryo.* The first, second, and third structures in this series belong to the *fruit,* whereas the others—viz., the testa, the albumen, and the embryo—are essentially parts of the *seed.* The uses of the various structures which surround the minute embryo are to protect it from injury, and, at the same time, to supply it with suitable nourishment till such time as it is able to take care of itself. Most people are familiar with the gray pearly "silver skin" which forms the outer covering or testa of the coffee bean. It envelops every part of the albumen, follows its foldings, and dips into the deep furrow on the face. By its tough, leathery nature it acts as an effectual protection to the delicate structures within. Before the bean is roasted the parchment and silver skin are removed, and then we have left the horny, folded albumen making up the bulk of the bean. It is this albumen, roasted and ground, which supplies the coffee of household use. In the economy of plant life, the albumen is intended for a very different purpose: it is a patrimony which the young embryo is supposed to utilize and adapt for the purposes of its growth and development. In fact, it is a supply of food specially and wisely adapted to promote its first impulses of life and energy. When examined under the microscope, the albumen consists of a number of cells, with walls more or less thick, forming a storehouse of nourishment in the form of starchy compounds, volatile oil, and other vegetable products. If in a fresh, mature bean we cut rather obliquely toward its base, we shall come upon a small cylindrical body, completely invested by the tissue of the albumen. It is about one-third the length of the bean, and looks like a small peg with a round head. This is the embryo of the future plant, and apparently now consists of only two parts. The narrow pointed part directed toward the base of the bean is the radicle. This, in the process of germination, will develop into the tap-root, while the round head, called by botanists the *plumule*, will be found, on examination, to consist of two very minute fleshy leaves—the cotyledonary or seed-leaves of the young plant. Between these minute leaves is a process called the *punctum vegetationis*, or growing-point of the ascending axis, destined, in process of time, to give rise to all the various structures of stem, branches, leaves, flowers, and fruit.

PROPAGATION BY SEEDS.

"For the raising of Liberian coffee from seeds the first requisite is a supply of well-ripened seeds, as fresh as possible. From the description of the various structures contained in a coffee seed it will be seen how delicate and sensitive these structures are. If the albumen be injured by damp or fermentation, or if it be exposed to the hardening and desiccating influences of a dry atmosphere, it will be rendered quite unfit as a food supply for the young seedling, and it is owing to these circumstances that imported seeds so often fail to produce healthy plants. In the case of well-ripened seeds, under favorable conditions, ninety-six to ninety-eight per cent. will germinate, and at least ninety-four per cent. will develop into fine trees. As in other seeds, it is necessary, in order to produce germination, that they receive the proper amount of moisture, heat, and air. The moisture required should be supplied by moderate but uniform watering, night and morning. Excess of water will have an injurious effect upon the young plants, and render them weak and sickly. The best soil for raising seeds is a mixture of loam and leaf-mould, or earth produced by rotten leaves, sifted and mixed with an equal volume of sand; the sand keeps the loam from adhering together when watered, and allows excess of water to drain off, while the loam retains as much water in the cavities of the soil as is required for the purposes of germination. Jungle soil, well sifted and mixed with an equal proportion of sand, generally forms an excellent soil for young plants. The seeds may be sown in deep boxes, or in beds formed in the open air. In any case, a good depth of soil is necessary, for even in a very young seedling the tap-roots are extremely long, and they require an abundant supply of good, rich soil to keep up their growth.

"The plants should be grown in partial shade or covered by thatched hurdles or "cadjans;" care should be taken not to cover them up too much; when established, the protection should be very gradually removed, according as the plants indicate their ability to bear the effects of light and sunshine. For transplanting purposes bamboo pots, baskets, or cow-dung pots may be used. Where easily obtained, bamboo pots are strongly recommended; they afford every protection for the tap-roots, and at the same time supply them with a good depth of soil. The cow-dung pots require more care in making, and, on young estates, the material may not easily be obtained; but, where it is possible to make them, they are superior to anything else for transplanting purposes. Once the young plant is established in the cow-dung pot it is safe, for, when buried in the soil, the material of the pot becomes softened by moisture, and is easily penetrated by the roots, thus forming a protection for the roots when handled, and ultimately a valuable manure to the plant.

"Seeds of Liberian coffee appear to take a longer time to germinate than the ordinary coffee. Seeds sown on January 2d appeared above ground and were two and a half inches high on February 1st. They remained apparently *in statu quo* for about a month, but by the end of March the two bright seed-leaves were fully developed. Two months longer are required to thoroughly establish them, so that, under ordinary circumstances, Liberian coffee-plants require about five or six months before they can be safely transplanted; and, when transplanted, too much care cannot be taken in handling the tender young rootlets and preserving them from injury.

"In germinating, it will be noticed that at first there is only a short, pale green stalk, surmounted by the rounded oval form of the parchment bean. The structures of the coffee-seed noticed in the last section have now become greatly altered. Under the stimulating effects of heat and moisture the embryo has pushed forth its radicle and, penetrating the soil, has begun its life's work of absorption: on the other hand, the ascending axis of the embryo has grown upward, and, drawing its first nourishment from the albumen enclosed in the parchment and testa, appears as a short stalk with a globose head. It should be here noticed that, in order to nourish the young plant, all the starchy compounds contained in the albumen have become changed, during germination, into sugar—a process analogous to what takes place with regard to starchy compounds in the animal economy. During the apparently stationary period, noticed above, the cotyledonary or seed-leaves are growing larger and larger within the parchment case. When they have exhausted their food supply the parchment covering, as well as the silver skin, falls off, and then the two fresh, bright green seed-leaves, being well supplied with moisture by the roots, begin their work of elaborating the juices and supplying the plant with its proper supply of food.

GENERAL REMARKS.

"The plants of Liberian coffee now in the Botanic Gardens consist of several groups planted at different periods since 1873. The largest trees, now nearly ten feet high, were sent from Kew, in Wardian cases, in March, 1874; they were transferred into bamboo pots a few months afterward. Out of twenty-four plants received, four were so severely attacked by leaf disease that they succumbed; the others suffered more or less, but ultimately recovered. Many of the latter, however, show that they were weakened by the disease, for they are short of primaries and lose their leaves more rapidly than the healthy ones. Mr. Ferdinandus, the foreman of the Gardens, who has given considerable attention to this coffee, is a strong advocate for partial shade for young trees at this elevation. He believes that in the low country near the sea, the air, though warmer, is full of moisture, and the progress made by the trees at Henaratgoda strengthens him in the opinion that the Liberian coffee requires a warm, moist, and stimulating climate. During the warm weather on the hills the air is evidently too dry for young plants, unless they are partly shaded; mulching with dead leaves, jak shavings, or even sawdust, is found very beneficial in dry weather. If the plants have a deep, rich soil and can send down their long tap-roots into it, they may dispense with shade and be all the better for the larger supply of light and air. The trees mentioned above came into blossom when eighteen months old, but none of it set. In March, 1876, another and a larger blossom was produced, which set abundantly. The berries were ripe in the following December, and from the seeds a large number of plants was raised. This was the only blossom produced in 1876. In the following year (1877) they blossomed early in March, and a good crop of fruit was produced by the close of the year. At the end of April, in the same year, and at intervals varying from two to three months, the trees were in partial blossom, and they have ever since borne berries in different stages of growth. The principal flowering time, however, is March, and the main crop of fruit is ripe by the middle or end of December.

"In 1875 a parcel of thirty seeds, packed in damp moss, was received from Mr. Bull; these germinated and grew up into healthy plants. The attacks of leaf disease were but slight, and the plants, in partial shade, are now doing well and are nearly five feet high. A leaf of one of these plants measures eighteen inches in extreme length and eight inches at the widest part. In outline it differs slightly from other specimens. Instead of having the wedge-shaped base narrowing as it approaches the petiole (stalk) of the leaf, the base is rounded and almost resembles the full oval outline of the extremity of the leaf. The variations in the outline of the leaves, in the number of petals, in the size and shape of the berry, and in the area of the flower-scar, are points which may well be noticed; for if they are associated with a more robust habit, with a greater immunity from leaf disease, and also with a larger production of the crop, it is evident that such varieties are deserving of great attention, and, as special varieties, would well repay careful and systematic culture. Mr. Ferdinandus, who has successfully raised several thousands of plants of this coffee, prefers trees with small concave leaves, globose berries, and large flower-scars; these are certainly the finest trees at Peradeniya, and they bear the best crops. Attention having been drawn to these variations in Liberian coffee it is quite possible that others may be noticed. As the cultivation extends we shall, no doubt, be able to gather more accurate information respecting them, and learn whether any special variety is adapted for special areas of cultivation, or for higher and lower elevations.

"A group of plants received from Mr. Bull in 1876 were soon afterward planted out in fresh jungle soil. Slightly shaded at first, they quickly established themselves, were topped at six feet, and now (March, 1878) they have shown their first blossom, which has abundantly set. One or two trees placed in rather thick shade have shown that under such conditions they become drawn up and attenuated, and their first primaries are three and a half feet from the ground. It is quite certain that anything beyond a very partial shade is not suitable for this coffee. As soon as the young trees have well established themselves in rich, deep soil they can bear, provided the air is moist, full exposure to the sun.

"In the third year the trees may be expected to produce a good crop, with a succession of blossoms every two or three months, according as the weather is favorable. The trees begin to throw out their secondaries in the third year, but apparently not so rapidly and regularly as the common coffee. It will be noticed that in branching, the Liberian coffee has an erect tree-like habit, and its primaries do not possess that horizontal and drooping habit which is so characteristic of C. Arabica. When rather large trees of Liberian coffee are attacked by leaf disease, the leaves show perforations scattered here and there over their surface; the fungus seems to be confined to isolated areas, and the leaves being so large, instead of causing them to fall off, a round hole is made through them, as if eaten by a caterpillar. Thus the greater part of the leaf-area is left intact, and it is enabled, in spite of leaf disease, to discharge its functions as an essential part in the economy of the plant. It can hardly be expected that a plant of this kind can be entirely free from the attacks of the many parasites which affect vegetable life in Ceylon. One tree of Liberian coffee has been attacked by borer, and the leaves of a small plant have been entirely destroyed by the caterpillar of the pearl moth; but cases of this nature, so far, are too isolated and possibly too accidental to allow any general conclusions to be drawn from them. That the Liberian coffee in the adult state is strong enough to resist attacks of leaf disease, and that it is well suited for cultivation in the extensive districts of the low country, are facts alone sufficient to render its cultivation in Ceylon one of the most promising undertakings in the island."

Small quantities of coffee are grown along the eastern coast of Africa, in Abyssinia, the Somali country, Mozambique, Madagascar, Natal, Re Union, and Mauritius; but the total yield, so far as its influence upon the supply of Europe and the United States is concerned, is insignificant, as the export capacity of all the places named does not exceed from six hundred to eight hundred tons annually. The product of the eastern provinces of Africa, taken in connection with the small crops raised on the west coast, makes Africa contribute between three thousand and four thousand tons to the world's production, the amount including coffee grown in Egypt and the interior countries of the continent.

CHAPTER XV.

EMPIRE OF BRAZIL.

WITHIN a few provincés of Brazil is produced more than one-half of the coffee-supply of the world.

The industry in that great empire will be better understood if some knowledge is possessed of the country, its government, inhabitants, and industrial development.

The government is monarchical, hereditary, constitutional, and representative. The reigning monarch is the Emperor Dom Pedro II., who succeeded to the throne of his father, Dom Pedro I., on the 7th of April, 1831, being little over six years old. He was declared of age, and assumed the reins of government on July 23, 1840, and was crowned July 18, 1841. He is an educated man, of liberal ideas, an indefatigable worker, and has proved himself a wise and capable ruler.

The empire of Brazil covers one-fifteenth of the surface of the globe, one-fifth of the New World, and three-sevenths of South America. It extends from about 5° 10′ north latitude to 33° 46′ south latitude, and from 34° 47′ 15″ to 74° 7′ 5″ west longitude of Greenwich. Situated in the eastern part of South America, it has a coast line, washed by the waters of the North and South Atlantic, of nearly five thousand miles. Its greatest length is two thousand six hundred miles, and its width, measuring from Ponta de Pedras, the most eastern point, to the most western point on the river Javari, is about two thousand eight hundred miles. It has an area of 3,288,110 square miles, divided into twenty provinces, besides the municipality of S. Sebastião do Rio de Janeiro, as follows: Amazonas, Pará, Maranhão, Piauhy, Ceará, Rio Grande do Norte, Parahyba, Pernambuco, Alagoas, Sergipe, Bahia, Espirito Santo, Rio de Janeiro, S. Paulo, Paraná, Santa

Catharina, S. Pedro do Rio Grande do Sul, Minas Geraes, Goyaz, and Matto Grosso.

Extensive mountain ranges and rivers of enormous size traverse the empire, so that vast plains and extensive valleys abound. Its principal river, the Amazon, is the largest on the globe, being, with its tributaries, navigable for over thirty thousand miles. This river empties into the ocean with a velocity so great "that at a distance of nearly one mile from the coast its current is still equal to four miles an hour, and navigators may drink of its waters after losing sight of land."

The climate of Brazil varies greatly in different parts of the empire, being hot and damp during the rainy season in the region from Rio de Janeiro, the capital, north to the Amazon, the mean temperature being 26° Centigrade (79° Fahrenheit). From the capital to the extreme southern point the heat diminishes, and the climate becomes cool, especially in the provinces of S. Paulo, Paranà, Santa Catharina, S. Pedro do Rio Grande do Sul, and part of Minas Geraes. The following particulars are given in a work published under the auspices of the Brazilian Government, entitled "The Empire of Brazil at the [Philadelphia] Exposition of 1876":

"As a rule, the rainy season commences in November, and lasts until June. These limits, however, vary according to localities. From the river Amazon to the Parnahyba it rains a great deal; thence to S. Francisco but little; and more again to the south. The immense valley of this river embraces the region which the natives call the *Sertão*, and has two very distinct seasons, the dry and the wet season, the former lasting from January to May, and the latter from June to December. In June all vegetation ceases, all seeds ripen; in July the leaves commence to turn yellow and to fall; in August vast tracts of land present the aspect of a European winter without snow, with two or three exceptions the trees being denuded of leaves. Where the old mode of preparation is in vogue, this is the most favorable season for the preparation of the coffee cultivated on the mountains. Being gathered, it is spread on the ground, which exhales no moisture, but, on the contrary, absorbs it. Surrounded by an atmosphere in the same conditions, the coffee dries rapidly without fermenting.

"From December to January the wet season sets in, and with the first rainfalls the rivers, which until then had been almost dry, with only here and there a few pools, which served as watering-places for cattle, or as a refuge for fish, swell immensely. Plants in a few days, as by a charm, reacquire their verdancy; the soil is covered with parti-colored flowers; alimentary plants grow quickly and produce abundantly."

The vegetation of this colossal empire, so richly endowed by nature, is beyond the powers of description. "In the mountain passes not far removed from the sea shore, the conjoint effects of heat and moisture produce a superfluity of vegetable life, which man's utmost efforts cannot restrain. Trees split for paling in the neighborhood of Rio de Janeiro send forth shoots and branches immediately, and this whether the position of the fragments be that in which they originally grew, or inverted. On the banks of the Amazon the loftiest trees destroy each other by their proximity, and are bound together by rich and multiform vines. In the province of Maranhão, the roots, grasses, and other plants, extending from the shores of pools, weave themselves, in time, into a kind of vegetable bridge, along which the passenger treads, unaware that he has left the firm earth, until the jaws of a cayman protrude through the herbage before him." Botanists pronounce the flora of Brazil unsurpassed by that of any other region in the world. There are already twenty thousand species known to scientists, many of which are invaluable as articles of food or medicine.

Almost every sort of wood can be obtained in the forests; among the most valuable trees being an uncultured palm growing in several of the provinces, almost every portion of it coming into use, even the leaves giving wax used in the manufacture of candles, the province of Rio Grande do Norte exporting 300,000 kilograms (660,000 pounds) over and above home consumption. It is, however, reserved for a foreign plant, Coffœa Arabica, to take the first place as a source of wealth—to be, in fact, the chief source of the prosperity of the empire. The productiveness of the soil is in some instances wonderful. Grain returns commonly one hundred and fifty fold; in some localities two hundred and fifty to three hundred, and on one of the coast islands four hundred fold has been frequently harvested. Rice yields as much as a thousand fold, and the cotton fields are unusually productive. These facts are interesting to the reader as showing that nature has done more for the coffee-fields of Brazil than for almost any other section of the coffee-growing belt.

The question of labor has for some time interested the planters of Brazil, and the problem they must solve is how to secure an abundance, for if crops increase without an addition to the population, there will be a scarcity. Already the wisdom of introducing Chinese laborers has been canvassed.

It is now a difficult matter to harvest properly a crop of over four million bags of coffee, in addition to giving proper care to other crops. A report recently published in Brazil states that "the only remedy is to curtail plantations to a point where production may about balance consumption, thus admitting easy harvesting and better preparation for market."

The population of Brazil is not definitely known, but it probably does not exceed 12,000,000 souls, including native tribes of Indians numbering about 2,000,000, and in 1876, 1,476,567 slaves. In a few years slavery will be abolished. By virtue of a decree of the empire, made in 1871, all persons born thereafter in Brazil were free, and freedom was given to the slaves employed in the public service or in the imperial household.

A correspondent of the London *Times*, in commenting upon the policy of gradual emancipation and certain evasions of the law, says: "The mere fact that the majority of colored freedmen have flocked to the cities and looked for domestic service may be taken as an earnest of what will become of sugar, cotton, and other plantations when the whole slave race has ceased to exist. It is supposed, indeed, that coffee may thrive in the hands of white laborers; but at the estate of Rio Bonito, where slave-labor is carried on with equal regard to economy and humanity, there is a firm conviction that the full enforcement of the law of 1871 must be a death-blow to their industry. And again, other planters, aware that the days of slavery are numbered, work their land to utter exhaustion, anxious to get as much profit out of it as they can with their slaves, and convinced that with final abolition their property will have to be abandoned as valueless." When a scarcity of labor presses upon the Brazilian planter, it is probable, however, that measures will be taken to enlist the services of that portion of the population now classed as aborigines, and numbering over two millions, besides drawing thousands from the low lands to the southern provinces, where a cooler climate makes hard work less wearing upon the system. Or if no such solution can be had, the power of machinery can be utilized, and history will record of its adaptation in Brazil a story similar to that it has written respecting the United States.

This power of agricultural machinery to compensate for a deficiency in the labor supply was most ably shown by Mr. Samuel B. Ruggles, of New York, in a speech made to the Cobden Club, at their annual dinner in London, on the 21st June, 1879. His subject was "The Agricultural Progress of the Nation in Cheapening the Food of America and Europe." In the course of his remarks he said:

"It may not be superfluous to add the prosaic fact, that our scanty population of 5,922,471 individuals, aged ten years and upward, engaged in agriculture in 1870, would have been wholly unable, with any human labor within their reach, to plough, sow, and plant the land, and to reap, mow, and prepare for market the immense crop of cereals and grasses represented in a yearly product of $2,447,189,141. That vast work was and could be accomplished only by the use of the efficient and various agricultural labor-saving machines and implements, mainly the fruits of American invention and enterprise, practically augmenting from five to tenfold, or, in mathematical phrase, raising to that higher power the unaided working capacity of the 5,992,471 individuals. In truth, it is this great and providential superaddition of force which now fully enables our country to discharge the sublime and beneficent duty to plentifully and permanently feed with vegetable and animal food large and constantly increasing portions of the populations of the outer world."

Brazil has already begun to use new machinery and adopt improved processes of cultivation and preparation upon the plantations. In the production of sugar the most improved machinery is being introduced, and we are informed, in a volume issued by the government, that "the culture and preparation of coffee, sugar, cotton, and tobacco, has been considerably improved by the introduction of new machinery and improved processes." The necessity for a division of labor is also recognized, and planters in many instances cultivate coffee, leaving to others its preparation for market. Central mills are being established by companies and worked upon a plan similar to that in operation in districts in this country where factories are placed for the manufacture of butter and cheese.

The empire further recognizes its duty to its subjects by fostering agricultural institutions. We find one institution where the pupils are trained so as to make of them excellent overseers or managers of large rural establishments, and the best assistants for the progress and improvement of agriculture. It is fortunate that the emperor takes a great interest in all these matters and devotes time and labor to bringing the schools to a high degree of excellence, and in encouraging all manner of industrial enterprises.

Confirming these conclusions we have further and decisive proof in the construction of electric telegraphs, lines of railways, and increased facilities for ocean navigation. The former were introduced in 1852, and we now find that Brazil is in telegraphic communication with the United States and Europe, and with the Argentine, Paraguayan, and Chilian Republics. The starting of a line of steamships to the port of New York wrought great changes in the coffee trade between the two countries. It is, however, in the development of railway communication that we find the greatest amount of work done, calculated to improve the internal affairs of the empire. In 1867, there were only six railroads in operation, of the aggregate length of 683 kilometres (424 miles), but every year since then has added to the number of miles built. Five years later fifteen lines were operated, with 1,026 kilometres (637 miles); in 1876, twenty-two lines, with 1,660 kilometres (1,031 miles); and in 1880, thirty-one lines, with 3,059 kilometres (1,900 miles) were worked, while lines were under construction, or survey, that would add 1,910 kilometres (1,187 miles) to those then in traffic.

The government has spent large sums of money in aid of railways. The main line is known as the Dom Pedro II. Railway, and is the trunk of the present system. It starts from Rio de Janeiro, the capital, crosses an important part of the province of Rio de Janeiro, has a branch traversing the province of S. Paulo, and another bringing to the coast the crops of the province of Minas Geraes, while its southern connections open a line to Santos. This road reaches several of the richest provinces of the empire, and its prosperity is chiefly due to its large traffic in coffee. The mania for building railroads has, however, resulted in an extension of lines into provinces where the traffic is insufficient to make the operating of the roads profitable. Those interested in further studying this subject will find it ably treated in Mr. Herbert Smith's work on "Brazil: The Amazons and the Coast," and also in the volume lately mentioned, published under the auspices of the Brazilian Government. It is sufficient for our purpose to know that within five or six years the railways have penetrated the large coffee-growing districts, and that the crop finds its way to market rapidly, and at far less cost than when planters sent their product to market on the backs of mules, which mode of conveyance was made uncertain, and at times impossible, by the bad condition of the roads during the rainy season. It has been sufficiently demonstrated that the government and planters of Brazil are alive to the importance of using the great factors that have revolutionized the commerce of the world within twenty years, viz., steam and electricity, and this is the more creditable, for this has been done in instances where it is certain the railways cannot, for many years at least, earn operating expenses, as some of them traverse long stretches of arid land where it is not probable that large quantities of either freight or passengers can ever be furnished. These developments have done much to cheapen the price of coffee, and their effect has been felt more during the past year than at any previous time.

CHAPTER XVI.

THE BRAZILIAN PRODUCT.

We now come to consider the position of Brazil, the veritable colussus among coffee-producers.

A coffee-plant was brought over in 1722, from the French colony of Cayenne to Para, in the Amazon district, where the cultivation, however, was only undertaken after the promulgation of a decree in 1761, exempting the new agricultural product from export duties. From the Amazon the culture extended to Maranhão, whence in 1774, two small trees were taken to the province of Rio and planted in a private garden, near the convent of Adjuda. The trees prospered, and subsequently an enterprising Belgian, named Molke, opened a regular coffee plantation amidst the great fields of sugar-cane and cereals which then constituted the chief wealth of the province. Such, we are told, were the beginnings of that immense culture which now supplies more than one half of the world's coffee.

The coffee industry in Brazil did not at the outset display that marvellous rapidity of growth, which had signalized the cultivation in the West Indies. While the island of Hayti, in little more than seventy-five years after the introduction of the plant, had exported nearly eighty millions of pounds of coffee per annum, Brazil, at the end of a period of about equal length, in 1820, did not export more than fourteen million pounds of the article. Cuba was then shipping a yearly average of twenty-five million pounds. From that time forth, however, the coffee production of Brazil began to assume remarkable proportions. Stimulated by the high prices of the staple and the adaptability of the country to coffee-raising, the planters of the province of Rio had commenced the wholesale conversion of the former sugar and other estates into coffee plantations. In 1830, the exports from Rio de Janeiro had already increased to 391,785 bags, or

27,985 tons. In 1840, they reached 1,068,418 bags, or in the ten years from 1831 to 1840 an average of 48,532 tons annually. From 1841 to 1850 the product increased to 98,907 tons, and from 1851 to 1860 to 143,671 tons annually. The curtailment of coffee consumption, consequent upon the civil war, in the United States—the chief market for Brazil coffee—discouraged production, and the yearly average exports from Rio, from 1861 to 1870 did not exceed 138,537 tons. From 1871 to 1875, however, the shipments advanced to an average of 155,912 tons per annum. The total exports from the empire have been as follows, the statement showing the quantity shipped from Rio de Janeiro and Santos, the countries to which the coffee was exported, and the total average supply of Brazil coffee for the past seven years:

Shipments from Rio de Janeiro.

(Bags of 60 kilos, 132 lbs.; 17 bags to the ton.)

Year.	United States.	Europe and Cape, etc.	Total.	Proportion to United States, Europe, etc.	
				U. S. Per cent.	Europe. Per cent.
1880	1,824,950	1,632,921	3,457,871	52½	47½
1879	2,245,091	1,253,982	3,499,073	64	36
1878	1,624,945	1,218,135	2,843,080	57	43
1877	1,633,700	1,122,085	2,755,785	59	41
1876	1,404,302	1,299,429	2,703,731	42	48
1875	2,001,427	1,111,749	3,113,176	64	36
1874	1,477,317	1,145,290	2,622,607	57	43
Total seven years.	12,211,732	8,783,591	20,995,323	58	42
Average per year.	1,744,533	1,254,799	2,999,333	58	42

Average per annum, 176,431 tons = 395,205,440 lbs.

Shipments from Santos.

(Bags, 60 kilos, 132 lbs.; 17 bags to the ton.)

Year.	United States.	Europe, etc.	Total.	Proportion.	
				U. S. Per cent.	Europe. Per cent.
1880	205,962	862,020	1,067,982	19	81
1879	210,305	946,631	1,156,936	18	82
1878	175,253	925,701	1,100,954	16	84
1877	87,431	606,084	693,515	12½	87½
1876	58,004	603,789	661,793	9	91
1875	126,514	719,372	845,886	15	85
1874	107,168	639,183	746,351	14	86
Total seven years.	970,637	5,302,780	6,273,417	15½	84½
Average per year.	138,662	757,540	896,202	15½	84½

Average per annum, 52,718 tons = 118,088,320 lbs.

Combined Shipments of Coffee from Rio and Santos.

(Bags, 60 kilos, 132 lbs; 17 bags to the ton.)

Year.	United States.	Europe, etc.	Total.	Proportion. U. S. Per cent.	Proportion. Europe. Per cent.
1880	2,030,912	2,494,941	4,525,853	45	55
1879	2,455,396	2,220,613	4,656,009	53	47
1878	1,800,198	2,143,836	3,944,034	45	55
1877	1,721,131	1,728,169	3,449,300	50	50
1876	1,462,306	1,903,218	3,305,524	43	57
1875	2,127,941	1,831,121	3,959,062	54	46
1874	1,584,485	1,784,473	3,368,958	47	53
Total seven years.	13,182,369	14,086,371	27,268,740	$48\frac{1}{5}$	$51\frac{4}{5}$
Average per year.	1,883,195	2,012,339	3,895,534	$48\frac{1}{5}$	$51\frac{4}{5}$

Average per annum, 229,149 tons = 513,293,760 lbs.
Average consumption per annum in Brazil, 20,000 tons = 44,800,000 lbs.
Total yearly production, 558,093,760 lbs.

Here we have the stupendous average of 558,093,760 pounds, or 249,149 tons of coffee, annually, for seven years, from the partially developed empire of Brazil. A large proportion of the government revenue is derived from a tax or duty imposed upon exports of coffee. The duty in Rio de Janeiro is thirteen per cent., and in Santos thirteen and a half per cent., based on the average quotation of coffee as fixed by the brokers every Saturday.

From the preceding tables it will be seen that the United States absorbs the larger portion of the Rio export, while Europe takes eighty-four and one-half per cent. of the Santos. During the past seven years Europe has taken an average of nearly fifty-two per cent. of the Brazilian crop exported.

With production being pushed in Central America and Mexico, and large supplies from the East Indies, Ceylon, and India, it is becoming a question of more than passing interest what effect the tremendous crops of Brazil will have upon prices, as the total supply is at present rather in advance of the world's requirements.

The coffee-tree seems to find the requisite conditions of climate and soil in almost every portion of the vast region known as Brazil, and nearly everywhere gives an abundant yield.

Coffee-culture extends from the Amazon to the province of San Paulo, and from the coast to the western limits of the empire—a surface exceeding 653,400 square kilometres. Within this territory it is estimated that there are about 530,000,000 coffee-trees, which cover an area of 1,400,000 acres.

The coffee-plantations situated on the high lands, and exposed to the east, are the most productive, but the industry prospers even in the bottom lands, although the product is said to be inferior in flavor and aroma. In Brazil the trees are usually planted five feet apart, but in many cases at much wider intervals, large quantities of vegetables, and even grasses, being often raised between the rows. The plant gives its first full crop in its fifth year, and continues to produce until about its twentieth year. In some instances plantations have lasted thirty years, and efforts are now being made to improve the culture so as to lengthen the life of the trees. This is chiefly sought by enriching the ground, and by a better system of raising the young plants, through which a more vigorous growth is obtained. During the period of bearing, the tree is calculated to produce, on an average, a total of thirty to forty pounds of clean coffee, although between six and twelve years of age the average is much higher. From the twelfth to the twentieth year the yield is irregular. Formerly small cuttings, taken from the old bushes, were used for the propagation of the coffee-tree; it is now, as in Eastern countries, principally raised from the seed. On the high lands the gathering of the crop begins in April or May, and continues until November. The "West India process" of separating the pulp, and then washing and drying, prevails on most of the large estates. Much progress seems to have been made, of late years, in the curing of the coffee-bean. Improved machinery has come into use, and much better grades are exported. It is interesting, in this connection, to note the following remarks from the pen of Professor Agassiz, written during his stay in Brazil:

"I have taken pains to ascertain the facts respecting the culture of coffee during the last fifty years. The immense development of this branch of industry, and the rapidity of the movement, especially in a country where labor is so scarce, is among the most striking economical phenomena of our century. Thanks to their perseverance, and the favorable conditions presented by the constitution of their soil, the Brazilians have obtained a sort of monopoly of coffee. More than half the coffee consumed in the world is of Brazilian growth. And yet the coffee of Brazil has little reputation, and is even greatly underrated.

"Why is this?

"Simply because a great deal of the best produce of Brazilian plantations is sold under the name of Java or Mocha, or as the coffee of Martinique or Bourbon. Martinique only produces six hundred sacks of coffee annually; Guadaloupe, whose coffee is sold under the name of the neighboring island, yields six thousand sacks—not enough to provide the market of Rio de Janeiro for twenty-four hours, and the island of Bourbon hardly more. A great part of the coffee which is bought under these names, or under that of Java coffee, is Brazilian, while the so-called Mocha coffee is often nothing but the small round beans of the Brazilian plant, found at the summits of the branches, and very carefully selected. If the *fazendeiros*, like the Java planters, sold their crops under a special mark, the great purchasers would learn with what merchandise they have to deal, and the agriculture of Brazil would be greatly benefited. But there intervenes between the *fazendeiro* and the exporter a class of merchants—half bankers, half brokers—known as *commissarios*, who, by mixing different harvests, lower the standard crop, thus relieving the producer of all responsibility, and depriving the product of its true characteristics."

The above remarks may be true with regard to that portion of Brazilian coffee exported from Santos, and which finds a market in Europe, but they are erroneous as regards the larger portion of the Brazilian product. That known as Santos is produced in the southern districts of the empire, and does not possess that rank and peculiar flavor that is characteristic of the coffee exported from the port of Rio de Janeiro, and which is so marked that it cannot be disguised. Selections of the choicest Rio beans might, however, if stored properly for two or three years, lose this peculiar smell and flavor, and become so mellowed by age as to approach more closely in drinking qualities those produced in the more northerly portions of South America.

SACKING AND WEIGHING.

The principal ports of Brazil from which coffee is exported are Rio de Janeiro, Santos, Bahia, Caravellas, and Ceará. The port of Rio exports over three-fourths of all the coffee that Brazil sends abroad. The coffee of the provinces of Minas Geraes, Espirito Santo, and the northern portion of San Paulo all has its market in Rio. Santos occupies the second rank in the magnitude of its exports.

The coffee of Brazil varies greatly in color and size. Most of the Rio coffee received here is a small-sized bean, varying in color from a light to a dark green, with some of a yellow hue, often denominated Golden Rio. Large quantities are artificially colored, in order to meet the requirements of certain sections where a prejudice exists in favor of some peculiar color. Various chemicals are used in the process, some of which are rank poison, while others are comparatively harmless. By simply washing in clear cold water it may easily be determined if the bean has been artificially colored. The flavor of most of the Rio coffee imported into the United States is, as has been before stated, quite marked and entirely different from that of any other sort; its smell and appearance, being also quite distinct and characteristic, preclude its substitution for other descriptions.

In the Rio market the coffee is classed either as high land or bottom land, and is branded as follows: Superior, Primeria boa (good firsts), Primeria regular (ordinary firsts), Primeria ordinaria (low firsts), Segunda boa (good seconds), Segunda ordinaria (low seconds). Bahia coffee, owing to its mode of preparation, does not rank as first quality; it is branded either S, SS, SSS.

The planters generally forward their coffee to a *commissario*, or factor, who acts as their agent. It is received in all sorts of lots and conditions from many different growers, no regularity being observed in the style of bag or the amount it contains. The factor sells his stock to the dealers or packers (*ensaccadores*), men that control large warehouses. The coffee is conveyed from the railway depot, in trucks or horse-cars, to a large room in the storehouse, level with the pavement. The sacks of coffee are piled on either side, each being numbered and further distinguished by some special mark. Samples are drawn from each bag, similar qualities are put together, and the coffee is then re-sacked in coarse bags, of uniform size, each made to hold sixty kilogrammes, or one hundred and thirty-two pounds. From the packers the exporter secures his supply, which is forwarded either by sailing vessel or steamer to the different ports of destination, the principal of which in the United States are New York, Baltimore, and New Orleans. Formerly New Orleans received the bulk of the supply, but since the war New York has been the chief market. Cargoes by sailing vessel are generally owned by one firm, while steamer cargoes are the property of many. Since July 1, 1872, there has been no import duty upon coffee. The first duty levied by our Government on this article was two and one-half cents per pound, imposed in 1789, afterward increased in 1790 to four cents per pound, and in 1794 to five cents, remaining at that figure until 1812, when it was advanced to ten cents, and so remained until the close of the war. In 1814 the duty was placed at five cents, remaining unchanged until 1828, when it was reduced to two cents, and in 1830 to one cent, and in 1832 made free, and so continued until the civil strife of 1861 was inaugurated, when four cents per pound was imposed, afterward increased to five cents, and so continuing until January 1, 1871, when it was reduced to three cents, and finally entirely abolished, July 1, 1872.

HOW COFFEE IS IMPORTED.

Supposing we have ordered our agent in Rio de Janeiro to forward to us one thousand bags of coffee of sixty kilos. each, the order is filled, the coffee placed aboard steamer or sailing vessel, and in due course of time landed in New York, Baltimore, or New Orleans, or perhaps sent to Hampton Roads for orders. The following will show the cost of the above purchase placed in warehouse in Brooklyn, in which city all Brazil coffee entering the port of New York is now stored.

Pro Forma Invoice of 1,000 Bags of Coffee, of 60 Kilos. each, Shipped from Rio de Janeiro to the United States.

1,000 bags coffee of 60 kilos. each = net kilos. 60,000, @ 6$350 per 10 kilos	*Rs. 38:100$000	
1,000 empty bags @ 700 reis..................	700$000	
		Rs. 38:800$000
Export duty on kilos. 60,000, @ 502 rs. per kilo. = Rs. 30,120$000 @ 13%..................	Reis 3:915$600	
Harbor-master (Capatazias) fees, 60 rs. pr. bag..	60$000	
Brokerage, 50 rs. pr. bag....................	50$000	
Shipping expenses (at 220 rs. = Rs. 220.000), sample, tins and box (Rs. 25$000), freight on same (Rs. 2$000), consul's certificate (included in sample, tins, etc.), cablegram (Rs. 100$000), stamps, petties, etc. (included in sample, tins and box).	347$000	
		4:372$600
		43:172$600
Commission, 2%..................		863$450
		44:036$050
Bill brokerage and stamps, ⅜ of 1%...........................		165$760
		Reis 44:201$810

RIO DE JANEIRO, September 19, 1879.

Conversion of Rio de Janeiro into American Currency.

Amount of pro forma invoice.................. Reis 44:201$810		
At 21½d. exchange at Rio £3,959 15		
$4.84½—⅛ per £ sterling		$19,161 00
Charges accruing in the United States:		
Freight per steamer to New York, 40c. per bag and 5% primage...	$420 00	
Marine insurance, 1% less 30 % — $\frac{7}{10}$ net, on $21,672 or invoice and £ value @ $5.50	151 70	
Banker's commission for credit = ¾ of 1% on $19,161....	143 72	
Bill stamps in London (nil).		
Labor at vessel, 4c. per bag; storage, one month, @ 4c.; weighing, 3½c.; fire insurance, 1½c. per bag; delivery (lighterage), 4c. per bag = 16½c. per bag.............	165 00	
Petty charges, *i.e.*, sampling, sewing, custom fees, etc., on bags, per bag, 3½c.; approximate for skimming of quality, —— bags @ ; furnishing new bags	35 00	
Cables at New York	5 00	
		920 42
Cost of 1,000 bags in store..............................		$20,081 42

* 1,000 reis = 1 mil-ries = 54½ cents, U. S.

Based on out-turn weight of 130.87 lbs. per bag (original weight 132 lbs.), cost per pound is equal to (free of brokerage) 15$\frac{36}{100}$c., cash, as removed according to condition of London credits, *i.e.*, the whole invoice, payable fifteen days prior to maturity in London of the ninety days' sight drafts drawn from Rio on day of shipment.

As previously stated, the rate of the Brazilian export duty varies every week in conformity with the average of the brokers' quotations of coffee for the preceding week.

For instance, on a basis of 424 reis per kilo., or 3$307 reis per bag, the rate of duty would be with

Good firsts,	quoted at Reis	5$000	 11	per cent.
Regular firsts,	"	4$700	 12	"
Ordinary firsts,	"	4$300	 13	"
Good second,	"	3$800	..... 14½	"
Ordinary,	"	3$400	..... 15½	"

The establishment of cable and steamer communication with Rio de Janeiro has done much to prevent the market from being controlled by large importers. The Rio telegrams are a feature of the market, and come to the public either through some importing house, a broker, or the Associated Press, quoting either per arroba or per 10 kilos. They state the average daily receipts in Rio de Janeiro, give the quantity of coffee purchased for Europe and the United States, the price of good average cargoes, stock at date, shipments to different places, and the cost of exchange on London.

The true method of getting at the cost in United States currency is to multiply the price by the exchange. The result will be in English pence, which should be converted into American gold in the ordinary way at the existing rate of London exchange. The brokers, however, get a result accurate enough for all practical purposes by multiplying the price by the exchange, deducting one-fourth of the amount so obtained, getting the free on board cost in Rio de Janeiro, to which must be added freight and charges. Samples of the coffee are placed in a broker's office as soon after arrival as the seller elects, and it is by the broker sold to the jobbers, the seller paying a brokerage of one-fourth or three-eighths of one per cent.

COFFEE WAREHOUSE.

If a jobber sells an invoice to a dealer who requires the coffee shipped, he merely gives to a firm of forwarders an order upon the warehouse, and the coffee is then covered with an additional sack, costing from 13½ to 17½ cents, and delivered by the forwarders to the freight line. The seller pays weighing charges, four cents; storage, four cents, and labor, four cents per bag. The large railways keep lighters at the warehouse docks, accepting a delivery of the coffee through their agents there stationed. When shipped by steamers running to Southern ports cartage is charged.

When sold by importers in large lots, an allowance of four cents per bag lighterage is made. On lots sold to interior points this is not granted, unless the purchase covers four hundred bags or over. Invoices are designated by letters. An invoice consists of a number of chops, designated by figures, each chop varying from the others in quality, style, or color. The coffee is divided into six grades, known as choice to fancy, prime, good, fair, ordinary, and common. These are subdivided and classed as follows:

Fancy.	Strictly fair.	Good ordinary.
Choice.	Fully fair.	Ordinary.
Strictly prime.	Fair.	Low ordinary.
Prime.	Barely fair.	Common.
Strictly good.	Low fair.	Peaberry.
Good.		

There is no standard of grade, nor is it deemed possible to establish one, owing to the changes wrought by time in the appearance of the beans. The grade varies with the size and quality of the crop and the condition of the market. Upon a quick and rising market coffee that ordinarily would be called fair suddenly becomes strictly fair or good, and on a depressed or declining market it may be termed barely or low fair.

The following definitions of what constitutes the different grades are generally accepted on the market, but nothing binds them as a standard:

Choice to Fancy.—Coffee that is entirely free from any imperfections, uniform in color and size of bean, and extremely sightly in appearance.

Prime, that which is free from imperfections, quite regular in color and size, but deficient in the rich, glossy appearance that marks choice to fancy.

Good, is that ranging from almost, to strictly clean, good in bean and color—in fine, what may be termed a nice, plain coffee. This is the average grade.

Fair, is that which is moderately clean, having now and then a few black or broken beans, or those mottled in color, or showing various slight imperfections.

Ordinary, is indefinite in color, and quite unsightly in appearance, being largely mixed with black beans and other imperfections.

Common, is a poor, unsightly coffee, filled with imperfections, such as black and broken beans, and of no definite color. This is the lowest grade of Rio excepting *triage*, a coffee which is exactly described by the word trash.

The first four grades may each be divided into three separate colors, viz., light, medium, and dark. The prime and fair grades are sometimes polished, and the good frequently. By prefixing the word "strictly" to each one of the first five grades (such as strictly choice, strictly prime, etc.) the selection of such grade may be secured.

Different sections of the country require coffee of some peculiar color, and to get this jobbers will, when it is scarce, pay an extra price for it. For instance, the Chicago market takes a medium to light green Rio and scarcely any dark green, and of what are known as skimmings takes only light-colored.

Cincinnati is partial to a yellow bean, but also takes a few greens, but of a darker hue than Chicago wants.

Louisville takes much the same style as Cincinnati, except that on green coffee it prefers a deeper color.

Texas requires the darkest kinds to be procured, and principally of low grades.

Dark green Rios are the favorite with St. Louis buyers.

Philadelphia buys heavily of low grades, absorbing whatever light or dark skimmings are offered.

The following tables show the export movement from Rio de Janeiro and Santos, and also the imports into the United States and the port of New York.

The exports of coffee from Rio de Janeiro have been as follows from 1800 to 1880. Prior to 1874 the sacks contained five arrobas, or 160 pounds; since that time they contain sixty kilos., or 132 pounds. The figures are for the crop year extending from July 1st to June 30th:

Year.	Sacks.	Tons.	Year.	Sacks.	Tons.
1800-1......	10	——	1849-50....	1,451,715	103,694
1813-14.....	12	——	1850-51....	1,392,361	99,455
1817-18.....	63,986	4,570	1851-52....	1,993,255	142,375
1818-19.....	74,247	5,303	1852-53....	1,809,861	135,704
1819-20.....	73,314	5,237	1853-54....	1,640,179	117,155
1820-21.....	97,500	6,965	1854-55....	1,986,224	141,873
1821-22.....	105,366	7,528	1855-56....	2,409,265	172,090
1822-23.....	152,048	10,861	1856-57....	2,100,313	150,022
1823-24.....	185,000	13,214	1857-58....	2,097,449	149,818
1824-25.....	224,000	16,000	1858-59....	1,833,416	130,958
1825-26.....	183,136	13,081	1859-60....	2,031,412	145,101
1826-27.....	260,000	18,571	1860-61....	2,122,625	151,616
1827-28.....	350,900	25,064	1861-62....	2,034,404	145,321
1828-29.....	369,147	26,368	1862-63....	1,486,207	106,158
1829-30.....	375,107	26,793	1863-64....	1,312,902	93,779
1830-31.....	391,785	27,985	1864-65....	1,495,697	106,835
1831-32.....	448,249	32,018	1865-66....	1,792,504	128,036
1832-33.....	478,950	34,211	1866-67....	1,867,312	133,379
1833-34.....	561,692	40,121	1867-68....	2,584,493	184,607
1834-35.....	560,759	40,054	1868-69....	2,200,156	157,154
1835-36.....	647,438	46,245	1869-70....	2,513,588	179,542
1836-37.....	715,893	51,135	1870-71....	2,107,630	150,545
1837-38.....	657,005	46,929	1871-72....	2,358,708	168,122
1838-39.....	766,696	54,764	1872-73....	2,402,414	171,601
1839-40.....	889,324	63,523	1873-74....	1,686,174	120,441
1840-41.....	1,068,418	76,316			
1841-42.....	1,028,368	73,455		Bags, 132 lbs.	
1842-43.....	1,174,689	83,906	1874-75....	3,087,676	181,628
1843-44.....	1,183,646	84,546	1875-76....	2,805,476	165,028
1844-45.....	1,269,381	90,670	1876-77....	2,708,236	159,308
1845-46.....	1,187,591	84,828	1877-78....	2,549,915	149,995
1846-47.....	1,522,434	108,745	1878-79....	3,577,437	210,461
1847-48.....	1,650,300	117,879	1879-80....	2,937,209	172,777
1848-49.....	1,706,544	121,896	1880-81....	4,225,245	248,544

The shipments of coffee from Santos have been as follows, from July 1st to June 30th, for the past seven years:

Year.	Bags.	Tons.	Year.	Bags.	Tons.
1874-75.........	829,753	48,809	1878-79.........	1,210,946	71,583
1875-76.........	754,993	44,590	1879-80.........	1,046,061	61,533
1876-77.........	628,903	37,143	1880-81.........	1,198,625	70,507
1877-78.........	998,442	58,970			

Importations of Brazil Coffee into the United States (Atlantic Coast), 1866 to 1881.

Year.	Bags.	Tons.	Year.	Bags.	Tons.
1866.........	808,040	57,586	1874*.......	1,454,841	88,872
1867.........	1,209,785	86,404	1875.........	2,139,463	126,075
1868.........	1,172,541	83,747	1876.........	1,490,662	87,842
1869.........	1,239,029	88,499	1877.........	1,903,849	112,190
1870.........	1,401,387	100,105	1878.........	1,836,155	108,202
1871.........	1,591,788	113,691	1879.........	2,561,628	150,953
1872.........	1,186,170	84,726	1880.........	1,957,934	115,379
1873.........	1,325,917	94,467			

Average for fifteen years, 1866–1881.... 1,551,946 bags, 99,916 tons.
Average for ten years, 1871–1880 ...... 1,744,841 " 108,240 "

Direct Receipts in New York of Brazil Coffee for the Year ending December 31st.

Year.	Total Bags.	Pounds.	Year.	Total Bags.	Pounds.
1857......	360,717	56,099,404	1869......	720,486	115,275,160
1858......	342,950	54,428,360	1870......	623,089	99,678,240
1859......	374,167	59,833,900	1871......	639,152	102,242,240
1860......	292,595	46,544,920	1872......	520,782	83,304,960
1861......	558,060	89,126,880	1873......	629,014	100,629,360
1862......	347,691	55,595,480	1874......	779,225	109,317,692
1863......	280,912	44,923,156	1875......	1,060,483	139,980,984
1864......	532,364	84,803,670	1876......	728,965	96,153,564
1865......	584,540	93,510,912	1877......	1,066,066	140,552,028
1866......	526,586	84,096,816	1878......	1,120,224	147,860,428
1867......	768,478	122,936,408	1879......	1,714,654	226,322,386
1868......	770,528	123,269,650	1880......	1,277,823	166,985,910

* Prior to 1874, large bags, 160 lbs.; 1874, large and small bags; after 1874, small bags.

CHAPTER XVII.

COFFEE CULTURE IN THE WEST INDIES.

The Dutch were the first to introduce the coffee-plant into the West Indies, as they had been the pioneers of its cultivation in the East. In 1710 a tree had been sent from Batavia to the Botanic Gardens of Amsterdam, where it prospered and produced fruit. Some of the young plants propagated from this parent stock were, in 1718, taken by the Dutch to their colony of Surinam, where the culture was carefully extended, as well as in Berbice and Demerara. But jealous monopoly has ever marked Dutch colonial policy, and the worthy tropical Hollanders were probably in no hurry to present their neighbors right and left with the valuable evergreens. The coffee-plant, however, found its way in a most provoking manner to the French island of Martinique. It is said that the Botanic Garden of Paris surreptitiously procured a cutting from the Amsterdam garden, and therefrom raised a vigorous tree. From this a slip was entrusted, for introduction into the West Indies, to a French officer named Declieux, who is reported, during an unusually long and stormy voyage, to have shared his daily ration of water with the young plant. The slip reached Martinique safely, in 1720, and became the parent of an immense progeny; for its descendants not only peopled the fields of Martinique and Guadaloupe, but in a few years spread to Jamaica, Porto Rico, Hayti, Cuba, the smaller Antilles and Central America, the Guianas, and the Brazils, where alone the prolific family numbers at the present day probably six hundred million members.

The progress of the coffee industry in the West Indies placed those islands for a time at the head of coffee-producing countries, but from that position they are now strangely fallen. The rapid decline of their coffee-industry is, indeed, a curious phenomenon, which many causes, chief among which may be named the abolition of slavery and the excess, some years ago, of production over consumption, with the consequent unremunerative prices, have conspired to accelerate. The French colonies of Martinique and Guadaloupe, the former of which alone exported 5,000 tons, or over 11,200,000 pounds of coffee in 1759, now export together only from 600,000 pounds to 1,000,000 pounds of the article, the whole going to France.

Cuba, which from 1830 to 1840 exported an average of over 25,000,000 pounds of coffee, and, as late as 1842, 15,710 tons, does not at the present day produce a sufficient amount for local consumption, but depends for its supply partly on importations.

In 1878–79 the area in Jamaica devoted to coffee-growing was 22,853 acres. The following interesting facts respecting Jamaica coffee are taken from a letter written by Mr. D. Morris to the *Ceylon Observer*, from the Botanical Department, Jamaica, in June, 1880. This gentleman says:

"The crop of last season was sold, in some instances, at 130*s.* per cwt. I had the pleasure, the other day, of visiting Radnor plantation. I found it a good type of Jamaica estates, most of which have been in cultivation for more than a century and a half. In some places the trees were poor and 'sticky,' but wherever the soil has been preserved, and especially in 'bosoms,' the trees were looking healthy and strong. In spite of 'no manure,' in spite of 'mammoty' weeding for generations, these trees were bearing good crops, and, moreover, the producer is able to obtain prices which Ceylon planters must envy.

"I have been trying to find out why the Blue Mountain coffee of Jamaica is always so good, and how it is that it obtains such high prices as compared with the fine and highly cultivated coffee of Ceylon. Is the coffee grown here a peculiar variety of C. Arabica? or is there something in the soil and climate which promotes the larger formation of the essential oils and secretions in the fragrant bean? Whatever it is, it cannot be in the superior cultivation, the more rational treatment of the crop, or the greater care in the curing. The only cultivation which the estates here receive consists in a rough 'hoe-weeding,' once or twice a year, with no pruning, except what the hoe does, no system of drainage, no terracing, and, as I mentioned before, no manuring! It is true that on one or two estates a higher style of cultivation is being inaugurated, but, as a rule, coffee cultivation in Jamaica cannot compare at all with what is being done in Ceylon. It may seem strange to a Ceylon planter, but all the work of pulping, curing, and preparing the coffee is done here on the estates by the superintendent or overseer, and when the coffee is sent down to Kingston it is ready for shipment and immediately put in barrels. This system, and the absence of large coffee-curing establishments, must necessarily increase the cost of curing, etc., but it appears to have been pursued here from time immemorial, and planters appear to like it.

"Owing to the large areas nominally included under one estate, the different 'coffee-fields' are sometimes two or three miles away from the works, lying in 'bosoms' of the hills, and only visited for the occasional 'hoeing' and picking of the crop. Out of a nominal acreage of 1,000 acres often there are only 160 to 200 acres, and sometimes only about 60 or 80 acres, under cultivation. The other parts are in 'reccinate' (jungle), or so steep that owing to 'breakaways' and rocks it is impossible to cultivate them. This gives a Jamaica coffee estate a very patchy appearance, and as cinchona has not yet been taken up generally by planters, the uncultivated areas greatly exceed those cultivated. Much more might be done with the suitable coffee lands if a regular system of nurseries were established and plants put out with greater care. At present new lands are planted up with 'suckers' (or rather seedlings) found under the trees. These are pulled up with little or no care, even when they have six or eight primaries, and after being carried in bundles on heads exposed to the full rays of the sun are put in holes, and allowed to take their chance without shade or shelter. It is strange to hear such plants called 'suckers,' but that is the orthodox term for them here, and it is on such plants that Jamaica planters entirely depend for their supplies and for planting up. I was much puzzled the other day with a remark made me by a planter respecting these said 'suckers.' I asked why these self-sown plants were called 'suckers,' when evidently they were nothing of the kind. I suggested 'seedlings' as an appropriate term. I was told: 'No, no, they are not seedlings; a sucker does not become a seedling till it is crowned.' This was still worse, and I had to give it up.

"With regard to the absence of nurseries and the planting up of land by weakly sown 'seedlings' it seems a pity that so much valuable land and so much time should be lost, when the remedy is so simple. The plants thus put in are often two feet high, and with several primaries (*i. e.*, crowned, as I found afterward). Their rootlets are torn and lacerated, and the check they thus receive in transplanting, and in being suddenly taken out from shade and exposed to the fierce rays of a tropical sun, results either in a large percentage being killed or in the plants being two or three years before they produce a maiden crop.

"But still, as the planters say, many of the plants do grow, and when they do they produce some of the best coffee in the world.

"In color, the best Jamaica coffee is darker and bluer than Ceylon coffee, and the beans smaller. Whether the color shows a larger proportion of oil I know not, but the sample appears to be greatly judged and valued according to color. The sample sent reminds one, in the size of the beans, of Mocha coffee, only the beans of the latter are generally of a dark yellow color. Nearly all West Indian and Brazilian coffees are bluish or greenish gray.

"The color of the bean must depend in some measure on the manner of pulping and drying, but, so far as I have noticed, the processes in Jamaica are much the same as in Ceylon, except that, possibly, here the cherry is allowed to stand longer before it is pulped.

"But to return to the question of high prices—Why does Jamaica coffee command such high prices? This subject, and especially in connection with Mocha coffee, must have occupied the attention of coffee-planters ever since coffee-planting began, but, so far, it appears not to have received a satisfactory solution. Is it temperature, atmospheric pressure, natural fertility, humidity of soil or air, amount of sunlight and excessive stimulation which produces the perfect elaboration of those subtle principles upon which the aroma and active qualities of coffee depend?

"With regard to Mocha and Jamaica coffee, there must evidently be a combination of very favorable conditions for the production of beans possessing such salutary and agreeable qualities; but from the subtlety and delicacy of the laws of vegetable assimilation, I fear it is almost impossible so to analyze and trace these conditions as to produce their parallel in other coffee-producing countries.

"As far as I have noticed, there is little disease on any of the cultivated plants of Jamaica. With the exception of the *Cemiostoma coffeeilum*, a little leaf miner similar to the *Gracilaria coffeefoliella* (NIETNER) of Ceylon, which cause the silvery tortuous markings and blotches on coffee-leaves, Jamaica coffee appears to be very free from disease. Our old friend the black bug is here, but it does not give annoyance except, sometimes, to badly cultivated and young coffee."

In the British colony of Jamaica the average annual shipments in the three years ending 1807, were about 11,000 tons. Seventy-five years ago the exports were placed at 9,821 tons, rising to 15,200 tons in 1814, but, subsequently, the production diminished, and exports fell off very largely. During the past ten or fifteen years exertions have been made to revive the coffee industry, to which the island is said to be peculiarly adapted, its product being noted for its superior quality.

The Blue Mountains, which extend lengthwise of the island, are admirably adapted for the cultivation of the coffee plant. The first trees were planted in 1728. In 1844 there were nearly seven hundred plantations on the island. The exports for seventeen years beginning with 1864 are given as follows:

Year.	Pounds.	Year.	Pounds.
1864	4,141,903	1873	7,199,144
1865	6,229,712	1874	10,351,570
1866	8,513,532	1875	7,136,000
1867	6,264,861	1876	8,708,000
1868	7,855,488	1877	9,532,544
1869	5,501,887	1878	9,411,584
1870	9,671,564	1879	10,832,080
1871	5,611,245	1880	10,088,864
1872	9,510,739		

The fine selections of Jamaica coffee command an extreme price on the London market, where this variety is highly prized for its very fine cup qualities. In style and flavor it rivals Plantation Ceylon. The bean has a bluish gray appearance, and is very uniform and handsome. The receipts in the United States of the best descriptions are very small, most of that imported being classed as ordinary. Jamaica coffee usually comes in bags of two hundred and fifty pounds and upward, subject to actual tare. Occasionally smaller packages are received, weighing about one hundred and fifty pounds. The ordinary bean is large, and varies in color from a dark green to almost white. Frequently samples show black beans and stones. The drinking qualities of ordinary Jamaica are not equal to those of a choice Cucuta Maracaibo, but are above those of what is known as Trujillo Maracaibo. The receipts in the United States have averaged seven hundred and eighty-three tons annually for the last ten years. The imports, from 1866 to 1881, into the United States were as follows:

Importation of Jamaica Coffee into the United States (Atlantic Coast), 1866 to 1881.

Year.	Packages.	Tons.	Year.	Packages.	Tons.
1866	9,680	808	1874	13,796	1,133
1867	6,276	467	1875	13,741	1,021
1868	8,428	284	1876	3,972	355
1869	3,356	267	1877	12,317	1,192
1870	5,708	552	1878	5,320	459
1871	7,724	679	1879	9,960	1,024
1872	8,100	721	1880	8,133	842
1873	3,441	399			

Average for fifteen years, 1866–81.......... 7,996 packages, 680 tons.
Average for ten years, 1871–80............ 8,650 " 783 "

HAYTI AND SAN DOMINGO.

The cultivation of coffee began in Hayti about 1735–40. The industry flourished under the protection of the French Government, declining after the island passed out of the hands of France.

In 1789 a crop of 80,000,000 pounds was produced on the island of Hayti. This island lies from three to five degrees below the northern limit of the coffee-growing belt. The country is mountainous, its elevated ranges being capable of cultivation nearly to their summits. The climate is especially well adapted to the growth of the coffee tree, the cultivation of which is being extended in the eastern part of the island, called St. Domingo, in contradistinction to the French or western part, which comprises the republic of Hayti. The many and rapid political changes, which have been more or less of a revolutionary character, have tended to retard the development of coffee-plantations. The cultivation of the tree is principally carried on by the natives, who are so careless in the preparation of the bean that much of the product comes to market very stony and dirty, thus reducing its value far below the standard which its drinking qualities would otherwise ensure. Improved machinery is employed to a very limited extent. Efforts are being put forth to induce an extension of coffee-culture, and to secure greater care in preparing the coffee for market, with a design to regain the ground lost during years of civil commotion. The bulk of the crop goes to Europe, and a considerable part of that received here is re-exported thither, where it is carefully picked over, selected, and graded. It reaches market in all sorts of bags, the buyer receiving actual tare. The bean is larger than the Rio bean, approaching very closely in style to ordinary Jamaica. In color it varies, some of it being classed with what is termed white coffee. The receipts of St. Domingo coffee at the port of New York have been for ten years as follows:

Importation of St. Domingo Coffee into the United States (Atlantic Coast), 1866 to 1881.

Year.	Bags.	Tons.	Year.	Bags.	Tons.
1866	38,900	2,258	1874	42,226	2,450
1867	49,388	2,866	1875	75,583	4,383
1868	68,810	3,995	1876	112,165	6,509
1869	83,790	4,701	1877	97,922	5,684
1870	70,692	4,102	1878	125,348	7,275
1871	59,978	3,480	1879	146,075	8,478
1872	62,834	3,741	1880	171,230	9,939
1873	46,326	2,679			

Average for fifteen years, 1866–1881.......... 83,418 bags, 4,836 tons.
Average for ten years, 1871–80............... 93,969 " 5,462 "

The total export from Port au Prince (Hayti) from the crop of 1877–78, was 179,904 bags, and from the crop of 1878–79, 143,939 bags. The average production of the island is about 26,000 tons, the crop not showing very great variation.

PORTO RICO.

Porto Rico furnishes a coffee that is in great favor in Spain and Italy, and also on the island of Cuba. The cultivation is carried on largely in the provinces of Mayaguez, Ponce, Guayanilla, Aguadilla, Arecibo, and St. Johns.

The exports have been as follows for the years mentioned:

Year.	Pounds.	Year.	Pounds.
1877	15,358,742	1874	21,189,382
1876	13,478,647	1873	27,168,951
1875	27,003,094		

Cuba absorbed more than half of the crop of 1877, taking 8,543,010 lbs.; Spain and Italy, 2,643,946 lbs.; Germany and Denmark, 1,027,648 lbs.; the balance going to England, France, the United States, and sundry other points.

The bean is somewhat similar in style to the Central American product, varying in color, but mostly greenish. The selections average larger in size than the Rio bean. In flavor this ranks as a mild coffee. A good deal of it has a peculiar taste, approximating to what is usually termed "hidey." The ordinary is not a good flavored coffee, but the finer qualities rank well.

Of the lesser islands Dominica and Trinidad yield about 3,000 tons each, the rest of the group in the West Indies not producing enough to give them a position as coffee-growing countries. The total production of all the West India Islands does not exceed 40,000 to 42,000 tons.

The receipts from Cuba and Porto Rico in all United States ports have been as follows:

Importation of Cuba and Porto Rico Coffee into the United States (Atlantic Coast), 1866 to 1881.

Year.	Bags.	Tons.	Year.	Bags.	Tons.
1866	3,794	330	1874	9,560	620
1867	860	54	1875	7,387	464
1868	25	2	1876	1,154	72
1869	342	28	1877	448	26
1870	70	10	1878	134	9
1871	1,099	69	1879	13,650	853
1872	14,533	908	1880	4,365	322
1873	10,137	639			

Average for fifteen years, 1866–1881............ 4,504 bags, 294 tons.
Average for ten years, 1871–1880............... 6,247 " 398 "

CHAPTER XVIII.

MARACAIBO AND LAGUAYRA COFFEE.

From seven to twelve per cent. of the supply of coffee received in the United States comes from the northern part of South America, and is known as Maracaibo, Laguayra, or Porto Cabello coffee. It is grown either in Venezuela or the United States of Colombia. Both countries are mountainous, and are divided into provinces or states. The valleys are long and beautiful, and on the mountain sides and the lowlands coffee, which is the principal article of export, is raised. Owing to defective cultivation and neglect, the trees do not yield well, in some instances only one-quarter of a pound per tree. Political anarchy and the scarcity of capital and labor have stood in the way of the full development of Venezuela's industry, as they also have, to a greater or less extent, in New Grenada, now called the United States of Colombia, Peru, and Ecuador, in all of which the coffee-plant will grow and prosper. Still, the northern states of South America, with their Central American neighbors, form a great zone of coffee production, the fourth in importance. In 1876 the export was 35,721,130 kilograms (78,750,803 pounds); in 1875, 31,082,417 kilograms (68,524,296 pounds), or an average for the two years of 33,401,773 kilograms (73,637,548 pounds) or 32,874 tons. Adding the product of New Grenada, there are about 35,000 tons available annually for export. The home consumption is about thirty per cent. of the crop. Officials in Venezuela estimate the total production at 50,000,000 kilograms (110,000,000 pounds).

Maracaibo coffee is known as Cucuta, Merida, Tovar, Bocono, and Trujillo. The first-named ranks as the finest. It is grown in the Province of Santander, in the United States of Colombia, and shipped from the town of San José to the port of shipment. The best Cucuta approaches Java in size and shape of bean. When first gathered, the Maracaibo crop is of a greenish color, assuming toward the close of the crop season a yellow cast, which adds to its value. The crop is variable, the quality being, as a rule, poor when the yield is large, and good when small.

The finer sorts are regarded by many as being equal to the best Java, and when roasted are often sold as Java, being possessed of a fine aroma. Before being roasted they are also used to mix with Java and sold as such; and on the principle that "Fleas have smaller fleas to bite 'em" there is probably more coffee shipped to this market, termed Cucuta, than is grown in the district of that name.

Next in order of merit comes Merida, then Tovar, Bocono, and Trujillo; the first named is sometimes equal to or superior to Cucuta; the last mentioned is the commonest, sometimes containing stones and dirt.

The coffee is grown on the western side of a range of mountains running northeast and southwest across the northwest corner of Venezuela. The plant was first introduced into the region in 1784 by a Catholic priest. The tree thrives best in the temperate region, but to some extent is cultivated in the *tierra caliente* (hot region), where, however, the product is of inferior quality. On the high lands the plant can be grown without shade, but in such instances the tree is short lived. Generally the young shoots are planted in parallel lines under the shade of large trees, the *Cucare.* The first crop is gathered when the tree is four or five years old, the harvest beginning in October. The berries are picked by hand and carried to a building where they are prepared for market by one of the two processes described in a previous chapter. Coffee that is prepared by means of a pulping machine is called *cafe descerezado*, and that which is subjected to the terrace or drying plan is termed *cafe trillado.* The latter is inferior, as the drying of the berries causes a deteriorating change in color, smell and taste of the bean. Good Venezuela coffee should have a light bluish-green color and a peculiar aromatic smell, and the beans should be of equal size and shape. In Venezuela 1,000 to 1,500 trees are planted upon a *fanegada* (one and three-quarter acres) of ground. A well-developed tree yields from one-half to one pound of coffee.

Laguayra coffee is grown on highlands in the province of Valencia, some six or eight miles from the capital city of Caracas, in Venezuela. A coast range of mountains extends through the northwestern part of the province of Caracas. The bulk of the crop is sent to Europe. The best coffee is shipped to the United States under the name of washed Caracas, Caracas Laguayra, and Trillados. The balance of the Laguayra crop forms the larger part of what is termed Puerto Cabello, the latter being the name of a shipping port further west on the Caribbean Sea. This coffee is known as Puerto Cabello Trillados, and graded upon the Rio basis, as the bean approximates Rio coffee in size and color. The last named is inferior to Maracaibo in quality. In the province of Coro a low grade of coffee is raised and shipped from Puerto Cabello as Laguayra or Maracaibo.

Maracaibo coffee is put up in thin sisal hemp bags, containing 130 pounds; the Laguayra in heavy burlap bags, usually holding 110 pounds, net; there is, however, no uniformity, as the coffee is received in all sorts of shapes. The bags are marked with the initial letter of the consignor or consignee, under which is a letter designating the province in which the coffee was grown. Too much reliance must not be placed upon these marks, as inferior coffee is often branded with the initial letter of a district growing a fine grade. The average imports of Laguayra coffee into the United States for ten years have been about 90,000 bags, or 5,139 tons.

Savanilla coffee is grown in the United States of Colombia, in and about the town of Ocana, on the western slope of the range from which the Cucuta crop is received. It ranks in the New York market below Maracaibo. Another variety of fine mountain coffee, quite equal to fine Cucuta, is grown in the same republic, and designated Bogota. It is shipped from the town of Honda.

Angostura is a large, spongy coffee, not much in favor here. It is raised in Venezuela and shipped from Cuidad, Bolivar, a town four hundred miles from the mouth of the Orinoco River. The tables below show the imports into Atlantic United States ports, of Maracaibo, Laguayra, and New Grenada coffee.

DRYING COFFEE ON THE TERRACE.

Importation of Maracaibo Coffee into the United States (Atlantic Coast), 1866 *to* 1881.

Year.	Bags.	Tons.	Year.	Bags.	Tons.
1866	52,611	2,890	1874	71,001	3,898
1867	55,387	3,041	1875	66,255	3,575
1868	93,271	5,122	1876	153,451	8,221
1869	53,706	2,949	1877	184,856	9,905
1870	117,218	6,437	1878	204,684	10,965
1871	102,302	5,616	1879	199,694	10,698
1872	170,305	9,351	1880	234,689	12,573
1873	98,042	5,383			

Average for fifteen years, 1866–1881........ 123,832 bags, 6,708 tons.
Average for ten years, 1871–1880........... 148,528 " 8,019 "

Imports of Laguayra and Puerto Cabello Coffee into the United States (Atlantic Coast), from 1866 *to* 1881.

Year.	Bags.	Tons.	Year.	Bags.	Tons.
1866........	62,550	3,072	1874.......	143,241	6,834
1867........	44,019	2,162	1875.......	144,177	7,451
1868........	62,884	3,087	1876.......	41,500	2,038
1869........	42,657	2,095	1877.......	132,083	5,995
1870........	36,931	1,619	1878.......	103,680	5,091
1871........	69,205	3,398	1879.......	61,383	3,014
1872........	126,502	6,210	1880.......	124,741	6,125
1873........	105,896	5,230			

Average for fifteen years, 1866–1881......... 86,763 bags, 4,228 tons.
Average for ten years, 1871–1880............ 105,241 " 5,139 "

CHAPTER XIX.

COFFEE PRODUCT OF CENTRAL AMERICA.

Coffee is the chief article of export from the Central American States. The climate and soil are well adapted to its cultivation. The finest coffee is raised on the highlands, and is possessed of a delicate aromatic flavor, while its drinking qualities equal, if they do not surpass, the better-known Java and Mocha. The States of Costa Rica and Guatemala lead in the cultivation of this variety, and then, in the order named, San Salvador, Nicaragua, and Honduras. In 1845 the Republic of Costa Rica passed a decree encouraging the development of coffee plantations. The sides of the magnificent hills about the towns of San José and Cartago were soon covered with coffee-trees, the planters rapidly growing rich from the product. Thirty-five years ago coffee culture in Costa Rica amounted to very little, while in 1876 the crop was 18,000,000 pounds; in 1877, 25,987,101 pounds; and in 1878, 18,065,206 pounds.

In the New York market the term Costa Rica was formerly applied to all imports of coffee from Central America, but recently the Central American product has further taken the distinctive names of the various states from whence it comes.

Definite statistical information respecting the crops of the different states in Central America is hard to obtain. An estimate made in February, 1881, by importers in this city largely interested in the Central American coffee trade, places the average crop of Guatemala at 300,000 to 350,000 quintals (30,000,000 to 35,000,000 pounds); Costa Rica, 300,000 to 350,000 quintals (30,000,000 to 35,000,000 pounds); Salvador, 150,000 quintals (15,000,000 pounds); Nicaragua, 25,000 quintals (25,000,000 pounds); Honduras, 10,000 quintals (10,000,000 pounds)—a total production for Central America of from 110,000,000 to 120,000,000 pounds, or say about 50,000 tons per annum. Costa Rica has produced a crop of 400,000 quintals (40,000,000 pounds), and Guatemala rising 300,000 quintals (30,000,000 pounds).* From Guatemala there were exported, in 1875, 7,302 tons; in 1876, 9,260 tons; in 1879, 11,251 tons. The crop of 1880–81 is estimated at 225,000 to 250,000 quintals, or 10,000 to 11,000 tons. The export from Salvador was, in 1877, 10,992,997 pounds, or 4,908 tons.

I regard the preceding estimate as representing a maximum crop, yet one of our leading importing firms, for many years in the Central American trade, places the average total annual crop of the five Central American states for the past five years at 70,000,000 pounds, or say 35,000 tons. The industry has made rapid advances for the past ten years, and the best informed persons in regard to it look for a continued increase.

A great diversity in modes of cultivation and preparation prevails. In some instances the planters use the most primitive methods, and upon other estates the most improved machinery is employed and the greatest care exercised in the cleaning and selection of the beans into different sizes. Costa Rica coffee differs in shape from Rio or Java, approximating more closely to

---

* According to Prof. Van Den Berg, President of the Java Bank, the production of coffee in Central America amounted in 1865 to 9,050,000 kilos. (19,951,630 pounds), and the average from 1876 to 1878 was 32,500,000 kilos. (71,649,500 pounds) per annum.

Dr. Neumann-Spallart gives the exports of San Salvador in 1877 at 54,710 centner (6,030,883 lbs.), and the total of Central America at 288,045 centner (31,751,200 lbs.). (Uebersichten über Production, etc.)

The French official "Annales du Commerce Extérieur," for March, 1880, No. 2,196, gives the value of the exports of coffee from San Salvador in 1876 at $1,209,362 (93.5 cents United States money); 1877, at $1,686,444; and 1878, at $1,180,069. It also gives the exports from Guatemala in 1878 at 20,935,900 pounds, valued at 16,748,702 francs.

The Consul-General of Guatemala at New York states that 25,201,685 pounds of coffee, valued at $4,032,270, were exported from Guatemala during the year 1879.

M. Darley de Thiersant, Consul-General and Chargé d'Affaires of France at Guatemala, reports the exports of coffee from the Republic of Nicaragua during the year 1878 to the value of $1,265,825 (of Central America). (Bulletin Consulaire Français, p. 65, 1ère Fascicule, 1880.)

the best grades of Maracaibo. In color it varies from a dark to a light grayish green. When roasted it has a heavier body than Java or Maracaibo, possessing a fine, rich flavor, considered by experts as equal to the finest kinds grown. It is worth noticing that in opposite quarters of the globe, Costa Rica and South India occupy the same north latitude, and that their respective growths approach one another in quality. The Costa Rica peaberry is a very fine coffee, that is often sold for Mocha. It is grown upon Mocha shoots, but it loses the hard flinty appearance of the true Mocha bean, and varies from it in size and color. The difference in climate and soil also changes its flavor from that of the true Arabian product.

The cultivation of the coffee tree in Guatemala is increasing, so much so that it is expected the export will reach 20,000 tons within the next five years. In 1875, the export was 7,302 tons, and in 1876, 9,260 tons. The yield on the Pacific slope reaches three pounds per tree, and in specially favored spots as high as five pounds, while on the Atlantic side, in the Vera Paz, or Coban district, only one pound is obtained. The Guatemala bean varies from a dark to a bluish green. Some of it runs unusually uniform in size, as it is carefully picked over several times. The finer grades are regarded as equal in flavor, and by some judges, superior to any other coffee grown. The Salvador bean is of a yellow cast, and is possessed of a very sweet smell. The product of Honduras is mottled in appearance, and the beans broken. Nicaragua produces but little, the whole of which goes to market as Costa Rica or Guatemala coffee.

Recently some 70,000 trees have been planted in the Chiriqui district, in the State of Panama, and this marks the beginning of the enterprise in that state.

A San Francisco trade report for the year 1880, says:

"We are slowly but surely obtaining the whole of the trade in Central American coffee grown on the Pacific coast. During the past year imports exceeded by over six and a half million pounds those of 1879, and by more than four million pounds those of the greatest importing year ever before noted. The shipments from Costa Rica during 1880 were unusually large, being augmented by that portion of the previous crop, which, owing to excessive and early rains in 1879, could not arrive at port of delivery during that season. Thus, the imports from that republic were 40,095 bags in the year just passed, against 24,414 bags in 1879, and 32,166 bags in 1878.

"The imports of Guatemala in 1880, have been 61,020 bags, against 40,028 bags in 1879, and 48,957 bags in 1878.

"The imports of Salvador coffee last year were, 32,455 bags, against 20,400 bags in 1879, and 21,371 bags in 1878."

"The imports of Central American coffee into Pacific coast ports in 1880 reached 18,853,826 pounds, or 8,461 tons, which, added to Atlantic Coast imports, make a total of 16,171 tons.

Importation of New Grenada and Costa Rica Coffee into the United States (Atlantic Coast), 1866 *to* 1881.

Year.	Bags.	Tons.	Year.	Bags.	Tons.
1866..........	7,889	390	1874..........	42,703	2,131
1867..........	9,755	488	1875..........	41,153	2,058
1868..........	16,011	801	1876..........	31,529	1,568
1869..........	9,637	482	1877..........	46,994	2,370
1870..........	12,296	614	1878..........	37,974	2,111
1871..........	22,364	1,112	1879..........	78,929	4,856
1872..........	30,272	1,506	1880..........	125,581	7,710
1873..........	36,634	1,824			

Average for fifteen years, 1866–1880 .... 36,648 bags, 2,001 tons.
Average for ten years, 1871–1880 .... 49,413 " 2,724 "

CHAPTER XX.

THE COFFEE INDUSTRY IN MEXICO AND OTHER COUNTRIES.

The coffee-tree finds a congenial home in Mexico and in Central America.

"It may be an unknown fact to many Americans," writes the Hon. John W. Foster, United States Minister to Mexico, "that at our very doors, in Mexico, our neighboring republic, there exists the agricultural capacity to produce all the coffee that can be consumed in the United States, and of a quality equal to the best grown in any country. Mexico, it is true, is exporting very little coffee and scarcely figures in the coffee-producing countries, but its capacity and adaptability for its production have been tested by more than fifty years of successful cultivation."

A correspondent of the *New York Herald* wrote to that journal in February, 1879, that "the peculiarly adaptable soil and climate, altitude, and condition of atmosphere necessary to the production of coffee are possessed by an area of no narrow limit in the State of Vera Cruz, while in the States of Jalisco and Michoacan the lands yielding coffee crops from perennial trees may be measured by the scores of leagues."

The government is encouraging the production, and if Mexico is spared political troubles, she is likely to add very largely to the world's supply within the next ten years. The same causes, however, which have in the past paralyzed the growth of the nation's general prosperity have equally retarded the progress of this branch of agriculture. The coffee production of Mexico has, heretofore, been almost entirely limited to supplying the home demand, which is quite large; but it is now creating a considerable foreign trade, the export to the United States for the year ending June 30, 1880, reaching a total of

6,789,693 pounds, valued at $1,265,970; 1879, 8,307,040 pounds; 1878, 6,337,063 pounds. The tree is grown chiefly in the States of Vera Cruz, Oaxaca, Tabasco, Colima, on the Sierra, and in the mountainous parts of Southern Mexico. The product is classed either as coast or mountain coffee, the distinguishing features of which are that while the bean of the coast coffee is light and spongy, that of the mountain product is hard and flinty. Mexican coffee is known in the New York market as Tabasco, Jalapa, Cordova, and Oaxaca. The first named is a coast coffee, generally of poor quality, as it is cultivated in the *tierra caliente* (hot region), lying along the coast of the Gulf of Campeche; it is the lowest grade of Mexican coffee. That designated Jalapa has a small, yellowish bean, rather short and wide, but irregular in size, imperfectly cleaned, and including many broken beans, and those covered with patches of the brown inner skin of the berry. The Sierra bean is small, with a greenish cast, and approximates in character to mountain coffee. It is grown on table-lands, and it is not, as a rule, nicely cleaned.

Cordova furnishes a larger and longer bean, uniform in size, well cleaned, and usually green in color. This coffee is often polished and used as a substitute for Rio. From the same district there is exported a large white bean that is called Mexican Java. All of the above, except that named Tabasco, are usually sold from first hands under the name of Cordova coffee. Oaxaca is a rough, green, mountain coffee, coming from the province of Oaxaca and surrounding districts. It has the dark green, semi-transparent appearance of a mountain coffee, but unfortunately is not properly hulled and cleaned, as much of it has the inner skin of the berry attached, and many of the beans are smashed, owing to the planters using a common roller instead of improved machinery. Were this coffee properly cleaned and carefully assorted, it would rival in appearance and flavor almost any upland coffee raised in Costa Rica and Jamaica. In Colima, on the west coast, is grown a berry usually called Tepic, the bean, when prepared, approaching in style the small flinty Mocha. Almost all of it is consumed in the province where grown, selling for forty to fifty cents per pound on the plantation, the select peaberry commanding from $1 to $1.25 per pound.

In flavor Tabasco is the mildest, Sierra next, then Cordova, which closely approaches Rio in strength, but is destitute of its harsh, pungent taste. Oaxaca coffee, if free from sour beans, drinks like the product of Costa Rica. White Cordova, or Mexican Java, approaches, when one year old, good Cucuta Maracaibo in flavor. Age greatly modifies the rank flavor peculiar to Mexican coffee. In 1879, 163,508 pounds were imported into San Francisco, and in 1880, 44,369 pounds. France takes a large part of the Mexican crop. The coffee is usually shipped in large grass bales, weighing from 220 to 260 pounds. Occasionally lots are received, especially the White Cordova, packed in bags made of native hemp, weighing 130 to 140 pounds, the package being tied with a heavy rope. Now and then half-bales are received, called pockets or mats, and weighing 80 to 100 pounds. Actual tare is allowed the purchaser.

PRODUCTION AT OTHER POINTS.

Along the west coast of South America, in the states of Peru, Ecuador, and Bolivia, plantations are found, but only from the latter state is any coffee exported. The largest quantity exported from Bolivia in any one year was 543 tons, and the smallest since 1867, 76 tons, the average for seven years—1870–77—being 307 tons annually.

The islands of the Pacific do not contribute any appreciable quantity to the world's supply. The Hawaiian Islands export an irregular quantity, as will be noted by reference to the following table of exports from Honolulu:

Year.	Pounds.	Year.	Pounds.	Year.	Pounds.
1861	45,000	1871	47,000	1875	166,000
1864	311,000	1872	393,000	1876	154,000
1869	341,000	1873	262,000	1877	131,000
1870	415,000	1874	75,000		

In 1878 the imports of Hawaiian coffee into the United States were 118,100 pounds; in 1879, 40,417 pounds; in 1880, 77,942 pounds. From the above figures it appears that Hawaiian coffee cultivation is declining, and this is probably due to the pushing of the sugar industry, which flourishes by reason of the reciprocity treaty with the United States, which admits sugar into ports of the country free of duty, this giving a monopoly to capitalists on the Pacific coast owning sugar refineries. These parties have opened large sugar estates in the Sandwich Islands, and are making the most of a treaty conferring quite extraordinary privileges, and having several years yet to run. The legislation which authorized this treaty was not above suspicion, and, while it may succeed in its object and enrich a few persons who were in a position to monopolize its benefits, it is unjust to our American sugar industry and opposed to the time-honored principle of no favoritism, which has heretofore ruled in the foreign policy of the United States.

In the island of Taviuni, in the Fiji group, there are some half dozen coffee-estates, ranging in area from fifty to three hundred acres. Coffee-trees here are just coming into bearing (1880). At the Sydney exhibition the first gold medal was awarded to an exhibit of coffee from Fiji. The leaf disease has, however, made its appearance on some of the estates. So far as its present relations to the world's supply are concerned, Fiji is scarcely worth the mention. Tahiti grows a few tons annually.

Is the United States to enter the lists as a coffee-producing country? From the Annual Report of the Agricultural Bureau (1879) it appears that coffee has been successfully cultivated within our own borders. A Mrs. Julia Atzeroth, of Braiden Town, Manatee County, Florida, sent to Commissioner Le Duc a branch of coffee grown in the open air, together with the following letter:

GEN. W. G. LE DUC, *Commissioner*, *Washington*, *D. C.*:

DEAR SIR—Yours of the 20th of last month arrived safe, and I can assure you that I felt greatly honored to find that you appreciate my experiment in growing coffee, and that mine should be the only coffee in the United States. I feel sure it can be successfully grown farther south, where frost never comes, and there is an abundance of land and soil suited to its growth. My trees are now attracting considerable attention. Many persons come to see them and ask for seed.

I have given some seed, and I will try to encourage its cultivation, to improve the country thereby. That is why I tried it, and now I feel satisfied it will be a success, if fairly tried. I came to this State some thirty years ago, and am one of the first settlers in Manatee. I would like to see you and tell you my experience in Florida. I would not exchange my home for any other State I know of. Florida needs nothing but energy and industry to make its people independent.

The department has supplied Mrs. Atzeroth with a number of young trees with which to enlarge her experiment, and also furnish other persons in the same locality, and farther south, with plants which should, if carefully planted and successfully cultivated, bear coffee within five years.

It is something to know that a lodgment has been effected on the coast of Florida, and though four trees, so far, are known to have been successfully grown and fruited, yet whether the coffee will ripen thoroughly and prove as profitable here as it has done in other countries is yet to be determined.

The following letter from a resident of Bogota, bearing on the subject of coffee-production in the United States, is of interest, because of its intelligent treatment of the subject, and the amount of information therein contained. Commissioner Le Duc is also entitled to much credit for his enterprise and originality in endeavoring to promote the agricultural welfare of the country, not only in this, but in many other directions.

To the HON. WM. G. LE DUC, *Commissioner of Agriculture, Washington, D. C., U. S. A.:*

SIR—I have noticed a circular issued by the department seeking information in regard to coffee. As I have frequently passed through the cold-country coffee region in this neighborhood, and have made it a point to inform myself as to the particulars of the culture and habits of the plant, I take the liberty of writing you as follows:

It is true that the coffee does not require a very hot climate. In fact, that which is raised in the colder regions is most highly esteemed and brings the highest price in the home and European markets.

Its upward range is limited by the frost-line, as is that of the orange, plantain, and bamboo. In a table compiled from Boussingault and Humboldt, the coffee appears as the hardiest of these, enduring a temperature one degree colder than the orange, three colder than the plantain, and five colder than the bamboo. Local authorities assure me this is a mistake as regards the orange, which is more hardy than the coffee. An English writer fixes on the bamboo as a test, saying that wherever it grows the climate is suitable for coffee. There seems to be no doubt that the coffee will endure more cold than the bamboo, so that the latter fails to serve as an indication of the *northern* limit of the coffee. And for this reason, both the coffee and the orange will grow at a height so cold as to prevent their having fruit. But as the Southern summer has a genuine hot-country temperature, the coffee would bear, as the orange does, in the season, if it could be carried through the winter.

This is the crucial point. Even in the plantations below the frost-line the coffee suffers at times from an extraordinary visitation of frost, or from the cold produced by a hail-storm, and it is generally admitted that a frost will kill it. On the other hand, it is said to grow, in peculiar circumstances, above the frost-line. Here in Bogota, for instance (temperature 60° F.), it will grow, without bearing, in the open air about the houses, but it will not live out on the plain where there are frosts so heavy as to often kill the potato. This is merely an illustration of the fact, well understood in the North, that a frost, like a dew-fall, and unlike a freeze, can be guarded against by a slight covering—the shade of a tree or building often serving to protect the vegetation in its vicinity while that more exposed is blighted. Now it is deemed essential that the coffee-plant should be shaded. The usual plan is to plant the coffee and the plantain together, so that the latter, by its rapid growth, may furnish shade before the coffee needs it. Some prefer to plant, also, certain fruit-trees to take the place of the plantain at a later date. The excessive heat of the summer in the Gulf States would certainly call for a liberal shading of the plantations. The question then arises as to whether the shade provided for summer would serve to protect the plants from frost in the winter. As I have no personal knowledge of the severity of the winter or of the character and habits of the trees available for this purpose, I cannot form even an opinion as to the probability of the success of the experiment. The question would still present itself whether it might not be feasible to protect the plants by keeping the ground wet, which is said to be sufficient to save the potatoes here, or by coverings of straw, or by smoldering fires raising clouds of smoke on exceptionally cold nights. I believe that the large profits of the coffee culture would warrant even these measures if they were found to serve the purpose.

The best crops that I have seen have been on a rich black loam, too rocky to be worked with the plow, and on the slopes of ravines. It is said that the plant dies out in a few years on clay soil. But the Liberian plant is said to flourish on such soil. It belongs, however, to the very hottest of climates. I attribute the better condition of the plants on sloping ground to the fact of their being more shaded. If the shedding of water more readily has anything to do with it, that could be effected on level ground by proper drainage. It is generally held that the coffee will not flourish on wet ground, though the best plants I ever saw were within a few feet of an unfailing stream.

The fact is that agriculture in tropical countries is done in such a slovenly manner; so few experiments are tried, and those few so carelessly; there is such a lack of accurate observation and comparison of notes, as well as of enterprise and sound judgment, that it is difficult to arrive at broad and accurate generalizations on many of these subjects. As a rule, each man attributes to the nature of the plant effects which arise from the accidents of his location or treatment.

As with all small fruits, the perfection of the coffee-berry depends on a good supply of moisture. In the tropics the principal crops follow immediately after the close of the rainy seasons, and if the rain fails the crops are light, as the berries dry up and fall off without ripening. The heavy summer rains in the Southern States would probably come just at the right time. But I should not advise any one to put in coffee on a piece of ground that could not be irrigated, though it is often done.

Practice varies in regard to the number of plants to the acre. After looking over a plantation, noting the plants in best condition, and making measurements, I determined, to my own satisfaction, that the best way, in a cold country, at least, is to plant in rows four yards apart and two yards apart in the row. The branches interlock in the row (which some regard as necessary), and the distance between the rows allows of moving about for cultivating and gathering. By trimming, the foliage can be made as open or as crowded as may be deemed best, while the wider spaces between the rows allow of the extension of the branches in that direction if they should be crowded in the other. This gives about 600 plants to the acre.

The yield is estimated sometimes as low as two pounds to the plant. But the same cultivator who gives me this figure says he is convinced that the increase of the yield indefinitely is only a question of improved cultivation. A more usual estimate is three pounds. A Scotchman in the neighborhood, who has brought more intelligence and care to the examination of the matter than any other cultivator here, claims to have plants under special cultivation that yield ten pounds each. This is about the figure claimed for the Liberian plant. No one could foretell what would be the result of transferring the plant to a country where it would have but one bearing season, instead of two, as here; but it is natural to suppose that it would exert itself with exceptional vigor in that one season. In all probability the more careful and judicious treatment that it would there receive would produce results even beyond those commonly attained in this country.

It is claimed that the Liberian plant, and perhaps some others in the hot country, are in full bearing at three years of age. This is not true of the colder country, where they just begin to bear at three years, and attain their maturity at from five to seven years. Here is the chief expense of getting up a plantation. The first investment has to lie unproductive, and the weeds have to be fought unceasingly through these years. When once the plants obtain their growth their shade keeps the weeds down almost without further attention.

It is usual here to estimate the expense roughly as half the value of the coffee. That raised in this neighborhood was sold last year in Bogota or Honda at about twenty cents per pound, and the planters counted that half clear; that is, they allowed ten cents a pound for expenses. The Scotchman above mentioned has satisfied himself that the cost of production is but five cents a pound.

I conclude, then, that coffee can be raised successfully over a large part of

California and in the Lower Colorado and Rio Grande Valleys, where irrigation is practicable ; that it is exceedingly doubtful whether it could be raised in the Gulf States ; that there may be a possibility of this being accomplished through careful experiment and persistent effort, having a view to the discovery of a method of cultivation adapted to the climate or to the production of a hardier variety, as was done in Russia in the case of wheat ; that the importance of the matter, viewed in relation not only to the aggregate cost of importations into the United States, but considered also as one of the most profitable branches of agriculture, which it certainly is, would justify almost any outlay necessary to test the question systematically and thoroughly.

WILLIS WEAVER.

BOGOTA, October 18, 1879.

CHAPTER XXI.

ADULTERATION OF COFFEE.

A PRIMARY requisite for making a good cup of coffee is, of course, *coffee.*

This might appear a superfluous statement, but, in reality, it deserves to be carefully kept in view by the consumer, considering the number of preposterous substances now in the markets of the world, from which many of our confiding and deluded fellow-men daily endeavor to extract the much-desired beverage.

The adulteration of coffee and the vast scale on which it is practised, are well-known facts.

I have already, for many reasons, dwelt on the advisability of the rule that every family should grind their own coffee. Were this rule invariably observed by the entire coffee-consuming public, coffee adulteration would soon be relegated into the limbo of lost arts. I have, indeed, heard of a contrivance patented, years ago, by an ingenious Englishman, for the purpose of moulding chicory and other substances into coffee-beans. But this form of adulteration, even though improved by the fertile minds of our countrymen, would ever be comparatively easy of detection, and consequently much less to be dreaded than adulterants in the treacherous disguise of the ground article.

Coffee consumers who, finding it impossible or inconvenient to do the grinding at home, purchase their coffee already ground (and they are numbered by thousands), tread a path beset with snares and delusions. All trouble in this direction can be avoided when resident quite a distance from the store or roasting establishment, by using the whole coffee sold in pound packages bearing the guarantee of well-known houses. The powder which they carry home from the retail grocery, in the fond belief that it is coffee, may not contain more than a mere sprinkling of the aromatic berry, while the rest is made up of worthless or even noxious substances, thrown in to make bulk and give color to the decoction when made.

All sorts of ingredients have been used in the sophistication of coffee, the range extending all the way from insipid vegetables to such abominations as the *baked liver* of animals.

In the works of English chemists and the reports of Parliamentary Committees, dating from ten to twenty-five years back, we find that chicory, roasted grain, roasted peas and beans, carrots, parsnips, potatoes, acorns, mangold-wurzel, lupins, sawdust, Venetian red, and fragments of the baked liver of oxen and horses were severally detected in samples of so-called ground coffee sold in the London shops (Hassall). So far, indeed, was the practice carried, that it was scarcely possible at that time to procure samples, no matter at what price, that were not largely adulterated. Appropriate legislation and the enlightenment of the public mind on this subject have since, to a great extent, checked these practices and led to a somewhat healthier condition of the coffee trade in the English market; but the evil still flourishes in the United States, although, so far as I am aware, nothing worse than ground peas, rye, and chicory are used for the purpose of adulteration.

The story is told of a traveller, who, stopping at a country hotel somewhere between the Mississippi and the Alleghanies, astonished the proprietor by engulfing cup after cup of the hotel's coffee. "You seem to be very fond of coffee, sir," could not but remark the host, as he tendered the stranger his fifth cup of the liquid. "I am indeed, sir," replied the other, gravely, "I always take *one* cup of coffee at breakfast, and I am still in hopes of arriving at that quantity before I leave this table. Will you favor me, sir, with another cup or two of this preparation?"

If that persistent coffee-drinker is yet in the land, he must still very often find himself in the necessity of resorting to the same expedient.

Nor are complaints like the following unfrequently seen in the public prints:

BAD COFFEE IN THE RESTAURANTS.

To the Editor of the Herald:

Please call the attention of the Board of Health to the article (bad coffee) served in city restaurants. It is damaging to the constitution of man, and should not be allowed to be sold.

E. K. Young.

The fact is, at very few, if any, of the average eating-houses, or restaurants, can a person procure a cup of unadulterated coffee. And in the vast majority of poorer households, the stuff which they purchase and use under the name of coffee is merely a compound of extraneous substances which have nothing in common with coffee but the color when roasted and ground.

The following statement occurs in a copy of the *Scientific American*, published toward the close of our late war:

"The editor of the *Baltimore American* lately visited the commissary department of one of the large military hospitals, and noticed several barrels of dried coffee-grounds, the purpose whereof excited his curiosity. The polite commissary informed him that they received twelve dollars a barrel for the grounds. 'But what is it purchased for?' he asked. 'Well,' said the commissary, hesitatingly, 'it is re-aromatized by the transforming hand of modern chemistry, and put up in packages, which are decorated with attractive labels and high-sounding names.'"

The principal adulterants, however, now resorted to in this country, as before stated, are chicory and roasted rye and peas. These ingredients are palmed off in vast quantities on the American coffee-drinker.

All of the so-called patent or proprietary *ground* coffees, which in various styles of showy packages and under seductive titles are commended to the consumer, consist of nothing but a mixture of those adulterants (chiefly rye and peas) with more or less of the genuine substance.

The high prices which have prevailed in the coffee market since 1871, and which are given in another chapter, have greatly stimulated the adulteration of coffee in the United States. The *American Grocer* of April 29, 1876, commenting on the general question of the coffee-supply, remarks:

"Another point to be taken into consideration, which has been almost completely lost sight of, is the rapid increase in the *ground-coffee* business, which has reached its present proportions within the past two years, and especially last year.

"The six hundred coffee and spice-mills of this country use over one thousand roasting-machines, with a capacity of 1,200,000 pounds a day. These mills grind and put up coffee, either in packages or in bulk, and, as a rule, wherever grinding is done, there adulteration is practised. A prominent manufacturer says the average basis for this business is the following proportion to every 1,000 pounds:

Roasted peas......................	400	pounds.
Roasted rye.......................	200	"
Roasted chicory...................	100	"
Other ingredients.................	50	"
Roasted coffee (best qualities).......	250	"
	1,000	pounds.

"This can be sold at a profit to the wholesale merchant at twenty cents currency per pound, allowing a discount of ten to twenty per cent., and is sold by retailers at twenty-five cents currency.

"The determined way in which the ground coffee business is being pushed, the great quantity now produced, and the low prices at which it is furnished render it evident that, sooner or later, the importer will find it an important element in his calculations determining the consumption of pure coffee in this country."

What was true in 1876 is true to-day, but we are happy to say, not to so great an extent. This is chiefly due to a reduction in the price of coffee, thus increasing the purchasing power of consumers; and to the general introduction of the coffee-mill into families and also into retail stores. Extremely high prices tend to increase the sale of adulterated coffee in packages, while cheap coffee curtails the demand to very narrow limits. Many brands of ground coffee that were popular from 1862 to 1870 did not contain more than five or ten per cent. of pure coffee, and yet they were endorsed as being of superior quality by letters of recommendation received from persons of distinction, probably in return for a gift of a box of so-called coffee.

The root of dandelion, first dried and ground, makes a very tolerable substitute for coffee, perhaps preferable to chicory, but it is not used to any considerable extent. Some years ago a brand of prepared coffee was put upon the market under the name of "Dandelion Coffee;" but only a small proportion was really the dandelion root, the article being largely composed of ground peas and rye, probably owing to the difficulty of procuring any considerable quantity of dandelion.

There are sold to a considerable extent, both in this country and in Europe, various preparations called "Coffee Essences." Some of these are in the form of liquids put up in bottles, others in the shape of dry, granular particles, which are usually compressed into rolls, or packets, which are neatly covered with foil, paper, and various colored labels. These preparations are, almost without exception, the veriest trash, being composed of burnt sugar in its various forms, principally of the commonest "Black Jack" syrup or molasses—the residuum left in the refining of sugars, which is mixed with chicory, the moisture of which is evaporated and the rest of it finally roasted, or burnt, to a point where, when again diluted with water, it gives a dark-colored liquid, somewhat resembling, *in appearance*, strong coffee. In some of these so-called coffee essences various chemicals are used to simulate the genuine coffee flavor, and in a very few of them there may be a trifle of genuine extract of coffee. It may be said that these worthless compounds are principally used to beguile the laboring classes, and others who are obliged to live in cheap boarding-houses, into the idea that the dark-colored liquid which is put before them under the name of coffee is a strong infusion of the genuine article, when, in reality, if there is any coffee at all in the decoction, it is infinitesimal in quantity, the dark-colored material being added to give it the appearance of strength. The expense of producing a strong, pure, dark-colored extract of coffee has heretofore placed the article beyond the purse of the poorer classes of consumers; hence, the almost universal use, in whole or in part, of substitutes, which, as above shown, are in turn frequently sophisticated by the use of these so-called "coffee essences."

It may not be amiss, in connection with the subject of coffee adulteration, to say a few words here of what is termed "glossing" roasted coffee. The "gloss," which is made of various starches, glues, and mosses, is applied to the coffee while hot, giving the coffee an even coating which hardens as it cools. It is claimed that the gloss fills up the pores of the coffee, retaining its strength and aroma, besides having a tendency to clear it when the coffee is boiled. I am inclined to think that these benefits are overrated, that they are more apparent than real, and that the practice tends to prevent that crispness of the coffee, which is desirable in grinding. On the whole, it tends rather to injure the flavor than to improve it.

Many good judges of coffee, however, dissent from this opinion, and so great has been the demand for the glossed roasted coffee that a patent has been claimed for the process, and an interesting discussion of its validity, in the shape of an extract from the *American Grocer*, will be found in the Appendix to this work.

After expatiating on the prevalence of adulterants in ground coffee, it is proper to state that the consumer has it usually in his power to solve, by several simple and practical experiments, the question as to whether a sample of ground coffee is adulterated or not, although, of course, the best way is to buy the coffee in the bean, and thus avoid all suspicion.

The following tests are suggested by Dr. Hassall, in his work on "Food:"

1. Notice whether the ground coffee "cakes" when pressed between the fingers or in the paper in which it is folded; if so, there is good reason to believe that it is adulterated, probably with chicory.

2. Place a few pinches of the suspected coffee upon some water in a wine-glass; if part floats and part sinks, it may be presumed that it is adulterated either with chicory, roasted grain, or some analogous substance. Ground coffee is enveloped in an oily substance which prevents its imbibing the water, while the other substances absorb the water and gradually subside to the bottom to a greater or less extent.

This test, however, sometimes gives imperfect results, as occasionally lard or similar stuff used in roasting the chicory will cause it to float. In most instances, also, part of the coffee subsides with the chicory and part of the latter remains on the surface with the coffee, and after a lapse of a short time both coffee and chicory fall to the bottom.

3. If the cold water to which a portion of ground coffee has been added quickly becomes deeply colored, it is an evidence of the presence of some roasted vegetable substance or burnt sugar; for, when coffee only is added to water, the liquid becomes scarcely colored for some time.

4. Make a boiling aqueous solution with the coffee; if it be an infusion of pure coffee, it will be found thin and limpid; if, on the contrary, it be adulterated with any substance containing much gum and starch (as rye, peas, etc.), it will be thick and mucilaginous.

Lastly, spread out, on a piece of glass, a little ground coffee and moisten it with a few drops of water; if you are enabled to pick out, by means of a needle, minute pieces of a substance of a soft consistence, the coffee is doubtless adulterated; for the particles of the coffee-seed are hard and resisting, and do not become soft even after prolonged immersion in water.

These simple means will usually suffice to detect the general fact of adulteration. To determine the character of the adulterants used, we must appeal to science; and for this purpose, as for so many others, the microscope proves the most powerful auxiliary and most reliable detective.

Viewed under the magnifying-glass, the component fibres and elementary structures of the different ground substances present peculiarities and characters that enable an experienced observer to identify, beyond a doubt, the particular adulterant or adulterants employed.

Chicory is distinguished by the size, form, and ready separation of the component cells of the root, as well as by the presence of an abundance of spiral vessels of the dotted form. Roasted cereals, beans, etc., by the respective size, form, and other characters of the starch granules of which the grains are principally composed. Figure 1 (Plate I.) gives the appearance, magnified to one hundred and forty diameters, of a fragment of roasted coffee; Fig. 2 (Plate I.), that of a fragment of roasted chicory;

PLATE I.

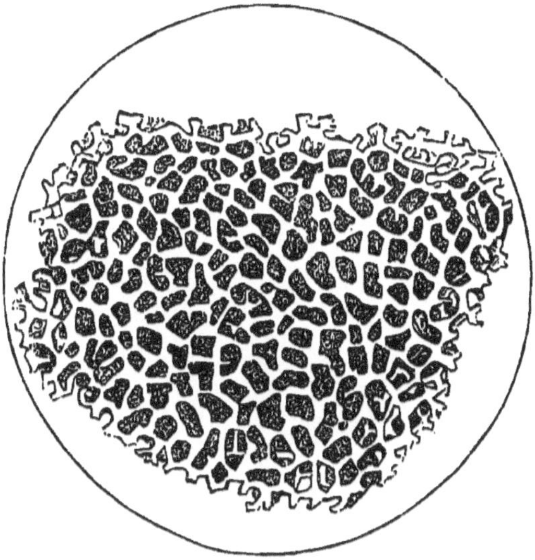

FIG. 1.—FRAGMENT OF ROASTED COFFEE.

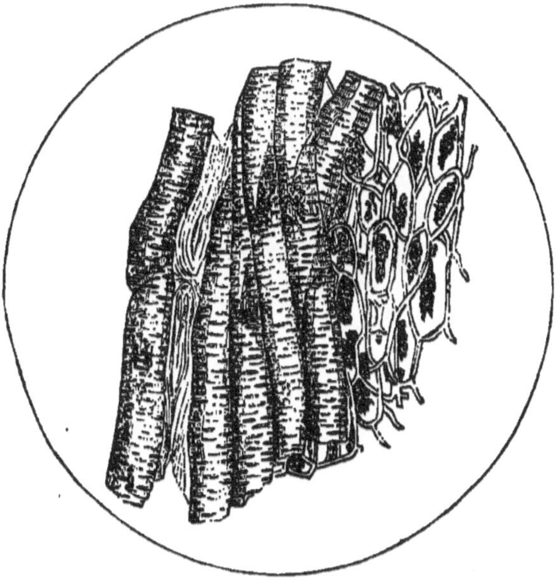

FIG. 2.—ROASTED CHICORY ROOT.

PLATE II.

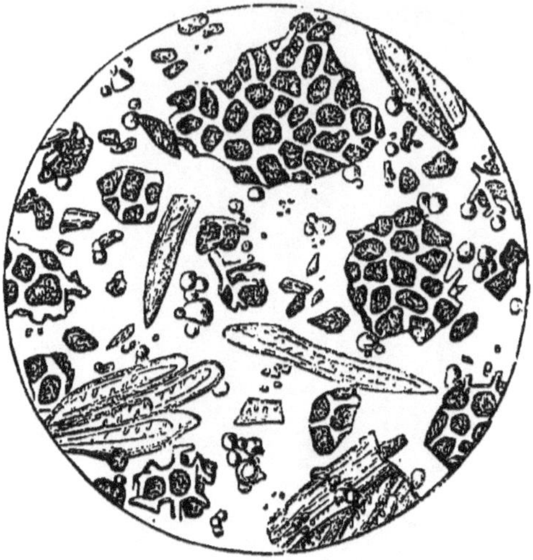

FIG. 1.—FRAGMENT GENUINE GROUND COFFEE.

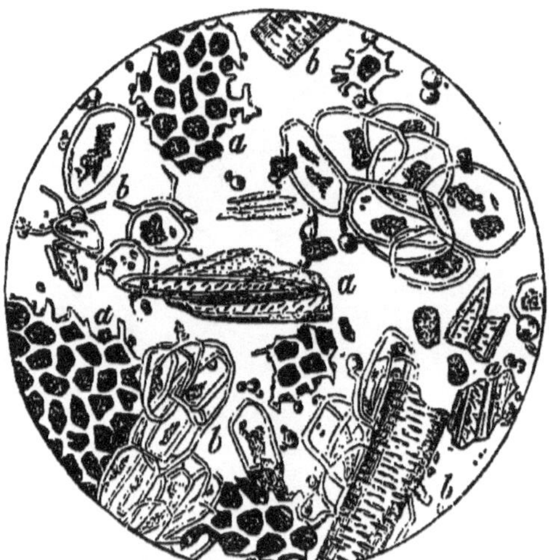

FIG. 2.—FRAGMENT GROUND COFFEE ADULTERATED WITH CHICORY.
a, *a*, Coffee. *b*, *b*, Chicory.

Fig. 1 (Plate II.) exhibits a fragment of genuine ground coffee; Fig. 2 (Plate II.), a sample of ground coffee adulterated with chicory, both magnified one hundred and forty diameters.

No fraud or absurdity ever lacked a voice raised in defence or extenuation; and an occasional good word has been put in for the mixture of other substances with coffee. Persons, I am willing to suppose, out of the patent-coffee business, may be found who think the admixture of chicory or other adulterants an improvement on pure coffee. But while there is no discussing the eccentricities of individual tastes, I have no fear of the spreading of such heresy. I have too high an opinion both of coffee and of my fellow-men to admit such a possibility. As to the statement that in some parts of Europe—in France, for instance—a majority of coffee-drinkers prefer the beverage with an infusion of chicory, I am inclined to think, with Dr. Hassall, that it is entirely incorrect. I am, indeed, convinced, as he is, that the undoubtedly large consumption of chicory in France is traceable merely to the practice of economy in small things, so characteristic of the middle and lower classes in that country, and not to the gratification of a peculiar taste. I have certainly never heard of anybody being avowedly invited there to take a cup of "chicory and coffee," and the following account, which has been going the rounds of the French papers, of how the President of the French Republic obtained a cup of pure coffee, indicates that chicory there, as well as here, is esteemed simply an adulteration.

HOW M. GRÉVY GOT A CUP OF COFFEE.

Everybody knows that M. Grévy never takes wine, not even at dinner. But like M. Thiers, he is a passionate lover of coffee. To be certain of having his favorite beverage of the best quality, he always, when he can, prepares it himself. Some years ago he was invited, with a friend, M. Bethmont, to a hunting party by M. Menier, the celebrated manufacturer of chocolate, at Noisiel. It happened that M. Grévy and M. Bethmont lost themselves in the forest, and, in trying to find their way, they stumbled upon a little wine-house, and, tired out, stopped for a rest. They asked for something to drink. M. Bethmont found his wine excellent, but, as usual, M. Grévy would not drink. He wanted coffee, but he was afraid of the decoction which would be brought him. He got a good cup, however, and this is how he managed it:

"Have you any chicory?" he said to the man.

"Yes, sir."

"Bring me some."

Soon the proprietor returned with a small can of chicory.

"Is that all you have?" asked M. Grévy.

"We have a little more."

"Bring me the rest."

When he came again with another can of chicory, M. Grévy said:

"You have no more?"

"No, sir."

"Very well. Now go and make me a cup of coffee."

CHAPTER XXII.

CHEMICAL ANALYSIS OF COFFEE—ITS MEDICINAL AND OTHER PROPERTIES.

It will prove profitable to examine briefly the verdict rendered by chemistry and physiology respecting the properties of coffee and its so-called substitutes. The researches of scientists inform us that coffee owes its individuality, if I may so term it, to three characteristic constituents: a volatile aromatic oil called caffeone; an element called caffeine, identical with the theine of tea ; and a kind of tannic acid, analogous to that of tea, called caffeic acid. Each of these elements possesses virtues and powers of its own, and plays a part in the general effect produced by coffee.

To the caffeone, or essential oil, which, when chemically separated by ether, presents the consistency of cocoa-butter, is due the peculiar and delicious aroma given out by coffee in roasting. Taken alone, the oil is found to produce a gentle perspiration and agreeable excitement, and to stimulate the mental faculties, while it retards, in a marked degree, the process of assimilation and, consequently, the waste of tissue. It exercises also an aperient effect on the bowels. Over-doses bring on sleeplessness and symptoms of congestion.

Caffeine, which is inodorous, but has a slightly bitter taste, in creases the nervous activity of the system ; the heart and pulse are quickened, the imagination enlivened. Administered in stronger doses, it causes trembling and a sort of intoxication, not unlike that resulting from alcoholic stimulants. It is said also to diminish the waste of organic tissue.

The caffeic acid, as it exists in the raw bean, has a decidedly astringent tendency. This, however, is modified in the roasting, and, besides, counteracted by the aperient properties of the caffeone. Some uncertainty seems to prevail, as yet, as to the full agency of this acid, some chemists ascribing to it the flavor and chief properties of coffee as a beverage.

United, acting and reacting upon each other, modified in their specific properties by their combination, these three elements give rise to the general properties of coffee, which are summed up as follows by Professor Johnstone: "It exhilarates, arouses, and keeps awake. It counteracts the stupor occasioned by fatigue, by disease, or by opium; it allays hunger to a certain extent, gives to the weary increased strength and vigor, and imparts a feeling of comfort and repose. Its physiological effects upon the system, so far as they have been investigated, appear to be that, while it makes the brain more active, it soothes the body generally, makes the change and waste of tissue slower, and the demand for food in consequence less. All these effects it owes to the conjoint action of three ingredients very similar to those contained in tea."

It is quite plain that this beneficent chemical trinity is entitled to the deepest reverence of the true lover of coffee, and deserves a high niche in the pantheon of gastronomic deities.

The identical principle of caffeine and elements analogous to caffeone and caffeic acid occur in tea, and closely allied principles in cocoa, as well as in the leaves and seeds of the South American plants which furnish the Yerba Mate, or Paraguay tea, and the Guarana bread of Brazil—thus seemingly forming a requisite in the diet of nearly the whole of mankind.

Neither these principles, nor analogous constituents, is found in any of the adulterants of coffee; the latter can have, therefore, none of the peculiar properties of coffee. They are purely and simply trash, and a fraud both upon the purse and the stomach of the consumer.

Dr. Hassall contrasts chicory and coffee in the following words:

"They differ from each other in their botanical nature, in chemical composition, and in physiological action and properties.

"Coffee is the fruit or seed of a tree, while chicory is the succulent root of a herbaceous plant. Now, it is a well-ascertained fact that, of all parts of vegetables, the fruit and seeds usually possess the most active properties; this is no doubt due to the circumstance of their being freely exposed to the influence of light and air—agencies which promote chemical changes in the plant, and so effect the elaboration of those complex organic substances on which the activity of vegetables depends. On the other hand, it must be manifest that, as the roots are removed from the influence of these powerful agencies, they cannot be so richly endowed with active properties; and, indeed, there are but few roots which contain either alkaloid or volatile oil—the constituents which give to coffee its peculiar virtues. The distinction, therefore, between the properties of the seeds and roots of plants is very important, and it is especially so in the case before us.

"The infusion of the one is heavy, mawkish, and nearly destitute of aroma; that of the other is light, fragrant, and refreshing.

"Coffee contains, as already shown, at least three active principles, viz.: the volatile oil, the tannin, and the alkaloid caffeine; in chicory there are no analogous constituents.

"Coffee exerts on the system marked and highly important physiological effects, of a beneficial character. There is no proof that chicory exerts any one of these effects, while it is very questionable whether the properties which it does possess are not really hurtful."

As to nutritiveness, chicory possesses only about one-half as much nitrogenous substance as coffee; and even that in no way benefits the drinker of the decoction, as these substances are almost entirely insoluble in water and are thrown away with the dregs. But, granting that a man should, for economy's sake, be content to drink a mixture of coffee and chicory, he could not with any certainty obtain even this. It has been proved that this substance, so largely used for adulterating purposes, is itself largely adulterated; in fact, all of the ingredients which have been detected in adulterated coffee, and which we have before enumerated, have also been discovered in powdered chicory. Parsnips, carrots, peas, and similar vegetables are chiefly used in this sophistication, and a compound is thus formed which can be sold under the market price at which genuine chicory can be had. Chicory is not grown to any extent in the United States, the attempts at culture and manufacture having given a poor, woody product, much inferior to that of foreign growth. The article is imported from Europe, where it is raised principally in Germany, France, Belgium, and

Holland. From July 1, 1878, to June 30, 1879, there were imported 4,002,566 pounds of chicory, valued at $144,688; during the same period the coffee imports amounted to 377,848,473 pounds, representing $47,356,819. In other words, supposing the ratio of consumption to importation and stocks to have been similar, for every one hundred pounds of coffee only 1.06 pound of chicory was consumed. This furnishes additional evidence of what I have already stated with regard to the adulterants employed by our manufacturers of patent coffees. They have at hand an abundance of the cheapest materials, and resort but very sparingly to the comparatively expensive article of chicory.

If I have allotted so much space to combating the claims of chicory, it is because these claims have obtained a certain currency, in spite of their apocryphal character, and also because, by reducing the very stronghold of plausible adulteration, the minor positions fall as a matter of course. The sooner the tampering with the purity of coffee is divested of all hypocritical pretences and given its proper name—sheer adulteration—the better it will be for the great consuming public.

The nutriment pretended to be derived from an infusion of roasted cereals is infinitesimal, the starchy matter of which they are mostly composed being reduced into charcoal during the roasting, and "a single mouthful of wholesome bread contains more nourishment than half a dozen cups of a beverage made from roasted corn."

The subjoined analysis of coffee, raw and roasted, is given by Professor Hassall:

	Raw.	Roasted.
Water	8.26	0.36
Cane sugar	8.18	1.84
Caffeine	1.10	1.06
Fat	11.42	8.30
Gluten	10.68	12.03
Extractive (caramel) gum, tannin.	14.03	26.28
Cellulose, etc.	42.36	44.96
Ash	3.97	5.17
	100.00	100.00

In another form, according to Payen, the analysis of unroasted coffee gives the following results:

Water	12.00
Flesh-formers	14.75
Heat-givers	66.25
Mineral matter	7.00
	100.00

The *Journal of Pharmaceutical Chemistry* contains the following in relation to the experiments of Dr. C. O. Cech, of St. Petersburg, upon the oil of roasted coffee:

"Although the coffee-bean belongs to our daily food, we are still uncertain of the chemical nature and composition of the products of roasting coffee, and of oil of coffee, one of the important characteristic constituents of the bean. The existence of a coffee oil makes itself known in a striking manner by its roasting, for this oil, driven out of the beans by the heat, is partially volatilized, and, together with other products of the roasting, produces the characteristic aroma of roasted coffee, an odor possessed by no other substance. In very strong black coffee, too, we can see this oil like little drops of grease floating on it. The amount of oil in coffee varies from eight to thirteen per cent., and at least half of this is lost in roasting, so that it would be a paying experiment to attempt to collect this oil, especially in large establishments where much coffee is burned and several pounds of oil are dissipated daily. In 1878, not less than five hundred thousand tons of coffee were consumed, so that the amount of oil that might have been collected was very considerable. Dr. Cech tried the experiment, in one of the large roasting establishments of Berlin, of connecting the roasting drum with a cooling apparatus and a receiver, so as to condense and collect the volatile and oily products of the roasting. At first there is scarcely any gas generated in the drums, but after the beans are browned and the whole mass has been heated to the temperature where the oil evaporates, such a quantity of the volatile aromatic oil is generated that it trickles down the walls of the chamber in which the beans are shovelled and cooled after coming from the drums. Unfortunately, the manipulations of roasting are at present such that this very co ing and reshovelling of hot beans must be done in the open a and is the reason that it is not possible to catch and conden the vapors so abundantly liberated. Practice has proven that the very moment when the beans turn brown and the first vapo begin to be given off it is absolutely necessary to pull the dru out of the roasting furnace and rapidly cool the coffee by shov ling and reshovelling in the air, or there is danger of its taking fi in the furnace and burning to a coal. Nevertheless it might feasible to connect the drums with an exhauster so as to conden the gases in a receiver, and at the same time cool the bean enou to prevent its taking fire. Cech has no doubt that the oil obtain in this manner would find use, at a profit, in making liqueurs. study the properties of oil of coffee, Dr. Cech pounded up fif pounds of different kinds of coffee in a mortar, and then extract it with alcohol and ether, obtaining about 1,200 grammes (tv and a half pounds) of oil of coffee. The beans extracted by hi were not of equal value as regards the yield of oil, for while son contained as high as thirteen per cent., other kinds fell belo eight per cent. The oil of coffee is a green, thick, transpare oil, and after some time a few long needles were deposited fro it. These proved to be caffeine. Since caffeine is not extract from the exhausted beans by ether, and very little of it is tak up by the alcohol employed, the coffee from which the oil h been extracted could be employed for the manufacture of caffeir The coffee oil became turbid in half a year, although it was ke in hermetically closed bottles. Small groups of crystals we formed in the middle of the liquid, and slowly settled to the bo tom, and at the end of three years the bottle was two-thirds fu of a dirty mass of crystals, consisting of the solid fatty acids, b the upper layer of the liquid remained for years transparent, cle and of a beautiful green color, proving that a portion of coffee consists of liquid oleic acid."

Recently there appeared in the *Physician and Surgeon*, a p per from the pen of Prof. Albert B. Prescott, of the Universi of Michigan, from which it appears that the tannin in the coff berry is not over about one-third the quantity of that in te leaves; it may be considerably less. Six samples of coffee we tested, as in the tea, for the amount of soluble tannin, and steeped in fifty parts of water.

Name of Coffee.	Price per pound.	Tannin Dissolved by— 5 Minutes' steeping.	10 Minutes' steeping.	20 Minutes' steeping.	30 Minutes' steeping.
1. Maracaibo	28 cts.	0.00	0.00	0.01	0.35
2. Mocha	22 "	0.00	0.00	0.02	0.60
3. Java	30 "	0.00	trace.	0.20	1.42
4. Rio	26 "	0.00	0.00	0.02	0.72
5. French Best ...	25 "	0.00	trace.	0.25	1.80
6. Arbuckle	25 "	0.00	0.00	0.00	0.09
Average......	——	——	——	0.08	0.83

Coffee and tea as beverages in actual use were also taken and analyzed and the amount of tannin estimated, with the result of showing that on an average the tea contained nearly four times as much tannin as the coffee. These results leave no doubt that the tea we drink contains at least four or five times as much tannin as the coffee we drink. Also, that the tea yields only a small proportion of its large quantity of tannin at five to ten minutes' steeping. And in case of poisoning by alkaloids, strong tea is better than coffee as an antidote.

As to the volatile oils. The essential oil of tea is a very small but a distinct constituent of good tea. The market value of good tea undoubtedly depends far more upon this volatile oil than upon all other constituents. Its presence is recognized and its proportions discerned by the expert, from the odor, when hot water is poured upon hot tea in a hot cup. This volatile oil is conjectured to be an organic stimulant. Coffee in the green state has no volatile oil. By the process of roasting an agreeable essential oil is developed, doubtless in part from the fat present. The effect of this essential oil on the human system is not at all known. It may cause the digestive disturbance sometimes due to coffee-drinking.

As to the food substances, tea contains pectin, gum, legumin, and other matters, yielding in all to boiling water, about thirty-two per cent. of its weight. Coffee contains after roasting one or two per cent. of glucose, ten to twelve per cent. of fat, nearly as much legumin, and a little gum. It yields twenty to twenty-fiv per cent. to water. It is likely that these food substances, as mod fied by roasting, disagree with the digestion of many person This may be why substitution of tea-drinking sometimes give relief to those suffering from drinking coffee.

It is to be hoped that more of our chemists will give attentio to this matter in the interests of economic science. As is we known, the quality of coffee improves by long keeping, and chemical analysis of coffee beans of different ages might indicat the cause of the improvement, and possibly its production by ar tificial means.

Prof. Johnston states that, weight for weight, tea yield about twice as much theine as coffee does to the water in whicl it is infused, "but as we generally use a greater weight of coffe than we do of tea in preparing our beverages, a cup of coffee o ordinary strength will probably contain as much theine as a cu of ordinary English tea. One cup of strong French coffee wil contain twice as much caffeine as a cup of weak French tea."

The two subjoined analyses serve to show the comparativ composition of the roasted berry and the tea-leaf.

	TEA. (Mulder.)	COFFEE. (Payen.)
Water	5.0	12.0
Gum and sugar	21.0	15.5
Gluten	25.0	13.0
Theine	0.5	0.75
Fat and volatile oil	4.0	13.0
Tannic acid	15.0	5.0
Woody fibre	24.0	34.0
Ash	5.5	6.71

The above analyses must not be relied upon for any othe purpose than that of a general comparison. It will be seen tha the theine is much understated in the tea.

Swallowed with the grounds, as is done in Turkey, coffe undoubtedly affords much nourishment. Mr. Payen states tha it contains more than twice the nutriment of soup, and thre times as much as tea. In the beverage, however, prepared as i is by us, the nitrogenous or flesh-forming matter, being mostly insoluble, remains in the dregs. Coffee slightly roasted contains the maximum of aroma, weight, and nutrition.

It is said that in Germany a decoction of roasted acorns is often used as a "substitute" for coffee. The acorns are gathered in autumn, when they are ripe, shelled, cut into pieces of the size of coffee-berries, and thoroughly dried. They are then roasted until they become of a cinnamon-brown color, ground, and treated as ordinary coffee-powder. It is pretended that this acorn coffee is "greatly liked by the people, and considered strengthening for consumptives and delicate children." I hope it is, for the sake of those who consume the beverage. As to being a substitute for coffee, it is only so in the sense in which anything becomes a substitute for another when put in its place. There is no more analogy between real coffee and this so-called acorn coffee than there is between a cigar made with tobacco-leaves and a cigar made with cabbage-leaves. The two latter, indeed, are put in the mouth and smoked in the same way, and so are the two former prepared and taken in the same way. But there the resemblance ends. For aught of common between the two substances, the acorn drink might as well be termed acorn tea, acorn chocolate, or acorn soup. It is fortunate that but little of such substances is used. The imports of acorn coffee and all other substitutes for coffee for the year ended June 30, 1879, amounted to only 5,012 pounds, and valued at $309.

With regard to the evil effects charged to the abuse of coffee by some authorities, the "National Dispensatory" says: "The consequences of an abuse of tea were declared to be similar to that of coffee long before chemistry had demonstrated the identity of theine with caffeine. Among their evil effects were enumerated the following: indigestion, acidity, heartburn, watchfulness, tremors, debility, irritability of disposition, and dejection of spirits. By some persons both tea and coffee were accused of producing paralysis. Most of these effects are more likely to follow the habitual use of tea than of coffee, perhaps because, as a general rule, more of the former than of the latter is consumed; and the spinal symptoms, such as painful muscular tension and cramp and persistent wakefulness, are more apt to be produced by tea.

In experiments undertaken with a number of selected health persons, the operation of caffeine has been found to vary exceeingly; by the same dose some were scarcely at all affected, whi others suffered from palpitation of the heart, a full, frequen or irregular pulse, irritable bladder, trembling limbs, headach roaring in the ears, flashes before the eyes, sleeplessness, phaı tasms, a sort of intoxication, and even delirium, when a very larg dose was taken, and a subsequent unfitness for bodily or ment labor."

These effects, which may be called poisonous, illustrate th danger of exceeding due moderation in the use of coffee, for the show that it may, if immoderately consumed, tend to develop morbid condition of the nervous system, which must render peculiarly liable to disease, although in a much less degree tha opium or alcohol. Indeed, the excessive use of coffee is muc more injurious to the spinal than to the cerebral functions. I its primary operation it agrees with those stimulants in excitin muscular and mental activity as well as cheerfulness, and in i after-effects it does not tend to produce narcotism or stupor, bı only that unsteadiness of the mind, and still more of the spin functions, which denotes exhaustion. It agrees with them, wit tobacco, with Chinese and Paraguay teas, and with various othe stimulants used by different nations, in the main features of i action. . . . . The moderation of tissue-waste, which, has been said, belongs to coffee in common with other articl having the same general action, and in use among different n tions, is illustrated by various well-established facts. The inhal itants of Central Africa, the native country of coffee, in their pred atory excursions are said to subsist entirely upon a mixture c coffee and butter, which is prepared in masses of the size of a bi liard-ball, one of which will keep a man in strength and spiri during a day's fatigue. Jomand says: "120 grammes (4 ounce of powdered coffee and 3 litres (8 pints) of an infusion made wit 200 grammes (6½ ounces) of different kinds of coffee enabled m to live for five consecutive days without lessening my ordinar occupations, and to use more and more prolonged muscular e ercise than I was accustomed to without any other physical injur than a slight degree of fatigue and a little loss of flesh." Th

Belgian coal-miners live and work efficiently upon a ration of solid food much less than that of the French miners, and yet perform more labor than the latter. The only difference in the quality of their food consists in the Belgians receiving a ration of coffee, and to this is attributed their superior endurance. . . . . It may seem at first sight irrational that a substance which restricts tissue-waste should be used for the very purpose of quickening certain functions, and especially those of the brain.

"It restricts tissue-waste, and yet it is used to quicken certain functions, especially those of the brain. The mental exhilaration, physical activity, and wakefulness it causes explains the fondness for it which has been shown by so many men of science, poets, scholars, and others devoted to thinking. It has, indeed, been called 'the intellectual beverage.'

"But all of these occupations involve increased functional activity, and therefore increased waste of tissue in the brain and spinal marrow, the very action which coffee is said to restrain. To reconcile these apparent incongruities, it has been maintained that coffee does not act primarily as a cerebral stimulant, but only secondarily by removing the vascular plenitude occasioned by prolonged study, by a full meal, and especially by alcohol, opium, or other agents which directly tend to load the brain with blood; that, if taken on an empty stomach, it does not quicken the functions of the brain, but, on the contrary, renders it dull and inapt for steady thought, creates general debility and nervousness, and frequently causes *hemicrania.*

"During digestion, however, the case is different, particularly if a full and stimulating meal has been taken; the mind grows dull and sluggish, a tendency to sleep arises, and everything indicates an increased amount of blood in the brain. In like manner prolonged mental labor produces cerebral plenitude and drowsiness. It is this condition, apparently, which coffee corrects by contracting the blood-vessels and relieving the brain of its oppressive load of blood. The habit of taking coffee at breakfast and after dinner is explained by the stimulant action (whether direct or indirect) which it exerts not only upon the nervous system generally, but especially upon the stomach and bowels. There can be no doubt that it quickens gastric digestion and relieves the sense of plenitude in the stomach, stimulates the secretion of bile, and augments the peristaltic action of the intestine, thereby promoting defecation. It is quite as certain that, used to excess, it paralyzes the digestive function in all its steps, and leads to further disorders, of which the chief are congestion of the liver, constipation, and hemorrhoids. Whether these effects are to be ascribed to a power in coffee to produce contraction of the capillary blood-vessels may be uncertain, but their reality is beyond doubt."

Dr. Guillasse, of the French navy, in a recent paper on typhoid fever, says: "Coffee has given us unhoped-for satisfaction; and after having dispensed it we find, to our great surprise, that its action is as prompt as it is decisive. No sooner have our patients taken a few tablespoonfuls of it than their features become relaxed and they come to their senses. The next day the improvement is such that we are tempted to look upon coffee as a specific against typhoid fever. Under its influence the stupor is dispelled and the patient rouses from the state of somnolency in which he has been since the invasion of the disease. Soon all the functions take their natural course, and he enters upon convalescence."

Dr. Guillasse gives to an adult two or three tablespoonfuls of strong black coffee every two hours, alternately with one or two teaspoonfuls of claret or Burgundy wine. A little lemonade or citrate of magnesia should be taken daily, and, after a while, quinine. From the fact that malaise or cerebral symptoms appear first, the doctor regards typhoid fever as a nervous disease, and the coffee acting on the nerves is peculiarly indicated in the early stages before local complications arise.

For a fuller description of its medicinal properties we refer the reader to the interesting article on Coffœa Arabica, to be found in the "National Dispensatory."

CHAPTER XXIII.

THE COFFEE TRADE.

Between the producers and consumers of coffee stands the trade which handles the article, taking it from the former and distributing it to the latter. The statistical data which are presented in other chapters sufficiently illustrate the importance of this branch of the commerce of the world—the coffee crop—which amounts in round numbers to eleven hundred million pounds, being worth from first hands not less than $135,000,000.

Coffee as a commercial staple is naturally inseparable from coffee as a popular beverage. Increased consumption at the breakfast-table leads to higher prices in the market, which in turn must stimulate production in the field. This extended production reacts on the value of the commodity and brings it again to a more accessible level, when, as experience has shown, consumption resumes its onward march and the rotation of cause and effect begins anew. But this general law of supply and demand, so easily stated, is in reality very complex in its workings. Consequences often apparently belie premises, or are so long postponed as meanwhile to puzzle or to injure.

Amsterdam was for many years the centre of the coffee trade, and it will not be amiss to study the earlier fluctuations of coffee in that market. One of the effects of the great European wars at the beginning of this century was to so entirely shut out the supply of coffee from the Continent that the price was forced up to almost fabulous figures. In Amsterdam, good ordinary Java sold in 1810 at from 105 to 115 Dutch cents * (about 42 to 46 cents, gold, in

* In all that pertains to the Amsterdam market, the *cents* are the *Dutch* cents, unless otherwise specified. Two and one-half Dutch cents are about equivalent to one American cent.

United States money) per pound; in 1811 for 215 cents (86 cents, U. S.) per pound; and in 1812 for 270 cents, or about $1.08 of our money, per pound. Meanwhile, stocks accumulated in England. After the fall of the French empire and the return of peace, a rapid distribution took place. From 1814 to 1817, prices ranged in Holland from 40 to 50 cents per pound in Netherlands currency, representing a very moderate value—from 16 to 20 cents of our money per pound. But the impetus given caused consumption to run ahead of production. The supply could not keep pace with the requirements, and Java coffee rose again to 92½ cents or 37 cents, U. S. In 1823 it still brought 75½ cents in the Amsterdam market (30 cents, U. S.). But the natural consequences of this long period of high prices began at this time to make themselves felt. For more than ten years coffee had been yielding enormous profits; under this powerful stimulus, the culture had taken a sudden and immense development. New plantations had been opened everywhere. The product of the millions of young trees now commenced pouring into the European markets. Production not only overtook the still increasing consumption, but, like the famous dog in headlong chase after the fox, it kept steadily ahead and gained more and more. Prices for good ordinary Java coffee in Holland tumbled to 37½ cents in 1825, and to 21 cents (a fraction over 8 cents, U. S.) in 1830. There they seemed to "touch bottom" for a while and rallied to 36 cents (14⅖ cents, U. S.) in 1835, and after a plunge to 23 cents (9⅕ cents, U. S.) during the great crisis of 1837, floated up to 33 cents (13⅕ cents, U. S.) in 1839.

The cheapness of coffee during these years no doubt contributed powerfully to the spread of its use among a numerous class of consumers to whom it had hitherto been denied. This era of popularizing the article, at the expense of the trade and of the producer, had not yet come to an end; darker days were yet in store for the coffee-grower.

Toward 1840 the yield of Java attained unprecedented proportions (68,414 tons in 1840), while, from the Western hemisphere, Brazil began to ship enormous crops, amounting in that year to more than 76,000 tons. Consumption could not keep pace. So low did prices fall that the Dutch Trading Maatschappy, a monopoly formed in 1824 for the collection, shipment to Holland, and sale of all the coffee that the government produced, was compelled in 1843 to fix 20 cents (8 cents, U. S.) as a minimum price for good ordinary Java, below which it advertised it would permit no sales. The measures devised by the company worked only temporary good. The minimum was raised to 22½ cents (9 cents, U. S.) in 1844, and, under a speculative combination formed by the Dutch merchants, prices advanced to 26 @ 27 cents for a while ($10\frac{4}{10}$ @ $10\frac{8}{10}$ cents, U. S.), only to collapse in 1845, with disastrous effect to those concerned. In 1846 the adoption of a minimum of 20 cents was again resorted to, which, in 1848, the Maatschappy was obliged to lower to 18 cents (7⅕ cents, U. S.), while forced sales out of private hands were made at 16 @ 17 cents (6⅖ @ 6⅘ cents, U. S.). This was far below the cost of production and handling. By this time the decline of the coffee industry in the West Indies became clearly visible. The neglected plantations went out of bearing, and coffee-production ceased almost entirely in that part of the world. A fitful reaction advanced prices one hundred per cent. from 1849 to 1850, but in subsequent years we find the appreciation of the staple struggling up through such quotations as 25½ cents (10⅕ cents, U. S.) in 1851; 23 cents (9⅕ cents, U. S.) in 1852; 33½ cents (13⅖ cents, U. S.) in 1853; 29½ cents (11⅘ cents, U. S.) in 1854; 34 cents (13⅗ cents, U. S.) in 1855 and 1856 (notwithstanding the importation in 1856 by the Maatschappy of 1,278,873 bags—the largest quantity ever imported, exceeding the average yearly supply by 300,000 bags); 40 cents (16 cents, U. S.) in the spring of 1857; 20 cents (8 cents, U. S.) and 22 cents (8⅘ cents, U. S.) at the end of that critical year; 34 cents (13⅗ cents, U. S.) in 1858; 38½ cents (15⅖ cents, U. S.) in 1859 and 1860; to 44 cents (17⅗ cents, U. S.) and 46¼ cents (18½ cents, U. S.) in 1861.

Then occurrred the great civil war in the United States, which, it is calculated, "diminished the consumption about two hundred thousand tons." A well-informed authority in coffee matters, writing about ten years ago, observes that but for that important event "the equilibrium between production and consumption would have been disturbed." It is urged that the continual encouragement afforded to consumption by low prices during so many years and the parallel discouragement of production had now reversed the position. The dispirited dog was now lapsing behind the game. Java, which in 1855 produced 76,596 tons (the largest crop ever known), barely kept up to previous averages, while consumption was still on a rapid increase. Brazil, it is true, had suffered no interruption to the development of her coffee culture, having had the good fortune of ministering to the growing wants of our prosperous republic; but the fast-swelling millions of this country would have continued to absorb any increase of her product. "The world would not," says the same authority, "have had coffee enough. The American war prevented this deficiency, which, without the large Brazil crop of 1866, would have been enormous." I am not prepared either to support or combat the foregoing opinion. The question is a complex and, at best, a theoretical one, requiring more study than it has been in my power to bestow upon it. I have merely stated this view of the matter as one in the light of which it may be curious to consider subsequent events in our coffee market and in Europe.

Our record of prices for the New York market opens with the year succeeding the financial panic of 1857.

—1858—

During this year the prices of coffee other than Java ruled lower than for several previous years. The average cost of fair to prime Rio in 1857 was 11.04 cents, and in 1858, 10.96 cents. The fluctuations in Brazil were between 9½ @ 10¾ cents, and 10¾ @ 12 cents, for fair to prime; St. Domingo, 7¾ @ 10 cents; Maracaibo and Laguayra, 10¼ @ 14 cents. The changes in Java were more marked, the lowest price being 13½ cents; the highest, 20 cents. At the opening of the year Java sold at 15½ @ 16½ cents, reached 20 cents in March, and declined in November to 13½ @ 14 cents—the low prices stimulating speculation.

—1859—

The market for all grades was remarkably steady, the prices of Java being confined within a variation of 2¼ cents; Brazil, ¾ @ 1 cent; St. Domingo, 2⅛ @ 2¼ cents; and Maracaibo, 1½ cent. Higher prices were obtained for Brazil coffee in November and

December of 1859 than at any time for nine years previous. Large sales of Rio were made late in the summer for export to Germany, an event of peculiar significance at that time.

—1860—

In this year there was a decrease of 46,352,227 pounds in the consumption, and yet prices reached a point for the principal kinds higher than any previously on record. The supply was short, the Brazil crop being deficient. The average cost of Brazil in 1860 was 13.69$\frac{1}{4}$ cents for fair to prime, against 11.61 cents in 1859, an advance of 18 per cent.; St. Domingo advanced from an average of 10.39 cents in 1859 to 12.39$\frac{7}{8}$ cents in 1860, an increase of 19$\frac{1}{3}$ per cent.; Maracaibo and Laguayra ruled nearly 16$\frac{5}{8}$ per cent. higher; while Java averaged 16.15$\frac{1}{4}$ cents, or 1.36$\frac{1}{4}$ cents above the average for 1859.

—1861—

At this time the country was troubled with civil war. The blockade of the Southern ports increased the receipts in New York, where the sales showed an increase over the previous year of 55 per cent. In the spring of 1861, at the time Fort Sumter was bombarded, business became depressed and prices declined. In July a duty of five cents per pound was proposed, and this gave life to the market, which became excited. In August, Congress placed the duty at four cents per pound, this action advancing prices and leading to large speculative transactions. Near the close of the year an additional duty of one cent per pound was levied, and made to cover coffee in bond. On January 1, 1861, fair to prime Brazil sold at 11$\frac{1}{2}$ @ 12$\frac{1}{2}$ cents, and in December at 18$\frac{1}{2}$ @ 19$\frac{1}{2}$ cents, out of bond. Java advanced from 15$\frac{1}{2}$ @ 16$\frac{1}{2}$ cents in January, to 24 @ 25 cents in December.

—1862—

In 1862 the effects of the war became more apparent, coffee being shut out of the Southern States. The consumption fell off 98,055,875 pounds, or 52.42 per cent.; prices ruled very much higher, those for Brazil being 64$\frac{1}{4}$ per cent. beyond those for 1861. During this year the use of substitutes began, and all manner of mixtures were sold with high-sounding names, and, strange to say, often bearing an endorsement from persons possessed of a national reputation.

The trade varied greatly during the year, being dull when news of defeat came to the Union armies, and active when a victory was chronicled. Brazil sold at 11½ @ 18½ cents in January, reaching its highest point, 31 @ 33 cents, in November—averaging 23 cents for the year, against 14 cents in 1861. Java sold up to 34 @ 35 cents, an advance from the lowest point of 9 @ 9½ cents.

—1863—

High prices led to a decrease in consumption, which was about 35,600 tons, as against an average of 89,600 tons for the ten years prior to 1861. The receipts were nearly 4,500,000 pounds lighter than the consumption. During this year prices varied as gold fluctuated in value. The average cost of Brazil was 31.18 cents, or 8.17 cents above that of the previous year. Java was worth 41 cents at the close of the year, its average cost being 37.04 cents per pound, an advance over 1862 of 9.54 cents.

—1864—

The consumption increased 36.84 per cent., the Government being a purchaser to the extent of 40,000,000 pounds. The market for most of the year was excited and irregular. At the beginning of January Rio sold for 22⅝ cents, gold, or 34¼ @ 34½ cents, currency. In July gold sold at 285, making the currency value of the same grade 53 cents, while its gold price was 18⅜ cents. Six months later the currency quotation was 45 @ 45½ cents, or 19 15/16 cents in gold, then selling at 227.

These wide fluctuations in price show to what great disadvantage dealers operated. In August, Java sold at 58 @ 60 cents, the lowest prices being made in January, when the market ruled steady at 40 @ 41 cents; averaging for the year 49 cents. The average currency cost of Maracaibo and Laguayra was 41.59 cents, against 31.93 cents in 1863.

—1865—

The consumption exceeded that of the previous year 19,059,653 pounds, or nearly 17½ per cent., due to the renewal of trade with the Southern States. It will be noted, by reference to the table of receipts of Java, that in 1864 they were unusually heavy, reaching 6,384,908 pounds at New York, while in 1865 only 178,000 pounds were received. On January 1, 1865, there was a stock in Boston and New York of nearly 118,000 mats of Java coffee. Prices were more uniform, and the trade transacted business upon a gold basis, so that from June, 1865, quotations are given in gold. The average cost of Rio was 20.65 cents, gold; Maracaibo, 21.3 cents, gold; Java, 25.82 cents, gold.

—1866—

The record for this year shows an advance of 23½ per cent. in consumption, but notwithstanding the increase the distribution still fell far behind that of the years preceding the war.

The average cost of all kinds, except Java, was below that of 1865, the average of Brazil for the year being 18.66 cents, gold, against 20.65 cents in 1865; St. Domingo, 17.12 cents, against 18.78 cents; Maracaibo, 19.45 cents, against 21.3 cents; Java, 26.08 cents, against 25.82 cents.

—1867—

Consumption continued to increase, and for this year exhibited a gain of 27¼ per cent., being the largest reported since 1859; the deliveries at New York were 132,335,511 pounds. For the country, exclusive of the Pacific Coast, the consumption was 203,506,671 pounds, a gain over 1866 of 43,587,790 pounds. Prices ruled lower, the average cost of fair to prime Rio being 17.24 cents, or 1.42 cent below the average price in 1866: Maracaibo averaged 17.69 cents, or 1.76 cent less than for the previous year: Java averaged 24.75 cents, against 26.08 cents in 1866.

—1868—

Lower prices prevailed, thereby stimulating consumption. The year's business was not very profitable to importers, but the deliveries were almost as large as in the days of free coffee. The average price of Brazil for the year was 15.73 cents, or 1½ cent below that of 1867; St. Domingo, 14.58 cents, or 1¼ cent lower; Maracaibo, 16.38 cents, or 1⅛ cent less, Java selling at a decline of 1⅛ cent; the average for the year being 23.41 cents, against 24.75 cents in 1867.

—1869—

The receipts were, 4,149,313 pounds more than in 1868, while the consumption increased 19,792,317 pounds, which led to a reduction in the stock, which was on December 31st, 16,717,682 pounds below the quantity held at the beginning of the year. In the spring of 1869 a large speculative business was done in Java, the transactions amounting to 100,000 mats, and absorbing all the stock on the spot, together with that to arrive. The highest price for the year was in June, when Java sold at 23½ @ 25 cents, the lowest in April, when it brought 21 @ 23 cents, the average for the year being 23.02. The average cost of Brazil, was 15.82; Maracaibo, 17.54.

—1870—

The imports for the year were the largest on record, as also was the consumption, which was 37,470,555 pounds larger than that of 1869, equal to a gain of 15⅝ per cent.

The market during this year was less disturbed by fluctuations than it had been for many previous years. Brazil averaged 16.33 cents, a higher price than had ruled since 1867; Java averaged 21.19 cents, against 23.02 cents in 1870, a decline of 1.83 cent.

—1871—

During this year the receipts and consumption were again increased, being heavier than for any previous year. The duty was reduced two cents per pound, and yet there was a decline in the average cost of Brazil of less than half a cent; Maracaibo, was 1¼ cent lower; Java, $\frac{1}{10}$ cent higher in comparison with 1870, when Java coffee sold at lower prices than for several years previous. In August of that year it became certain that the Brazil and Java crops were short, and a very active trade was done, especially in Java, of which 100,000 mats were sold. The deliveries of Java fell, in 1871, 540,000 piculs below 1870, the Sumatra crop of 1872 was 65,700 piculs below that of 1871, and Brazil exported, in 1872, 425,000 bags less than in 1871. In September the activity continued, and during October there was much excitement, wide fluctuations marking speculative operations. In August, Brazil sold at 14¼ @ 15¾ cents, and in October, at 19 @ 20½ cents; Java advanced from 12¾ @ 13 cents, in August, to 16¼ @ 16½ cents during the latter part of December.

—1872—

The decline in the receipts from 322,700,479 pounds in 1871, to 277,636,258 pounds in 1872, was due to a short crop in the Brazils, from whence the bulk of supplies came, and to the failure of the Java crop. On July 1st, the remaining duty of three cents was removed, and yet the average gold price of fair to prime Rio was 2½ cents above that of 1871; Maracaibo and Laguayra, averaged nearly 2 cents higher, while Java was 21.3 cents, as against 21.29 cents the year preceding, the lowest price being made in November, when it sold at 18½ @ 19½ cents; the highest in January, when it was held at 23 @ 25 cents.

—1873—

The effect of the short crops was seen during this year in the marked advance in prices. Brazil, Java, Ceylon, and West India countries were short in their supply, the exports from Rio falling over 51,000 tons below those of 1872, while the Sumatra crop, which was very short in 1872, was in 1873, 46,380 piculs below the average per year for the five years from and including 1867 to 1871.

The highest price of Brazil sorts was reached in September, when fair to prime sold at 21¾ @ 23 cents, averaging for the year 19.99 cents, against 18.42 cents in 1872; Java sold during the same month at 25½ @ 27 cents, and in December, at 30 @ 34 cents, an advance over the price on January 1st of 11 @ 13 cents per pound. The average price of Java for the year was 23.63 cents, against 21.3 cents in 1872.

—1874—

This year was marked by large speculative transactions, accompanied by wide fluctuations in price. The growth of consumption in Europe and America, light stocks and diminished crops led to a great advance on the Continent of Europe, as well as in the New York market. The reign of high prices, however, was short, and the decline was hastened by reports of a large crop in Brazil, at that time placed at 212,000 to 220,000 tons, against a yield of 155,000 to 160,000 tons in 1873–74; it reached over 235,000 tons. The Java crop was 125,000 to 130,000 piculs in excess of the previous year, while Ceylon was expected to exceed 1873–74, by nearly 50 per cent., or 300,000 cwt. The year opened with fair to prime Brazil cargoes held at 25 @ 27 cents, advancing three weeks later to 26¼ @ 28¼ cents. In June, the same grades sold at 17 @ 19½ cents; September, 15¾ @ 19 cents, the average cost for the year being 21.08 cents, against 19.99 cents in 1873. Java sold on January 1st, at 31 @ 35 cents, dropped to 22 @ 25 cents in June, then advanced, selling at 24 @ 28 cents during November and December, averaging for the year 26.68 cents. With a declining market from the beginning of the year, and a variation in price of 8 to 10 cents per pound, importers and dealers sustained considerable loss, and the year closed with a bad record so far as profits were concerned.

—1875—

In 1875, the imports increased greatly, showing a gain of $26\frac{7}{20}$ per cent., while the consumption increased only $8\frac{13}{16}$ per cent. The resnlt was that the year closed with a heavy stock, viz., 21,161 tons, against 2,705 tons December 31, 1874. Prices averaged 2.07 cents per pound lower on Brazil, being 19.01 cents, against 21.08 cents in 1874. Fluctuations in Java were confined to a difference of 3 @ 4 cents, the average for the year being 26.71 cents, against 26.68 cents in 1874, or only 3 cents per 100 pounds higher than the average of the previous year. It will be noted that free coffee brought no benefit to consumers, who paid higher prices from the time the duty was removed.

—1876—

The record of this year contains many features of interest. The receipts fell off 85,869,661 pounds, or 38,335 tons. The consumption exceeded the imports 34,738,078 pounds, while the stock at the close of the year was redneed to only 1,795 tons, a quantity smaller than was ever held at the same date within a quarter of a century. With increased consumption, diminished supplies, and a reduced stock, prices would ordinarily seek a higher level, but the facts are that they ruled lower than in 1875, the average cost of Brazil sorts being 17.97 cents, against 19.01 cents in 1875; Maracaibo sold at an average of 17.02 cents, or 3.52 cents lower than in 1875, Java declining 5.14 cents. Early in the year mild coffee sold at higher prices than at any other time in 1876, all kinds declining in mid-summer, advancing as the year drew to a close, the Brazil sorts reaching their highest point in December, when fair to prime sold at 19 @ 20 cents, against an average for the year of 17.97 cents. Mild sorts did not quite recover the decline. The market during most of the year was irregular and unsettled.

—1877—

Notwithstanding that the general trade of the country was greatly depressed throughout the year, and prices higher than in 1876, there was a small advance in consumption. With the exception of one year the imports were the largest in the history of the trade. The average price of Brazil during the year exceeded that of 1876 by 1.75 cents; Maracaibo ruled 1.9 cents higher, while the average cost of Java was 2¼ cents above the year previous. The fluctuations were wider, Java selling at 22 @ 23 cents in December, and up to 24½ @ 25½ cents in July, at which time Brazil sold at 19¾ @ 20¾ cents, against 17½ @ 19 cents in November. The receipts were with one exception the largest on record, reaching a total of 341,214,438 pounds. The consumption was larger than in 1876, and was larger with two exceptions than for any previous years. Prices fluctuated considerably, being lowest toward the close of December.

—1878—

This year marked a new era in the coffee trade, not only in this country, but wherever the article was produced or consumed. Then it was that the large crops made it apparent that the time, previously predicted, when the production would exceed consumption had come, and that the control of the existing speculative syndicate would soon terminate. During the year prices of all varieties declined, and with the exception of Java, ruled lower than in January. Prime cargoes of Brazil declined from 18¾ to 15¾ cents, the average price for the year being about 3¼ cents below that of 1877; Maracaibo declined 3⅜ cents, and St. Domingo, 3⅕ cents, while the average yearly cost of Java was 1⅛ cent less. In January, Java sold at 21 @ 23 cents, declining in April to 20½ @ 21½ cents, and ruling at 23 @ 23½ cents in December. There was an advance during the year of 6,466 tons in consumption, while the receipts fell 5,297 tons below those of the previous year.

—1879—

The course of prices in 1879 was downward, excepting for Java. There was a great gain, both in the receipts and consumption on the Atlantic Coast, the former advancing 50,980 tons, and the latter, 36,869 tons, the stock being 11,163 tons heavier on December 31, 1879, than at the corresponding date 1878. During this year Europe made an advance in consumption, and yet prices fell. During the fall of 1879, however, in New York, the coffee syndicate made another effort to advance prices, and this was greatly aided by the general improvement in business. Fair Rio coffee, advanced from 13½ cents in September, to 17 cents in November, Maracaibo gained 3 cents in price within two months. and St. Domingo went from 10½ to 14 cents during the same time. So rapid was the increase in the demand for merchandise that prices of all kinds were greatly advanced, legitimate trade being for a time supplanted by speculative operations. The great advance during the last two months of 1879 checked trade, as dealers generally believed that the large crops produced in Brazil and the East Indies, in connection with the stimulus given to production in Mexico and Central America, warranted lower prices for coffee.

—1880—

This year was one of reaction, and the history of the trade for the twelve months is a record of loss and disaster such as never was experienced before in the coffee trade in the United States.

Considering the large supplies, prices ruled high in January, 1880, fair to prime Rio selling at 15½ @ 17 cents; Maracaibo, 13½ @ 17 cents; Padang Java, 22 @ 24 cents.

The deliveries in the early part of the year were large, but during the spring and summer months they were comparatively light. During the summer there was an attempt made by heavy holders of East India coffee to control the supply of Brazil on the spot, and to arrive, and their free purchases carried the price of fair Rio, which, under the influence of a dull spring trade, had dropped to 14¼ cents, up to 16¼ cents, and loaded them with a heavy stock. Large receipts in Rio de Janeiro, however, and the general statistical position, made buyers timid; the combination being unable to sustain the market, prices declined rapidly, and they soon found themselves owners of an immense stock of Java and Brazil coffee that showed a loss of from three to five cents per pound. The enormous shrinkage caused the failure of the two largest coffee firms in America, and the sudden death of a leading member of the combination threw affairs into confusion, and thus led to the breaking up of the three largest coffee houses in the United States. The loss sustained by the trade in New York and Boston, between July, 1880, and January, 1881, is estimated at between $5,000,000 and $7,000,000.

—1881—

At the commencement of 1881 there was a stock at Atlantic coast ports of 19,353 tons, and when the holdings are compared with the stock held at the beginning of 1880, it will be noted that on January 1, 1881, there were 95,429 bags of Brazil held at New York, against 223,249 bags on the 1st of January, 1880, a difference of 127,820 bags; while of Java and Singapore there were 169,639 mats, or 133,363 mats more than were held at the beginning of 1880. When prices are compared, it will be seen that during 1880 there was a greater decline in the price of mild coffee than in that of Brazil sorts, and this led to an increased demand for Central American, Mexican, and Venezuela, as well as low grade East India coffee, of which there was an unusually large stock—the largest, in fact, that this market ever carried of grades termed low grade Java. The comparative cost of the different sorts on the 1st of January, 1880 and 1881, and on the 1st of May in each of the two years, is shown by the following table:

	Jan. 1, 1880.	Jan. 1, 1881.	Decline.	May 1, 1880.	May 1, 1881.	Decline.
Java, Gov't bags	23 @ 24	14½ @ 16	8½ @ 8	21 @ 22	14½ @ 16	7½ @ 6
Java, Grass mats	24 @ 25½	15 @ 20	9 @ 5½	23 @ 24	14½ @ 20	8½ @ 4
Singapore......	17 @ 20	14 @ 15	3 @ 5	14 @ 16	12 @ 14	2 @ 2
Ceylon.........	16 @ 19	11 @ 13	5 @ 6	15 @ 17	11 @ 13	4 @ 4
Maracaibo......	14 @ 19	11 @ 13	3 @ 6	13 @ 17	10 @ 13	3 @ 4
Laguayra.......	14 @ 16½	11 @ 13	3 @ 3½	13¼ @ 14⅝	11 @ 14	2¼ @ ⅝
Jamaica........	14 @ 16	10 @ 12	4 @ 4	13 @ 16	10 @ 12½	3 @ 3½
Costa Rica.....	15½ @ 18	12 @ 16	3½ @ 2	13 @ 18	12 @ 15	1 @ 3
St. Domingo....	13 @ 15	10 @ 11	3 @ 4	12 @ 14	9½ @ 11	2½ @ 3
Mexican	15½ @ 17½	12 @ 13	3½ @ 4½	14 @ 16	12 @ 13	2 @ 3
Rio—fair.......	15½	13	2½	14½ @ 14⅝	11¼ @ 11½	3¼
Rio—prime......	16½	14	2½	15½ @ 15⅝	12¼ @ 12½	3¼

In the European markets prices show the same marked disparity, supplies accumulating in spite of low prices. In London the comparative prices on May 1st were as follows:

London Coffee Quotations.	Floating Cargoes.		Ex Quay.		
	1880.	1881.		1880.	1881.
	s. d. s. d.	s. d. s. d.		s. d. s. d.	s. d. s. d.
Rio—Low superior................	65 0 @ 66 0	55 0 @ 56 0	2/6 @ 3/ more obtainable if landed.	67 0 @ 67 6	58 0 @ 59 0
Rio good first.	63 6 @ 64 6	53 0 @ 54 0		65 6 @ 66 6	55 0 @ 56 0
Channel good first.	61 6 @ 62 6	50 0 @ 51 0		64 0 @ 64 6	52 0 @ 54 0
Good Channel....................	59 6 @ 60 6	46 0 @ 48 0		61 6 @ 63 0	46 0 @ 48 0
Fair Channel....................	57 6 @ 58 6	43 0 @ 44 0		57 6 @ 59 6	42 0 @ 45 0
Low fair Channel................	55 0 @ 56 6	37 0 @ 40 0		54 0 @ 56 0	38 0 @ 39 0
Low and irregular...............	52 0 @ 53 0	35 0 @ 36 0		50 0 @ 52 0	36 0 @ 36 6
Santos—Good average.............	61 6 @ 63 6	50 0 @ 51 0		61 0 @ 62 6	51 0 @ 52 0
Fair average....................	60 0 @ 61 0	48 0 @ 49 0		59 6 @ 60 6	50 0 @ 51 0
Washed Brazil—Good to fine.......	——	——	LANDED.	84 0 @ 86 0	67 0 @ 70 0
Medium colory...................	——	——		75 0 @ 80 0	61 0 @ 63 0
Grayish	——	——		70 0 @ 73 0	57 0 @ 60 0
Bahia—Ordinary mixed (S)........	46 0 @ 47 0	36 0 @ 37 0		47 0 @ 49 0	34 0 @ 36 0
Fair ditto......................	48 0 @ 49 0	40 0 @ 41 0		50 0 @ 51 0	41 0 @ 43 0
Good greenish...................	53 0 @ 55 0	42 0 @ 44 0		55 0 @ 59 0	46 0 @ 48 0
Ceylon—Plantation low mid.......	——	——		89 0 @ 89 6	79 0 @ 81 0
Good ordinary...................	——	——		63 0 @ 64 0	55 0 @ 57 0
Holland—Java, good ordin'y. cents.	39⅓	36		——	——
New York—good cargoes....cents.	15¼	12¼		——	——
Hamburg—real ordinary.....pfeng.	62	47		——	——

The consumption has, however, very naturally increased under the stimulus of low prices. The average monthly consumption for the first four months of the years 1879, 1880, and 1881, was 13,805 tons for the Atlantic coast, against an average per month for the first four months of 1881, of 15,217 tons, an increase over the corresponding time in 1880 of 2,821 tons. At London an increase was reported of 344 tons for the first four months of 1881 over the same time 1880. Still it is apparent that the supply of coffee is increasing in a faster ratio than consumption, and this is not likely to be disturbed for some years unless some great calamity overtakes the crop, while if a disaster should come to some one of the great consuming countries similar to the war that occurred in this country from 1861 to 1865, prices would reach an unusually low level.

We here present the range of prices for the year 1880, as taken from the report of the Chamber of Commerce, which shows at a glance the great decline that occurred between January and December. The average prices for the month and for the year were per 100 pounds.

Brazil—Fair to Prime Cargoes.

1880.	1st.	10th.	20th.	Average for the month.		
				1880.	1879.	1878.
January	15½ @ 16¾	15¾ @ 17	15½ @ 16½	$16.16⅜	$15.42	$17.87
February	14¾ @ 15¾	14¾ @ 15¾	15½ @ 16½	15.50	14.79⅕	17.08
March	15½ @ 16½	15 @ 16¼	14¾ @ 15¾	15.62½	14.16⅗	16.54
April	14¾ @ 16	14½ @ 15¾	14 @ 15	15.00	14.20⅘	16.37
May	14¾ @ 15¾	14½ @ 15½	14½ @ 15½	15.08⅓	13.58⅕	17.00
June	14¼ @ 15½	14½ @ 15½	14¾ @ 15¾	15.04	13.75	16.20
July	15 @ 16	15 @ 16	14¾ @ 15¾	15.50	14.00	16.12
August	15 @ 16	15¼ @ 16¼	15¾ @ 16¾	15.83	14.04	16.70
September	15¾ @ 17	16 @ 17	15 @ 16¼	16.16⅜	14.70	17.16
October	14½ @ 16	13¼ @ 14½	13¾ @ 13¾	14.46	16.33	16.50
November	13¾ @ 15	13½ @ 14½	13¼ @ 14¼	13.96	16.91	15.54
December	13 @ 14	11¾ @ 13	13 @ 14	13.12	16.37½	15.04
Average for the year				$15.12	$14.85½	$16.51

Java—(Padang.)

1880.	1st.	10th.	20th.	Average for the month.		
				1880.	1879.	1878.
January	23¾ @ 22	23¾ @ 24	23¾ @ 24	$23.87½	$23.25	$22.16
February	23¾ @ 22	23¾ @ 24	23 @ 24	23.75	24.25	21.50
March	23 @ 23	23 @ 24	23 @ 24	23.50	23.91⅔	21.16
April	22 @ 22	22 @ 23	22 @ 23	22.50	24.25	21.00
May	22 @ 22	21 @ 22	20 @ 22	21.66⅔	24.25	21.25
June	20 @ 22	20 @ 22	19½ @ 21	20.75	24.25	21.66
July	19½ @ 22	19½ @ 21	21 @ 22	20.66⅔	24.25	22.50
August	21 @ 22	21 @ 23	21 @ 23	21.83⅓	24.00	24.00
September	21 @ 22	21 @ 23	21 @ 23	22.00	23.58	24.37
October	21 @ 22	21 @ 23	29 @ 23	21.66⅔	24.50	23.58
November	20 @ 22	20 @ 22	28 @ 20	20.33⅓	24.79	23.37
December	18 @ 22	18 @ 20	26 @ 18	18.33⅓	24.37½	23.25
Average for the year				$22.62 7/12	$24.14	$22.48

Maracaibo and Laguayra.

1880.	1st.	10th.	20th.	Average for the month.		
				1880.	1879.	1878.
January	13½ @ 16½	14 @ 16½	14½ @ 17	$15.33⅓	$15.17	$17.25
February	14½ @ 17	14½ @ 17	15 @ 18¼	16.04	15.58⅓	16.33
March	15 @ 18¼	15 @ 18¼	15 @ 18¼	16.62½	14.66⅔	15.75
April	15 @ 18¼	15 @ 18¼	15 @ 18¼	16.62½	14.00	15.50
May	14 @ 17	14 @ 17	14 @ 17	15.00	14.00	15.33
June	14 @ 17	12¾ @ 16	12¾ @ 16	14.75	13.91	15.50
July	13½ @ 16¼	13½ @ 16¼	14 @ 16¼	14.95⅚	13.75	15.33
August	14 @ 17	14 @ 17	14½ @ 17¼	15.62½	13.75	14.91
September	14½ @ 17¼	14½ @ 17¼	14½ @ 17¼	15 87½	13.75	15.25
October	13 @ 17	14 @ 17	13¼ @ 15	15.04	15.08	15.50
November	13¼ @ 15	13¼ @ 15	13 @ 14½	14.00	16.58	14.75
December	12¼ @ 13½	11⅝ @ 13	11¼ @ 13	12.45⅚	16.21	14.83
Average for the year				$15.52 5/12	$14.70	$15.52

The consumption of the country, according to Moring's tables, was 10,847 tons below that of 1879, but 28,277 tons above the average for the ten years 1871–80, and 5,294 tons above the average for the three years 1878–80, thus showing that the demand was comparatively steady.

The deliveries of Rio and Santos coffee in the United States from January 1st to December 31st, during the years 1878, 1879, 1880 and 1881 to August 1st, were as follows:

Deliveries of Rio and Santos Coffee in the United States from January 1st to December 31st.

	1881. Bags.	1880. Bags.	1879. Bags.	1878. Bags.
January	195,879	201,901	172,119	146,818
February	181,604	198,157	199,557	166,516
March	230,565	176,193	205,629	164,404
April	161,859	167,292	202,186	122,513
May	189,665	110,316	156,242	182,347
June	206,227	142,178	157,441	115,504
July	137,582	160,287	185,981	137,389
August	——	189,675	177,757	149,124
September	——	135.495	226,053	136,604
October	——	248,773	236,989	188,883
November	——	233,046	166,836	186,217
December	——	240,420	158,212	211,838
Total	1,303,421	2,203,733	2,243,002	1,908,157

The consumption on the Pacific Coast was about 6,100 tons, against 4,400 tons in 1879, and 5,400 tons in 1878. The receipts on that coast in 1880 from Central America reached 137,568 bags, or 18,789,973 pounds, against 11,891,445 pounds in 1879, and 13,918,223 pounds in 1878. The California dealers report an increasing demand from States east of the Mississippi, which gain is largely due to an increase of population, to improved means of transportation, and to the good quality of the coffee received from Salvador and Guatemala, and these factors are likely to give the California market greater prominence than it has hitherto enjoyed.

The following statement shows in detail the import into San Francisco:

	Imports for Years			
	1880. Pounds.	1879. Pounds.	1878. Pounds.	1877. Pounds.
Rio, Mocha, etc	524,270	1,389,249	141,702	221,170
Hawaiian	77,338	40,212	114,282	141,265
Costa Rica	5,059,748	3,102,611	4,111,914	4,328,171
Guatemala	8,171,510	5,731,108	6,717,319	6,766,450
Salvador	4,683,282	2,923,782	3,046,574	3,330,980
Nicaragua.........	1,039,286	150,999	42,416	95,139
Mexico	72,140	24.427	20,856	79,257
Java...............	583,693	268,033	1,058,641	445,400
Tahitian	2,691	47,626	——	——
Manila	175,417	201,776	264,779	603,074
Singapore.........	95,887	2,247	3,213	296,800
Hongkong.........	——	7,392	——	——
Ceylon............	504,000	——	——	51,121
Chile	10,484	——	——	——
Panama...........	5,695	——	——	——
Guayaquil.........	9,882	——	——	——
Amapala..........	10,238	——	——	——
Unspecified	91,519	——	——	——
Total	21,123,366	13,889,462	15,621,698	16,358,827

These figures differ slightly from those contained in other statements, and we therefore present another table, showing the total receipts, stock, exports, and consumption for five years, 1876 to 1880:

	1880. Pounds.	1879. Pounds.	1878. Pounds.	1877. Pounds.	1876. Pounds.
Total..............................	20,444,961	12,229,659	15,398,252	16,179,220	10,455,728
Stock January 1st................	1,229,200	2,034,504	1,802,115	500,000	1,594,200
Total supply......................	21,674,161	14,264,163	7,200,367	16,679,220	12,049,928
Deduct exports and shipments overland	4,447,230	3,171,780	2,969,310	3,673,840	485,046
	17,226,951	11,092,383	14,231,057	13,005.380	11,564,882
Deduct stock December 31st	3,532,266	1,229,200	2,034,504	1,802,115	1,200,000
Consumption	13,694,686	9,863,183	12,196,553	11,203,265	10,364,882

The consumption on the west coast is likely to increase rapidly, as the Western territories are filling up with immigrants, and the facilities for distributing merchandise are extending every year. Now that the Southern Pacific Road is open, New Orleans may prove a formidable competitor for the trade of the South-West and the Pacific Coast. The average price of Guatemala coffee in San Francisco for eleven years, as compared with the yearly average price for fair to prime Brazil cargoes in New York, was as follows:

Year.	Average price Guatemala for year per 100 lbs.	Yearly average price for fair to prime Brazil cargoes in New York.	Year.	Average price Guatemala for year per 100 lbs.	Yearly average price for fair to prime Brazil cargoes in New York.
1870..........	$19.12½	$16.33	1876	$20.52	$17.97
1871..........	17.31	15.91	1877	19.88½	19.72
1872..........	18.88½	18.42	1878	17.41½	16.51
1873..........	19.83	19.99	1879	16.71	14.85½
1874..........	22.65½	21.08	1880	15.18	15.12½
1875..........	20.34	19.01			

In examining the following table, showing the highest and lowest price of fair to prime Rio coffee in New York from 1849 to 1880, it will be noted that since 1850 there has been a steady appreciation in price, and that the market has always been subject to wide fluctuations.

The average yearly price of fair to prime Rio coffee in New York for thirty years, as reported to the New York Chamber of Commerce, was as below:

Year.	Per 100 lbs.	Year.	Per 100 lbs.	Year.	Per 100 lbs.
1850..........	$10.79	1861	$14.01	1871	$15.91
1851..........	9.41	1862	23.01	1872	18.42
1852..........	8.84	1863	31.18	1873	19.99
1853..........	9.77	1864	42.49	1874	21.08
1854..........	10.41	1865	20.65	1875	19.01
1855..........	10.41	1866	18.66	1876	17.97
1856..........	11.03½	1867	17.24	1877	19.72
1857..........	11.04	1868	15.73	1878	16.51
1858..........	10.96	1869	15.82	1879	14.85½
1859..........	11.61	1870	16.33	1880	15.12
1860..........	13.60				

From 1861 to June, 1865, quotations are in currency; after the latter date in gold.

Coffee was taken from the free list August 6, 1861, and a duty imposed of 4 cents per pound; increased December 25, 1861, to 5 cents per pound; reduced January 1, 1871, from 5 to 3 cents per pound, and abolished July 1, 1872.

The following table exhibits the lowest and highest price of Padang Java yearly from 1858 to 1880, and the average price for each year. Prior to 1865 quotations are in currency, from that date in gold; the Appendix furnishes a table showing the fluctuations in gold during the existence of a premium on the same:

Year.	Lowest.	Highest.	Average for year.	Year.	Lowest.	Highest.	Average for year.
	Cents.	Cents.	Cents.		Cents.	Cents.	Cents.
1858	13½	20	16.13	1870	19	23	21.19
1859	13¾	16	14.79	1871	17½	26½	21.29
1860	14¼	18½	16.51	1872	18½	25	21.30
1861	15½	25	18.38	1873	19	34	23.63
1862	24½	35	27.50	1874	22	35	26.68
1863	33	41	37.04	1875	24	30	26.71
1864	40	60	49.10	1876	18	26	21.57
1865	24	51	25.82	1877	22	25½	23.82
1866	24	28½	26.08	1878	20½	25	22.48
1867	24	27	24.75	1879	23¼	24¾	24.14
1868	21	27	23.41	1880	18	24	22.62
1869	21	25	23.02				

Is the present valuation of coffee to be maintained, or are we to look forward again to an era of low prices?

To this interesting question very different answers are returned. Some predict that the range of low prices of former years has passed away forever, while others will only see in the rise of coffee since 1871 a gigantic manipulation of the staple. The advocates of the first-mentioned theory argue that in past years the consumption of coffee has increased in a greater ratio than the productive area under cultivation; that in the most important coffee-producing country—Brazil—the supply of labor has become insufficient; and that, besides, the Brazilian planters, enriched by their profits, can now afford to hold off from an unfavorable market and command their own terms. It is retorted from the opposite camp that general production has already received a powerful development from the high prices of the last five or six years—a development visible in the increased yield of the West Indies, and of Central and South America; and that with regard to Brazil, the newly-acquired wealth of the planting class must necessarily tend to counteract the scarcity of labor by facilitating the introduction of improved machinery in its stead. If it was profitable, they say, to raise coffee years ago, when it could be laid down here at 8 to 12 cents per pound, what must it be now at 12 to 16 cents per pound?

In view of these conflicting opinions, it is well to keep in mind some peculiarities of coffee-culture and of the staple itself, which may sometimes mislead calculation or temporarily suspend logical results. It takes, as we have seen, from three to four years for new coffee plantations to come into bearing; hence the necessity for a considerable outlay of capital to open a plantation; hence, also, ample working room for speculative operations to move in, before the field can possibly respond to the market. And speculation finds still further assistance in the nature of the article, which, not deteriorating, but improving with age, constitutes an excellent security on which to borrow money.* There is, therefore, no doubt that a "ring," backed by sufficient capital, could for a long time keep up an artificial situation; and, in the present instance, it cannot be denied that the embarrassing economical problems resulting from the want of hands in the coffee-producing countries of the western world, the unprogressive condition of Java's industry for many years, leaf-disease in Ceylon, and the increasing aggregate consumption indicate a plausible foundation for at least a temporary advance. But, on the other hand, it must not be forgotten that the area for coffee culture in the world is practically unlimited, and that new centres of immense production have already sprung up in regions overflowing with cheap labor, while in spite of the supposed disadvantages of the Brazilian planter the average yearly export from Rio de Janeiro for the seven years from 1874 to 1880 reached 229,149 tons, an unprecedented figure.

I now pause to consider the consumptive requirements of the world, my figures, as far as possible, being based on actual returns in the United States, England, France, and Germany, while for other countries I have availed myself of the latest accessible statistical tables, using quite freely as a basis those collated by Dr. Van Den Berg (Historical and Statistical Notes, Java, 1880).

---

* It is true that the lessons of 1880, and the downfall of the leading spirits in the great coffee syndicate are likely to render such operations less liable to influence the market in future. If, however, serious disaster should reduce the Brazil crop in as great a proportion as the 1880–81 Java crop has been cut down, the fact alone would generate new speculative ventures.

CHAPTER XXIV.

COFFEE-CONSUMPTION OF THE WORLD.

The United States consumes nearly one-third of the exports of coffee from all producing countries, having absorbed from a total production of about 525,000 tons, an average of 156,482 tons per annum for the last five years, of which about seventy-three per cent. was the product of Brazil. There seems to be a steady increase in the quantity taken, it having risen from an average of 79,848 tons annually from 1857 to 1861, to 156,482 tons annually from 1876 to 1880. The tables of H. E. Moring & Co. make the consumption on the Atlantic coast for 1880, 168,678 tons, and the average for the five years from 1876 to 1881, 151,900 tons. The Pacific coast consumption averaged for the same period 5,080 tons, making a total for the United States of 156,980 tons, or 498 tons more than the net imports as reported by the United States Bureau of Statistics. One notable feature is the disposition among consumers in favor of mild coffee; and with the opening of direct railway communication with our sister republic of Mexico, a greater disparity than now exists between the imports of coffee from Brazil and those from other countries may be anticipated. In order to study correctly the progress of coffee consumption in the United States, it will be necessary to examine the subject somewhat in detail.

We first present the quantities and values of tea and coffee imported into and exported from the United States, together with the net imports and the estimated imports per capita of population, from 1859 to 1880 inclusive. The net imports represent the approximate consumption, those of tea being placed in comparison with coffee in order to show the relative consumption of two articles the active principle of which is identical in each. It is estimated that one pound of tea will go as far in supplying a family, as four pounds of coffee.

When tea and coffee were subject to duty, the imports for consumption, *i.e.*, the imports on which duties were paid each year, represented approximately the actual consumption of these articles; but, since the duty has been removed, all imports of tea and coffee are entered for immediate consumption on their arrival from a foreign country, and go immediately into the hands of the importer, the entry for consumption being merely a technical name of the means by which the goods are delivered directly from the custody of the government to that of the importer.

Of the tea and coffee entered for consumption on arrival a considerable amount is afterward exported.

All the exports shown in the table are of foreign tea and coffee previously imported, and, therefore, the imports less the exports (or the net imports) form the nearest approximation which can be given to the consumption of these articles in the United States.

It is interesting to note, in studying the table upon the next page, the fluctuations in the per capita consumption of tea and coffee. Thus we find that the minimum distribution of tea and coffee was in 1863–65, that of tea falling to one-half pound per capita, or just one-third of the quantity used in 1881. We also find that the quantity of coffee used per head was about the same in 1881 as in 1859. Thus, it would appear that it took from the year 1863, when the consumption was only 2.2 pounds per head, until 1880, for the country to reach the same ratio of distribution as existed prior to the war. From 1873 to 1879 all the business industries of the country were depressed, labor was largely unemployed and immigration light, and very naturally a heavy reduction in the use of tea and coffee was anticipated.

The decline, however, was small, that of tea varying from one-quarter to one-half pound per capita, and coffee fluctuating between 6.2 pounds and 7.3 pounds, a fact the more remarkable, as wages were low and the financial condition of the country poor.

Quantities and Values of Tea and Coffee Imported into and Exported from, and Net Imports into, the United States, and the Estimated Imports per Capita of Population, from 1859 *to* 1881, *inclusive.*

Year ended June 30th.	Tea.						
	Imports.		Exports.		Net Imports.		Per Capita of Population.
	Lbs.	Dollars.	Lbs.	Dollars.	Lbs.	Dollars.	Lbs.
1859	29,268,757	7,388,741	6,149,468	2,461,563	23,119,289	4,927,178	0.76
1860	31,696,657	8,915,327	5,369,729	1,085,203	26,236,928	6,930,124	0.84
1861	26,117,956	6,977,283	5,101,289	1,556,630	21,016,657	5,420,653	0.66
1862	24,868,421	6,545,664	1,531,644	636,906	23,336,777	5,906,758	0.71
1863	29,761,037	8,013,772	2,739,997	1,032,723	27,021,040	6,981,049	0.80
1864	37,229,176	10,649,880	1,378,154	671,956	35,851,022	9,977,924	1.04
1865	19,568,318	4,956,730	2,719,129	1,912,797	16,849,189	3,043,933	0.49
1866	42,992,736	11,124,231	1,481,290	612,095	41,511,446	10,610,296	1.17
1867	39,892,658	12,415,087	513,084	199,400	39,379,574	12,215,687	1.09
1868	37,843,612	11,111,560	2,217,749	711,751	35,625,863	10,399,809	0.97
1869	43,754,354	13,687,750	2,944,329	947,461	40,810,025	12,740,289	1.08
1870	47,408,481	13,863,273	4,868,010	1,374,056	42,540,471	12,489,217	1.10
1871	61,364,919	17,254,617	6,469,974	1,929,830	44,894,945	15,324,787	1.26
1872	63,811,003	22,943,575	4,441,401	1,260,408	59,369,602	21,684,167	1.46
1873	64,815,136	24,466,170	1,060,196	454,641	63,754,940	24,011,679	1.53
1874	55,811,605	21,112,234	1,670,252	871,956	54,141,353	20,240,278	1.26
1875	64,856,899	22,673,703	1,565,595	714,185	63,291,304	21,959,518	1.44
1876	62,887,153	19,524,165	1,726,908	874,574	61,160,245	18,649,592	1.35
1877	58,347,112	18,181,467	1,508,937	676,566	56,838,175	15,504,901	1.22
1878	65,366,704	15,660,188	2,243,515	737,544	63,123,189	14,922,624	1.32
1879	60,194,673	14,577,518	1,303,138	362,092	58,891,535	14,215,526	1.11
1880	72,162,936	19,782,631	2,258,167	799,263	69,894,769	18,983,368	1.39
1881	81,843,988	21,014,818	2,713,139	779,395	79,130,849	20,235,418	1.58

Year ended June 30th.	Coffee.						
	Imports.		Exports.		Net Imports.		Per Capita of Population.
	Lbs.	Dollars.	Lbs.	Dollars.	Lbs.	Dollars.	Lbs.
1859	264,496,534	25,086,029	17,615,566	1,823,760	246,820,948	23,262,279	8.1
1860	202,144,733	21,883,797	20,095,206	2,268,691	182,049,527	19,615,106	5.8
1861	184,499,655	20,668,297	6,589,203	777,485	177,910,452	19,790,812	5.5
1862	122,799,311	14,192,195	9,785,633	1,382,070	113,013,678	12,810,125	3.4
1863	80,461,614	10,396,860	5,652,846	1,081,462	74,808,768	9,314,398	2.2
1864	131,022,782	16,221,586	3,178,296	871,260	127,844,486	15,350,326	3.7
1865	106,463,062	11,241,706	22,147,017	5,716,053	84,316,045	5,525,653	2.4
1866	181,413,192	20,531,784	5,618,309	901,857	175,794,883	19,629,927	5.0
1867	187,236,580	20,696,259	5,964,592	881,128	181,271,988	19,815,131	5.0
1868	248,983,900	25,288,451	7,900,980	845,705	241,082,920	24,442,746	6.5
1869	254,160,993	24,531,743	10,765,395	1,020,231	243,395,598	23,511,512	6.5
1870	235,256,574	24,234,879	4,083,000	410,836	231,173,574	23,824,043	6.0
1871	317,992,048	30,992,869	5,257,012	498,560	312,735,036	30,494,309	7.9
1872	298,805,946	37,942,225	3,467,462	408,574	295,388,484	37,533,651	7.3
1873	293,297,271	44,109,671	6,851,027	1,143,076	286,446,244	42,966,595	6.9
1874	285,171,512	55,048,967	3,285,636	705,860	281,885,876	54,343,107	6.6
1875	317,970,665	50,591,488	6,834,014	1,280,154	311,136,651	49,311,334	7.1
1876	339,789,246	56,788,997	8,884,457	1,625,932	330,904,789	55,163,065	7.3
1877	331,639,723	53,634,991	9,890,715	1,567,058	321,749,008	52,067,933	6.9
1878	309,862,540	51,914,605	12,821,426	2,086,366	297,061,114	49,828,239	6.2
1879	377,848,473	47,356,819	15,092,846	2,311,068	362,755,627	45,045,251	7.3
1880	446,850,727	60,360,769	6,721,889	944,573	440,128,838	59,416,196	8.8
1881	455,169,534	56,775,391	31,918,062	4,396,558	423,276,472	52,379,833	8.4

Note.—The population is estimated for years other than census years, 1860, 1870, and 1880.

As far back as 1856–57 the consumption per capita was larger than the average for the past five years, which, according to Moring's tables, was 7.09 pounds per head. The last-named authority places the consumption at the figures given below:

Year.	Population.	Tons.	Per Capita.
1876	46,000,000	134,109	6.53
1877	47,000,000	135,238	6.45
1878	48,000,000	141,949	6.62
1879	49,000,000	179,525	8.21
1880	50,000,000	168,678	7.56
Average 5 years	48,000,000	151,900	7.09

The quantities of tea and coffee taken for consumption prior to 1859 were as follows:

Year ended—	Tea. Retained for Home Consumption.		Tea. Consumption per Capita of Population.	Coffee. Retained for Home Consumption.		Coffee. Consumption per Capita of Population.
	Pounds.	Dollars.	Pounds.	Pounds.	Dollars.	Pounds.
September 30—						
1830	6,878,091	1,532,211	0.53	38,363,687	3,180,479	3.0
1840	16,883,099	4,007,144	0.99	86,297,761	7,615,824	5.05
June 30—						
1850	28,199,591	3,982,054	1.22	129,791,466	9,918,472	5.55
1851	13,504,774	3,452,496	0.57	148,992,505	12,489,671	6.2
1852	25,587,668	5,927,143	1.03	180,712,687	13,372,124	7.3
1853	19,291,884	7,024,526	0.75	185,999,243	14,380,383	7.3
1854	19,236,113	4,933,553	0.73	150,246,403	13,377,972	5.7
1855	19,763,593	4,937,610	0.72	175,150,440	15,486,423	6.4
1856	18,181,470	5,250,608	0.64	223,638,479	20,321,142	7.9
1857	16,500,285	4,344,963	0.57	216,655,977	19,809,854	7.5
1858	28,766,577	5,877,387	0.97	174,497,161	16,779,870	5.9

The Annual Reports of the New York Chamber of Commerce make the consumption of the Atlantic coast, and ports on the Gulf of Mexico, for the five years 1876 to 1880, inclusive, as follows:

Consumption of the Ports.

		1880. Tons.	1879. Tons.	1878. Tons.	1877. Tons.	1876. Tons.
Taken from	New York	122,698	127,336	94,695	86,455	83,953
"	New Orleans	15,291	12,996	11,014	12,326	10,750
"	Baltimore	26,287	30,681	28,899	28,099	31,105
"	Philadelphia	176	704	1,172	1,965	798
"	Boston	429	478	345	279	244
"	Other ports	4,535	7,046	6,247	6,782	8,208
Total		169,416	179,241	142,372	135,906	135,058

The above statement shows an average annual consumption for the past five years of 151,808 tons on the Atlantic coast, which, added to the figures for the Pacific coast, makes a total consumption in the United States of 156,888 tons, as against 156,980 tons, as given in H. E. Moring & Co.'s tables, and 156,482 tons, according to the Government returns.

The same authority reports the deliveries at New York (including coastwise receipts), from 1851 to 1880, inclusive, as follows:

Deliveries at New York (including Coastwise Receipts) for the past Thirty Years.

Year.	Tons.	Year.	Tons.	Year.	Tons.
1851	30,276	1861	46,339	1871	70,532
1852	32,833	1862	30,073	1872	69,713
1853	25,304	1863	28,842	1873	68,863
1854	29,842	1864	38,346	1874	82,801
1855	33,446	1865	48,754	1875	77,135
1856	36,903	1866	51,122	1876	84,087
1857	27,184	1867	59,078	1877	86,621
1858	43,819	1868	67,105	1878	94,741
1859	37,366	1869	67,289	1879	127,677
1860	29,859	1870	68,735	1880	122,995

Average per year, 1851–1860 .... 32,683 tons.
Average per year, 1861–1870 .... 50,568 "
Average per year, 1871–1880 .... 88,516½ "
Average per year, 1876–1880 .... 103,224 "

A study of the preceding tables, especially in reference to the per capita consumption, bears out the rule that the extent to which an article of diet, like coffee, is used depends largely upon its cheapness. It may also be safe to assume that the shrinking and retrenchment process that occurred in our community between the years 1873 and 1879 tended to diminish consumption. Our laboring population was forced to economize and renounce some of its comforts, and, had it not been for the long period of depression that made itself felt with severity from 1876 to 1879, the growth in consumption would probably have been very much larger than is shown by the record.

During the first four months of 1881, coffee declined two to six cents per pound, and the consumption for that period shows a gain over the same time in 1880 of 11,284 tons, this fact bearing out the above statement.

A period of high prices, it is evident, carries within itself a double influence (increased production and decreased consumption) which must limit its extent; and this must hold true so long as the productive capacity of the globe, with regard to coffee, is not reached.

On the whole, to one glancing collectively over the complicated pros and cons of the question, the outlook (whatever may have been the statistical position in the recent past) seems to point to no inadequacy of the general production, while, at the same time, altered circumstances may prevent in our main country of supply a return to rates existing under a different system of labor and a different distribution of wealth.

It will be interesting to follow, in the next few years, the phases of a problem which affects almost every breakfast-table in the land. A glance at the consuming power of Europe will enable us to better understand the relation of the world's supply of coffee to its demand.

The total distribution of coffee in Europe, taking the figures for the past three years, will average 383,521 tons annually.

In detail the position of coffee in the leading depots of Europe on December 31st, for the last three years, was reported by Messrs James Cook & Co., of London, as follows:

	Imports.			Stocks, December 31st.		
	1880.	1879.	1878.	1880.	1879.	1878.
	Tons.	Tons.	Tons.	Tons.	Tons.	Tons.
Holland	81,210	67,790	67,630	29,340	22,620	24,160
Antwerp	45,500	44,740	36,070	8,700	3,300	4,200
Hamburg	87,750	84,100	79,750	13,000	7,500	11,000
France	86,000	100,287	87,416	42,000	37,420	34,321
Bremen	6,100	7,340	7,500	470	70	150
Trieste	11,200	12,810	13,260	3,550	4,300	1,840
Genoa	7,040	8,490	6,630	1,520	1,730	1,420
On Continent	324,800	325,557	298,256	98,580	76,940	77,091
Great Britain	77,797	80,870	63,670	19,497	15,285	15,405
Total	402,597	406,427	361,926	118,077	92,225	92,496

The supply and distribution of three years was as follows:

	1880.	1879.	1878.	Average for Three Years.
	Tons.	Tons.	Tons.	Tons.
Total stock January 1st	93,131	86,960	102,321	94,137
" imports to Dec. 31st	402,597	406,427	361,926	390,317
" supply for 12 months...	495,728	493,387	464,247	484,454
Deduct stock, Dec. 31st	118,077	92,225	92,496	100,933
Distribution in 12 months.....	377,651	401,162	371,751	383,521

The distribution in 1877 amounted to 340,053 tons; in 1876, to 378,958 tons, the average per year, for the five years 1876 to 1880, being 373,915 tons.

The kinds of coffee most in favor for consumption in England are East India, Plantation Ceylon, and Jamaica. Of Brazil, the consumption is small. In Great Britain there is a duty of 1½d. per pound on raw, and 2d. per pound on roasted coffee.

A brief mention of trade customs in England will be of interest in view of the intimate business relations between the United States and the United Kingdom. The terms of public sale (for in Great Britain coffee is sold almost entirely at auction) are one month's credit, with discount at the rate of five per cent. per annum allowed to the buyer if settlement is made before the month expires. A discount of one per cent. is allowed on all coffee, except Brazil, Guatemala, New Grenada, Laguayra, and

Honduras, which carry two and a half per cent. All sorts of coffee are sold in the London market, except French West India and Celebes. Hayti and Padang Java are seldom offered.

The bulk of the supply offered at the public sale comes from the East and West Indies, Ceylon, and Central America. Cargoes are purchased for any continental port, generally Hamburg, Antwerp, Havre, Trieste, or Marseilles, and occasionally for Bremen, Copenhagen, or Stockholm. The cargoes thus sold are nearly all Brazil coffee, though in some few instances they include shipments from Porto Rico, and still more rarely from Manila.

The following market report illustrates the manner of doing business in the London market, and illustrates the relative prices, per cwt., of the various kinds:

Auction—April, 1881.

Ceylon—1,460 casks, 940 barrels and bags:		
small	63s 0d	70s 0d
low middling to middling	81s 0d	86s 0d
good middling to good bold	88s 0d	98s 0d
good to fine bold	101s 0d	110s 0d
peaberry	100s 0d	107s 0d
East India—5,680 cases and bags:		
Mysore, medium to bold	115s 0d	125s 6d
small	90s 0d	95s 6d
Coorg, etc., gray	72s 0d	78s 0d
medium	78s 0d	85s 0d
good to bold	90s 0d	107s 0d
peaberry	98s 0d	106s 0d
Old Crop, small to bold	63s 0d	89s 0d
Guatemala—6,295 bags—part sold:		
good to fine ordinary foxy	68s 0d	60s 6d
grayish to fine ord. greenish	63s 0d	66s 0d
bold to good greenish	72s 0d	77s 0d
good to fine colory	85s 0d	92s 0d
Mocha—270 packages—part sold:		
short berry (mixed)	98s 0d	—
Jamaica—1,090 packages—small part sold:		
old palish (mixed)	46s 0d	47s 0d
Santos—1,580 bags—part sold:		
fair to good greenish	51s 0d	53s 0d
washed mottled pale	62s 0d	—
African—80 bags:		
fair reddish	47s 0d	—
Rio—340 bags—withdrawn.		
Washed Rio—690 bags—		
without reserve	67s 0d	68s 0d
Central American.. 850 bags.	chiefly bought in.	
Costa Rica .... 250 bags.		
New Granada...... 440 bags.		
Porto Rico....... 1,700 bags.		
Manila .... 100 bags.		
Java .... 120 bags.		

The following table shows the imports, consumption, and stocks of coffee in England on December 31st of each year from 1869 to 1880:

Year.	Imports.	Consumption.	Stocks, Dec. 31st.	Year.	Imports.	Consumption.	Stocks, Dec. 31st.
	Tons.	Tons.	Tons.		Tons.	Tons.	Tons.
1869	77,416	12,904	29,468	1875	79,487	14,307	17,696
1870	80,286	13,674	30,762	1876	68,082	14,685	9.058
1871	85,711	13.664	24,757	1877	80,414	14,413	18,596
1872	74.227	13,917	14,765	1878	63,484	14,656	15,395
1873	81,876	14,192	12,516	1879	80,469	15,238	15,285
1874	70,246	13,952	13,750	1880	77,797	14,540	19,497

The per capita consumption of coffee in the United Kingdom is very small, tea being the favorite beverage, the consumption of which in 1879 was 160,652,187 pounds, or 4.80 pounds per head; and in 1880, 158,576,334 pounds, or 4.66 pounds per head. The consumption of coffee between the years 1843 and 1880, inclusive, is given in the following table:

Consumption in United Kingdom, 1843–80, *inclusive.*

Year.	Pounds.	Per Head.	Year.	Pounds.	Per Head.
1843	29,979,404	1.10	1862	34,664,155	1.18
1844	31,352,382	1.14	1863	32,986,116	1.11
1845	34,293,190	1.23	1864	31,591,122	1.06
1846	36,754,554	1.30	1865	30,748,349	1.02
1847	37,441,373	1.33	1866	30,944,363	1.03
1848	37,077,546	1.37	1867	31,567,760	1.05
1849	34,399,374	1.24	1868	30,608,464	1.01
1850	31,166,358	1.14	1869	29,109,113	0.94
1851	32,504,545	1.18	1870	30,629,710	0.99
1852	34,978,432	1.27	1871	31,010,645	0.98
1853	36,983,122	1.34	1872	31,661,311	1.00
1854	37,350,924	1.34	1873	32,330,928	1.01
1855	35,764,564	1.28	1874	31,860,080	0.99
1856	34,995,944	1.24	1875	32,526,256	1.01
1857	34,367,484	1.21	1876	33,342,288	1.02
1858	35,338,111	1 24	1877	32,830,224	0.99
1859	34,492,947	1.20	1878	33,393,248	1.00
1860	35,674,881	1.23	1879	34,696,256	1.04
1861	35,375,675	1.21	1880	32,569,824	0.96

"If we examine closely the statistics of coffee-consumption in England," remarks Mr. Simmonds, "we find that in the first four years of the century it was only an ounce per head; in the five years ending 1809 it averaged three ounces. It then increased in the next quinquennial period to six ounces, at which proportion it remained steady till 1825–29, when it advanced to eleven ounces, increased in the next five years to fifteen ounces, averaged about a pound per head for the following ten years, and then kept steady at about a pound and a quarter till 1861, since which period it has been gradually declining contemporaneously with the increased consumption of tea, and notwithstanding a reduction of duty." In 1880 we find that the people of England were using nearly five pounds of tea to each pound of coffee consumed.

The causes of this movement of the two staples in opposite directions would certainly form an interesting subject of inquiry. Are we to see here the operation of that "British pride," which, in a French opinion already quoted, had so much to do with the first adoption of coffee in England, or that general law which prompts the metropolis to become a consumer of the products of its dependencies—a law exemplified in the case of Spain and Portugal, which to this day continue to use chocolate long after the colonies from which they drew the article have become independent states. But, if the trade of China is to all intents and purposes British trade, and the East generally is next to British, do not the British colonies of Ceylon and India produce coffee in increased quantities? If the higher price of coffee has not prevented the spread of its popularity on the continent—in France, for instance—can we look to that cause with regard to wealthy England, where habits of economy among the people prevail to a much more limited extent? Or, is it entirely a preference of taste, a special congeniality of tea to the British temperament—a peculiar adaptability to British diet—as some will have it?

Professor Lehman considered that the preference of the English for tea was due to the larger supply of plastic material afforded by their diet—a fact which rendered desirable the proportionately greater nervous stimulus which is caused by tea, while the populations of France and of Germany, being much lighter "feeders," found an important element in the retardation of the assimilative process by the influence of coffee.

The table below exhibits the imports, consumption, and stocks of coffee in France on December 31st, from 1869 to 1880:

Year.	Imports.	Consumption.	Stocks on Dec. 31st.	Year.	Imports.	Consumption.	Stocks on Dec. 31st.
	Tons.	Tons.	Tons.		Tons.	Tons.	Tons.
1869......	84,568	50,327	31,332	1875.....	91,209	48,013	25,068
1870......	67,378	72,665	2,935	1876.....	86,597	53,487	30,189
1871......	59,407	40,155	2,262	1877.....	74,178	47,810	29,735
1872......	41,464	16,708	10,682	1878.....	87,416	54,105	34,321
1873......	73,895	44,884	19,852	1879.....	100,327	56,825	38,924
1874......	64,838	38,706	15,311	1880.....	88,040	57,722	40,904

The new French tariff imposes the following rates of duty upon coffee, given in francs and centimes per 100 kilos:

	New tariff.	Old tariff.
Coffee berries and nibs	156.00	150.00 to 170.00
Coffee roasted and milled	208.00	

The average consumption from 1876 to 1880 was 53,990 tons (120,937,600 pounds), which, divided among a population of 37,405,000 persons, shows a use of 3.23 pounds per capita.

In Germany the use of coffee is very general. For the last five years the consumption averaged 101,655 tons per annum, which, with a population of 43,000,000, makes it 5.3 pounds per capita. The consumption from 1869 to 1880, inclusive, was as follows:

	Tons.		Tons.		Tons.
1869	81,368	1873	97,775	1877	95,779
1870	98,350	1874	90,033	1878	99,284
1871	86,400	1875	100,612	1879	112,594
1872	92,585	1876	106,398	1880	94,222

Coffee in Holland is entered free of duty, and the consumption is very large; it is difficult to obtain an accurate statement of the quantity used. The imports for the last five years averaged 5.3 pounds per capita. The following table gives the amount for each year, from 1869 to 1880, inclusive:

	Tons.		Tons.		Tons.
1869	59,160	1873	70,490	1877	84,240
1870	69,040	1874	63,900	1878	67,630
1871	80,630	1875	81,620	1879	67,790
1872	45,360	1876	55,950	1880	82,620

The people of Belgium, being fond of coffee, used from 1872–77 an average of 21,718 tons (48,649,000 pounds) per annum, which is equivalent to nine pounds per capita.

The enormous consumption in Holland is accounted for by the climate, by the want of good drinking-water, but, principally, by the great cheapness of coffee in that country. "At the present prices," said a Dutch writer in 1868, "coffee is in Holland the cheapest of all articles of food."

The nations of Northern Europe, it will be noticed, are heavy coffee-drinkers, with the exception of Russia, which is essentially a tea and spirit drinking nation.

The average annual import into the Netherlands from 1873 to 1877 was 101,567 tons; the export for the same period averaged 70,839 tons per annum, thus making the consumption 30,728 tons per annum, or 68,830,720 pounds, which, on a basis of population of 4,000,000, is equal to seventeen pounds per capita. Dr. Van Den Berg furnishes the following statement:

	Kilos.	Tons.
1863—1867.		
General import	81,494,000	80,038
" export	67,534,000	66,328
Probable consumption	13,960,000	13,710
1868—1872.		
General import	92,916,000	91,257
" export	74,689,000	73,355
Probable consumption	18,227,000	17,902
1873—1877.		
General import	103,416,000	101,569
" export	72,127,000	70,839
Probable consumption	31,289,000	30,730

The above statement shows a remarkable increase, the present consumption amounting to about eighteen pounds annually per capita, based on a population, from 1873 to 1877, of 3,850,000 persons.

In Austria the consumption, according to the returns from 1874 to 1878, was 36,587 tons (81,953,960 pounds) per annum, which, with a population of 37,000,000, gives a per capita use of 2.21 pounds.

Switzerland uses 8,200 tons per annum, which, divided among 2,750,000 inhabitants, gives to each 6.68 pounds.

Italy, from 1873 to 1877, consumed 12,635 tons (28,303,000 pounds), or equal to 1.05 pounds per capita, placing the population at 27,000,000.

In Spain, cocoa or chocolate is used in preference to coffee, of which a small quantity is imported, the amount varying from 2,250 to 3,150 tons per annum. Coffee pays customs duty, per kilogram, 2 reals vellon; municipal duty, per kilogram, 1.08 reals vellon; transitory duty, per kilogram, 1.08 reals vellon; total customs duty, per kilogram, 4.16 reals vellon. The duties on coffee amount to about 39 per cent. on cost. Portugal is a very small consumer, also Greece, the two countries not taking, as an extreme figure, over 2,500 tons per annum. The statistics relative to the other parts of Europe show that in Russia, Sweden, Norway, Asiatic and European Turkey, and Denmark, about 50,000 tons of coffee are used annually.

Bringing together the figures showing the consumption in the different parts of Europe and the United States, we have the extent of the present demand made by coffee-consuming countries upon the coffee-plantations of the world:

	Tons.
Average yearly consumption in the United States, 1876—1880	156,482
" " " United Kingdom, 1876—1880	14,896
" " in France, 1876—1880	53,990
" " in Zollverein (Germany), 1876—1880	101,655
" " in Belgium, 1872—1877	21,718
" " in Netherlands, 1873—1877	30,730
" " in Austria, 1873—1878	36,587
" " in Italy, 1872—1877	12,635
" " in Switzerland, 1873—1878	8,150
" " in Spain and Portugal, estimated	3,000
" " in other countries in Europe, partly estimated	52,500
Average annual consumption, Europe and North America	492,343

The quantity of coffee consumed per annum in Europe, according to the above table, is 335,861 tons, or 38,054 tons less than the distribution as given in the trade circular of Messrs. James Cook & Co., of London. An accurate estimate of the quantity consumed in Europe and North America cannot be made, owing to the lack of official statistics in some countries, to the unknown quantity held as stock beyond first hands, to the want of reliable figures showing re-exports from importing countries, and to the imperfection of existing data; yet it can be closely approximated, and we feel safe in making the statement that 500,000 to 510,000 tons is a full estimate for present requirements in this country and in Europe.

The compilation of Dr. Van Den Berg makes the total consumption of Europe and the United States 479,000,000 kilos, or 493,482 tons. The rest of the world dependent upon the coffee-exporting countries for a supply does not require annually more than 12,000 tons, so that we can safely say that a supply of 510,000 tons will be ample to meet the wants of the coffee-consuming countries of the world. Brazil has furnished for the past three years an average of 241,765 tons; Java, 89,797 tons; Ceylon, 43,022 tons; India, 16,077 tons; the West Indies, 40,000 tons; Central America, 50,000 tons; Venezuela and New Grenada, 35,000 tons; Mexico, 5,000 tons; Arabia, 4,000 tons. Thus, leaving all other minor producing points out of our calculation—which will balance any over-estimate for Central America—we have from the countries named above a supply of 524,661 tons. From this showing it appears that supply is fully abreast of demand, despite leaf-disease in Ceylon, while the excess of stocks held at the beginning of 1881 will quite balance the short Java crop of 1880–81.

To what extent new plantations that are to come into bearing in South America, Mexico, and Central America, will add to the supply, is a problem that only time can enable us to solve. There is everything in the situation to warrant a range of prices much lower than those ruling from 1862 to 1879, the more so as there is little chance of speculative rings being formed, for Europe is not given to such operations, and American coffee-merchants have during the past year been taught a lesson that will not soon be forgotten.

CHAPTER XXV.

THE KING OF THE COFFEE TRADE.

FIVE-AND-FORTY years ago, or thereabouts, a bright, ambitious youth left his home in Rhode Island and came to New York, bringing with him a first-class reputation as an accountant. In fact, his business tact and ability were of so high an order that they soon commanded attention. He made a connection, in 1836, with one of the largest and most respectable firms on the east side of the city, engaged in the grocery business.

This young man possessed in an eminent degree the faculty which marks most men of note—that of keeping his own counsels. Although possessing great confidence in his own abilities, he was modest and unobtrusive in manner, and pursued his ambitions in a resolute but quiet way, which, for the time being, attracted but little attention.

There is nothing special to record regarding the next fifteen years of his life, other than to say that his social position was all that could be desired, and his progress and reputation as a merchant rapid for those days. In 1851 he was admitted a junior partner in the proud firm he had so long and faithfully served—a firm standing at the very head of the coffee trade. The senior member of the firm was one of those merchant-princes of whom New York was, and is still, justly proud. In financial as well as trade circles the name of this man was a tower of strength, while socially he occupied a first place. To be associated with such a man as a partner was no small honor, and our Rhode Island youth estimated the privilege for all that it was worth, and undoubtedly looked forward to the day when the senior should retire and the junior succeed to his place. That day came after various changes, in 1868, and the book-keeper of 1836 became the head of a large firm, with a clear half-million to his credit.

Ambitious to make his mark in the business world, and to become the peer of his illustrious predecessor, he launched out boldly, and in 1869 we find him engineering a great speculation in coffee. Old bankers shook their heads ominously, and doubted his ability to wear the laurels won by the merchant-prince who formerly directed the firm's affairs. The bankers felt that prudence dictated a conference with the new man at the helm, especially as he was inclined to enter upon bold speculative operations. To them, in substance, the merchant said: "Whatever else I know, I think I know the coffee trade thoroughly. I shall act upon my own judgment, and by it 'sink or swim.'"

Those who are familiar with the coffee trade will by this time have recognized the pen-picture we have drawn as that of B. G. Arnold, the well-known "King of the Coffee Trade." For more than ten years he ruled the coffee market of this country as absolutely as any hereditary monarch controls his kingdom, and his influence was felt throughout the commercial world. Our tables of prices bear eloquent testimony of his power, and it is known that the operations of a single year succeeding the interview with the bankers above noted yielded his firm a profit of one million two hundred thousand dollars. In the social world he filled a large place. At his palatial residence the President of the United States was a guest, and the periodical receptions were social events. But all things come to an end, and in accordance with this immutable law, the control which Mr. Arnold and his associates exercised over the coffee market finally ceased. For the first five years of the decade 1870–1880, the coffee market had been steadily forced up until abnormally high prices were reached; these stimulated production, and in 1876, while in Java, the writer, in a letter to the *American Grocer*, used the following words: "As a consequence of these high prices many new coffee-gardens have been planted, and these are just beginning to bear and must inevitably have an effect upon the future market. The quantity of government coffee raised in Java last year, which was rather a poor year, was 494,000 piculs, while the crop of 1876, which is a good year, is 1,266,000 piculs. It is also said that the production has proportionately increased in Sumatra and other coffee-bearing islands of the Malay Archipelago, and that the average yield during the next few years must be very large. If the same causes produce like effects in other coffee-producing sections of the globe, we may reasonably look forward to moderate prices for this staple in the future."

The sequel is known to all: production outran consumption, prices went down, down, down, despite the desperate and more or less successful efforts made at times to rally the market, until the final result came in the disastrous failures in 1880, which swept away the leading houses of the coffee trade in the United States. The chief cause of this disaster seems to have been an inability on the part of the leading spirits in the coffee trade to look on both sides of the question, a result which inevitably comes sooner or later in all speculative transactions.

As usual, since the great failures in the coffee trade, there have been plenty of persons ready to say unkind things of the chief actors in the drama; but, while there can be but one opinion as to the welfare of the public being subserved by the failure of speculative combinations, all who know Mr. B. G. Arnold are ready to concede that the failure of such a man is, in one sense, a public misfortune. As an industrious, energetic, and upright merchant, faithfully fulfilling every engagement; as a charitable and public-spirited citizen, fully performing his duty to society, the character of Mr. Arnold stands out in bold relief and is worthy of all commendation.

He still continues in business with his son, Mr. F. B. Arnold, and, with his intimate knowledge of the staple and his long business experience, it is not improbable that there may come another phase to this romance of trade, and "the king will have his own again."

CHAPTER XXVI.

THE TROPICS' BEST GIFT.

How little do the millions throughout the civilized world, who sit at their breakfast-tables, realize the labor and pains which have been taken to place before them the fragrant cup which, if good, makes everything good!

From the time when the little seedling first shoots above the ground in the tropics, it is watched and shaded, pruned and cultured by the dusky sons of toil; nor is the task near ended when the planter sees his hopes realized in the red, ripe berry.

Let us trace it from hand to hand until it reaches the table of the consumer. In its gathering and preparation a vast amount of labor is required; then comes its transportation to the seaboard, where it is weighed, stored, sampled, assorted, and sold, oftentimes passing through the hands of several owners before shipment to the country where it is destined to be consumed. Here it is placed in great warehouses and the same formalities are again observed. After leaving the plantation and before reaching the consumer, it has paid tribute to the transporter to the shipping port, to the laborers, warehousemen, brokers, merchants, and bankers of that country; to the ships which carry it abroad; to the custom-houses of importing countries, to their stevedores, storage warehouses, insurance companies, and bankers; to the brokers who sample and sell it, the weighers who weigh it, and the wholesale merchants who buy it. Then comes its cartage or lighterage, its roasting and sale to retail merchants, and its transportation to the point where it is finally distributed and consumed. Twelve hundred millions of pounds of coffee annually pass through this routine, and probably a hundred millions of people, besides the consumers, are directly or indirectly benefited. Factories have been brought into existence to manufacture the machinery required in the cultivation and preparation of this staple; great mills work throughout the whole year on the bagging required for the packages; warehouses worth millions have been provided for its storage; mighty fleets of vessels are created and maintained for its carriage on the sea, and railroads for its transportation on land. Governments find it a chief source of customs revenue. In the eleven years, 1861 to 1872, the import duty on coffee yielded nearly one hundred millions of dollars to the United States Government. In England, France, Germany, and other countries, it contributes largely to the national treasuries, while in Brazil the export duty on coffee is the chief source of revenue. All this from a little berry which hardly more than two centuries since was scarcely known in commerce, and whose chief development has been within the last century. Surely, it must have some precious properties to thus command the homage of the civilized world!

It has been said of wine that

> " It warms the heart and stirs the blood
> Till it leaps in the veins like a bounding flood."

It has also been said that "wine is a turncoat: first a friend, and then an enemy." But coffee is an ever-faithful, steadfast friend, and whether in torrid, or temperate, or frigid climes, everywhere throughout the civilized world, in the king's palace or the laborer's hut, it is eagerly prized, for it cheers and comforts, brightens and blesses, as doth no other substance under the sun.

Brillat Savarin said, "A last course at dinner wanting cheese is like a pretty woman with only one eye;" and if this be true of cheese, is it not doubly so of coffee, and without coffee and cheese would not a dinner be like a beautiful woman with both "windows of the soul" lacking? Certain it is that since Savarin's time all gourmets have concurred in adding coffee as the appropriate and crowning luxury of a perfect dinner; when coffee is served, then "the feast of reason and flow of soul" begins, and without the fragrant cup dulness prevails.

It is a striking fact that coffee is pre-eminently a promoter of the social element; from its earliest use this has been a notable feature. It has also indirectly been an aid to liberty and freedom of speech, for when it attracted men together they naturally discussed events, and free discussion is the parent of liberty. As stated elsewhere, its use in Moslem countries met with strong opposition from both the civil and religious authorities; and in English history we find that, in 1675, Charles II. attempted to suppress the then new institution of coffee-houses by a royal proclamation in which it was stated that they were the resort of disaffected persons, "who devised and spread abroad divers false, malicious, and scandalous reports, to the defamation of His Majesty's government and to the disturbance of the peace and quiet of the nation." On the opinion of legal persons being taken as to the legality of this step, an oracular deliverance was given to the effect that "the retailing of coffee might be an innocent trade, but, as it was used to nourish sedition, spread lies, and scandalize great men, it might also be a common nuisance."

That coffee promotes sociability among men cannot be doubted any more than that its twin sister, the fragrant leaf of China and Japan, promotes sociability among women, and in the above official announcement of the advisers of Charles II. the ladies have an argument which they can throw in the teeth of the sterner sex, if any be so unkind as to intimate that tea-parties are the source of much scandal and gossip.

The active stimulating element is the same in both coffee and tea; in the former it is known as caffeine, while in the latter it has been designated theine. As explained elsewhere, they are chemically identical, and their effect upon the nervous system, when taken in equal quantities, is precisely similar. Considering its importance from an economic and therapeutic standpoint, this substance does not seem to have received from scientific men the attention which it deserves. This subtle principle embodied in Arabia's fragrant berry has outlived prejudice, has triumphed over opposition; religious and political bigotry, aided by military force, has failed to suppress it; and may we not claim that it has fairly won the first place in the world's social and domestic economy, and that it is truly the tropics' best gift?

STATISTICAL TABLES

SHOWING THE

IMPORTS, EXPORTS, CONSUMPTION, RECEIPTS, AND PRICES OF COFFEE IN THE UNITED STATES AND FOREIGN MARKETS.

STATISTICAL TABLES

SHOWING THE

IMPORTS, EXPORTS, CONSUMPTION, RECEIPTS, AND PRICES OF COFFEE IN THE UNITED STATES AND FOREIGN MARKETS.

TABLE I.

Imports, Exports, Consumption, and Stock of Coffee in the United States, Atlantic Coast, from 1854 *to* 1880, *inclusive.*

Year.	Imports. Total tons.	Exports. Total tons.	Consumption. Total tons.	Stock, Dec. 31st. Total tons.
1854	81,460	5,641	80,125	8,700
1855	106,345	6,958	93,919	14,168
1856	103,100	3,945	97,423	15,900
1857	97,265	13,097	77,038	23,030
1858	101,635	3,800	112,167	8,700
1859	110,950	8,593	99,380	11,677
1860	82,957	3,760	79,068	11,786
1861	81,360	3,537	83,502	6,107
1862	44,000	4,613	39,728	5,766
1863	33,602	1,445	35,589	2,334
1864	64,868	9,484	48,700	9,018
1865	59,632	2,413	57,191	9,046
1866	73,834	2,237	71,391	9,252
1867	101,037	2,897	90,807	10,585
1868	106,130	5,065	99,642	18,088
1869	108,107	7,092	108,479	10,625
1870	126,133	2,542	125,407	8,811
1871	144,065	2,575	141,344	8,954
1872	124,100	2,588	121,303	9,109
1873	120,831	3,066	120,303	5,951
1874	122,174	1,931	123,913	2,281
1875	159,393	3,496	136,649	20,529
1876	119,285	3,855	134,109	1,850
1877	151,123	4,141	135,238	13,594
1878	145,907	6,302	141,949	11,250
1879	197,810	7,495	179,525	22,040
1880	176,694	10,777	168,678	12,279

TABLE II.

Receipts and Consumption of Coffee in the United States, 1851 *to* 1880, *inclusive.*

Year.	Receipts. Tons.	Consumption. Tons.	Year.	Receipts. Tons.	Consumption. Tons.
1851	96,448	82,243	1866.........	73,836	71,392
1852	91,760	91,514	1867.........	101,038	90,851
1853	86,210	78,432	1868.........	106,255	99,643
1854	81,461	80,125	1869.........	108,307	108,679
1855	106,345	97,490	1870.........	126,134	125,407
1856	103,086	97,422	1871.........	144,062	141,343
1857	97,264	77,038	1872.........	123,944	121,303
1858	101,632	112,167	1873.........	120,146	120,150
1859	110,949	99,379	1874.........	124,960	126,200
1860	82,937	79,067	1875.........	157,862	137,321
1861	81,359	83,502	1876.........	110,550	135,058
1862	43,999	39,727	1877.........	152,327	135,906
1863	33,598	35,589	1878.........	147,030	142,372
1864	64,868	48,699	1879.........	198,010	179,241
1865	59,631	57,208	1880.........	176,581	166,463

In the above statement of consumption we have included only the direct receipts at the ports, the *coastwise receipts* being embraced in the calculation at the port of original entry.

TABLE III.

Comparative Prices, New York Market, 1858 *to* 1880, *inclusive.*

Year.	Brazil.	Java.	Maracaibo	Year.	Brazil.	Java.	Maracaibo
1858.......	10.96	16.13	12.04	1870	16.33	21.19	17.47
1859.......	11.61	14.79	11.80	1871	15.91	21.29	16.22
1860.......	13.69	16.15	13.83	1872	18.42	21.30	18.18
1861.......	14.01	18.38	15.38	1873	19.90	23.63	20.51
1862.......	23.01	27.50	24.31	1874	21.08	26.68	20.87
1863.......	31.18	37.04	31.93	1875	19.01	26.71	20.54
1864.......	42.40	49.10	41.59	1876	17.97	21.57	17.02
1865.......	20.65	25.82	21.30	1877	19.72	23.82	18.92
1866.......	18.66	26.08	19.45	1878	16.51	22.48	15.52
1867.......	17.24	24.75	17.69	1879	14.85	24.14	14.70
1868.......	15.73	23.41	16.38	1880	15.12	22.(2	15.52
1869.......	15.82	23.02	17.54				

The highest price of Rio in 1864 was 53½ cents, in July; lowest, 33¼ cents, in January. Java sold in August of that year at 60 cents, and in January at 40 cents, currency. From 1861 to 1865 quotations in currency, after that date in gold.

TABLE IV.

Cargo Prices of Fair to Prime Rio Coffee in New York, Duty Paid, Monthly, from 1825 to 1880, inclusive.

Year.	Lowest.	Highest.	Average prices.	Duties.
1825.......	16 —March	19 —May	16¾ @ 17¼	5 cents per pound.
1826.......	14 —September	17 —January ..	14½ @ 15½	"
1827......	14 —September	15 —February .	14 @ 14½	"
1828.......	12 —September	15 —January ..	12¾ @ 13⅛	"
1829.......	12 —June......	13 —January ..	12 @ 12¾	"
1830.......	10 —September	12 —January ..	11 @ 11¼	"
1831.......	10 —January ..	13 —November.	11 @ 11½	2 "
1832.......	12 —May	14 —November.	12½ @ 12⅝	1 "
1833.......	11 —May	14 —March	12 @ 12¾	Free.
1834.......	11 — —	12 — —	11 @ 12	"
1835.......	11 —January ..	13 —January ..	11½ @ 12⅛	"
1836.......	11 —January ..	13 —March	11 @ 12	"
1837.......	9 —July..... ..	12 —February .	9¾ @ 11½	"
1838.......	9 —March	12 —December.	9½ @ 11½	"
1839.......	9 —December.	12 —April.....	10 @ 11¾	"
1840.......	9 —July	12 —October...	9½ @ 10¾	"
1841.......	9 —June......	11 —February .	9½ @ 10½	"
1842.......	6 —December.	10 —January ..	7¼ @ 9½	"
1843.......	6 —September.	9 —May	6½ @ 8	"
1844.......	6 — —	7 — —	6 @ 7	"
1845.......	5 —July	8 —October ..	6 @ 7½	Free in Am. ships.
1846.......	6 —October...	8 —January ..	6½ @ 7⅜	" "
1847.......	6 —June......	8 —January ..	6¾ @ 7¼	Free.
1848.......	5 —August ...	8 —January ..	5½ @ 6⅜	"
1849.......	5 —January ..	10 —December.	6½ @ 7⅛	"
1850.......	7 —May	14 —February .	10 @ 11¼	"
1851.......	7 —November.	11 —February .	8½ @ 9¼	"
1852.......	7 —February .	10 —May......	8 @ 9	"
1853.......	8 —January ..	12 —December.	8½ @ 10	"
1854.......	8 —December.	12 —January ..	9 @ 11¼	"
1855.......	8 —January ..	12 —September	9⅛ @ 10¾	"
1856.......	9 —July	12 —January ..	10 @ 11½	"
1857.......	10 —January ..	12 —July	10½ @ 11½	"
1858.......	9 —February .	12 —November.	9¾ @ 11	"
1859.......	10 —January ..	13 —December.	10½ @ 12	"
1860.......	11 —February .	15 —August ...	13 @ 14	"
1861.......	11 —January ..	17 —December.	12½ @ 15	"
1862.......	10 —February .	33 —December.	21 @ 23	5 cents per pound.
1863.......	26 —September.	33 —December.	29⅝ @ 31	"
1864*......	11¾—July	22⅝—April	15½ @ 17	"
1865.......	14 —December.	18½—June......	15 @ 17	"
1866.......	10½—July	16½—March	12½ @ 15⅛	"
1867.......	9 —December.	14½—April	10¾ @ 13¾	"
1868.......	8½—January ..	12½—March	9¼ @ 11¾	"
1869.......	8¾—January ..	12 —April	9¼ @ 11¾	"
1870.......	9½—January ..	13¼—April	11⅞ @ 12½	3 "
1871.......	10½—January ..	18 —December.	12 @ 14	"
1872.......	14½—April	19 —June......	15½ @ 18	From July 1, free.
1873.......	17¼—March	27 —December.	19½ @ 21	Free.
1874.......	16¾—September.	28 —January ..	19¾ @ 22	"
1875.......	15¾—March	21½—September	18¼ @ 19⅝	"
1876.......	16½—August ...	19½—January ..	17¼ @ 18¾	"
1877.......	15 —November.	21¼—January ..	18 @ 19	"
1878.......	14 —December.	18¾—January ..	15⅝ @ 17½	"
1879.......	13 —May	18 —November.	14 @ 15⅝	"
1880.......	11¾—December.	17 —January ..	14¼ @ 16	"

* Gold prices.

Cargo Prices of Rio Coffee in New York at the Beginning of each Month, 1825 *to* 1845, *inclusive.**

Month.	1825	1826	1827	1828	1829	1830	1831	1832	1833	1834	1635
January	16@17	16@17	14@15	14@15	12@13	12@—	10@—	—@13	13@—	11@12	11@12
February	16@17	16@—	14@15	13@14	12@13	12@—	10@—	—@13	13@—	11@12	11@12
March	16@17	16@—	14@15	13@14	12@13	12@—	10@—	—@13	13@14	11@12	12@—
April	16@17	16@—	14@15	13@—	12@13	11@12	11@—	—@13	12@13	11@12	12@—
May	19@—	16@—	14@15	12@13	12@13	11@12	11@—	12@—	11@12	11@12	12@13
June	17@13	14@15	14@—	13@—	12@—	11@—	11@12	12@13	11@12	11@12	12@13
July	17@—	14@15	14@—	13@—	12@—	11@—	11@12	12@—	12@—	11@12	12@13
August	17@—	14@15	14@—	13@—	12@—	10@11	11@12	12@—	12@—	11@—	12@13
September	17@—	14@15	14@—	12@13	12@13	10@11	11@12	13@—	12@13	11@12	11@12
October	17@—	14@15	14@—	12@13	12@13	11@—	11@12	13@14	12@13	11@12	11@12
November	17@18	14@15	14@15	12@13	12@13	11@12	12@13	14@—	12@13	11@12	11@12
December	17@—	14@15	14@15	12@13	12@13	11@12	12@13	13@—	12@13	11@12	11@12
Average	16.84@17	$14\frac{5}{6}$@$15\frac{1}{4}$	14@15	$12\frac{5}{8}$@$13\frac{1}{6}$	12@13	$11\frac{1}{12}$@$11\frac{3}{5}$	$10\frac{11}{12}$@$12\frac{2}{7}$	$12\frac{1}{4}$@$13\frac{1}{8}$	$12\frac{1}{12}$@$12\frac{3}{4}$	11@12	$11\frac{1}{2}$@$12\frac{2}{3}$

Month.	1836	1837	1838	1839	1840	1841	1842	1843	1844	1845
January	11@12	10@12	10@11	10@11	9@11	10@11	8@10	6@ 9	6@ 7	6@ 7
February	11@12	10@12	10@12	11@12	9@11	11@—	8@10	7@ 9	6@—	6@—
March	12@13	11@12	9@11	11@12	9@11	10@11	8@ 9	6@ 8	6@ 7	6@ 7
April	11@13	10@12	9@11	10@12	9@11	9@10	7@ 9	6@ 8	6@ 7	6@ 8
May	12@—	10@12	9@10	10@12	9@10	9@10	8@10	6@ 9	6@ 7	6@ 8
June	11@12	10@12	9@10	10@12	9@10	9@10	8@10	6@ 8	6@ 7	6@ 7
July	11@12	9@11	9@11	10@12	9@10	9@10	7@10	7@ 8	6@ 7	5@ 7
August	11@12	9@11	9@11	10@12	9@10	10@11	7@ 9	7@ 8	6@ 7	6@ 7
September	11@—	9@11	10@12	10@12	10@11	10@11	7@10	7@ 8	6@ 7	6@ 8
October	11@12	9@11	10@13	10@12	10@12	9@11	7@ 9	7@ 8	6@ 7	6@ 8
November	11@—	10@11	10@12	10@12	11@—	9@11	7@ 9	6@ 7	6@ 7	6@ 8
December	11@12	10@11	10@12	9@11	10@11	9@10	6@ 9	6@ 7	6@ 7	6@ 8
Average	$11\frac{1}{8}$@$12\frac{2}{9}$	$9\frac{3}{4}$@$11\frac{1}{6}$	$9\frac{1}{8}$@$11\frac{1}{5}$	$10\frac{1}{12}$@$11\frac{5}{6}$	$9\frac{5}{12}$@$10\frac{6}{11}$	$9\frac{1}{4}$@$10\frac{1}{6}$	$7\frac{1}{2}$@ $9\frac{1}{6}$	$6\frac{5}{12}$@$8\frac{1}{12}$	$6\frac{7}{12}$@7	$5\frac{11}{12}$@$7\frac{7}{11}$

* Finance Report, United States, 1863.

Cargo Prices in Gold, "in Bond," for Fair to Prime Rio Coffee in New York, from 1846 *to* 1880 *inclusive.*

Month.	1846	1847	1848	1849	1850	1851
January	7¼@ 8	7½@ 7¾	6½@ 7½	6¼@ 6½	11 @12	10 @11½
February	7¼@ 8	7 @ 7¾	6¾@ 7¼	6¾@ 7	14 @14½	11 @11½
March	7⅝@ 8¼	7¼@ 8	6½@ 7¼	6⅝@ 7	13 @13½	10½@11¼
April	7 @ 8	7¼@ 8	6⅞@ 7½	6½@ 7	12 @12½	10 @10¾
May	7 @ 8	7¼@ 7⅞	6¼@ 7½	6 @ 7¼	9 @ 9½	9½@10
June	7¼@ 8	6⅞@ 7¾	6¾@ 7¼	6 @ 7¼	7¾@ 9½	8½@ 9½
July	7¼@ 8	7 @ 7¾	6½@ 6¾	6 @ 7½	9 @10½	8½@ 9½
August	6⅞@ 8	6¾@ 7¾	5¾@ 6¾	6¼@ 7⅝	9 @10¼	8 @ 9
September	6¾@ 7½	7 @ 7¾	5¾@ 6⅞	6¾@ 8	9 @11	8 @ 9
October	6½@ 7½	6½@ 7½	6½@ 6¾	7¼@10	9⅝@12½	8 @ 9
November	6¾@ 7½	7 @ 7⅜	5½@ 6⅞	9½@10½	10¼@11½	7½@ 9¼
December	7¼@ 8	6¼@ 7¾	6½@ 6¾	9½@11½	10 @11¼	7½@ 9¼
Average	6.99@7.90	6.94@7.75	6.19@7.06	6.68@8.07	10.28@11.54	8.90@9.98

Month.	1852	1853	1854	1855	1856	1857
January	8 @ 8¾	8½@ 9¾	11¼@12½	9 @10½	10 @12¼	10 @11½
February	7½@ 9½	8¾@ 9¼	9½@11¾	9 @10½	10 @12½	10 @11¼
March	8¼@ 9½	8¾@10	9½@12½	9 @11¾	10½@12½	10½@11¾
April	8½@10	8¾@10	10 @11½	10 @11¾	10½@12	10½@12
May	8¾@10⅛	9 @ 9¾	9½@11½	10 @11	10½@12	10¾@12
June	8¼@ 9¾	8 @ 9¾	9¼@11½	8¾@10¾	9½@11¾	10¾@11¾
July	8¼@ 9⅝	8 @10	8¾@11	8¾@11	9½@12	11 @12
August	8¼@ 9½	8½@10	9 @11	10 @11½	10¼@11¾	11½@12½
September	8 @ 9¼	9 @12	9 @11⅝	10 @12	10¼@11¾	11 @12¼
October	8 @ 9¼	9¾@11¾	10 @12	10 @11¾	10½@12	11 @12
November	8 @ 9¼	10 @11¾	9½@11¾	10 @11½	10¼@11½	10½@11
December	8½@ 9¾	10¾@12	9 @10½	9½@12½	10 @11¼	9½@10¾
Average	8.19@9.52	8.98@10.54	9.40@11.57	9.58@11.37	10.15@11.94	10.68@11.73

Month.	1858	1859	1860	1861	1862	1863
January	9½@10¾	10¾@12	11½@12½	11½@13	12.96@14.90	14.65@16.71
February	10¾@11½	10¾@12	11½@12¾	11½@13¼	13.35@15.33	13.32@15.49
March	10¼@11½	10¾@12¼	12½@14¼	11¾@13½	14.61@17.06	15.97@17.58
April	10¾@11½	11 @12¼	13¼@14½	12¼@14	13.72@17.16	15.39@16.71
May	10¼@11½	11 @12¼	13½@14	12¼@13½	13.39@16.29	15.61@17.15
June	11¼@11½	11 @12	13 @14¼	11¾@14	13.67@15.76	15.41@17.14
July	10½@10¾	10¾@12	13½@14½	12 @14½	13.18@14.48	16.57@17.91
August	10½@11½	10¾@11¾	15 @15¾	8¾@11	14.21@15.09	16.63@17.62
September	10½@12	12 @12¾	13¾@16½	9¾@11¾	13.14@14.41	14.77@18.13
October	12 @12¾	11¾@12¾	14 @15¾	11¼@13	12.51@16.01	16.61@17.64
November	10¾@12	11½@13	14 @15	11½@13	15.98@20.17	15.94@17.97
December	10¾@12	11½@12¾	13 @13¼	12½@14½	17.51@20.17	16.19@18.18
Average	10.60@11.56	11.10@12.23	13.21@14.27	11.87@13.25	14.04@16.40	15.44@17.35

Cargo Prices in Gold, "in Bond," for Fair to Prime Rio Coffee in New York, from 1846 *to* 1880 *inclusive*—(Continued).

Month.	1864	1865	1866	1867	1868	1869
January	17.03@17.35	14.91@16.53	13½@15½	11 @13	8½@11¼	8¾@11½
February	16.86@17.01	15.63@17.33	13½@16	11½@14	8½@11½	9¼@11¾
March	17.99@18.16	15 @16½	13¾@16½	12 @14	10¼@12½	9½@11¾
April	18.16@21.04	14 @16½	13 @16	12 @14½	10½@12½	9¾@12
May	19.93@21.33	14½@18	13 @15½	12 @14	9¾@11½	9½@12
June	14.91@15.85	16½@18½	11½@15	11¼@14	9¾@11½	9 @11½
July	11.66@15.73	15½@17½	10½@14	10½@14	10 @12	9½@12
August	13.30@15.67	14½@16	12½@15	10¼@13¾	9½@11½	9¼@11¾
September	15.67@17.47	15 @17¼	12½@14½	10¼@14	9 @11¾	9 @11¾
October	12.66@13.58	15 @17	13 @15	9½@13¾	8¾@11¾	9 @12
November	12.09@14.27	14½@17½	13 @14½	9½@13	8½@11½	9 @12
December	13.68@16.09	14 @15½	11¾@14	9 @12¾	8½@11½	9 @11¾
Average	15.44@17.01	14.92@16.98	12.00@15.12	10.78@13.78	9.27@11.73	9.21@11.81

Month.	1870	1871	1872	1873	1874	1875
January	9½@12	10½@13½	16¾@18½	18 @19¾	26 @28	18¼@19¾
February	10¼@12¼	10½@13¼	16¾@18¼	18¼@19¾	23 @25	17¾@19
March	10¼@12¼	10¾@13¼	15½@17	17¼@18½	22¾@24¾	15¾@17¾
April	11 @13¼	10¾@12¾	14½@16	17¼@18½	19¾@22¼	17¼@19
May	10¾@13¼	10½@12½	16¼@18¼	18½@19½	17½@20	17 @18¾
June	10¼@12½	10½@12	17½@19	18¼@19½	19½@21¾	17 @18¾
July	10¼@12½	11 @12½	16¼@18	18½@19¾	19¾@21¾	18½@19¾
August	9¾@12¼	11½@13¼	16 @18	21 @22¼	17¾@20	19¼@20½
September	10 @12¼	12¼@14	15½@17½	21½@22¾	16¾@20	20¼@21½
October	10 @12½	15¾@17¼	15½@18	20 @22¾	18 @20½	20 @21¼
November	10¼@12¾	14 @15¾	15¾@18¼	20 @22¼	18 @20	18¾@20
December	10¼@12¾	16¼@18	16¼@18½	24½@27	17¾@19½	18¼@19½
Average	11.68@12.56	12.02@13.98	15.00@17.96	19.40@21.02	19.71@21.98	18.17@19.63

Month.	1876	1877	1878	1879.	1880
January	18 @19½	20 @21¼	17 @18¾	14½@16¼	15½@17
February	16½@18¾	19½@21	16¼@18	14 @15¾	14¾@16½
March	17¼@18¾	19½@20¾	15¾@17	13¼@14½	14¾@16½
April	17¼@19	18½@20	15¾@17	13¼@15	14 @16
May	17¼@18½	19 @20½	16 @17¾	13 @14¼	14½@15¾
June	16¾@18	19¼@20¼	15½@17¾	13¼@14¼	14½@15¾
July	17 @18¼	19¾@20¾	15½@17	13¼@14¾	14¾@16
August	16½@17¾	19 @20¼	16 @17½	13½@14¾	15 @16¾
September	17½@18½	16 @16¼	16½@18	13½@16	15 @17
October	17¾@19	16 @16¼	15¼@16	15½@17½	13¼@16
November	18¼@19½	15 @15¼	14½@16¼	16 @18	13¼@15
December	17¾@19	15¼@15½	14 @16	15½@17¼	11¾@14
Average	17.25@18.71	18.04@19	15.61@17.42	14.04@15.69	14.23@16.02

TABLE V.—Price of Java Coffee in New York, 1858 to 1880, *inclusive.*

Date.	1858	1859	1860	1861	1862	1863	1864	1865	1866	1867	1868	1869
January 1	15½-16½	13¾-14¾	14¾-15	15½-16½	25½-28½	33 -33¾	40 -41	— -50	27 -28½	24¾-25¼	27 - —	21 -24
January 10	15½-16½	14 -14½	16 -15½	15½-16½	25 -26	33½-34	40 -41	— -50	27½-28½	24½-25	25 -25½	21 -24
January 20	15½-16½	14 -15	14¾-15½	15½-16¼	26 -27	33½-34	40 -41	50 -51	27½-28½	24½-25	24½-25	21 -24
Average for the month	16	14.29	16	15.96	26	33.58	40½	50.16	27.92	24 83	25.67	22½
February 1	15½-16½	14¼-15	15 -15½	15¾-16¼	26 -26½	35 -36	40 -41	47 -49	27 -28½	25 -25½	24 -25	21 -23½
February 10	15½-16½	14¼-15	14½-15¾	15¾-16½	25 -27	35½-36	41 -42	47½-48½	27½-28½	24½-25	24 -25	21 -23½
February 20	16 -15½	14¼-15½	15 -16	15½-16½	25 -27	35 -37	41 -42	47 -48	27½-28½	24¾-25¼	24½-25½	21 -23½
Average for the month	16.08	14.71	15¼	16.04	25.41½	35.92	41.17	47.83	27.92	25	24.67	22¼
March 1	16½-17	14½-15½	15¼-16	16½-17½	25 -26½	39 -40	41 -42	46 —	27½-28½	24¾-25	24½-25½	21 -23½
March 10	18 -20	14½-15½	15¼-16	16½-17¼	25 -26½	38 -38½	43 -44	45 -46	27½-28½	24½-25	24½-25½	21 -23½
March 20	18 -20	14 -15	15½-16½	16½-17¼	26	38 -39	43 -44	35 -37	27½-28	24½-25	24½-25½	21 -23½
Average for the month	18¼	14.83	15½	16.92	26.16⅔	38¾	42.83	42.66	27.92	24¾	25	22¼
April 1	19 -20	14 -15	15½-16½	16½-17½	25	38 -38½	45 -46	32 -35	26¾-27½	25 -25¼	23½-24½	21 -23½
April 10	19 -20	14 -15	15½-16	16¾-17½	25 -26	37 -38	47½-50	32 -34	26½-27½	25 -25½	23½-24½	21 -23¼
April 20	18½	14½-15	15½-16	18¾-17½	25½-26	37 -38	52½-55	32½-35	26½-27	24¾-25	23½-24½	21 -23
Average for the month	19.17	14.58	15.87½	17.08	25¾	37¾	49.33	33.41	26.96	25.08	24	22.16
May 1	18 -19½	14½-15	15½-16	16½-17	25 -26	37 -38	52½-55	33½-36	25 -26	24 -25	23 -24	23 -25
May 10	18	14½-15	15½-15¾	16½-17	24½-25	37 -37½	50 -52½	32 -35	25½-26	24 -25	23 -24	23 -25
May 20	15¾-18	14½-15	15½-16	16½-17	24¾-25½	36½-37½	50 -51	31½-33½	25½-26	24 -25	23 -24	23 -25
Average for the month	17.71	14¾	15.70	16¾	25½	37.21	51.83	33.58	25.67	24½	23½	24
June 1	15¾-17½	14 -15	15½-16	16½-17	24½-26	36½-37	50 -51½	35½-36½	25¼-26	24 -24½	23½-23½	23½-25
June 10	15¾-18	14 -15	15½-16	16 -17	24½-25½	— -37	49 -50	33 -34½	25 -26	24 -24½	22½-24	23½-25
June 20	15½-18	14 -15	15½-16	17 -17½	25 -25½	— -37	49 -50	33 -34	24½-25½	24 -24½	22½-24	23½-24½
Average for the month	16¾	14½	15¾	16.83	25⅛	36.92	49.92	34.41	25.38	24¼	23.17	24.17

TABLE V.—Price of Java Coffee in New York, 1858 to 1880, *inclusive—Continued.*

Date.	1858	1859	1860	1861	1862	1863	1864	1865	1866	1867	1868	1869
July 1	15 -17	14 -16	15½-16	16 -17½	25 -25½	35½-36½	49 -50	24 -24½	24 -25½	24 -24½	22½-23½	23 -24½
July 10	14½-17	14 -15	15½-16	17 -18	25½-26	35½-36	55 -57	24 -25	24 -25	24 -25	22½-23½	23 -25
July 20	14½-17	14 -15	15¾-16½	16½-18½	26 -27	36 -36	55 -57	24 -25	24 -25	24 -25	22 -23½	22½-25
Average for the month	15.83	14½	15.87½	17¼	25.83½	35¾	53.83	24.41	24.58	24.42	22.92	23.83
August 1	15 -16½	14 -15	16½-18	18½-19½	26 -27	34 -35	55 -57	25 -26	24 -25	24¼-25	22 -23½	22¾-24¼
August 10	14¾-16	14 -15	16½-18½	19 -20	26 -27	35½-36	57 -58	25 -26	24 -25	24 -25	21½-23½	23 -24¼
August 20	14¾-16	14 -15	16¼-17½	19 -20	26½-27	35 -36	58 -60	25 -26	25 -26	24 -25	21½-25½	23½-25
Average for the month	15½	14½	17.20	19½	26.58½	35¼	57½	25½	24.83	24.54	22.58	23.79
September 1	14¼-15½	15¼-16	16 -17½	19 -19½	26½-27	34½-35	58 -59	26 -26½	25 -26	24 -25	21½-22¼	22 -25
September 10	14¼-15½	15 -16	16¼-17½	19½-20	26½-27	35 -36	58 -58½	26 -27	25 -26	24 -24½	21½-23½	22 -25
September 20	14½-15½	15 -16	16½-18	19 -20	26½-27	36½-37½	56 -56	27 -27½	25½-26	24 -24½	21½-23	21 -24
Average for the month	14.91	15.54	16.95	19½	26¾	35¾	57.42	26.66	25.58	24.38	22.29	23.17
October 1	14¾-16¼	15¼-16	16½-18	20 -21	26½-27	36½-37½	45 -46	— -30	25 -26	24 -24¾	21 -22½	22 -24
October 10	14½-15½	15 -16	16½-18	20 -21	27½-28½	38 -40	42½-45	32 -34	25½-26¼	24 -25	21 -23	22 -24
October 20	14 -15	14¾-15½	16¼-17½	19½-21	— -30	38 -39	45 -46	32 -34	26 -26	24½-25	21 -23	22 -24
Average for the month	15	15.41	17½	20.42	28¼	38.17	44.92	32	25.62	24.54	21.92	23
November 1	13½-14	14¾-15½	16¼-17½	— -21	31 -32¼	38 -40	48 -50	29 -32	25 -25¾	24½-25	21¼-23½	22 -23½
November 10	14 -15	14¾-15½	16½-17½	21 -23	34 -35	39 -40	50 -52½	28 -32	25 -26½	24½-25	21½-24	22 -23½
November 20	14 -14½	14¾-15½	16¼-17½	21 -21½	34 -35	39 -40	48 -50	28 -29	25 -25½	24½-25	21 -24	22 -23½
Average for the month	14.17	15½	16,91⅔	21¼	33.54	39.33	49¾	29.66	25.29	24¾	22.62	22¾
December 1	14 -15	14½-15	16¼-17½	21½-22	34 -35	39 -40	— -50	28 -29	25 -26	24½-25½	21½-23¾	22 -22½
December 10	13¾-14	14½-15	16 -16½	23 -24	34 -35	40 -41	50 -52	27 -28	25 -25½	26 -27	21½-24	22 -23
December 20	13¾-14½	14¼-15	16 -16½	24 -25	34 -34½	40 -41	49 -50	27 -28	25 -25¼	26 -27	21 -23½	21½-22½
Average for the month	14.17	14.71	16.45	23¼	34.41⅔	40.16	50.17	27.83	25.29	26	22.54	22.41
Average for the year	16.13	14.79	16.15¼	18.38	27½	37.04	49.10	25.68	26.08	24¾	23.41	23.02

Note.—From July 1, 1865, all the quotations were in gold.

Date.	1870	1871	1872	1873	1874	1875	1876	1877	1878	1879	1880
January 1	21½-22½	19 21½	23 -25	19 -21	31 -35	26 -30	25 -26	23 -25	22 -23	23 -23½	24¾-22
January 10	21½-22½	17½ 20	22½-25	19¾-22	30 -35	26 -29	24½-25½	23 -25	22 -23	23 -23½	23¾-24
January 20	21½-22½	19 21	23 -25	21 -23	30 -34½	26 -29	24½-25½	22½-24½	21 -22	23 -23½	22¾-24
Average for the month	22	19.66	23.91	20.96	32.58	27.66	25	23.83	22.16	23.25	23.87½
February 1	21½-22½	18 -21½	23 -24½	20½-22	30 -34	28 -30	24 -25	23½-24½	21 -22	24 -24½	24¾-22
February 10	19½-21½	18 -22	23 -24½	20 -22	29 -33	26 -29	23 -24	23 -24	21 -22	24 -24½	23¾-24
February 20	19 -21½	18 -22	23 -24½	20½-22½	28 -32	26 -29	22½-23½	23 -24	21 -22	24 -24½	23 -24
Average for the month	20.92	19.92	23¾	21.16	31	28	23.66	23.66	21.50	24.25	23.75
March 1	20 -21½	18 -22	22 -24	20½-22½	28 -31	26 -29	22½-23½	23 -24	21 -22	24 -24½	24 -22
March 10	20 -21½	18 -22	22 -23½	20 -22	28 -31	26 -28	22½-23½	23 -24	20½-21½	23½-24	23 -24
March 20	20 -21½	18 -22	22 -23½	20 -22	26 -29	26 -28	22 -23	23 -24	20½-21½	23½-24	23 -24
Average for the month	20¾	20	22.83	21.16	28.83	27.16	22.83	23.50	21.16	23.91⅔	23.50
April 1	20 -21½	18 -22	21 -23	20 -22	25 -28	25 -27	22 -23	23 -24	20½-21½	23½-24	23 -22
April 10	20 -22	18 -22	21 -23½	20 -22	25 -27	24 -26	22 -23	23 -24	20½-21½	23½-24	22 -23
April 20	20 -22	18 -22	21 -23	20 -21½	24 -27	25 -26	22 -23	23 -24	20½-21½	24 -24½	22 -23
Average for the month	20.92	20	22.08	20.92	26	25½	22½	23.50	21	24.25	22.50
May 1	20 -22	18 -22	20½-23½	20 -21½	23½-26	25 -27	22 -23	22 -23	20½-22	24 -24½	23 -22
May 10	20 -22	18 -22	21½-23½	20½-22	23 -25½	25 -27	21½-22½	23½-24½	20½-22	24 -24½	21 -22
May 20	21½-22½	18 -22	22 -23½	21 -23	23 -27½	24 -26	19 -22	23½-24½	20½-22	24 -24½	20 -22
Average for the month	21.33	20	22.38	21.33	24¼	25.66	21.66	23½	21¼	24.25	21.66⅔
June 1	21½-22½	18 -22	22 -23½	21 -23	22 -25	24 -26	19½-22½	24 -25	20½-22	24 -24½	20 -22
June 10	21½-22½	18 -22	22 -23½	21½-23	22 -25	24 -26	19½-22	24 -25	20½-22	24 -24½	20 -22
June 20	20 -22	18 -22	22 -23½	21½-23½	22 -26	24 -26	18½-21	24 -25	22 -23	24 -24½	19½-21
Average for the month	21.66	20	22¾	22½	23.66	25	20.50	24.50	21.66	24.25	20.75
July 1	20 -22	18 -22	19½-22	21 -23	22½-27	25 -27	19 -21½	24½-25½	22 -23	24 -24½	19½-22
July 10	20 -22	18 -22	19½-22	21½-23½	23½-28	25 -27	19 -21½	24½-25½	22 -23	24 -24½	19½-21
July 20	19½-22	18 -22	19 -21	21½-23½	23½-28	25 -27	18½-21	24½-25½	22 -23	24 -24½	21 -22
Average for the month	20.92	20	20½	22½	25.42	26	20.08	25	22½	24.25	20.66⅔

TABLE V.—PRICE OF JAVA COFFEE IN NEW YORK, 1858 TO 1880, *inclusive—Continued.*

Date.	1870	1871	1872	1873	1874	1875	1876	1877	1878	1879	1880
August 1	19½-22	18 -22	19 -21	22½-24	23½-28	25 -27½	18½-21	24½-25½	23 -23½	24 -24½	21 -22
August 10	19¼-22	20 -23½	19 -21	23½-25½	23½-28	25 -27½	18½-21	24 -25	23¾-25	23½-24	21 -23
August 20	19½-22	20 -23½	19 -21	24½-26	23½-28	26 -28	18 -20½	23½-25	23¾-25	23½-24	21 -23
Average for the month	20¼	21.17	20	24.33	25¾	20½	19.58	24.58	24	24	21.83⅓
September 1	19½-23	19 -22½	19 -21	25 -27	23 -28	26 -28	18 -20½	23½-25	23¾-25	23½-24	21 -22
September 10	19 -22	21 -23	19 -21	25½-27	22½-28	26 -28	19 -21½	23½-25	23¾-25	23½-24	21 -23
September 20	19 -22	21 -23	18¾-20	24½-26	22½-27	26 -28	19 -23	23½-25	23¾-25	23 -23¼	21 -23
Average for the month	20.58	21.58	10.79	24.33	25.16	27	20	24.25	24.37	23.58	22
October 1	19 -22	23 -24	18¾-20	25 -27	22½-27	26 -30	19 -23	23½-25	23 -24	24 -24½	21 -22
October 10	20½-23	24 -26	18¾-19½	24 -25½	22½-27	27 -30	19 -23	23½-25	23 -24	24½	21 -23
October 20	20½-23	24 -26½	18¾-19½	23½-25½	23 -28	27 -30	19 -23	23 -23½	23½-24	24½-25	19 -23
Average for the month	21.33	24.42	19.21	25.08	25	28.33	21	23.91	23.58	24.50	21.66⅔
November 1	21 -23	25 -26½	18½-19½	26 -28½	24 -28	27 -29	19 -22½	22½-23	23¼-23½	24½-25	20 -22
November 10	21 -23	24 -25½	18½-19½	26 -28½	24 -28	26 -28	19 -22½	22½-23	— -23½	24¼-25	20 -22
November 20	21 -23	22½-25	18½-19½	25½-28½	24 -28	26 -28	19 -22½	23 -23	— -23½	24¾-25	18 -20
Average for the month	22	24.76	19	27.17	26	27.33	20.75	22.66	23.37	24.79	20.33⅓
December 1	20½-22	22½-25	18½-19½	28 -31	24 -28	26 -28	19 -22½	22 -23	23 -23½	24½-25	18 -22
December 10	20 -22	23 -25	18¾-19¾	30 -32	24 -28	26 -27	20 -23	22½-23½	23 -23½	24½-24¾	18 -20
December 20	20 -22	23 -25½	19 -21	30 -34	24 -28	25 -26	20 -23	23 -24	23 -23½	23½-24	16 -18
Average for the month	21.08	24	19.37	30.83	26	26.33	21¼	23	23.25	24.37½	18.83⅓
Average for the year	21.19	21.29	21.30	23.63	26.68	26.71	21.57	23.82	22.48	24.14	22.62 7/12

TABLE VI.

Comparative Monthly and Yearly Prices for Three Years.

Month.	BRAZIL—Fair to Prime Cargoes. Average for the Month.			MARACAIBO AND LAGUAYRA. Average for the Month.		
	1880	1879	1878	1880	1879	1878
January	$16 16⅔	$15 42	$17 87	$15 33⅓	$15 17	$17 25
February	15 50	14 79⅓	17 08	16 04	15 58⅓	16 33
March	15 62½	14 16⅔	16 54	16 62½	14 66⅔	15 75
April	15 00	14 20⅚	16 37	16 62½	14 00	15 50
May	15 08⅓	13 58⅓	17 00	15 00	14 00	15 33
June	15 04	13 75	16 26	14 75	13 91	15 50
July	15 50	14 00	16 12	14 95⅚	13 75	15 33
August	15 83	14 04	16 70	15 62½	13 75	14 91
September	16 16⅔	14 70	17 16	15 87½	13 75	15 25
October	14 46	16 33	16 50	15 04	15 08	15 50
November	13 96	16 91	15 54	14 00	16 58	14 75
December	13 12	16 37½	15 04	12 45⅚	16 71	14 83
Average for year	$15 12	$14 85½	$16 51	$15 52$\frac{5}{12}$	$14 70	$15 52

Month.	ST. DOMINGO. Average for the month.			JAVA. Average for the Month.		
	1880	1879	1878	1880	1879	1878
January	$13 37½	$11 00	$15 83	$23 87½	$23 25	$22 16
February	12 83⅓	10 75	14 37	23 75	24 25	21 50
March	13 60	10 75	13 91	23 50	23 91⅔	21 16
April	13 00	10 75	13 50	22 50	24 25	21 00
May	13 00	11 25	13 20	21 66⅔	24 25	21 25
June	12 41⅔	11 25	13 62	20 75	24 25	21 66
July	12 25	11 25	13 33	20 66⅔	24 25	22 50
August	12 25	11 25	12 75	21 83⅓	24 00	24
September	12 25	11 25	12 83	23 00	23 58	24 37
October	12 00	11 91	12 50	21 66⅔	24 50	23 58
November	11 50	14 50	12 50	20 33⅓	24 79	23 27
December	11 16⅔	14 41	11 75	18 33⅓	24 37½	23 25
Average for year	$12 63⅓	$11 69	$13 34	$22 62$\frac{7}{12}$	$24 14	$22 48

TABLE VII.

Receipts of Sundry Kinds of Coffee, not enumerated specifically, into the United States (Atlantic Coast), 1866 *to* 1880, *inclusive.*

Year.	Bags.	Tons.	Year.	Bags.	Tons.
1866	8,401	633	1874	121,479	6,869
1867	16,859	1,052	1875	40,977	2,567
1868	16,666	1,024	1876	47,707	3,221
1869	22,423	1,173	1877	71,567	4,877
1870	16,569	791	1878	64,884	4,246
1871	37,675	2,337	1879	98,669	7,239
1872	73,852	4,702	1880	109,172	6,967
1873	70,605	4,489			

Average, 15 years (1866 to 1880) .... 54,500 bags, 3,486 tons.
Average, 10 years (1871 to 1880) .... 73,659 " 4,751 "

TABLE VIII.

Circular Estimating and Proclaiming, in United States Money of Account, the Values of the Standard Coins in Circulation of the Various Nations of the World.

1881.
DEPARTMENT No. 1.
Secretary's Office.

TREASURY DEPARTMENT,
BUREAU OF THE MINT,
WASHINGTON, D. C., January 1, 1881.

HON. JOHN SHERMAN, *Secretary of the Treasury:*

SIR—In pursuance of the provisions of Section 3,564 of the Revised Statutes of the United States, I have estimated the values of the standard coins in circulation of the various nations of the world, and submit the same in the accompanying table. Very respectfully,

HORATIO C. BURCHARD, *Director of the Mint.*

Country.	Monetary Unit.	Standard.	Value in U. S. Money.	Standard Coin.
Austria	Florin	Silver	40.7	
Belgium	Franc	Gold and silver.	19.3	5, 10, and 20 francs.
Bolivia	Bolliviano	Silver	82.3	Bolliviano.
Brazil	Milreis of 1000 reis.	Gold	54.6	
British Possessions in N. A.	Dollar	Gold	$1 00	
Chili	Peso	Gold and silver.	91.2	Condor, doubloon, and escudo.
Cuba	Peso	Gold and silver.	93.2	1/16, 1/8, 1/4, 1/2, and 1 doubloon.
Denmark	Crown	Gold	26.8	10 and 20 crowns.
Ecuador	Peso	Silver	82.3	Peso.
Egypt	Piaster	Gold	04.9	5, 10, 25, 50, and 100 piasters.
France	Franc	Gold and silver.	19.3	5, 10, and 20 francs.
Great Britain	Pound sterling	Gold	4 86.6½	½ sovereign and sovereign.
Greece	Drachma	Gold and silver.	19.3	5, 10, 20, 50, and 100 drachmas.
German Empire	Mark	Gold	23.8	5, 10, and 20 marks.
India	Rupee of 16 annas.	Silver	39	
Italy	Lira	Gold and silver.	19.3	5, 10, 20, 50, and 100 lire.
Japan	Yen	Silver	88.8	1, 2, 5, 10, and 20 yen, gold, and silver yen.
Liberia	Dollar	Gold	1 00	
Mexico	Dollar	Silver	89.4	Peso or dollar, 5, 10, 25, and 50 centavos.
Netherlands	Florin	Gold and silver.	40.2	
Norway	Crown	Gold	26.8	10 and 20 crowns.
Peru	Sol	Silver	82.3	Sol.
Portugal	Milreis of 1000 reis.	Gold	1 08	2, 5, and 10 milreis.
Russia	Rouble of 100 copecks	Silver	65.8	¼, ½, and 1 rouble.
Sandwich Islands.	Dollar	Gold	1 00	
Spain	Peseta of 100 centimes	Gold and silver.	19.3	5, 10, 20, 50, and 100 pesetas.
Sweden	Crown	Gold	26.8	10 and 20 crowns.
Switzerland	Franc	Gold and silver.	19.3	5, 10, and 20 francs.
Tripoli	Mahbub of 20 piasters	Silver	74.3	
Turkey	Piaster	Gold	04.4	25, 50, 100, 250, and 500 piasters.
United States of Colombia	Peso	Silver	82.3	Peso.
Venezuela	Bolivar	Gold and silver.	19.3	5, 10, 20, 50, and 100 Bolivar.

TREASURY DEPARTMENT, WASHINGTON, D. C., January 1, 1881.

The foregoing estimation, made by the Director of the Mint, of the value of the foreign coins above mentioned, I hereby proclaim to be the values of such coins expressed in the money of account of the United States, and to be taken in estimating the values of all foreign merchandise, made out in any of said currencies, imported on or after January 1, 1881.

JOHN SHERMAN, *Secretary of the Treasury.*

TABLE IX.—Premium on Gold at New York, 1862 to 1878, *inclusive.*

The following statement exhibits the lowest and highest premium on gold at New York for each month, and for each year, from the suspension of specie payments, on December 30, 1861, to the resumption of the same, on January 2, 1879:

Years.	January.	February.	March.	April.	May.	June.	July.	August.	September.	October.	November.	December.	Lowest and Highest for the year.
1862..	101¼–103⅛	102⅛–104¾	101⅛–102⅝	101⅛–102¾	102⅛–104⅛	103⅜–109⅞	108¾–120⅛	112⅝–116¼	116⅛–124	122 –133⅛	129 –133¼	128⅝–134	101⅛–134
1863..	133⅛–160¾	152⅝–172½	139 –171⅞	145⅛–157⅞	143⅝–154⅞	140½–148⅜	123¼–145	122⅛–129⅞	126⅞–143¼	140⅞–156¾	143 –154	148⅛–152¾	122⅛–172½
1864..	151⅛–159⅜	157⅛–161	159 –169⅞	166¼–184¾	168 –190	188¼–250	222 –285	231⅛–261¾	191 –254⅛	189 –227¾	210 –260	212¾–243	151⅛–285
1865..	197¼–234⅜	196⅜–216¾	146⅛–201	143⅝–154⅛	128⅝–145⅛	135¼–147⅝	138⅝–146⅛	140¼–145⅝	142⅞–145	144⅛–149	145⅝–148¾	144⅝–148⅜	128⅝–234⅜
1866..	136¾–144⅝	135⅞–140⅜	125 –136⅜	125 –129⅜	125⅛–141⅜	137⅝–167¾	147 –155¼	146⅛–152⅛	143¼–147⅛	145⅜–154⅜	137⅜–148⅝	131¼–141¾	125 –167¾
1867..	132 –137⅞	135¼–140⅜	138⅝–140⅜	132⅝–141⅞	134⅞–138⅞	136⅜–138¾	138 –140¾	138⅞–142⅜	141 –146⅜	140¼–145⅝	138¼–141⅛	133 –137⅞	132 –146⅜
1868..	133¼–142⅛	139⅜–144	137⅞–141¼	137⅜–140¾	139⅛–140⅝	139⅜–141¼	140⅛–145¼	143⅜–150	141⅛–145⅛	133¾–140⅛	132 –137	134¾–136¾	132 –150
1869..	134⅝–136¾	130⅞–136¼	130¼–132⅜	131¼–134¾	134⅝–144¾	136⅜–139⅝	124 –137¾	131¼–136⅝	130¾–162⅛	128¼–132	121⅛–128⅜	119⅜–124	119⅜–162⅛
1870..	119⅝–123¼	115 –121⅛	110¼–116⅜	111⅜–115⅝	113¾–115⅛	110⅞–114¾	111⅛–122¾	114¾–122	112¾–116⅜	111⅛–114¼	110 –113⅜	110⅜–111½	110 –123¼
1871..	110⅜–111¼	110⅞–112¼	110⅛–111⅜	110⅛–111¾	111 –112¼	111¾–113⅜	111¾–113⅜	111⅝–113¼	112¾–115⅜	111⅜–115	110⅞–112⅝	108⅜–110⅞	108⅜–115⅜
1872..	108⅛–110⅛	109⅜–111	109¾–110⅜	109⅞–113¼	112⅛–114⅞	113 –114¾	113⅜–115¼	112⅛–115⅝	112¾–115⅛	112¼–115⅛	111⅞–114¼	111⅜–113⅜	108⅛–115⅝
1873..	111⅝–114¼	112⅞–115⅛	114⅝–118½	116¾–119⅛	116⅝–118⅝	115 –118¼	115 –116⅜	114⅞–116¼	110⅞–116⅛	107⅝–111¼	106⅜–110⅜	108⅜–112⅝	106⅛–119⅛
1874..	110⅜–112⅜	111⅜–113	111¼–113⅝	111¾–114¾	111⅞–113⅛	110⅜–112¼	109 –110⅞	109¼–110¼	109¼–110⅜	109¾–110⅞	110 –112¾	110⅜–112⅞	109 –114⅞
1875..	111¾–113⅞	113 –115⅝	114¾–117	114 –115⅜	115 –116½	116 –117½	112 –117⅛	112⅜–114¾	113⅜–117⅜	114⅛–117⅝	114⅛–116⅜	112⅝–116¼	111¾–117⅝
1876..	112⅞–113¼	112¾–114⅛	113¾–116	112⅝–113⅞	112¼–113¼	111⅞–113	111⅞–112¾	109⅜–112⅛	109¼–110⅜	106⅞–113¼	108⅛–110⅛	107 –109	107 –115
1877..	105¼–107⅛	104⅛–106⅛	104¼–105⅜	104⅜–107⅞	106⅛–107⅞	104¾–106⅜	105⅛–106⅜	103⅞–105⅜	102⅞–104	102⅜–103⅜	102⅜–103⅜	102⅛–103⅜	102⅜–107⅞
1878..	101¼–102⅞	101⅝–102⅞	100¾–102	100⅛–101¼	100¼–101¼	100⅝–101	100⅜–100¾	100⅜–100¾	100⅛–100⅜	100¼–101⅞	100⅛–100⅜	100⅛–100⅜	100⅛–102⅞

NOTE.—Lowest and highest during the seventeen years of suspension: lowest, 100⅛, December 17, 1878; highest, 285, July 11, 1864.

TABLE X.—Cost of Exchange in Rio de Janeiro.

Comparative Table, showing Lowest and Highest Rates of Exchange from 1850 *to* 1879, *inclusive—in Rio de Janeiro—from Official Quotations.*

Year.	London. Pence Sterling pr. Milreis.	Paris. Reis pr. Franc.	Hamburg. Prior 1873—Reis pr. Mark Banco. Since 1873—Reis pr. Reichsmark.	Year.	London. Pence Sterling pr. Milreis.	Paris. Reis pr. Franc.	Hamburg. Prior 1873—Reis pr. Mark Banco. Since 1873—Reis pr. Reichsmark.
1850.....	26¼–31	312–348	565–648	1865....	22⅛–27¼	355–415	675–775
1851.....	27⅜–31	308–350	570–648	1866....	22 –26	372–430	700–800
1852.....	26⅛–28¼	344–360	630–665	1867....	19¾–24⅜	392–450	740–875
1853.....	27⅛–29⅛	328–355	600–655	1868....	14 –20	432–655	890–1,120
1854.....	26⅛–28⅝	340–373	640–675	1869....	18 –20	480–525	900–965
1855.....	27 –28⅛	345–360	640–660	1870....	19⅝–24⅛	400–485	742–890
1856.....	26⅞–28⅛	341–354	645–662	1871....	22 –25⅞	374–420	708–772
1857.....	23⅝–28	343–365	648–695	1872....	24 –26⅛	358–388	685–735
1858.....	22¾–27	358–420	675–720	1873....	25⅛–27	350–376	444–451
1859.....	23⅛–26⅞	360–415	670–800	1874....	24¾–26¾	357–381	416–470
1860.....	24⅛–27⅛	353–390	670–740	1875....	26⅜–28⅜	339–360	436–444
1861.....	24¼–26¾	356–395	680–730	1876....	23¾–26¾	357–401	447–495
1862.....	24¾–27¾	345–380	657–710	1877....	23 –25⅛	370–416	467–498
1863.....	26⅝–27⅞	341–356	646–668	1878....	21¼–24⅝	398–448	467–519
1864.....	25¾–27¾	343–370	654–685	1879....	19⅛–23⅛	411–495	514–604

TABLE XI.—The World's Production of Coffee.

(From *Ceylon Directory*.)

Countries.	Estimated Area under Cultivation.	Present Maximum Export of Coffee.	Estimated Local Consumption.	Total Maximum Production.
	Acres.	Tons.	Tons.	Tons.
Brazil (including exports from Rio, Santos, Bahia, Pernambuco, and Ceara)...........	1,500,000	240,000	60,000	300,000
Java and Sumatra........................	1,200,000	90,000	20,000	110,000
Ceylon..	263,000	50,000	5,000	55,000
India...	150,000	25,000	7,000	32,000
Central America (between United States and Venezuela)........................	210,000	40,000	5,000	45,000
Venezuela, Peru, Bolivia, and Guianas........	220,000	40,000	8,000	48,000
Hayti or San Domingo........................	200,000	28,000	7,000	35,000
Cuba and Porto Rico........................	130,000	17,000	8,000	25,000
West Indies..................................	40,000	5,300	3,500	8,800
Arabia, Madagascar, Mauritius, Réunion, Abyssynia, Mozambique, and north-east coast of Africa..................................	220,000	7,500	22,500	30,000
Natal..	800	60	60	100
Liberia and West Coast from Loanda to Cape de Verde Islands, including Lagos, Sierra Leone, Gambia, Gold Coast, Elmina, St. Thomas, St. Helena, etc., etc..........................	100,000	4,500	10,000	14,500
Manilla, Celebes, and rest of Eastern Archipelago and Australia........................	45,000	5,000	3,000	8,000
Sandwich Islands and rest of Pacific Isles, including Fiji and New Caledonia............	12,500	1,200	1,000	2,200
Total..	4,291,300	553,550	160,060	713,600

The value of the world's production of coffee (over 14,000,000 cwts.) would be about 50,000,000 pounds sterling in the wholesale markets.

TABLE XII.—The World's Consumption of Coffee.

(From the *Encyclopædia Britannica*, 1877-78.)

Countries.	Total Imports of Coffee for Consumption.	Average Per Head.	Increase in Ten Years.
	Pounds.	Pounds.	Pounds.
France	98,635,000	2.73	.41
Belgium	49,771,000	13.48	4.88
Switzerland	18,779,500	7.03	——
Russia, European	14,740,920	0.19	——
Sweden	26,555,213	6.11	2.83
Norway	17,636,080	9.80	3.50
Denmark	26,035,652	13.89	9.00
Holland	72,395,800	21.00	——
Hamburg (Germany)	178,715,936	——	——
Austria (1871)	76,876,576	2.13	——
Greece	2,131,367	1.42	——
Italy (1871)	28,511,560	1.00	——
United Kingdom	32,330,928	1.00	——
United States	293,293,833	7.61	——

Total.......... 936,409,365 lbs., or 8½ millions cwt., 425,000 tons, excluding home consumption in producing countries.

The *Ceylon Directory* estimates the world's consumption (usual, not maximum) as follows:

	Tons.
Continent of Europe	300,000
United States and Canada	140,000
Mexico, Central America, and the West Indian Islands	28,000
Brazil and the rest of South America	86,500
Asia, including Java and the Eastern Archipelago	76,000
Africa *	35,000
United Kingdom	15,000
Australasia and Pacific Isles	6,000
Total	686,500

This is the average in a year of abundant production. In 1820 the world's consumption of coffee was not more than 150,000 tons.

TABLE XIII.

Prof. Van Den Berg's Estimate of the Coffee Production of the Whole World.

Countries.	1855	1865	1870
	Kilos.	Kilos.	Kilos.
Asia	107,650,000	140,560,000	151,000,000
Africa	4,000,000	4,000,000	4,000,000
South America	185,715,000	231,000,000	261,390,000
Central America	3,500,000	9,050,000	32,500,000
West Indies	29,300,000	36,800,000	41,800,000
Australasia	——	300,000	150,000
Total	330,165,000 324,950 tons.	421,950,000 415,285 tons.	490,840,000 483,087 tons.

* Cape Colony has imported from Rio as much as 60,000 cwt. of coffee in one year. Algeria, at the other end of the Continent, also imports 60,000 cwt.—Compilers.

TABLE XIII.—*Continued.*

MacCulloch's "Commercial Dictionary," ed. 1854, estimates the coffee production of the whole world, about 1852, as follows:

	Tons.
Mocha, Hodeida, and other parts of Arabia	8,000
Java	62,000
Sumatra and remaining Archipelago	8,000
Brazil and remainder of South America	110,000
Hayti	15,000
Cuba and Porto Rico	17,000
British West Indies	2,000
Ceylon and British India	17,000
Netherlands West Indies	5,000
French West Indies and Bourbon	7,000

Total..............251,000 tons, or fully 255,000,000 kilos.

Messrs. Jacobson, of Rotterdam, estimated September 5, 1860:

	Half kilos.
Brazil	324,000,000
Netherlands India	144,000,000
Ceylon	60,000,000
St. Domingo	50,000,000
Venezuela and Costa Rica	30,000,000
Manilla, Mocha, and British India	25,000,000
Cuba, Porto Rico	15,000,000
Jamaica and remaining West Indies	12,000,000

Total, 660,000,000 half-kilos, or 330,000,000 kilos, or 324,787 tons.

And lastly, the present coffee production is noted in Prof. Dr. X. von Neumann Spallart's "Uebersichten über Production, Verkehr und Handel," ed. 1878, p. 92, as follows:

	Zol. Centners.
Brazil	4,800,000
Netherlands India	2,100,000
Ceylon	1,016,000
Hayti	620,000
Venezuela	598,000
British India	307,300
Porto Rico	234,000
Costa Rica	223,500
Guatemala	190,800
Colombia	140,000
San Salvador	74,300
Philippines	72,500
Aden (Arabia)	63,700
Straits Settlements	46,100
French Possessions in America and Africa	24,500
Nicaragua	15,000
Ecuador	11,000
Cuba	10,800
Soudan	10,000
St. Domingo	4,400
Liberia	1,500
Hawaii	1,400

Total, 10,564,800 Zoll. centners, or 528,240,000 kilos, or 519,896 tons.

TABLE XIV.

Prof. Van Den Berg estimated, in 1879, the consumption of coffee in the non-coffee producing countries to be as follows:

Countries.	Total Kilos.	Per Head, Kilos.	Countries.	Total Kilos.	Per Head, Kilos.
Norway	7,250,000	3.96	United States	147,000,000	3.75
Sweden	9,960,000	2.27	Canada	200,000	0.26
Denmark	4,500,000	2 37	Argentine Republic	1,330,000	0.76
Russia	7,625,000	0.10^{6}	Chili, Peru, Uru-		
England	14,970,000	0.45	guay, etc.	1,000,000	—
Netherlands	31,250,000	8.12	Cape Colony	3,000,000	3.50
Belgium	22,110,000	4.14	Natal	700.000	2.00
Germany	90.320,000	2.32	Algiers	2,150,000	—
Austria-Hungary ..	37,250,060	1.	Australia, New Zea-		
Switzerland	8,340,000	3.02	land	1,000,000	—
France	50,000,000	1.38	Persia	1,000.000	—
Italy	12.865,000	0.47	British India	1,000,000	—
Spain	2,750.000	0.16	Siam, China, Japan,		
Portugal	1,500,000	0.34^{5}	etc.	*pro mem.*	—
Greece	1,000,000	0.75			
Turkey	20,000,000	—		489,070,000	

or 481,845 tons, against a *production*, as estimated above, of 490,840,000 kilos, or 483,087 tons.

The increased production of coffee in the last years thus scarcely keeps pace with the increased consumption, and a serious failure of the crops must immediately cause a deficiency that would occasion a considerable rise in prices.

But, on the other hand, we should not lose sight of the fact that the consumption can suddenly decline very considerably through fiscal measures, and with the present state of affairs in Europe it would not be advisable to look upon this eventuality too slightingly.

A diminished consumption must, in its turn, necessarily lower the prices of this article, and for Netherlands, "that has made her financial prosperity wholly dependent on the prices of coffee, and where the rise or fall of a single cent in the prices of coffee either enriches or impoverishes the exchequer by a million" (D. C. Steijn Parvè: "Overzicht van het Handelsverkeer tusschen Nederland en Engeland," p. 102—"Review of the Commercial Relations between Netherlands and England"), it is therefore of great importance that the sale of coffee should everywhere remain as free and unobstructed as possible, in order that the consumption may increase uninterruptedly in the same proportion as the production will, by degrees, probably develop itself.

Her own interests should prompt Netherlands to set the example to other countries in this matter; and a prudent policy seems also to require that the system should be gradually abandoned that makes it almost an impossibility for the stranger to procure the coffee he requires for his own consumption at the place of production itself.

N. P. VAN DEN BERG.

BATAVIA, November, 1879.

TABLE XV.

Stock of Coffee in the Principal Depots of Europe, January 1, 1842, *to* 1881, *inclusive.*

Year.	Tons.	Year.	Tons.	Year.	Tons.
1842........	49,900	1856.......	51,600	1869.......	102,358
1843........	63,650	1857.......	72,000	1870.......	125,896
1844........	70,750	1858.......	96,650	1871.......	83,292
1845........	74,000	1859.......	61,600	1872.......	82,186
1846........	68,350	1860.......	53,200	1873.......	55,955
1847........	68,650	1861.......	46,000	1874.......	62,576
1848........	63,950	1862.......	62,800	1875.......	68,847
1849........	60,900	1863.......	56,000	1876.......	105,993
1850........	50,500	1864.......	64,000	1877.......	72,693
1851........	47,700	1865.......	57,700	1878.......	105,580
1852........	50,700	1866.......	57,400	1879.......	87,978
1853........	56,450	1867.......	56,500	1880.......	93,131
1854........	59,100	1868.......	85,270	1881.......	116,981
1855........	54,700				

TABLE XVI.

Comparative Statement of Imports, 1850 *to* 1880, *inlcusive.*

Year.	Holland.	Hamburg.	England.	United States.
	Millions lbs.	Millions lbs.	Millions lbs.	Millions lbs.
1850..............................	85	62	46	145
1851..............................	106	81	46	153
1852..............................	156	72	48	194
1853..............................	118	88	48	199
1854..............................	113	87	54	162
1855..............................	142	94	53	191
1856..............................	166	76	47	236
1857..............................	136	92	46	241
1858..............................	139	67	47	189
1859..............................	122	78	52	264
1860..............................	124	77	64	202
1861..............................	134	100	66	184
1862..............................	146	80	72	123
1863..............................	127	85	91	80
1864..............................	150	69	84	132
1865..............................	118	101	100	106
1866..............................	146	80	111	181
1867..............................	150	104	114	187
1868..............................	151	132	176	249
1869..............................	133	146	173	254
1870..............................	190	88	180	235
1871..............................	181	144	192	318
1872..............................	102	121	166	299
1873..............................	158	137	184	293
1874..............................	143	150	157	285
1875..............................	183	181	178	318
1876..............................	125	175	158	340
1877..............................	169	188	180	332
1878..............................	151	179	142	310
1879..............................	155	188	180	378
1880..............................	185	197	174	447

TABLE XVII.

Consumption in the German Zollverein, 1836 *to* 1880, *inclusive.*

Year.	Tons.	Year.	Tons.	Year.	Tons.
1836........	26,652	1851.......	45,287	1866.......	72,247
1837........	26,574	1852.......	47,259	1867.......	76,961
1838........	28,364	1853.......	47,295	1868.......	84,623
1839........	28,515	1854.......	55,805	1869.......	81,368
1840........	32,963	1855.......	61,234	1870.......	98,350
1841........	34,806	1856.......	57,517	1871.......	86,400
1842........	35,698	1857.......	61,035	1872.......	92,585
1843........	38.224	1858.......	67,131	1873.......	97,775
1844........	38,780	1859.......	68,260	1874.......	90,033
1845........	41,334	1860.......	65,464	1875.......	100,612
1846........	40,945	1861.......	72,478	1876.......	106,398
1847........	45,761	1862.......	67,414	1877.......	95,779
1848........	40,954	1863.......	66,804	1878.......	99,284
1849........	46,493	1864.......	69,942	1879.......	112,594
1850........	36,687	1865.......	72,765	1880.......	94,222

TABLE XVIII.

Consumption of Coffee in France, 1832 *to* 1880, *inclusive.*

Year.	Tons.	Year.	Tons.	Year.	Tons.
1832........	10,216	1849.......	17,780	1865.......	42,633
1833........	9,185	1850.......	15,029	1866.......	43,910
1834........	10,707	1851.......	18,271	1867.......	47,265
1835........	10,118	1852.......	21,218	1868.......	52,303
1836........	11,002	1853.......	19,548	1869.......	50,327
1837........	12,279	1854.......	21,316	1870.......	72,665
1838........	11,886	1855.......	26,228	1871.......	40,155
1839........	11,886	1856.......	22,790	1872.......	16,708
1840........	14,145	1857.......	27.505	1873.......	44.834
1841........	12,678	1858.......	27,701	1874.......	38,706
1842........	14,833	1859.......	29,764	1875.......	48,013
1843........	14,145	1860.......	33.694	1876.......	53.487
1844........	15,226	1861.......	36,935	1877.......	47,810
1845........	15,619	1862.......	37,132	1878.......	54,105
1846........	16,503	1863.......	38,900	1879.......	56,825
1847........	16,503	1864.......	39,784	1880.......	57,722
1848........	14,538				

TABLE XIX.

Quantities and Values of Tea and Coffee Imported into and Exported from the United States, from 1858 *to* 1881, *inclusive.*

Year ended June 30th.	Tea.				Coffee.			
	Imports.		Foreign exports.		Imports.		Foreign exports.	
	Pounds.	Dollars.	Pounds.	Dollars.	Pounds.	Dollars.	Pounds.	Dollars.
1858	32,995.021	7,261,815	4,228,444	1,384.428	189,211.300	18,369.840	14,714,139	1,589,970
1859	29,268,757	7,388,741	6,149,468	2,461,563	264,436,534	25,086,029	17,615,586	1,823,750
1860	31,696,657	8,915,327	5,369,729	1,985,203	202,144,733	21,883,797	20,095,206	2,268,691
1861	26,117,956	6,977,283	5,101,289	1,556,630	184,499,655	20,568,297	6,589,203	777,485
1862	24,739,983	6,545,654	1,531,644	638,906	122,799,311	14,192,195	9,785,633	1,382,070
1863	29,761,037	8,013,772	2,739,997	1,032,723	80,461,614	10,395,860	5,652,846	1,081,462
1864	37,229,176	10,549,880	1,378,154	571,956	131,622,782	16,221,586	3,778,829	871,260
1865	19,568,318	4,956,730	2,719,129	1,912,797	106,463,062	11,241,706	22,147,017	5,716,053
1866	42,992,738	11,123,231	1,481,290	612,935	181,413,192	20,531,764	5,618,309	901,837
1867	39,892,658	12,415,037	513,084	199,400	187,236,580	20,696,259	5,964,592	881,128
1868	37,843,612	11,111,560	2,217,749	711,751	248,983,900	25,288,451	7,900,980	845,705
1869	43,754,354	13,687,750	2,944,329	947,481	254,160,993	24,531.743	10,765,395	1,020,231
1870	47,408,481	13.863.273	4,868,010	1,874,056	235.256,574	24,234.879	4,083,000	410.836
1871	51,364,919	17,254.617	6,469,974	1,929,830	317,992,048	30,992,869	5,257,012	498,500
1872	63,811,003	22,943,575	4,441,401	1,259,408	298,805,946	37,942,225	3,467,462	408,674
1873	64,815,136	24,466,170	1,060,196	454,641	293,297,271	44,109,671	6,851,027	1,143,076
1874	55,811,605	21,112,234	1,670,252	871,956	285,171,512	55,043,967	3,285,636	705,860
1875	64,856,899	22,673,703	1,565,595	714,185	317,970,665	50,591,488	6,884,014	1,280,154
1876	62,887,153	19,524,166	1,726,908	874,574	339,789.246	56,788,997	8,884,457	1,625,932
1877	58,347,112	16,181,467	1,508,937	676,566	331,639,723	53,634,991	9,890,715	1,567,058
1878	65,866,704	15,660.168	2,247,116	737,544	309,882,540	51.914,605	12,821,426	2,086,366
1879	60,194,673	14,577,618	1,303,138	362,092	377,848,473	47,356,819	15,092,846	2,311,568
1880	72,162,936	19,782,631	2,268,167	799,263	446,850,727	60,360,769	6,721,889	944,573
1881	81,843,988	21,014,813	2,713,139	779,395	455,189,534	56,775,391	31,913,062	4,395,558

TABLE XX.

Quantities and Values of Imported Tea and Coffee Retained in the United States for Consumption, and the Estimated Consumption per Capita of Population, during the Years 1830, 1840, *and from* 1850 *to* 1881 *inclusive.*

Year Ended	Tea.			Coffee.		
	Retained for Home Consumption.		Consumption per Capita of Population.	Retained for Home Consumption.		Consumption per Capita of Population.
September 30—	Pounds.	Dollars.	Pounds.	Pounds.	Dollars.	Pounds.
1830	6,873,091	1,532,211	0.53	38,363,687	3,180,479	3.0
1840	16,883,099	4,067,144	0.99	86,297,761	7,615,824	5.05
June 30—						
1850	28,199,591	3,982,054	1.22	129,791,466	9,918,472	5.55
1851	13,504,774	3,452,496	0.57	148,992,505	12,489,671	6.2
1852	25,587,668	5,927,143	1.03	180,712,687	13,372,124	7.3
1853	19,291,884	7,024,526	0.75	185,999,243	14,380,383	7.3
1854	19,236,113	4,933,553	0.73	150,246,403	13,377,972	5.7
1855	19,763,593	4,937,610	0.72	175,150,440	15,486,423	6.4
1856	18,181,470	5,250,603	0.64	223,638,479	20,321,142	7.9
1857	16,500,285	4,344,963	0.57	216,655,977	19,809,854	7.5
1858	28,766,577	5,877,387	0.97	174,497,161	16,779,870	5.9
1859	23,119,280	4,927,178	0.76	246,820,948	23,262,279	8.1
1860	26,326,928	6,930,124	0.84	182,049,527	19,615,106	5.8
1861	21,016,667	5,420,653	0.66	177,910,452	19,790,812	5.5
1862	23,336,777	5,906,758	0.71	113,013,678	12,810,125	3.4
1863	27,021,040	6,981,049	0.80	74,808,768	9,314,398	2.2
1864	35,851,022	9,977,924	1.04	127,844,486	15,350,326	3.7
1865	16,849,189	3,043,933	0.49	84,316,045	5,525,653	2.4
1866	41,511,448	10,510,296	1.17	175,794,883	19,620,927	5.0
1867	39,379,574	12,215,637	1.09	181,271,988	19,815,131	5.0
1868	35,625,863	10,399,809	0.97	241,082,920	24,442,746	6.5
1869	40,810,025	12,740,269	1.08	243,395,598	23,511,512	6.5
1870	42,540,471	12,489,217	1.10	231,173,574	23,824,043	6.0
1871	44,894,945	15,324,787	1.26	312,735,036	30,494,309	7.9
1872	59,369,602	21,684,167	1.46	295,338,464	37,533,551	7.3
1873	63,754,940	24,011,529	1.53	286,446,244	42,966,595	6.9
1874	54,141,353	20,240,278	1.26	281,885,876	54,348,107	6.6
1875	63,291,304	21,959,518	1.44	311,136,651	49,311,334	7.1
1876	61,160,245	18,649,592	1.35	330,904,789	55,163,065	7.3
1877	56,838,175	15,504,901	1.22	321,749,006	52,067,933	6.9
1878	63,123,188	14,922,624	1.32	297,061,114	49,828,239	6.2
1879	58,891,535	14,215,526	1.11	362,755,627	45,045,251	7.3
1880	69,894,769	18,983,368	1.39	440,128,838	59,416,196	8.8
1881	79,130,849	20,235,418	1.53	423,276,472	52,379,833	8.4

Note.—The consumption of tea and of coffee in the United States, for each year from 1830 to 1866, inclusive, is estimated by subtracting the amount exported from the amount imported. For the years 1867 to 1880, inclusive, the amount of the respective articles entered for consumption at the custom-houses is taken as the consumption. The population is estimated for years other than the census years 1830, 1840, 1850, 1860, 1870, and 1880. In 1870 it was 38,558,371; in 1880 it was 50,152,866.

TABLE XXI.

Weights in Use in Coffee-Producing Countries, with their Equivalents in United States Currency.

Metric denominations and values. Names.		No. grams.		Equivalents in denominations in use.	
Millier or tonneau	=	1,000,000	=	2,204.6	pounds.
Quintal	=	100,000	=	220.46	pounds.
Myriagram	=	10,000	=	22.046	pounds.
Kilogram or kilo	=	1,000	=	2.2046	pounds.
Hectogram	=	100	=	3.5274	ounces.
Decagram	=	10	=	0.3527	ouuce.
Gram	=	1	=	15.432	grains.
Decigram	=	0.1	=	1.5432	grain.
Centigram	=	0.01	=	0.1543	grain.
Milligram	=	0.001	=	0.0154	grain.

Brazil.

Metric system obligatory from January 1, 1873.

Tonelada (ton for shipping) = 2,240 pounds avoirdupois.
Arroba = 32.38 pounds.
Quintal = 130.06 pounds.

Mexico.

Quintal = 101.61 pounds.

Philippines—Manilla.

Picul = 140 pounds.

Zollverein.

Centner = 110.24 pounds.

Prussia.

Centner = 113.44 pounds.

Bremen.

Centner = 127.5 pounds.

Vienna.

Centner = 123.5 pounds.

Netherlands.

Old Pond = 1.0893 pound.

Colonies.

French metric system adopted in 1816.

1 Picul = 100 catties = 10 gautang (coffee) = 135.6312 pounds avdp.

New Grenada, or United States of Colombia.

French weights.

Ceylon.

English weights used.

Candy = 545 pounds avoirdupois.

England.

16 ounces = 1 pound, lb.
28 pounds = 1 quarter, qr.
4 quarters = 1 hundredweight, cwt.
20 hundredweight = 1 ton.

United States.

Same as England in custom-house operations. Common usage calls 100 pounds a hundredweight, 25 pounds a quarter.

Cental = 100 pounds.

TABLE XXII.—Prices of Good Ordinary Java in Holland, 1871 to 1880, *inclusive*.

(In Dutch cents—2½ Dntch cents equivalent to one U. S. cent.)

1871	35	36½	33	34½	32½	43	
1872	43	44½	40½	47	44	49½	
1873	49½	57½	50	65½			
1874	65½	72½	50	59½	53	55½	
1875	55½	53	61	58			
1876	58	52	54	50	55		
1877	55	58	50	54			
1878	54	47	49	45	49	40½	
1879	40½	42½	41	42	40½	50	48
1880	48	39½	41	38	40	37	38½

TABLE XXIII.—Exports of Coffee from Rio de Janeiro for each Calendar Year, 1817 to 1880, *inclusive*.

Year.	Sacks, 5 Arrobas each.	In thousands of U. S. Pounds.	Tons.	Year.	Sacks, 5 Arrobas each.	In thousands of U. S. Pounds.	Tons.
1817	63,986	10,364	4,570	1850	1,343,484	217,644	97,386
1818	74,247	12,028	5,308	1851	2,040,405	330,546	147,565
1819	73,314	11,877	5,237	1852	1,906,472	308,848	137,879
1820	97,500	15,795	6,965	1853	1,638,210	265,390	118,477
1821	105,386	17,073	7,528	1854	1,988,197	322,088	143,789
1822	152,048	24,632	10,861	1855	2,408,256	390,137	175,169
1823	185,000	29,970	13,214	1856	2,098,812	339,927	151,753
1824	224,000	36,288	16,000	1857	2,099,780	340,164	151,859
1825	183,136	29,668	13,081	1858	1,830,438	296,532	132,380
1826	260,000	42,120	18,571	1859	2,030,266	328,903	146,832
1827	350,900	56,846	25,064	1860	2,127,219	344,609	153,844
1828	369,147	59,802	26,368	1861	2,069,627	335,280	149,678
1829	375,107	60,767	26,793	1862	1,485,220	240,606	107,413
1830	391,785	63,469	27,985	1863	1,350,109	218,718	97,642
1831	448,249	72,616	32,018	1864	1,480,134	239,782	107,045
1832	478,950	77,590	34,211	1865	1,801,952	291,916	130,319
1833	561,692	90,994	40,121	1866	1,934,896	313,453	139,934
1834	560,759	90,843	40,054	1867	2,659,753	430,880	192,357
1835	647,438	104,885	46,245	1868	2,265,185	366,960	163,821
1836	715,893	115,975	51,135	1869	2,564,975	415,526	185,508
1837	657,005	106,435	46,929	1870	2,209,456	357,932	159,791
1838	766,696	124,205	54,764	1871	2,357,961	381,990	170,532
1839	889,324	144,070	63,523	1872	2,011,098	225,798	145,445
1840	1,068,418	173,084	76,316	1873	1,984,670	321,517	143,534
1841	1,028,368	166,596	73,455		Sacks, 60 Kilos or 132 Lbs.		
1842	1,152,608	186,722	83,358				
1843	1,165,631	188,832	84,300	1874	2,644,995	349,139	155,588
1844	1,232,935	199,735	89,168	1875	3,190,010	421,081	187,648
1845	1,191,641	193,046	86,181	1876	2,787,501	367,950	163,971
1846	1,511,096	244,798	109,285	1877	2,847,756	375,904	167,515
1847	1,641,560	265,933	118,719	1878	2,914,420	384,703	171,436
1848	1,710,715	277,136	123,721	1879	3,507,559	462,998	206,329
1849	1,459,968	236,515	105,587	1880	3,436,108	453,566	202,124

STATEMENT SHOWING THE QUANTITY AND VALUE OF COFFEE IMPORTED INTO THE UNITED STATES, BY CUSTOMS DISTRICTS, FOR EACH FISCAL YEAR FROM 1871 TO 1880 INCLUSIVE.

[Compiled specially for this work.]

Customs districts into which imported.	1871		1872		1873		1874		1875		1876		1877		1878		1879		1880	
	Pounds.	Dollars.	Pounds.	Dollars.	Pounds.	Dollars.	Pounds.	Dollars.	Pounds.	Dollars.	Pounds.	Dollars.	Pounds.	Dollars.	Pounds.	Dollars.	Pounds.	Dollars.	Pounds.	Dollars.
Alaska, Alaska	[illegible]	[illegible]	[illegible]	[illegible]	[illegible]	[illegible]	[illegible]	[illegible]	[illegible]	[illegible]	[illegible]	[illegible]	[illegible]	[illegible]	[illegible]	[illegible]	[illegible]	[illegible]	[illegible]	[illegible]
Aroostook, Me.	[illegible]	[illegible]	[illegible]	[illegible]	[illegible]	[illegible]	[illegible]	[illegible]	[illegible]	[illegible]	[illegible]	[illegible]	[illegible]	[illegible]	[illegible]	[illegible]	[illegible]	[illegible]	[illegible]	[illegible]
Baltimore, Md.	[illegible]	[illegible]	[illegible]	[illegible]	[illegible]	[illegible]	[illegible]	[illegible]	[illegible]	[illegible]	[illegible]	[illegible]	[illegible]	[illegible]	[illegible]	[illegible]	[illegible]	[illegible]	[illegible]	[illegible]
Barnstable, Mass.	[illegible]	[illegible]	[illegible]	[illegible]	[illegible]	[illegible]	[illegible]	[illegible]	[illegible]	[illegible]	[illegible]	[illegible]	[illegible]	[illegible]	[illegible]	[illegible]	[illegible]	[illegible]	[illegible]	[illegible]
Boston and Charlestown, Mass.	[illegible]	[illegible]	[illegible]	[illegible]	[illegible]	[illegible]	[illegible]	[illegible]	[illegible]	[illegible]	[illegible]	[illegible]	[illegible]	[illegible]	[illegible]	[illegible]	[illegible]	[illegible]	[illegible]	[illegible]
Brazos de Santiago, Tex.	[illegible]	[illegible]	[illegible]	[illegible]	[illegible]	[illegible]	[illegible]	[illegible]	[illegible]	[illegible]	[illegible]	[illegible]	[illegible]	[illegible]	[illegible]	[illegible]	[illegible]	[illegible]	[illegible]	[illegible]
Bristol and Warren, R. I.	[illegible]	[illegible]	[illegible]	[illegible]	[illegible]	[illegible]	[illegible]	[illegible]	[illegible]	[illegible]	[illegible]	[illegible]	[illegible]	[illegible]	[illegible]	[illegible]	[illegible]	[illegible]	[illegible]	[illegible]
Buffalo Creek, N. Y.	[illegible]	[illegible]	[illegible]	[illegible]	[illegible]	[illegible]	[illegible]	[illegible]	[illegible]	[illegible]	[illegible]	[illegible]	[illegible]	[illegible]	[illegible]	[illegible]	[illegible]	[illegible]	[illegible]	[illegible]
Champlain, N. Y.	[illegible]	[illegible]	[illegible]	[illegible]	[illegible]	[illegible]	[illegible]	[illegible]	[illegible]	[illegible]	[illegible]	[illegible]	[illegible]	[illegible]	[illegible]	[illegible]	[illegible]	[illegible]	[illegible]	[illegible]
Charleston, S. C.	[illegible]	[illegible]	[illegible]	[illegible]	[illegible]	[illegible]	[illegible]	[illegible]	[illegible]	[illegible]	[illegible]	[illegible]	[illegible]	[illegible]	[illegible]	[illegible]	[illegible]	[illegible]	[illegible]	[illegible]
Chicago, Ill.	[illegible]	[illegible]	[illegible]	[illegible]	[illegible]	[illegible]	[illegible]	[illegible]	[illegible]	[illegible]	[illegible]	[illegible]	[illegible]	[illegible]	[illegible]	[illegible]	[illegible]	[illegible]	[illegible]	[illegible]
Corpus Christi, Tex.	[illegible]	[illegible]	[illegible]	[illegible]	[illegible]	[illegible]	[illegible]	[illegible]	[illegible]	[illegible]	[illegible]	[illegible]	[illegible]	[illegible]	[illegible]	[illegible]	[illegible]	[illegible]	[illegible]	[illegible]
Detroit, Mich.	[illegible]	[illegible]	[illegible]	[illegible]	[illegible]	[illegible]	[illegible]	[illegible]	[illegible]	[illegible]	[illegible]	[illegible]	[illegible]	[illegible]	[illegible]	[illegible]	[illegible]	[illegible]	[illegible]	[illegible]
Fernandina, Fla.	[illegible]	[illegible]	[illegible]	[illegible]	[illegible]	[illegible]	[illegible]	[illegible]	[illegible]	[illegible]	[illegible]	[illegible]	[illegible]	[illegible]	[illegible]	[illegible]	[illegible]	[illegible]	[illegible]	[illegible]
Galveston, Tex.	[illegible]	[illegible]	[illegible]	[illegible]	[illegible]	[illegible]	[illegible]	[illegible]	[illegible]	[illegible]	[illegible]	[illegible]	[illegible]	[illegible]	[illegible]	[illegible]	[illegible]	[illegible]	[illegible]	[illegible]
Genesee, N. Y.	[illegible]	[illegible]	[illegible]	[illegible]	[illegible]	[illegible]	[illegible]	[illegible]	[illegible]	[illegible]	[illegible]	[illegible]	[illegible]	[illegible]	[illegible]	[illegible]	[illegible]	[illegible]	[illegible]	[illegible]
Huron, Mich.	[illegible]	[illegible]	[illegible]	[illegible]	[illegible]	[illegible]	[illegible]	[illegible]	[illegible]	[illegible]	[illegible]	[illegible]	[illegible]	[illegible]	[illegible]	[illegible]	[illegible]	[illegible]	[illegible]	[illegible]
Key West, Fla.	[illegible]	[illegible]	[illegible]	[illegible]	[illegible]	[illegible]	[illegible]	[illegible]	[illegible]	[illegible]	[illegible]	[illegible]	[illegible]	[illegible]	[illegible]	[illegible]	[illegible]	[illegible]	[illegible]	[illegible]
Minnesota, Minn.	[illegible]	[illegible]	[illegible]	[illegible]	[illegible]	[illegible]	[illegible]	[illegible]	[illegible]	[illegible]	[illegible]	[illegible]	[illegible]	[illegible]	[illegible]	[illegible]	[illegible]	[illegible]	[illegible]	[illegible]
Mobile, Ala.	[illegible]	[illegible]	[illegible]	[illegible]	[illegible]	[illegible]	[illegible]	[illegible]	[illegible]	[illegible]	[illegible]	[illegible]	[illegible]	[illegible]	[illegible]	[illegible]	[illegible]	[illegible]	[illegible]	[illegible]
New Bedford, Mass.	[illegible]	[illegible]	[illegible]	[illegible]	[illegible]	[illegible]	[illegible]	[illegible]	[illegible]	[illegible]	[illegible]	[illegible]	[illegible]	[illegible]	[illegible]	[illegible]	[illegible]	[illegible]	[illegible]	[illegible]
Newburyport, Mass.	[illegible]	[illegible]	[illegible]	[illegible]	[illegible]	[illegible]	[illegible]	[illegible]	[illegible]	[illegible]	[illegible]	[illegible]	[illegible]	[illegible]	[illegible]	[illegible]	[illegible]	[illegible]	[illegible]	[illegible]
New Haven, Conn.	[illegible]	[illegible]	[illegible]	[illegible]	[illegible]	[illegible]	[illegible]	[illegible]	[illegible]	[illegible]	[illegible]	[illegible]	[illegible]	[illegible]	[illegible]	[illegible]	[illegible]	[illegible]	[illegible]	[illegible]
New London, Conn.	[illegible]	[illegible]	[illegible]	[illegible]	[illegible]	[illegible]	[illegible]	[illegible]	[illegible]	[illegible]	[illegible]	[illegible]	[illegible]	[illegible]	[illegible]	[illegible]	[illegible]	[illegible]	[illegible]	[illegible]
New Orleans, La.	[illegible]	[illegible]	[illegible]	[illegible]	[illegible]	[illegible]	[illegible]	[illegible]	[illegible]	[illegible]	[illegible]	[illegible]	[illegible]	[illegible]	[illegible]	[illegible]	[illegible]	[illegible]	[illegible]	[illegible]
New York, N. Y.	[illegible]	[illegible]	[illegible]	[illegible]	[illegible]	[illegible]	[illegible]	[illegible]	[illegible]	[illegible]	[illegible]	[illegible]	[illegible]	[illegible]	[illegible]	[illegible]	[illegible]	[illegible]	[illegible]	[illegible]
Oregon, Oreg.	[illegible]	[illegible]	[illegible]	[illegible]	[illegible]	[illegible]	[illegible]	[illegible]	[illegible]	[illegible]	[illegible]	[illegible]	[illegible]	[illegible]	[illegible]	[illegible]	[illegible]	[illegible]	[illegible]	[illegible]
[illegible], N. Y.	[illegible]	[illegible]	[illegible]	[illegible]	[illegible]	[illegible]	[illegible]	[illegible]	[illegible]	[illegible]	[illegible]	[illegible]	[illegible]	[illegible]	[illegible]	[illegible]	[illegible]	[illegible]	[illegible]	[illegible]
Paso del Norte, Tex., and New Mexico	[illegible]	[illegible]	[illegible]	[illegible]	[illegible]	[illegible]	[illegible]	[illegible]	[illegible]	[illegible]	[illegible]	[illegible]	[illegible]	[illegible]	[illegible]	[illegible]	[illegible]	[illegible]	[illegible]	[illegible]
Passamaquoddy, Me.	[illegible]	[illegible]	[illegible]	[illegible]	[illegible]	[illegible]	[illegible]	[illegible]	[illegible]	[illegible]	[illegible]	[illegible]	[illegible]	[illegible]	[illegible]	[illegible]	[illegible]	[illegible]	[illegible]	[illegible]
Pearl River, Miss.	[illegible]	[illegible]	[illegible]	[illegible]	[illegible]	[illegible]	[illegible]	[illegible]	[illegible]	[illegible]	[illegible]	[illegible]	[illegible]	[illegible]	[illegible]	[illegible]	[illegible]	[illegible]	[illegible]	[illegible]
Pensacola, Fla.	[illegible]	[illegible]	[illegible]	[illegible]	[illegible]	[illegible]	[illegible]	[illegible]	[illegible]	[illegible]	[illegible]	[illegible]	[illegible]	[illegible]	[illegible]	[illegible]	[illegible]	[illegible]	[illegible]	[illegible]
Perth Amboy, N. J.	[illegible]	[illegible]	[illegible]	[illegible]	[illegible]	[illegible]	[illegible]	[illegible]	[illegible]	[illegible]	[illegible]	[illegible]	[illegible]	[illegible]	[illegible]	[illegible]	[illegible]	[illegible]	[illegible]	[illegible]
Philadelphia, Pa.	[illegible]	[illegible]	[illegible]	[illegible]	[illegible]	[illegible]	[illegible]	[illegible]	[illegible]	[illegible]	[illegible]	[illegible]	[illegible]	[illegible]	[illegible]	[illegible]	[illegible]	[illegible]	[illegible]	[illegible]
Portland and Falmouth, Me.	[illegible]	[illegible]	[illegible]	[illegible]	[illegible]	[illegible]	[illegible]	[illegible]	[illegible]	[illegible]	[illegible]	[illegible]	[illegible]	[illegible]	[illegible]	[illegible]	[illegible]	[illegible]	[illegible]	[illegible]
Providence, R. I.	[illegible]	[illegible]	[illegible]	[illegible]	[illegible]	[illegible]	[illegible]	[illegible]	[illegible]	[illegible]	[illegible]	[illegible]	[illegible]	[illegible]	[illegible]	[illegible]	[illegible]	[illegible]	[illegible]	[illegible]
Puget Sound, Wash. Ter.	[illegible]	[illegible]	[illegible]	[illegible]	[illegible]	[illegible]	[illegible]	[illegible]	[illegible]	[illegible]	[illegible]	[illegible]	[illegible]	[illegible]	[illegible]	[illegible]	[illegible]	[illegible]	[illegible]	[illegible]
Richmond, Va.	[illegible]	[illegible]	[illegible]	[illegible]	[illegible]	[illegible]	[illegible]	[illegible]	[illegible]	[illegible]	[illegible]	[illegible]	[illegible]	[illegible]	[illegible]	[illegible]	[illegible]	[illegible]	[illegible]	[illegible]
Salem and Beverly, Mass.	[illegible]	[illegible]	[illegible]	[illegible]	[illegible]	[illegible]	[illegible]	[illegible]	[illegible]	[illegible]	[illegible]	[illegible]	[illegible]	[illegible]	[illegible]	[illegible]	[illegible]	[illegible]	[illegible]	[illegible]
Saluria, Tex.	[illegible]	[illegible]	[illegible]	[illegible]	[illegible]	[illegible]	[illegible]	[illegible]	[illegible]	[illegible]	[illegible]	[illegible]	[illegible]	[illegible]	[illegible]	[illegible]	[illegible]	[illegible]	[illegible]	[illegible]
San Diego, Cal.	[illegible]	[illegible]	[illegible]	[illegible]	[illegible]	[illegible]	[illegible]	[illegible]	[illegible]	[illegible]	[illegible]	[illegible]	[illegible]	[illegible]	[illegible]	[illegible]	[illegible]	[illegible]	[illegible]	[illegible]
San Francisco, Cal.	[illegible]	[illegible]	[illegible]	[illegible]	[illegible]	[illegible]	[illegible]	[illegible]	[illegible]	[illegible]	[illegible]	[illegible]	[illegible]	[illegible]	[illegible]	[illegible]	[illegible]	[illegible]	[illegible]	[illegible]
Savannah, Ga.	[illegible]	[illegible]	[illegible]	[illegible]	[illegible]	[illegible]	[illegible]	[illegible]	[illegible]	[illegible]	[illegible]	[illegible]	[illegible]	[illegible]	[illegible]	[illegible]	[illegible]	[illegible]	[illegible]	[illegible]
St. Johns, Fla.	[illegible]	[illegible]	[illegible]	[illegible]	[illegible]	[illegible]	[illegible]	[illegible]	[illegible]	[illegible]	[illegible]	[illegible]	[illegible]	[illegible]	[illegible]	[illegible]	[illegible]	[illegible]	[illegible]	[illegible]
Superior, Mich.	[illegible]	[illegible]	[illegible]	[illegible]	[illegible]	[illegible]	[illegible]	[illegible]	[illegible]	[illegible]	[illegible]	[illegible]	[illegible]	[illegible]	[illegible]	[illegible]	[illegible]	[illegible]	[illegible]	[illegible]
Vermont, Vt.	[illegible]	[illegible]	[illegible]	[illegible]	[illegible]	[illegible]	[illegible]	[illegible]	[illegible]	[illegible]	[illegible]	[illegible]	[illegible]	[illegible]	[illegible]	[illegible]	[illegible]	[illegible]	[illegible]	[illegible]
Willamette, Oreg.	[illegible]	[illegible]	[illegible]	[illegible]	[illegible]	[illegible]	[illegible]	[illegible]	[illegible]	[illegible]	[illegible]	[illegible]	[illegible]	[illegible]	[illegible]	[illegible]	[illegible]	[illegible]	[illegible]	[illegible]
Wilmington, N. C.	[illegible]	[illegible]	[illegible]	[illegible]	[illegible]	[illegible]	[illegible]	[illegible]	[illegible]	[illegible]	[illegible]	[illegible]	[illegible]	[illegible]	[illegible]	[illegible]	[illegible]	[illegible]	[illegible]	[illegible]
Total	[illegible]	[illegible]	[illegible]	[illegible]	[illegible]	[illegible]	[illegible]	[illegible]	[illegible]	[illegible]	[illegible]	[illegible]	[illegible]	[illegible]	[illegible]	[illegible]	[illegible]	[illegible]	[illegible]	[illegible]

TREASURY DEPARTMENT, BUREAU OF STATISTICS,
March 10, 1881.

JOSEPH NIMMO, JR.,
Chief of Bureau.

APPENDIX.

APPENDIX.

PATENTS ON ROASTED COFFEE.

NEW YORK, January 12, 1878.

Editor American Grocer :

We are paying a royalty on roasted and glazed coffee. Some parties claim to hold a patent for the use of starch, gelatinous, and saccharine substances for the purpose, as well as the method of application to roasted coffee. We are informed that roasters in Chicago and in some other parts of the country decline to pay them royalty, and if you can inform us on what grounds they decline, and whether there are other patents, and, if possible, whether their patents will stand the test of law, you will much oblige, yours truly,

BEARDS & COTTREL.

Perhaps some of the roasters declining will inform you, through us, of their reasons for declining to pay a royalty, and we can give no opinion as to the value of an untested patent. We ascertain that the American Glazed Coffee Association own three patents: No. 63,987, issued to Thomas N. Berry, Lynn, Mass., April 23, 1867, for preparing coffee for transportation, claims 1 ounce French isinglass and 4 ounces water, the mass mixed and moulded to form; No. 73,486, issued to John Arbuckle, Jr., Alleghany City, Pa., January 21, 1868; the roasted coffee is coated with a preparation composed of Irish moss, ½ ounce; gelatine, ½ ounce; isinglass, ½ ounce; white sugar, 1 ounce; eggs, 24 —the first three are boiled in water and the moss strained clear; claim the coating of roasted coffee with any gelatinous or glutenous matter for the purpose of retaining the aroma of the coffee, and also to act as a clarifying agent; also patent No. 91,870, issued to E. E. Rhinehart, Pittsburg, Pa., June 29, 1869, claims the mode of cooling or glazing roasted coffee by mixing therewith, before cooling, a mucilaginous or other suitable substance. The obtaining of these three patents for substantially the same articles and purpose shows the facility with which patents are obtained, and that in many cases their real value is questionable until tested in higher courts. We find, also, an English patent, No 3,131, issued to William Pidding, November 28, 1866, which antedates and originates the ideas set forth in the patents owned by the association:

"English patent, No. 3,131, William Pidding, November 28, 1866 (not sealed), subjects the green coffee to cutting up into particles and grains, then to desiccation and roasting. In some cases prefers to swell the berry by subjecting to steam at low temperature, in closed vessels. The granulated and roasted coffee is subjected to pressure, with or without humid heat, between cellular plates or indented rollers, producing cakes or balls of different shapes; then subjects them to a coating of gelatinous matter, whether composed of pure gelatine, gum, starch, or starch gum, used either separately or in combination. This coating is used as a preservative of aroma and purity, the coffee being made air-tight. In some cases intends to use the various gelatinous matters in a dry state or powder (or solution), mixing the same with the granulated coffee, and subjecting the same to a humid heat and pressure, to produce cakes or balls. The cakes, etc., by either process are subjected to heat of a temperature sufficient to harden them and render them portable."

As this patent is not sealed, it is incomplete, but, under a decision of Judge Strong, in the October Term of 1876, it may be of some value. The following is the decision:

SUPREME COURT OF THE UNITED STATES.

Corset Patent.—Moritz Cohn, appellant, vs. The United States Corset Company, John H. Lane and William Lyall.

[Appeal from the Circuit Court of the United States for the Southern District of New York.—Decided October Term, 1876.]

A patent is invalid if the invention claimed is found to be patented or described in a printed publication prior to the patentee's invention or discovery

thereof, and it is enough if the thing patented is described, and not the steps necessarily antecedent to its production.

Thus, when the invention claimed is an article, it is not necessary, in order to render the patent void, that the prior publication should also contain a description of the process by which such article was made.

Unless the earlier printed and published description does exhibit the later patented invention in such a full and intelligible manner as to enable persons skilled in the art to which the invention is related to comprehend it without assistance from the patent, or to make it or repeat the process claimed, it is insufficient to invalidate the patent.

Mr. Justice Strong delivered the opinion of the court.

A careful examination of the evidence in this case has convinced us that the invention claimed and patented to the plaintiff was anticipated and described in the English provisional specification of John Henry Johnson, left in the office of the Commissioner of Patents on the 20th of January, A.D. 1854. That specification was printed and published in England officially in 1854, and is contained in volume second of a printed publication circulated in this country as early as the year 1856. It is therefore fatal to the validity of the plaintiff's patent if, in fact, it does describe sufficiently the manufacture described and claimed in his specification. The plaintiff's application at the Patent Office was made on the 30th of January, 1873. In it he claimed to have invented "a new and useful improvement in corsets." After reciting that previous to his invention it had been customary, in the manufacture of corsets, to weave the material with pocket-like openings or passages running from edge to edge, and adapted to receive the bones, which are inserted to stay the woven fabric, and which serve as braces to give shape to and support the figure of the wearer, but that it had been necessary, after the insertion of the bones into said pocket-like passages, to secure each one endwise by sewing, he proceeded to mention objections to that mode of making a corset. He specified two only. The first was that it involved much hand labor, and consequent expense, in sewing in the bones, or securing them endwise in the woven passages; and the second was that the arrangement or placement of the bones in the passages had to be determined by hand manipulation, and that it was therefore variable and irregular, such as frequently to give to the corset an undesirable shape or appearance near its upper edge. These objections he proposed to remove, and to produce a corset in which the location or position endwise of the bones shall be predetermined with the accuracy of the jacquard in the process of weaving the corset stuffs or materials, thereby effecting the saving of labor and expense in the manufacture. He therefore declared his invention to consist in having the pocket-like openings or passages into which the bones are put closed up near one end, and at that point at which it is designed to have the end of each bone located. . . . . Amendments were then made until his present patent was at last granted, dated April 15, 1873. In the specification which accompanies it, the patentee omits what he admitted at first—that prior to his invention it had been customary, in the manufacture of corsets, to weave the material with pocket-like openings or passages running through from edge to edge, and he makes the further admission that it had been customary to weave the material with such passages all stopped and finished off at uniform distances from the edge. He therefore disclaims "a woven corset with the pockets stopped and finished off at a uniform distance from the edges," and he disclaims also "a hand-made corset with pockets of varying lengths stitched on," and his claim is, "a corset having the pockets for the reception of the bones formed in the weaving, and varying in length relatively to each other, as desired, substantially in the manner and for the purposes set forth."

"NOTES BY THE WAY."

HAVING been often asked why I did not collect and publish a series of letters written while on a trip around the world in 1876, most of which appeared in the *American Grocer* under the above title, or that of "Wayside Scenes, Thoughts and Fancies," I have embraced the present opportunity to do so, not because I think these letters of much general interest, but being written from a grocer's point of view, and touching somewhat often upon the food products of the Orient, they have been received with much favor by dealers in such articles, and they doubtless find an appropriate place in a work devoted to good things for the inner man. I therefore begin with

ACROSS THE PACIFIC.

STEAMER ALASKA,
PACIFIC OCEAN, August 26, 1876.

A long sea voyage is always somewhat monotonous, but a person disposed to look at the bright side of life can generally pick out some items of enjoyment to compensate for the general lack of that commodity. "Life-on-the-ocean-wave" people will please take note of this observation and the opinion of your correspondent. Somebody has said that "Doubtless God might have made a better berry than the strawberry, but doubtless God never did;" and it is possible that infinite power might create a more unnatural element for the human race to exist upon than the sea, but in my humble opinion infinite power never did. Tuesday, August 1st, at noon, found me on board of the steamship Alaska, at San Francisco, bound for Yokohama, and as the lines were cast off and the huge bulk of the steamer moved slowly out into the bay, the usual greetings were exchanged between friends on ship and friends on shore. Moving rapidly down the beautiful bay of San Francisco and out through the Golden Gate, the shores of America rapidly receded and were soon an indistinct line in the distance. One of the first things that strike a passenger on the ships of the Pacific Mail Steamship Company is the omnipresent Chinaman—Chinese waiters, Chinese cooks, Chinese firemen, Chinese sailors, and Chinese steerage passengers are everywhere to be seen. Indeed, the only white men on board the ship are the officers and cabin passengers. I asked our captain if there were no white sailors on board, and was surprised to receive the answer, "No, nothing below a boatswain, and one of those is a Chinaman." We have only about twenty-five cabin passengers, among whom are three missionaries, three young Japanese returning home after finishing their education in the United States, two officers of American men-of-war going out to join their ships, and the balance is made up of tourists and commercial men bound for different parts of the world. In the steerage are one hundred and sixty Chinese, mostly men, but also including a few women and children, returning to their homes in China. Some of these speak English quite well. Said one of them to me, in answer to an inquiry as to why he was going back to China: "Go China to gettee wifee, then go back Californee." I asked him if he had one picked out, and he said, "No, I buy one." I asked him how much she would cost, and he said: "Ninety dollar buy nice one with small footee." I asked him why he preferred those with small feet, and he answered: "Chinawoman big footee may be run around after other Chinaman, but Chinawoman small footee you leave her home, you find her there when you come back." By subsequent inquiry I found that the money paid to the bride's parents is considered a sort of dowry, but there is so little sentiment indulged in, and the bride has so little to say about her likes and dislikes, that it is very natural to esteem it a sort of a bargain and sale. Indeed in Japan, China, India, and all Eastern countries, the females have little scope for the exercise of their preferences as to whom they will marry.

For several days we have been making an average of two hundred miles per day, which is not very fast, but we are heavily laden, and on a long voyage like this, the company—principally for the consideration of economy in coal—do not drive their ships as is done on the Atlantic. Besides, the Alaska is one of the old side-wheel pattern of ships, and not very fast, although quite steady and comfortable. Twice the monotony of our voyage has been broken by an alarm of fire, which, however, turned out to be only a false alarm for the purpose of exercising the officers and crew in the fire-drill, which appears to be very perfect and efficient. Yesterday, in four minutes from the giving of the alarm, the hose was uncoiled, run aft, and six streams from the steam-pumps were pouring over the side in a way so vigorous that it must have proved very effective in case they were directed on a fire. The crew are also occasionally exercised at boat-drill, so as to perfect them in getting out and lowering the boats in case of need. A few evenings ago, just before retiring for the night, we had a beautiful view of a lunar-bow or "moon-rainbow," the largest and most distinct that I ever saw. On Sundays, regular service is held night and morning, usually celebrated in the morning by one of our American missionaries, and in the evening by two English missionaries who are destined for Japan. The chief amusements for week-days are sea-quoits, otherwise known as "bull," and reading and music. Altogether we manage to wear away the time as pleasantly as could be expected. Thus far we have had the usual variety of weather, clear or cloudy, dry or wet, smooth or rough, but old voyagers on the Pacific say that, taken altogether, the weather has been very good. On the 16th we reached the 180th meridian of longitude, and "the event of the voyage" took place, namely, *losing a day*. I had often heard of this, but never fully realized it until I had passed through the operation myself. It is briefly this—that in going round the world westward you constantly gain in time four minutes to the degree or parallel of longitude; consequently, when you arrive at the 180th parallel and are half-way round, from Greenwich, you have gained twelve hours, and, for the sake of convenience in navigation, this is called *a day*, in order to prevent twelve o'clock at night from being twelve o'clock in the daytime.

The occasion of crossing the line is generally signalized by some kind of ceremonies, and in our case an oil-barrel painted to resemble a buoy was dropped overboard, a gun fired, and the passengers of course all rushed on deck to find out what the firing meant. They were referred to the buoy, which was now plainly visible astern, as being the buoy which marked the 180th parallel of longitude. Of course they accepted this statement as "gospel truth," and due note was made of it in diaries, but after the joke had been carried sufficiently far it was duly explained by the captain, much to the enjoyment of the few who were in the secret, and the chagrin of those who had been taken in.

We have now been out twenty-three days, and have made 4,577 miles. If nothing happens, twelve hours more will bring us to the end of our voyage—a voyage which, although we consider it long, is less than half the time formerly occupied by our clippers in crossing the same space. Nine years ago the first steamer of this line crossed the Pacific Ocean, and for all the purposes for which oceans are valuable, for the use of commerce, reduced the distance between Asia and America one-half. Many may not appreciate the significance of this, but it means that the commerce of the Indies—the prize for which all the great nations of the earth have contended during the last two thousand years—has been brought within the grasp of the youngest nation. All that it needs is a wise and liberal policy on the part of our statesmen. Natives of China and other countries whose shores are washed by the Pacific Ocean must be guaranteed, when they come to this country, the same right that our Constitution has given the citizens of every country who have come to us since we have been a nation. The only important line of American steamships now afloat should be kept going by the same means that have fostered all British lines until they were strong enough to make their way unassisted—liberal subsidies for frequent mail service.

Frequent communication with, and simple justice in the treatment of the natives of the Indies will give us their trade. They will send us their tea, silk, coffee, and spices, and take our flour, petroleum, machinery, and other manufactured goods in vast quantities. Already entire cargoes of flour are shipped to China from our Pacific Coast, and the steamer upon which I am writing has more than a thousand tons of flour, dried fish, machinery, and other American products on board, destined for China and Japan.

JAPANESE NOTES.

TEA CULTURE IN JAPAN.

KOBE, JAPAN, September 15, 1876.

It is always hard for travellers and correspondents to ascertain bottom facts, and when successful they do not always possess the technical knowledge which enables them to present understandingly the facts which they have gathered. In all my experience in the tea trade in the United States, and from the various descriptive articles which I have read, I never obtained a clear idea of the processes by which this important staple was produced.

During my visit in Japan I was therefore anxious to obtain all possible information upon this subject. At the shipping ports even I found a considerable conflict of opinion between tea merchants upon various important points, and I therefore determined to visit one of the principal tea-producing districts in the interior, and, if possible, see for myself just how things were done. Armed with letters from the American Consul at Hiogo, Mr. Neuwitter, to the Governor of Kioto Fu, in which is situated the celebrated Yamashiro tea district, I proceeded to Kioto, which is some fifty miles in the interior. I was courteously received, provided with an interpreter from the Government School of Agriculture, and advised to visit the town or village of Uji, in the Yamashiro district, of which an ancient translation of an old Japanese book says:

"The village Uji, which lies in the east of Yodo, is very famous for tea in this country. There are very old tea trees, at least two or three hundred years old.

"The ground in this village is so fit for tea-trees that no other place can be equal in Japan. Almost all people of this village live in planting the tea-trees, and taking care of the plants.

"A great many quantities of tea are sent out all over this country, and even foreign countries. That is most principale production in this country. In the spring, women and girls pick the leaves of the plants, and that is very beautiful sight.

"It is in the direction of the southwest from this city, and the distance to the village from Sanjio is 3 Ris."

Taking *jinrikishas*, each drawn by two strong and active coolies, we passed through the outskirts of Kioto and over a beautiful rolling country, for some six or seven miles, to the locality above mentioned. The lowlands along this section are occupied by rice-fields, while the uplands are cultivated principally for tea. There is considerable variety in the mode of cultivation, but the prevailing system seems to be to plant in rows, about six feet apart. Three or four plants are usually planted together in hills, which are about three feet apart, and these, as they grow larger, fill nearly the whole space which is originally left between the hills, thus making an almost continuous row. The plants are raised from the seed, and take from three to four years to mature sufficiently to yield the first crop. After that they are picked continuously for many years.

During the winter and early spring, in the districts yielding the best varieties of tea, the plants are covered with mats, which serve the double purpose of protecting them first from the cold, which might injure the plants, and later, from the sun, which tends to make the leaves tough, and injures the delicacy of the flavor. The first picking, which is considered the best, takes place the last of April, or the beginning of May; the second, about a month later; while the third, which is often omitted, particularly when prices are low, takes place usually during the month of July.

The tea-plant is a species of camellia, bearing a thick and glossy leaf, which, when green, has no tea flavor, or rather, has a flavor very unlike the cured leaf known to us as tea. Left to themselves, the plants would probably grow to a considerable height, but they are pruned and trimmed down, so that they are seldom more than three or four feet high. This results in a large number of small branches, producing small and tender leaves, which are the only ones sought for, although in rapid picking different sized leaves will naturally be taken, together with a considerable quantity of stems and other trash. Immediately upon being picked they are taken to the buildings, where they are cured. A considerable number of the flat baskets, in which the tea is brought from the field, are placed over a steaming apparatus for a few seconds, the steam permeating the mass and wilting the leaves; this gives them a dark green color, and enables the leaf to be rolled or doubled up, so that there is less liability to crumble when fired. They are then thrown upon large paper pans, beneath which a gentle charcoal fire is maintained. They are here toasted or fired for several hours, varying somewhat with the degree of heat maintained, during which they are constantly rolled and stirred with the hands, so as to make the leaf as compact as possible. This completes the curing process, so far as the natives are concerned. The tea is then placed in large baskets, to await the sorting process. This is more or less carefully done according to the market for which the tea is destined and the number of grades which are desired. This process, as well as much other work connected with tea culture, is principally done by women and children. A small quantity of dried leaf is placed on a smooth tray or table before the sorters, who with a pair of chopsticks dexterously pick out the stems and coarse leaves, which are thrown aside as refuse. In the finer qualities they also separate the large from the small leaves, the latter being the most highly esteemed, and bringing much the highest price. After the tea is thus assorted it is sifted, to extract the dust and broken leaves, and packed to be sent to market. The finer qualities are generally placed in large earthenware jars, such as we sometimes see in the American market, but by far the larger portion is placed in chests holding from seventy-five to one hundred pounds. Some of the smaller tea farms often sell their product to the larger farmers or small country merchants, who pack it as above and send it to market. In passing along the narrow roads I occasionally saw quantities of tea packed in paper bales, being thus taken to neighboring merchants, who make a business of purchasing for shipment to the larger markets at the seaports and elsewhere.

We now come to the important part of the preparation of tea for the foreign market. At the principal shipping ports are established numbers of foreign houses, which make a business of buying the tea as it comes from the natives, and preparing it for export. These firms possess large warehouses, called "go-downs," which are provided with numbers of stone or mason-work furnaces, in each of which is placed an iron kettle, in which the tea is refired, to expel the surplus moisture, and to give it the rich "toasty" flavor which is desired by American consumers. During this process it loses from five to ten per cent. in weight from the moisture and dust which are taken out. The tea is taken as it comes from the country in boxes and jars, weighed, and dumped into a large pile, and thoroughly mixed to insure uniformity in the quality of each lot. Sometimes, when a particular grade or style is desired, different lots will be mixed together to produce the quality and style required. Each of the kettles is in charge of a Japanese workman, or workwoman, and these come along in regular file with their little baskets, and receive a quantity of tea sufficient for one charge. This they take back and place in their kettle, and keep constantly stirring it with their hands until it is sufficiently dried or toasted. They then take it out of the kettle, carry it back to where they received it, get a fresh charge, and keep repeating this operation. After it is fired, it is sifted to remove the surplus dust, re-packed into new half-chests, many of which are made from the old chests which come down from the country. Inside of each of these half-chests is placed a lining of lead, weighing, upon an average, about three and one-half pounds. This is soldered up air-tight, and the lid of the package nailed on. It is then matted, faced, ratanned, and is ready for shipment. A tea "go-down," when firing, presents a very animated and interesting spectacle. Different establishments vary in size, but some of them have as many as two hundred to three hundred furnaces, and, with all the other help required in carrying on the various parts of the process, such as receiving, packing, delivering, etc., in the busy season, employ five or six hundred hands, and turn out as many packages of tea per day. Men, women, and children are all employed in the different parts of this work, and the average wages paid are about twenty cents per day. For this sum a Japanese will work ten or eleven hours over a "go-down furnace," in a temperature which I can only compare to that of the stokehole of an ocean steamer, which, measured by the thermometer, ranges anywhere from 100 to 130 degrees.

IMPRESSIONS OF JAPAN.

NAGASAKI, September 18, 1876.

Coming here from our Pacific Coast during the month of August, when everything there, owing to the long absence of rain, is dry and brown, one is agreeably impressed with the contrast which the green hill-sides and valleys of Japan present, and this contrast between the verdure and foliage of the two countries is no greater than that between the respective people, their manners and customs. As we sailed through the entrance to the Bay of Yokohama, our attention was first attracted to the fleets of quaint fishing-boats, manned by nearly naked copper-colored crews, and, as soon as our steamer cast anchor in the harbor, it was surrounded by a throng of queer-looking boats called "sampans." In appearance they are a little like a Venetian gondola, but are unpainted, and, instead of being rowed, are sculled with a long double-jointed oar, which, although it looks clumsy, is very effective in native hands. I shall never forget my first trip to the shore in a "sampan," propelled by three or four of these half-naked boatmen, their lithe bodies bending in time with a weird chant, with which they accompanied their efforts. On landing, another surprise presented itself in the shape of a "*jinriksha*," which is the ordinary mode of conveyance on land here. The "*jinriksha*" is a sort of exaggerated baby-carriage on two wheels, and is drawn by either one or two men, usually by one, at a rate of speed which, perhaps, is not as fast as a London cab, but is certainly faster than the average rate of our hacks and omnibuses in America. At first they were only used in the smooth streets of the cities, which are here macadamized and usually very level, but they proved so effective and popular, that they are now used in all the principal towns and cities of the empire, and long trips through the country are made with them. It is no uncommon thing for a "*jinriksha*" drawn by two men, to accomplish forty or even fifty miles per day, across the country, where the roads are by no means perfect or level. The first one was invented by a Japanese about nine years ago, and it is estimated now that there are upward of a hundred thousand in the country, and the number is increasing very rapidly. Some four or five thousand have recently been put in operation in China, where they bid fair to be as successful as here. Japanese houses are generally mere skeletons constructed of wood, in the country roofed with straw, in the cities with tiles somewhat similar to the old Dutch pattern; they are arranged with screens which slide in grooves, and which, in warm weather, can, if desired, be taken out on all four sides; the rooms are also simply separated with screens or sliding paper partitions about six feet high. They have no chairs or bedsteads, everybody sitting cross-legged on the floor, which is composed of thick, heavy grass mats, which also serve the purpose of a bed at night. Shoes, which consist either of wooden clogs or straw sandals, are invariably removed before entering the house, which is thus always kept neat and clean. Rice and fish are the principal articles of diet, and chopsticks, as in China, are used to convey the food to the mouth, no knife or fork being used. Tea is the universal drink, although *saki*, a malt liquor brewed from rice and barley, is used to a considerable extent. It is not strong and fiery like distilled liquor, but will intoxicate if taken in sufficient quantities. Costumes are scanty, especially in summer time, and in the country many of the males go naked with the exception of a scanty cloth around the loins. This is also true of the boatmen at the seaports, but in the cities all classes are obliged by law to wear a sort of wrapper called *kimona.* Women are, as a rule, more fully dressed, but they, as well as the men, usually go bareheaded. In the higher classes some affect the European costume, and all are more completely clad than the lower classes. Infants are never carried in the arms, but on the back, supported by a shawl or scarf, and clinging tightly, even when quite small, to the neck and shoulders of the person carrying them. They are generally confided to the care of the other children who are too young to work, or of very old and superannuated persons. It is no uncommon thing to see a little girl of five or six years, with an infant fastened upon her back, entering into sports with children of her own age, without seeming to heed, in the slightest degree, the burden she is carrying. While the language of adult Japanese is as different as can well be imagined from that of Europeans, I have noted that babies' cries sound quite natural. Indeed, I believe that the language of babies is the same all the world over. Perhaps when the tongues were confounded at the building of the Tower of Babel, babies were not included, as they could hardly assist in the building of the tower. In color the Japanese are principally of a light copper-color, the better classes being somewhat lighter than the peasantry, and the women of all classes lighter than the men. Their hair is, almost without exception, of a glossy black, and is usually coarse and strong. The women dress it most elaborately, and much time is given to its care. With the men, the higher classes usually wear it as Americans do, but others shave a space about four inches wide, extending from the forehead back to the crown, and wearing the rest of it long, it is gathered up in a sort of quoue, and, being carefully tied, projects from the back of the head forward over the top. This style, however, savors somewhat of barbarism, and is discouraged by the government, which has also prohibited the tattooing of men's bodies, which practice was formerly quite prevalent, and was most elaborately done. For beasts of burden they have oxen and horses, but these are used as pack animals, there being no wheel vehicles used to any extent among the Japanese; indeed, nearly everything is carried on the shoulders of men. Previous to the introduction of "*jinrikshas*," people were carried in "*kagos*," a sort of chair, slung on long poles; and now nearly everything, from vegetables and market produce to earth and fertilizing material, is carried in baskets or buckets slung on poles something like the neck-yokes used in maple-sugar camps in the United States to carry the sap from the trees to the boilers. In Yokohama I saw a piece of low ground, which was to be used for a building site, being filled in with earth thus carried in baskets on men's shoulders a distance of several squares; and here in Nagasaki our steamer was coaled by a double line of coolies (as the working class here is somewhat erroneously called), composed of about an equal number of men and women, extending from the coal-junk to the deck of the steamer, who quickly passed small grass baskets filled with coal from hand to hand, and thus kept up an almost continuous stream of coal, somewhat as buckets of water are sometimes passed at a fire where there are no engines. Everything is done in a small and ineffective way. Lawns are clipped with large shears; the earth is cultivated in miniature patches with great thoroughness and minuteness of detail, but with equal slowness and tediousness. Of course such things can only be in a country where labor is very cheap. The average wages of a laborer here is only about twenty cents per day; skilled artisans can be obtained for from twenty-five to thirty cents, and in some places even less than these figures rule. Policemen get from five to seven dollars per month. I expressed my surprise to the Japanese gentleman from whom I received this information, and asked him how much a policeman could get board for per month, and was told that for two dollars and a half per month a single man could get good ordinary board, the fare consisting principally of rice and fish. Rice is worth here from $1.50 to $1.75 per picul of one hundred and thirty-three pounds, or about $1\frac{1}{8}$c. to $1\frac{3}{8}$c. per pound. At first thought it seems as if there might be a profit to import it into the United States, but our duty of $2\frac{1}{2}$c. per pound, together with freight, insurance, and premium on gold, bring it up to a figure where there is no margin. They *do* know how to cook rice here, though, and for the benefit of grocers and consumers in the United States I investigated the matter: Only just enough cold water is poured on to prevent the rice from burning at the bottom of the pot, which has a close-fitting cover, and with a moderate fire the rice is steamed rather than boiled until it is nearly done; then the cover is taken off, the surplus steam and moisture allowed to escape, and the rice turns out a mass of snow-white kernels, each separate from the other, and as much superior to the usual soggy mass we usually get in the United States as a fine mealy potato is superior to the water-soaked article. I have seen something approaching this in our Southern States, but I do not think even there that they do it as skilfully as it is done here, and in the Northern States but very few persons understand how to cook rice properly. I am sure that if cooked as it is here, the consumption of this wholesome and delicious cereal would largely increase in America. But to resume my remarks about the rates of labor, old residents say that the above-named prices are much higher than they used to be, and complain bitterly of the high cost of labor.

This is doubtless the result of the progressive policy which has ruled in Japan during the last twelve years—a policy which was begun by the Tycoons, and which was taken up and improved by the present government, of which the Mikado is the head, and in which he takes an active part. Wonderful progress has been made in developing the material resources of the country, and the present government deserve great credit for the progressive policy which they have so vigorously pursued. The Japanese are naturally bright and intelligent, and while they have never, until lately, had an adequate educational system, yet the majority can read and write, and books are plenty and cheap. During the past few years foreign languages have been taught in their principal schools, and a few of them now speak English quite well. Some of their attempts, however, are quite amusing, although probably not more so to us than our efforts to speak their language are to them. I append a circular of a hotel-keeper at Kioto, which is rather quaint and amusing. Just as I was departing he handed me a number of them, and desired me to place them in the hands of my friends.

(Picture of Kioto Maruyama.)

ENTREATY.

The undersigned respectfully informs visitors to Kioto ond Biwa, that he will conduct (under his personal supervision) a first class hotel situate at Maruyama Kioto Japan. The buildings are so situated that the whole city of Kioto can be clearly seen there, being on one side surrounded by hills covered with beautiful flowers, and presenting the finest scenery in the country.
No inconvenience about meal and sleepiny. &c.

Various Kinds of wines. Beer, and other European liquors, sold at possibly fairest price

The proprietor wishes the visitors to come without changing their part—prejudice.
charge for meal and stoppage per day
2 yen and 50 sen (2 dollars and 50 cents).
But every one may desire his own agreeable charge.
ya-ami's Hotel, (old jeutei,s)
At maruyama, Kioto,
Japan.

Altogether my impressions of Japan are most pleasant. The scenery, in many of its features, is beautiful and unique; the people possess a much higher order of intelligence and ability than I had expected, and I have everywhere met with so much kindness and hospitality that I can hardly realize that up to within a very few years the country was closed to foreigners, and they were looked upon as national enemies by the great mass of the people.

JAPANESE ENGLISH.

To the American reader the following "Extracts from the Diary of a Member of the Japanese Embassy to Europe in 1862–63" will be likely to prove interesting. In commenting upon the difficulty of intelligibly describing all that he saw, this gentleman says:

"More than this, I did not learn the crab-movement method of writing (meaning the Western system of writing across the page, in contradistinction to the Japanese method, which is perpendicular), nor did I become practised in the shrike-tongued languages, by which means I could make inquiries and form opinions, or obtain a knowledge of these people, their customs, manners, and dispositions. I am now writing merely what I heard and saw. It is to be feared that there will be very little of fact and a great deal of conjecture. A judgment concerning the whole must not be formed from a partial description."

He describes the British man-of-war, in which they embarked, and her crew, as follows:

"Name of ship Odin (the meaning of which is not understood); length, 191 feet; breadth, 42 feet; capacity, 2,000 tons; steam, 560 horse-power; masts, 3; paddle-wheels, 2; big guns, 8; middle-sized guns, 24; captain, lord—official title; Hay, name; officer of first rank, lieutenant—official title; Briggs, name; small lieutenants, 3; compass-considerers (quartermasters), 7; officers of steam department, 7; officers (gun-room officers?), 12; total number on board, 310 men."

In describing some of the institutions at Hong Kong, he says:

"We went into a government building two stories high, by 68 yards long, by 24 yards broad. We asked in writing what house it was; a man answered in the same way, 'No. 99, Soldiers' House' (99th regiment), whereon I think, although I do not know clearly the entire number of houses, it cannot be less than ninety-nine, which is of itself plain. May we not say that they are very numerous? In the afternoon I returned to the hotel, and in the evening went in suite to the Governor's house, where I saw barbarous dancing. For music they had flutes, fiddles, and drums. In dancing, each man takes a woman by the hand and all the couples come forward. They spread and met, assembled and dispersed, advanced and retired, then suddenly went swiftly round and round. While doing this they did not sing. I retired early, as I did not care to listen to the music, for all the sounds seemed alike and very die-away. All Western countries have this, and they call it 'tansu' (dance).

"First month, tenth day.—Soon after ten o'clock went out to walk in the broad place outside the town to see the soldiery. There were together five hundred men with muskets. They advanced and retired quickly, then spread out and closed up again, loaded and fired all very exactly by companies and sections, so that their movements seemed as if made by one hand and one foot."

His first experience on a railroad is thus described:

"The baggage had already been landed from the ship and put into the steam-carriage. So, at two o'clock, we mounted the carriage and set off westward by the power of steam as quick as lightning. The inside of it is divided into three parts, in each of which eight people sit face to face. Just behind, six steam-carriages were connected with us, all filled with people. These carriages can be increased or decreased in number, according to the number of travellers and the quantity of their baggage. The steam power of the carriage at the head of it can run like lightning one thousand or ten thousand miles, with a train of carriages three hundred yards long behind it. How wonderful and surprising this is! The carriage-way is made of iron thresholds, a little less than two inches broad, six inches high, and more than six or eight yards long, connected together. The two thresholds are about ten feet apart, and these lines, stretching along for many thousand miles, form the road of the steam-carriage. At every twenty yards are planted posts about eighteen feet high, on which are hung, in small or great numbers, all the lightning-news long wires. If there be a river in the road an iron or stone bridge is thrown across; if they meet with a hill, they pierce its belly and make a tube-like opening through it. As it is dark in these openings, in every division of the carriage there is a glass lamp overhead in the centre, which is put in and lighted from the roof; but the ground in Western countries is generally flat and level, with hardly any mountains rising up at all."

After describing the beauties of the Viceroy's palace in Cairo, he adds:

"But the Viceroy lives at Alexandria during the winter and spring, and only resides in this castle in the summer time. Hence it follows that, while the castle and the Buddahall are so beautiful, the houses of the people fall to ruins. Princes who neglect their people may find a mirror here."

Alluding to the Pyramids, he says:

"South of the city, about a mile distant, are three great stone towers of wonderful shape. Each is about six hundred feet square and of the same height. They were built more than three thousand years ago, and are the most wonderful sight in the world. They are full of confused and unreadable characters, written on stone, and there is no one to make the meaning clear; but lately some Westerns, who are fond of this thing, have considered them minutely and have discovered the meaning for the first time, as it may be seen in their books."

In describing the streets of Malta, he mentions that at every twenty-four yards is an iron lamp-post, in which "gassu" is lighted after dark for the convenience of the passers-by.

Alluding to manning the yards and saluting the Japanese flag by the English frigate Marlborough, he says:

"Just as we were going out of the harbor's mouth we met an Englishman about two hundred and seventy feet long called Marlborough. She hoisted the morning-sun flag (Japanese) and fired a salute of fifteen guns, in consequence of which the chief Imperial Envoy went on board of this ship and returned again after a short time. The morning-sun flag was then flown again and fifteen guns fired. The sailors stood in line upon the wood of the sails (yards), so as to complete the ceremonies with which illustrious guests are sent on their boat. In my opinion this is not an unimportant matter, since it depends upon the dignity or meanness of the country. This, therefore, was to call the attention and command the respect of every ship in the harbor. If the morning-sun flag goes to any part of the five continents the same is done. How gratifying and pleasant is this. When our ship left Malta, several of the soldiers sent from England to garrison that island, their time being up, were relieved from their duties and took passage on the ship to return to their country, bringing with them their families, including their wives and male and female children. Last night a little girl of the age of two years died, and this morning at ten o'clock the body was wrapped in cloth and brought to the stairs of the ship, where preparations were made to bury it in the water. The captain performed the duties of priest, put on his complimentary clothes and sword, and taking off his hat uncovered his head while he read the prayers. The officers, about fifteen in number, took off their hats also and prayed. A cannon-shot was fastened to the corpse and it was then buried in the sea, while all the spectators made sour noses."

In mentioning the bill of fare, he alludes to ham as "hotui," literally, "fire thigh."

On arriving at Ceylon notice of the arrival was published in the newspapers there, and is alluded to by him as follows:

"This morning the master of the hotel sent us the newspaper which was published the day before. In it our countrymen's journeys to the Western countries, our entrance into port the day before, and arrival on shore the day before was written. This is entirely done to make money by, and for no other purpose, and as by chronicles of the talk of the town it is only light and flimsy and not to be relied upon, but the quickness of its appearance was astonishing."

While in Paris there is an entry as follows:

"To-day met the physician to the King of Holland at the hotel. He is rather more than fifty years old; he has read Chinese books, and also understands some Japanese; so we communicated with him by writing and also conversed a little, and, although it was like scratching an itching place through one's shoe, yet it afforded some little pleasure to the heart of the traveller."

In describing the audience with the Emperor and Empress, he says:

"After passing through about three rooms we came to the audience-hall, where the Emperor, Empress, and Imperial Prince were seated. Outside of the throne were a number of female officials arranged in line; some among them had theatre-glasses, with which they used to look at our countrymen, who felt consequently much confused."

In describing the theatre in the palace at Versailles, he says:

"At the rear of the building was a room like our dancing-pleasure place, where Japanese nobles amuse themselves with dance-girls, which is used for acting plays before the Emperor."

In alluding to their reception at Dover, in England, he says:

"Then there came forth from the crowd a man about fifty years of age, who walked and hopped about like a sparrow, and sending forth a loud voice, cried: 'Yapanishee;' this person came formerly to Hakodate and dwelt there. He is an Englishman, and now stepping from the crowd to congratulate our countrymen on their safe arrival, took off his hat, and holding it in his hand, shouted in a high voice: 'Peyapeppe hore' (hip, hip, hurrah); the meaning of which is not clear, but it appears to be a congratulatory expression. Upon this all united in the same sound with one voice. Thus they welcomed us without cease by shouting in a loud voice in a most unpleasant manner."

In speaking of the furnishing of the hotel in London, he says:

"In every room, on the round table, was placed one copy of the whole book of the New Covenants translated into Chinese. I had heard of this before, which is, in fact, the book of the religion of the Western foreigners; a knowledge of it ought to be hated and disliked very much."

In speaking of London, he says:

"Of soldiers who go around at night there are twelve thousand (policemen), who do this to prevent robberies and fires and spies from hostile countries."

In speaking of the paintings and decorations at Windsor Castle, he says:

"Here on the walls were hung several thousand framed pictures of landscapes, angels, men, birds, beasts, flowers, trees, fruits, and vegetables. They were all accurately done, and certainly very admirable; in fact, all might be called wonderful, but foreigners only honor those who represent things as they really are, and respect what is like something with material form; they do not understand anything of the voices of spirits and the manifestations of the gods. Well, well, it is a great pity!"

While in London, he says:

"I went this afternoon to Regent's Park, name of a place. This is the garden which I spoke of before, where numerous families of large and small birds, beasts, fishes, and reptiles are collected. The extent of it is about six hundred yards square. In all the Western countries these birds and beast gardens, plant and tree gardens, universal-things-halls (museums), etc., are maintained by the government, and the lower classes are permitted to go in and look; wherefore, I think that these places are made in order to please the common people, and at the same time to profit them by increasing their knowledge of universal things. But from every spectator they take a little sight-money, according to the barbarous custom of always trying to make a profit, which we should think very mean. Ah! ah! If they gain by it, they also lose. To adopt what is proper and to reject that which is bad, how fine a thing this is."

The diary is continued at great length, but the above will enable us to "see ourselves as others see us"—not a bad thing to do occasionally. Although expressed in quaint and unfamiliar language, coupled with occasional errors, yet underlying the whole of it there is a basis of good sense, coupled with an eminent spirit of fairness which I believe to be representative of Japanese character.

A JAPANESE DINNER—JAPANESE PRODUCTS, PROGRESS, ETC.

Accepting the invitation of a Japanese friend who had resided some years in America, we were conducted to a hotel, or restaurant, pleasantly situated upon the banks of the river Sumida, which flows through the eastern portion of Tokio (Yedo). Removing our shoes, according to the invariable custom of the Japanese, we were shown into a clean, airy, upper room, looking out upon the river. We were asked if we would take a bath, which we declined, and our friend then explained to us that the Japanese, in hot weather, usually take a bath before dining, and afterward don a loose robe of thin, gauzy material, which is furnished by the proprietor of the hotel, and which they wear during the meal. We seated ourselves cross-legged upon the floor, which was covered with matting, the only furniture in the room. While waiting for the meal to be prepared, a small bronze brazier, or vessel, containing burning charcoal, was brought in, together with tiny Japanese pipes and mild Japanese tobacco, with which we were expected to amuse ourselves until the arrival of the first course, which consisted of sweetmeats called *quashi*, and was served upon small lacquered plates, placed upon trays, or tables, about three inches high, composed of the same material. It is hard to describe the character of these sweetmeats, but one of them was a small square or brick of a kind of jelly, of a golden color; another was a small scarlet ball, of a substance that tasted not unlike our marsh-mallow confections, and the third was of greenish color, and somewhat similar in taste. We understood that the ingredients of which these were composed were principally rice-flour and sugar. With this course tea was served in delicate porcelain cups, upon each of which was a fragment of a Japanese poem, or legend, of which the following is a specimen:

"How many times, my host, do you laugh in the month?

"Whenever we meet, we ought to have a pleasant time.

"You see that the beauties of spring vanish as running water;

"And the flower that scatters to the wind to-day opened but yesterday."

The second course was "chawan-mori," a sort of soup with eggs, somewhat similar to soup "a la Colbert." It was served in a bowl, but no spoons were provided, it being expected that the guests would use chop-sticks for the eggs and drink from the bowl the liquid portion. This soup was by no means unpalatable, and with a spoon would have been considered quite tolerable anywhere.

The third course was composed of a variety of fish with the collective name of "kuchi-tori sakana;" the first was a kind of shell-fish (awabi); the second the meat of the lobster (ebi); and with these, served as a relish, was a small fruit called "youzo," a species of citron

The fourth course consisted of a sweetened preparation of boiled beans, served with green ginger-root. and another variety of fish called "tai," fried.

The fifth course, called "sachi-mi," consisted of raw fish, served upon a delicate lattice-work of glass, and accompanied with two kinds of sauce, one dark in color, salt in flavor, and tasting as if composed of soy and anchovies, the other a preparation of horse-radish.

The sixth course was called "miza-gai," and consisted of "koi," a variety of boiled fish, served with pears and a kind of raw shell-fish, very much resembling our American scallops, cut in small squares.

The seventh course was composed of rice served perfectly plain, in small porcelain cups; this is called "meshi."

The eighth and last course, called "skemono," was a sort of salad, composed of egg-plants and small cucumbers

With each course, after the first, was served "saki," a fermented liquor manufactured from rice, and, in character, something between ale and wine. Some writers have fallen into the error of describing "saki" as a distilled liquor, but we were assured that this is not correct, and it is made by a process somewhat similar to brewing.

It is not disagreeable in flavor, but has a larger percentage of alcohol than our malt liquors, and exhilarates more quickly. Indeed, in this respect, it is somewhat similar to champagne. It is served hot from small porcelain vases, and it may be said to be the national drink of the Japanese.

When near the end of the dinner we were surprised by the appearance of some singing-girls, who proceeded to favor us with some music. They sang in the nasal falsetto tone common in the East, and accompanied themselves upon an instrument resembling a guitar, called Chami-Sen (or Shamisen). It has three strings, which are struck or thumbed with a piece of ivory somewhat resembling a paper-cutter. One of these girls also accompanied the music with a sort of dance, consisting of a series of graceful motions that were half pantomime and half posturing.

It may be summed up that, as an entertainment, it was pleasing from its novelty, but the *menu* would hardly be called satisfactory to a European palate.

Fish and rice are the staple articles of Japanese diet, and without either of these the nation would find it hard to exist. The soil is fertile, and apparently vegetables grow well here. Sweet potatoes, ordinary potatoes, turnips, carrots, squashes or pumpkins, egg-plants, and pears are grown, but do not enter largely into the people's diet. Beans are an important article, and from these is manufactured tofu or tofe, literally bean cheese, an article which is largely used by the poorer classes, and which is peddled from door to door as berries and vegetables are in America. Radishes are also grown to some extent, and some varieties of them are very large and not unlike beets. They are rather coarse in grain and texture, but not so much so as their size might indicate. The young bamboo is also eaten to some extent, and a variety of mushrooms are used in making sauces and relishes. A species of maize is raised, but it is very inferior to the American Indian corn, and is not used to any great extent. Tomatoes have been introduced from the United States within the last few years, and are received with considerable favor. Cakes and unleavened bread of various kinds are made from rice flour, and at the seaports bread made from flour imported from California is beginning to be used by the natives.

Of fruits, oranges, peaches, pears, apricots, plums, persimmons, raspberries, mulberries, and currants are indigenous here, but none of them grow in great perfection, and most of them are quite inferior in quality. Apples and strawberries have been introduced to some extent from other countries, but, although they can be grown here, do not seem to take kindly to the soil. The pears are round, mostly of a russet color, coarse in grain, not sweet, and seem to be a sort of cross between the apple and the pear. Water and musk melons are largely grown, but these are also inferior to the American productions of the same kind. The climate is not unlike that of our middle States, but there is more moisture, which keeps the vegetation constantly green. The general impression which one gets on coming here is that Japan is a beautiful country, and that her inhabitants are making great efforts to adopt what is best and most progressive among other nations. Railroads and telegraphs have been constructed between principal cities in the interior, steamship lines established along the coast and to China, lighthouses erected and connected by telegraph with the principal ports of entry, harbors improved, breakwaters constructed, mines opened, and a mint established, besides which the entire administration of government has been changed; a judicial and police system based upon the French, an educational and postal system like that of America has been adopted, while the army has adopted the Prussian and the navy the English system of organization and tactics. In short, they have taken the best from the organizations of the principal nations of the earth, and utilized it for the benefit of the Japanese people, and the wonderful part is that all this has been done within ten years. It is said that the Mikado also contemplated the adoption of a state religion, and with this view sent for leading missionaries of the different Christian sects resident in Japan to confer with them, but they differed so widely in their views, each claiming that *they* were right while all the others were wrong, that the Mikado concluded that there was more of the spirit of peace and goodwill in the Buddhist and Shintu beliefs than in the religion of "the Westerns."

CHINESE NOTES.

STEAMER NAGOYA MARU,
OFF COAST OF CHINA, September 21, 1876.

I was awakened this morning by our stopping to take on board the pilot. Looking from the window of my state-room, I saw that the water was yellow with mud, and I knew that we must be in the "Yellow Sea of China" and nearing shore—the shores of a country that have been a romantic mystery to me all the days of my life. The "Celestial Empire" and "flowery land" of my boyhood's dreams, whence came our tea and silk! The land of great walls and porcelain pagodas, of Shanghai roosters and fire-crackers! How I used to dream of the time when I would "grow big" and enjoy an eternal elysium of the latter—"have just as many as I wanted;" and how well I remember when a short, stumpy boy at school, who was my particular antipathy, described the difference in our build by maliciously calling me "Shanghai!" and how I tried to get even with him by retorting "Shorty!" How, as I grew older, the romance surrounding this country was heightened by my becoming familiar with the saying, "When our ship comes home from China," and learned that with the occurrence of that auspicious event every wish, no matter how extravagant, could be gratified. Later, when I came to New York, a green country boy, the illusion was kept up by finding that the richest and most noted merchants were in the "China trade;" the Careys, the Lows, the Olyphants, the Cryders, and a host of others, were living illustrations and confirmations of all I had heard and read—veritable "China Astors." And so I am prepared to appreciate and enjoy the magnificent, the wonderful, the Celestial Empire which I am so rapidly approaching. I remember now something about my geography saying that Shanghai is situated near the mouth of the "Yang-tse-kiang" River; how hard it used to be for me to pronounce that jaw-breaker! Indeed I never could do it except in connection with the "Hoang-ho," the other great river of China, and I used to sit for hours ringing the changes upon these two names. But we have passed the lightship, crossed the bar, and are entering the mouth of the river—the Yang-tse, from which we pass into the Woosung, a branch of the Yang-tse, upon which Shanghai is built, some fourteen miles up from the sea. The shores are low, densely populated, and carefully cultivated on each side. As we pass along, the Chinese fishermen are letting curious nets down into the water from off bamboo stagings, each of which has a funny little crow's nest of a booth to shelter the fishermen. Chinese cattle, with curious horns projecting straight back from the head, and birds, which are unfamiliar to us, are seen at intervals as we sail along. Presently the masts of large class shipping become visible over a low neck of land, rounding which we enter the harbor of Shanghai.

SHANGHAI, September 24, 1876.

Steamers and sailing vessels are lying at the wharves, and farther down are anchored in the stream opposite the "Bund" (the street lying along the river). This is lined with substantial buildings, some of them magnificent in their size and solidity, and presenting, as far as the eye can reach, a handsome and imposing appearance. Other streets running back from the water are built up closely with heavy, solid stone buildings for a distance of several squares. This is the foreign settlement or "concession," as it is called. Back of this lies the native city, containing about a quarter of a million inhabitants. Below the foreign shipping in the stream is a forest of masts belonging to the native junks, of which, seemingly, there are thousands. These penetrate to every part of the empire through the great system of canals (of which China has more miles than any other country on the globe), and have much to do with making Shanghai the great commercial *entrepot* that she is. Some of the sailing vessels at anchor in the stream are of the veritable old clipper-ship type, which, before the days of screw steamers, monopolized the carrying trade of the East. It does one good to look at them, even now, with their beautiful models and tall, gracefully tapered spars—"sky-scrapers" we used to call them; but they have had their day, and all-conquering steam now rules even the furthermost parts of the globe. Just before us lie the handsome steamers of the "Peninsula and Oriental" and the "Messageries Maritimes" lines, which furnish direct through steam communication with Liverpool and Marseilles weekly. Along the "French Bund," as it is called, for nominally the Bund is divided into the French, American, and English concessions, lie the steamboats of the "Shanghai Steam Navigation Company," which ply upon the "Yang-tse," and once controlled the entire trade of that great river. They are of American build, on the familiar model of our river and sound steamboats, and are largely owned by American capital. They still do a large and remunerative trade, but have to sustain a vigorous opposition from an English company which was organized some few years since, and it is understood that the investment does not now pay nearly so well as it once did. Indeed, all commerce here appears to be in a very depressed state, and the great merchants who formerly controlled this trade so absolutely that it was almost a monopoly, have been steadily losing money for a term of years, and speak anything but encouragingly of the future. Some of the great buildings along the Bund are untenanted, and many of them are for sale. It is claimed by some that ocean cables and steam communication have ruined the China trade. Doubtless it has spoiled the monopoly which the few once enjoyed, but at the same time it has opened the trade to many who do not despise the closer margins that now prevail everywhere in the commercial world. It is an easy life that residents here have been living, and it is possible that in the future a closer competition for trade may make greater exertions necessary. To one who has been used to the bustling, business life of New York, it seems as if there were several men here employed to do one man's work. Every clerk has his assistant in the shape of a Chinaman, or "boy," as he is called here, to run at his beck and call; to pull a punkah (a large fan) over him to create a breeze when it is warm, and even to perform the personal services of a valet. The Anglo-Saxon race loves to take its ease, and it soon becomes a sort of second nature to accept and even demand these little "conveniences." Chinese barbers come to your room to shave you, and a resident here informed me that his "boy" always shaved him before he got up in the morning, and that, if he did it so unskilfully as to wake him up, he used to kick him. All the waiters and coolies here are called "boys," no matter how old they may be. It sounds strangely to American ears to hear this, but at our hotel the other day, I heard a little toddler of not more than four or five years shouting "boy" quite lustily, to attract the attention of a hotel waiter old enough to be his grandfather, and he afterward ordered him about as peremptorily as he would a pet dog or kitten.

To-day we visited the native city. It is simply a conglomeration of little wooden structures, huddled together, apparently without plan or design. The streets are simply narrow lanes, not wide enough for any wheeled vehicles, and reeking with dirt and smells in every direction. It is surrounded by a high brick wall, and intersected here and there with small canals, which, apparently, are the only means of carrying off the refuse of the city.

On each side of these narrow lanes are situated the native shops, which are also manufactories and the dwellings of the people. Shops for the sale of curious ivory carvings, medicine, coffins, dry-goods, groceries, and every conceivable thing which these people use, were crowded together in every direction, as far as we went. Restaurants and tea-houses are frequent, and occasionally one comes to a temple or joss-house. In every corner is placed a little booth for the sale of something or other. One of these we noticed had a large stock of crickets or singing grasshoppers, each one enclosed in a little bamboo-basket, and all were singing in a shrill, piercing note, like that of the locusts and "katydids" at home. We were told that they were great favorites with children here, and it is said that the women also keep them as pets, and amuse themselves occasionally by making one cricket fight another, waging considerable sums upon the result. Upon the whole, my first impressions of China are not very favorable; no fault of China, perhaps, but of my imagination. Another illustration of the truth there is in the saying that there is more enjoyment in anticipation than in realization. However, I may, before leaving this country, have reason to change my present imoressions.

TEA CULTURE IN CHINA.

The methods followed in cultivating tea in China are almost precisely similar to those pursued in Japan, a detailed account of which was given in a previous letter. There is some difference, however, in the mode of preparation, and, indeed, this varies considerably in China in different districts, which produce different kinds of tea. The leaf, however, is essentially the same all over China, and all the different varieties of black and green are produced by a difference in the curing and manipulation. In certain districts, however, they are more in the habit of producing special kinds, unless the market should so shape that some other variety commands a better price; when it does, the production changes at will from green to black or black to green. The great tea-producing sections are in the interior of China, and more largely in the sections tributary to the Yang-tse-kiang River than any other. The tea is mostly grown by small proprietors or farmers, who cure it sufficiently to transport it to the native dealers, who collect and ship it to the treaty ports, where it is again sold to the large dealers, who refire it, assort it into grades, and, in turn, sell it to the foreign merchants, who export it to the different parts of the world.

When it is first picked, if destined for green teas, it is thinly spread upon bamboo trays and exposed to the sun for an hour or two, then thrown into firing-pans and rapidly moved about for, perhaps, five minutes. The heat develops the moisture and thoroughly wilts the leaves, which are then drawn quickly out and placed upon the rolling-tables. They are then rolled with the hands (and sometimes with the feet) in such a way as to produce the style of tea most desired—a more circular motion being necessary for "Gunpowders" and "Imperials" than for "Young Hysons" and "Hysons." They are then replaced in the firing-pans and kept moving by the rapid motion of the hands of the workmen for a length of time, varying somewhat with the degree of heat, but usually for an hour and a half or two hours. The leaves are then quite well dried and their color fixed, and it may now be said to be a natural-colored green tea. After it gets into the hands of the large native merchants at the shipping ports, however, it is refired, and during this process a little coloring matter is added—principally gypsum and indigo—in order to give it the handsome, glossy "face," such as is popular in the American market. With black teas the treatment is entirely different, the leaves being simply dried by the producer, during which process the tea is slightly rolled; and it remains in this condition until it reaches the hands of the wholesale merchant, who refires it and manipulates it in such a way as to materially change the flavor. Indeed, it may be said that this manipulation at the tea-firing "go-downs" is the most important part of the process, as different flavors can be produced at will, and upon the assorting and sifting depends the fineness of each grade. In some sections, during this manipulation by the large dealers, artificially flavored teas are produced. In Canton we saw large quantities of tea of ordinary quality being scented by flowers gathered from a variety of jasmine, which produces a white, deliciously fragrant blossom. A layer of tea is placed in the bottom of a large basket and a few flowers scattered upon it, then another layer of tea and another layer of flowers, and so on, until the basket is full. The flowers are generally placed in the tea in the afternoon, and allowed to remain there over night, when it is found that the tea has absorbed most of their fragrance, and is certainly very much improved. The flowers are then removed by sifting, and the tea refired to drive off the moisture that it may have gathered from the blossoms; it is then ready for packing. This scenting is done with both black and green teas, but probably to a greater extent with the varieties known as "Scented Caper" and "Flowery Pekoe," which go mostly to England, where they are used for mixing purposes.

During my stay here I have been favored with an inspection of the Chinese customs statistics for the past ten years, and have collected some interesting facts. Although tea has been a principal item in the business of my firm, and I have kept a general run of the quantities exported each year to the United States, I never had seen an analysis of the total exports, and it therefore proved a most interesting study. I found that of the 1,818,000 piculs (a picul is 133⅓ pounds) exported in 1875, 1,438,000 piculs were black, 210,000 piculs green, 167,000 piculs "brick," and about 3,000 piculs "dust." Brick tea goes entirely to Russia, overland, by camel-trains, and instead of being, as I had always supposed, a very superior article, it is very inferior in quality, being composed largely of the dust and siftings from all sorts, kinds, and qualities of tea, together with more or less tea of ordinary quality, which is also ground up into dust, moistened and compressed into shapes somewhat larger than our ordinary building brick. In addition to this, Russia takes about 90,000 piculs of black tea, consisting almost entirely of Congous, of which about 38,000 piculs go overland and 52,000 by sea, principally to Odessa. There are also considerable quantities of both leaf and brick taken overland to Siberia and Mongolia, the quantity of this exported being estimated for the year 1875 at 22,000 piculs of leaf tea, and 125,000 of brick tea. I had always supposed that Russia took considerable quantities of green tea, but I find that all of the leaf teas imported by her are Congons. America is the largest consumer of green tea, she having taken, in 1875, 130,000 piculs, against 70,000 piculs for England and 77,000 for India, no other country taking any green tea to any considerable amount. In blacks, however, America makes but a poor showing—namely, 92,000 piculs in 1875, against 1,100,000 for Great Britain, 106,000 for Australia, 88,000 for Russia, 12,000 for the Continent of Europe, 10,000 for New Zealand, 10,000 for Java, 3,800 for South Africa, 3,400 for British America, 2,200 for Cochin-China, 2,000 for Singapore and the Straits, 1,000 for Siam, 900 for Japan, 200 for India, and a few scatterings. Of all this immense quantity of black tea, only 117,000 piculs are Oolong, 1,189,000 are Congou, 41,000 Souchong, 35,000 Pouchong, 1,900 Flowery Pekoe, 37 Orange Pekoe, 46,000 Scented Caper, and 1,100 mixed. Of the 91,903 piculs taken by America, 16,778 are Congou, 69,586 Oolong, 3,647 Souchong, 1,812 Pouchong, 24 of Orange Pekoe, and 56 of mixed.

I could go on making a further analysis and comparison of figures, which might be of interest to the trade, but it is said that "figures are dry" and "comparisons are odious," and I am fearful of tiring the reader with too many of them. By the foregoing, however, it will be seen that Great Britain is the great consumer of tea; that the United States comes next, and Russia third, while the whole Continent of Europe, aside from Russia, takes but 12,360 piculs—less than one-eighth of the quantity taken by Australia. London being the great tea mart of the world, it is probable that some portion of the immense quantities sent to that port are re-exported, but it must be remembered that, in addition to all the tea which England imports from China, she receives about 31,000,000 pounds, or 233,000 piculs, grown in her own possessions (India). This also was mostly Congou or Souchong. The United States also imported about 25,000,000 pounds, or 188,000 piculs, from Japan; and, in looking over these figures, it becomes apparent that about ninety per cent. of all the tea exported from China, Japan, and India is consumed by people speaking the English language, and of this over seventy-five per cent. is taken by Great Britain and her colonies.

The production of tea has very largely increased during the past ten years, probably in a greater ratio than that of any other of the great staples of commerce. At the risk of tiring the reader, I append the figures showing the export of tea from China to foreign countries for the past ten years: Piculs—in 1866, 1,192,138; 1867, 1,330,974; 1868, 1,475,210; 1869, 1,528,149; 1870, 1,380,998; 1871, 1,679,643; 1872, 1,774,663; 1873, 1,617,763; 1874, 1,735,379; 1875, 1,818,387. By this it will be seen that the quantity exported from China has increased in ten years about fifty per cent., and to this great increase must be added the tea exported from India and Japan, amounting last year to about 120,000 piculs, where ten years ago little or none was exported. Putting these figures together, we find that the available supply has increased in ten years nearly one hundred per cent. It cannot be said that the consumption has increased in anything like the same ratio. Have we not, therefore, in these figures a satisfactory reason for the great decline in the prices of tea during this period—a decline which many of the old merchants in the tea trade have claimed to be excessive, and for which they profess they can see no good reason? It is probable, also, that this material reduction in the cost of tea has had more or less to do with influencing the coffee market. Three or four years ago a short crop in some of the principal coffee-producing countries was made the pretext, both in Europe and America, for largely advancing the price. Gravely written articles appeared in the most influential commercial journals in Europe and America, claiming that the consumption of coffee was increasing much faster than the production, and that this range of prices was not only legitimate, but that prices would probably attain a still higher range. Experience, however, has shown that the high prices stimulated production in all coffee-producing countries; the available supply everywhere increased, and the tremendous decline in the price of tea, making that by far the cheaper beverage, was "the last straw that broke the camel's back," and prices tumbled. Whether they will soon rise again or not depends, of course, somewhat upon circumstances; but all the indications at present point to increased production and a low range of prices in these two articles, which constitute so large an item in the domestic economy of the world.

CHINESE MANNERS, CUSTOMS, AND PECULIARITIES.

From Shanghai to Hong-Kong is 819 miles, but the fine steamer Ava, of the "Messageries Maritimes" line, upon which we took passage, made this distance in sixty-three hours—not a bad run for a heavily laden screw steamer. The cargo of this ship, by the way, is itself worthy of mention, being composed almost entirely of raw silk, which China merchants were hurrying forward to the French market, in order to avail themselves of the very high prices now ruling. The cargo of the Ava consisted of about ten thousand bales, worth, upon an average, over five hundred dollars a bale, or, in round numbers, *five millions* for the cargo. It is said to be the most valuable cargo ever carried by any ship. At any rate, $5,000,000 represents a goodly number of eggs to be carried in one basket. Soon after leaving Shanghai, the coast, which, at the mouth of the "Yang-tse" is low and flat, rises into a rugged range of mountains, which continues, with now and then a break, all the way to Hong-Kong. For the greater distance we passed quite close to the coast, which was fairly lined with a continuous fleet of quaint Chinese fishing-junks, which, when occasion offers, take a hand in piracy as well. At first I was inclined to doubt the stories which I heard of their enterprises in this line, but the records at Hong-Kong show that it is only about six years since they captured a sailing-vessel at the very entrance of the harbor of Hong-Kong, and now, notwithstanding the coast is closely patrolled by gunboats of both the Chinese and foreign governments, any vessel that goes ashore, or becomes disabled along the Chinese coast, is in great danger of being captured. It is not often that these rascals are taken, as, with their knowledge of every bay and inlet on the coast, and the light draught of water of their junks, it is quite difficult to follow them successfully; but occasionally a junk is caught outside that cannot give account of itself, and it is taken to Hong-Kong and dealt with according to law. The following advertisement, which I clipped from the *Hong-Kong Press* of September 26th, illustrates an occasion of this kind:

PUBLIC AUCTION.

IN THE VICE-ADMIRALTY COURT OF HONG-KONG, IN RE SUNDRY PIRATICAL GOODS AND THE JUNK "SING WOH LOONG."

The Undersigned has received instructions from MALCOLM STRUAN TONNOCHY, Esq., Marshal of the above Court, to Sell under a Decree of Appraisement and Sale, at 3 o'clock P.M.,

THIS DAY,

the 26th September, 1876, at Yow-ma-tee,—

ONE JUNK,

SUNDRY CLOTHING, MUSKETS, SWORDS, &c., &c.,

TERMS OF SALE.—Cash before delivery in Mexican Dollars, weighed at 7.1.7. All Lots, with all faults and errors of description, at purchaser's risk on the fall of the hammer.

J. M. ARMSTRONG,
Government Auctioneer.

Hong-Kong, 25th September, 1876.

Hong-Kong is a pretty little city, nestled close down upon the shores of one of the most beautiful bays in the world, and under the shadow of steep hills, whose peaks seem almost to overhang the city. It is an English colony, but included in the two or three thousands of foreign population is a sprinkling of almost every nation under the sun; France, Spain, Russia, and Germany all contribute their quota, and the variety is made up with Parsee merchants from India, Portuguese from Macao, Malays from the Peninsula and Straits, and the ever-present Chinese, who have gathered upon this little island, and clustered around the outskirts of the foreign settlement, until they now number upward of two hundred thousand. Among them are some of the shrewdest and wealthiest merchants in China. One man was pointed out to me who began his business life as a "comprador," and by his shrewdness and application has acquired a large fortune, owning quite a fleet of steamers, which ply, not only between Chinese ports, but the principal cities of the East. The "comprador," by the way, is an institution in Chinese commercial matters. "Comprador" is a Spanish word, signifying buyer, and in Chinese commercial life the "comprador" is not only a buyer but also a seller and general business manager; and while nominally occupying a subordinate capacity in the great houses of the East, he is the active business man through whose hands most of the business of the house passes. It is said that he has a keen eye for commissions or brokerages, and in addition to his salary, takes them from both buyer and seller. Certain it is that some of the "compradors" here are reputed to wield a larger capital than the houses whom they nominally serve. The necessity for the "comprador" originally grew out of the inability of foreign merchants to speak Chinese sufficiently well to conduct their business with the native merchants. It was, therefore, found necessary to employ a capable Chinaman, who could speak English, to facilitate these negotiations, and the "comprador" gradually became an institution. A few years ago an effort was made by the leading foreign houses to do without them and educate their clerks, so that they would be able to perform the "comprador's" functions; but it failed, and the "comprador's" influence is now again supreme.

There are many peculiarities in life here in the East which impress a visitor as being novel and curious. Sedan chairs, suspended on two long poles, the ends of which are placed on the shoulders of two coolies, are the means generally employed for getting about—no wheeled vehicles, not even *jinrikshas*, having yet been employed to any extent for this purpose. On the water, "sampans," a species of boat, are used, and in their way they are quite as much of a curiosity as the chairs. In China they are somewhat different from the Japanese sampan, and those in Hong-Kong are modelled more after the fashion of an ordinary boat. In the centre of them, however, most of them have an awning or canopy, to shield passengers from the sun and rain, while the ends are occupied by those who propel the boat. These are largely women and children. Indeed, whole families make these sampans their home, both by day and night. In a little locker, in one end, they keep a small brazier for cooking their meals, and they eat, sleep, and raise families within this narrow compass. It is no uncommon thing to see a woman sculling a boat with a young infant strapped upon her back, and children which an American mother would feel sure were in imminent danger of falling overboard, take a hand in propelling or steering the boat. Children, from one to three years of age, may be seen toddling about with a small buoy or life-preserver, composed of cork or other light material, strapped upon their breasts, so that in the event of their tumbling overboard they will not sink; and occasionally an unruly youngster of this age is seen with a string, one end of which is tied around his body and the other fastened to a ring-bolt, or other fixture of the boat, by which he can be hauled in, in case of falling into the water. Thousands of people thus live, and apparently thrive, in a way which to a European is incomprehensible. All these boats have eyes painted upon them near the bow, and further north this custom prevails universally. It is, doubtless, connected with some Chinese superstition, although I have not been able to ascertain precisely what it is. The story is current of a Chinaman who, being asked the reason for the custom, replied: "Junk no have eye, how can see? No can see, how can sabe?" (Understand, or know.)

The language known as "pigeon English," is also a queer institution. Originally growing out of the attempts of the Chinese to speak English, many imperfect and senseless expressions came to have a given significance and meaning, and to these, additions have gradually been made until now a recognized dialect has been formed, which is composed of all sorts of words, from all sorts of languages, but which is sufficiently perfect for ordinary communication between the natives and foreigners. Two prominent words in the vocabulary are "pigeon" and "catchee." With a Chinaman all business is "pigeon," and "catchee" signifies *get*. A Chinaman, desiring to ask you what business you are doing here, says, "What pigeon catchee you?" If you wish to tell a Chinese waiter to get two bananas and leave them up stairs in your room, you say, "Go catchee banana two piecee and leave my room top side." If he cannot get any, he comes back and reports, "No can catchee." Or "Bring me a glass of water" may be translated, "Go catchee one glass water, come bring this side."

The life of Europeans here is very different from that at home. A cup of coffee, with perhaps a little toast and eggs, is served in the morning at seven or eight o'clock, and between twelve and one o'clock the regular breakfast takes place, sometimes called "tiffin" or lunch, but which is really a substantial dinner. At 7.30 P.M., dinner is served, which is a heavy meal, not materially differing from tiffin. I have not yet gotten used to the heavy meals so late at night, but it seems to agree with those who live here, and probably has some good reason for having become a custom, although as yet I have heard none. As a rule, foreigners here take life easily, and I think enjoy more real comfort than in any place I have ever seen. Every dining-table has a "punkah" hung over it, which, during meal time, is pulled backward and forward by a boy, and a comfortable breeze thus constantly maintained.

The "pyjama" is also an institution not known in America. It consists of a loose garment, made of silk or other very light material, made up in two pieces, one being a pair of wide, loose drawers, and the other a sort of a jacket or shirt. They are very neatly made, and make quite a respectable suit; they are worn in place of night-gowns at night and in the privacy of one's own house, and on shipboard they are used to some extent as a morning and evening dress. I speak from personal experience when I state that no one knows what the perfection of comfort is until they have thrown off their clothes which they have worn during the sweltering heat of a tropical day, taken a cool and refreshing bath, put on their "pyjama" and sat down to dinner with a good appetite.

Another feature which attracts the attention of Americans is the carrying of everything on poles, instead of upon wheeled vehicles, as we do in America. As soon as your trunks are landed, a rope is passed around them and they are whisked up on a pole, and carried on the shoulders of two laborers or coolies, as they are called here, who trot off with them quickly and noiselessly. All merchandise is handled in the same way, and one often sees a heavy package of merchandise suspended on two poles, and carried by four or more coolies, instead of two, as in the case of the smaller and lighter pieces. It is said that much of the tea in the back country is thus carried long distances, sometimes hundreds of miles to the rivers, where it is placed upon boats and floated down to the seaports.

CANTON MANUFACTURES—SWEETMEATS, PRESERVED GINGER, SOY, ETC.

Many people are familiar with the appearance and taste of these articles, and I, in common with many others, have eaten them for years, but I had little idea just how they were prepared, and of what they consisted. So, when in Canton, I made it a part of my business to investigate these items.

The process of making preserved ginger is as follows: The ginger root, a large white variety, is first dug and the outer skin scraped off. This is chiefly done in the country surrounding Canton, where it is raised. It is then shipped down to the city in boats, carefully washed, and thrown into large kettles, where it is boiled for about twenty-four hours. It is then taken out and thrown into salt water, and allowed to remain there about twenty-four hours more. After this it is taken out, the rough edges trimmed off with a knife, and thrown upon tables, which are surrounded with operators, holding in each hand a kind of three-pronged fork, with which they prick the root until it is thoroughly punctured through and through. It is then washed in fresh water and dried in the sun for a time, after which it is again placed in large kettles, containing about an equal weight of sugar, and boiled for about twelve hours; it is then taken from the kettles and put into large earthen jars. The syrup is poured over it, and it is allowed to remain therein for several days—sometimes weeks—when it is boiled up again for a short time, and is then ready for packing. It is put up in jars and half-jars, such as all dealers are familiar with, and packed in cases containing six jars or twelve half-jars.

In all the various manipulations the Chinese are particularly dexterous. I was much interested in watching the process of putting the network of rattan over the jars, by which they are carried and handled. A workman would seize a piece of rattan, twist it into two rings just big enough to go over the top and bottom, and with another slender strip would weave a network between these two rings so quickly that I could hardly believe that it had been accomplished by an individual, and not by some marvellous machine. The pasting of the papers over the tops of the jars is also a curious piece of work. One end of a long strip of paper is first stuck to the edge of the jar, and the strip is then twisted over and over, each time receiving a little dab of paste, until the jar is hermetically sealed, and all this is done with such exceeding quickness and dexterity that you can hardly follow the motions of the operator's hands.

"Soy" has always been a mystery to me, as I fancy it has been to most other people who have dealt in or used it. I was therefore anxious to see a soy factory, and, taking a boat one day, we proceeded two or three miles up the river to where one was in operation. I found that the principal ingredient, or base, is a white bean known as "pak-toh," which, so far as I could judge, is very like any other small white bean. These are boiled, heavily salted, and put into big earthen jars, holding, perhaps, half a barrel each, where they are allowed to remain for about ten days, during which period fermentation takes place. They are then mashed up with a species of olive, which is picked and boiled, and this mixture is placed in neat cloth bags, into which water is poured and allowed to filter through. The liquid is then taken out, and placed in clean jars, and thickened with a heavy-bodied Chinese molasses; and this is *soy.* Thinned down with water, the Chinese use it as a sauce, and although when thick it is rather disagreeable than otherwise, when thin it has certainly a toothsome flavor and gives a zest and relish to meats, fish, etc. Most of the soy manufactured here is shipped to England, where it is used in large quantities as a base for the manufacture of sauces.

Tea, silk, and matting are the largest items of manufacture in Canton, and of these by far the largest proportion goes to England and the Continent. America, however, takes large quantities of matting and considerable silk, but the teas which we import from China are principally from Shanghai, Foochow, and Amoy. Canton is also celebrated for her silk embroideries and ivory carvings, and in both of these her workmen are particularly skilful. Embroidered crape and silk shawls, which the ladies would pronounce "just lovely," and which even the unappreciative men admit to be handsome, can be had here at prices which certainly show that there is a large profit absorbed somewhere between the purchaser in Canton and the fashionable shops on Broadway. Ask an American shopkeeper how it is, and he will tell you that it is owing to "high duties and the freight, insurance, and other charges" to which they are subject; but the duty is only sixty per cent., and freight, insurance, and other charges will all be covered by ten per cent. more, and there is still a very large margin to be accounted for, which can only be done upon the hypothesis of large profits to the dealer. However, these articles are hardly as staple as groceries, and perhaps it is wrong to eye the margin of profit through grocers' spectacles.

A VISIT TO CANTON—A FLOATING CITY—FEMALE HOTEL-RUNNERS—A CHINESE DINNER—DOG, AND CAT-MEAT RESTAURANTS—CHINESE TAILORS—KITES, CURRENCY AND OTHER PECULIARITIES.

Canton is situated on the Chan-Kiang, or Canton River, eighty-four miles up from the sea. The river is navigable for large vessels to this point, but, as there is but little room for merchant shipping, the greater part of the important productions of Canton are lightered down the river to Whampoa, some fourteen miles, where usually a considerable number of vessels are waiting for cargoes. For the first forty-five miles the river is lined on each side by hills or bluffs of considerable height, but higher up the land gradually becomes more level, and expands into a wide valley, in which Canton is situated.

As we approach the city, the first objects seen are the pagodas with their many stories towering one above the other, and a number of tall, square buildings, several stories higher than those by which they are surrounded. These latter we afterward learned were pawn-shops, and are substantially built of fire-proof material to afford security against fire and thieves. As we proceed up the river, the junks and smaller floating craft become more plenty, and for a mile or more below the landing-place of the steamers the river banks on both sides are lined with a dense mass of these craft of all sorts and sizes. As soon as the steamer touched the wharf, we were favored with our first experience of a female hotel-runner. I saw two young women making for me in a precipitate manner, and "wondered what was up," until they each exhibited an ivory card, upon one of which was inscribed the name of the "Canton Hotel," and on the other that of the "International Hotel." Having decided to go to the latter, a signal from our young woman brought a number of assistants, also females, to her aid, who seized our trunks and boxes in a jiffy, whisked them through the mass of half-naked, struggling and noisy Chinamen who were blocking the gangway, pulled the luggage and ourselves both into the neat hotel boat or "sampan," and vigorously sculled us across the river to the hotel, which is situated immediately upon the river-bank, and from the windows of which we could look upon the animated and novel scene. The smaller sampans or passenger-boats were very generally sculled by women, while the larger ones, which carry merchandise, seemed to be propelled by men.

There are thousands and tens of thousands of women employed in conveying passengers from one part of the city to another, and having no other home at night than the boat they propel during the day. The floating population of Canton is certainly a most novel and interesting feature, and it is said that there is nothing like it in any part of the world. There are passenger-sampans and freight-sampans, war-junks and merchant-junks, country boats and city boats, and even stationary boats, which are permanently anchored and used for music-halls, lodging-houses, etc.; but by far the greater part of this immense floating city is, during daylight, constantly in motion, plying hither and thither in every direction, and presenting a kaleidoscope of form and color long to be remembered. Sitting in the reading-room of our hotel at almost any time of the day, the sound comes up from this floating population "as the noise of a multitude." Whether you take a boat upon the river or a walk upon land, however, one is constantly impressed with the wonderful industry and activity of this people. Everybody seems to be working for a living. The streets are very narrow, seldom more than ten, and often not more than six feet wide; on either side, in the better portions of the city, there is a succession of brilliant shops, with gorgeous signs painted upon boards, which are hung perpendicularly instead of being placed laterally as in other parts of the world. The attendants are civil and diligent in the exhibition of their wares, but never importunate. In very many of these shops is a niche for a "Joss" or household god, to which offerings are made at intervals; and at the door of nearly every one of them is a little stone grotto or niche, in which at evening a light is placed, together with "Joss-sticks," which slowly burn and moulder away until they are consumed. The observance of their religious customs seems to be a prominent feature in the life of the Chinese, and, while there is evidently much superstition which to a European is absurd, it is also evident that the regard for his religion must be very strong in the average Chinaman to make him so faithfully observe all its forms.

I had heard so much of the peculiarities of Chinese diet that I was anxious to try a genuine Chinese dinner, and we therefore had our interpreter take us to a celebrated Chinese restaurant, kept by one "Chi-Hung," where we ordered a first-class native dinner. First, tea was served with dried melon-seeds, which our interpreter explained were to keep us busy until they could bring the other things. The first regular course consisted of shrimp-salad served with "soda eggs" (eggs boiled in a strong solution of soda-water and having an alkaline taste), together with a sauce made from soy and English malt vinegar; there was also an assortment of fruit consisting of sliced pears; "Yung-toh" (a star-shaped fruit tasting somewhat like gooseberries); "Pumlo" (a large, bitter orange); shelled almonds and pear-wine. The next course was the celebrated "bird's-nest soup," which was thickened with shreds of boiled chicken and hard-boiled eggs cut very fine; a little dried ham was also grated upon the top of the dish. These birds' nests, which are considered the greatest delicacy by the Chinese, are simply a sort of gelatinous substance which is gathered from the sea by a species of swallow in Java and Sumatra, and built up into nests. These nests are gathered by the natives, usually just as they are being finished, and before they have been soiled by the birds, and are shipped to Canton. As they are received here, they look more like a piece of crude, rather dingy glue bent up in the shape of a swallow's nest, such as we have at home, but much smaller. They are prepared by being soaked in water, thoroughly scoured to remove the dirt, cut up into thin strips, and it is then in substance, appearance, and taste nearer like Cooper's gelatine than any other substance with which I can compare it. To my taste it cannot be considered a delicacy, but as served to us it was certainly a very palatable dish. Course No. 3 consisted of pigeon's eggs served with chicken and ham, in a sort of stew; this was also a very good dish. Course No. 4 was composed of dried oysters stewed with mushrooms, young bamboo-shoots and cucumber, with a very little mixture of salt pork, for the purpose of giving it richness and flavor. Course No. 5 was composed of sharks' fins cut into thin strips and stewed with eggs; these fins also tasted much like gelatine. No. 6 consisted of boned-duck, boiled; it was stuffed with mushrooms, bamboo-shoots, dates, and various aromatic herbs—a very good dish. Course No. 7 consisted of boiled snails with salad; the orthodox way of eating these is to break off the small point of the shell, which destroys the vacuum, and then a gentle suck at the larger end places the toothsome morsel at your disposal. I tried one and it was very good, but I had hardly become accustomed to the idea of eating snails, and did not feel hungry enough to eat more. Course No. 8 consisted of boiled rice with "conch" water, which, as near as we could understand, was simply rice-water, with a few grains of rice left in it. Tea was served, and this ended the dinner. Large basins of hot water were then brought to wash our hands in, and small towels or napkins to dry them with. I also forgot to mention that there were small pieces of Chinese paper brought with the first course, which were intended to be used as napkins. Altogether, the viands may be said to be fairly palatable, and we could have made a good meal had we not already eaten a moderate dinner at the hotel just before starting, as we were fearful that we would not be able to appreciate Chinese cookery sufficiently well to satisfy our appetites. I then told our interpreter that I was very much dissatisfied at not having a *regular* Chinese dinner; that I wanted some cats and dogs, or rats and mice, such as Chinese eat; that, if we could not get it there, we must go to some place where we *could* get it. He assured me, in the gravest manner, that such things were not eaten by the Chinese, except occasionally by the poorer classes, when they could get nothing better. He volunteered, however, to go with us and try and find a place where we could procure "such tings." After paying our bill we started out in search of a dog-and-cat-meat restaurant.

After a long walk through the narrow streets, and making various inquiries, our interpreter turned into an alley-way, and stopping in front of a dark, dingy little eating-house, pointed triumphantly to the claws that were still attached to a hind-quarter of what might be mistaken for the fat hind-quarter of a young pig, and ejaculated "Dog!" After satisfying ourselves that this was the veritable article, he also showed us a kettle in front of which was an inscription in Chinese, which, he said, translated into English, read: "Black cat, served hot." I told him I wanted to try some, which fact he communicated to the proprietor, who escorted us up a pair of rickety bamboo stairs into a dirty little room on the second floor, in which there were four small tables with benches at their sides. Sitting down at these, we soon had the satisfaction of seeing two liberal-sized plates of stewed cat and dog before us. The cat was cut into much finer pieces than the dog, but both dishes looked and tasted, for all the world, like stewed rabbit. Owing to the two previous meals which I had discussed, my appetite was not very good, and I could hardly do more than taste of these two dishes. Proceeding down-stairs, I asked to be shown any live dogs and cats that might be on hand awaiting their fate, but, with the exception of one small, half-starved cat, there was nothing of the kind to be seen. I am sure that the dog was genuine, because I saw the feet attached to the hind-quarter, but I could not vouch for the other dish being genuine cat, because there were no identifying marks to be seen. This ended our experience with Chinese viands, and from what I have seen, and the inquiries which I have made in China, I am satisfied that the stories which have been current all over the world in relation to the Chinese habitually eating cats and dogs, or rats and mice, have been greatly exaggerated. Indeed, it may be said to be the romance of travellers rather than a statement of things as they actually exist. The principal article of flesh diet among the Chinese is pork; of this they use immense quantities, mostly, so far as I can judge, in a fresh state. Poultry, especially ducks, are also a very large item, and from these they very skilfully take out the bones, press them flat, salt and dry them and use them as preserved provision. So great a demand is there for these, and ducks not making very good mothers, the Chinese have invented hatching establishments, where immense numbers of ducks' eggs are accumulated, and, by keeping up a uniform degree of artificial heat, they are successful in hatching out nearly the whole of them. We visited one of these establishments near Canton, and found it very interesting. As soon as the ducks are hatched, they are sold to parties all over the country, who make a business of rearing them for market; they pay about two cents each for them when just out of the shell, and when reared obtain from twenty-five to fifty cents for them, according to size and condition. Rice, however, is the article of largest consumption among the Chinese, and probably fish comes next. Eggs are also largely used, and almost everywhere in Chinese native towns one can get fish, rice, and eggs in perfection, and, of course, with these there is no need of going hungry. Storks are also eaten in China, and in passing along the streets of Canton it was no uncommon thing to see large numbers of white storks exposed for sale. At first we wondered why they did not fly away, as they apparently were not fastened; but on investigating this matter we found that their eyes were sewed up, so as to make them entirely blind, in which state they never fly—certainly an original Chinese way of accomplishing the same object that we in America do by clipping the wings of birds that we do not wish to have "make themselves wings."

The Chinese also have a way of surmounting the traditional obstinacy of the pig, which is rather original and amusing. Every pig is put into a bag-shaped bamboo basket; these baskets are just large enough to receive him, and frequently we saw coolies trotting along the streets of Canton with a pig in a basket slung on a bamboo pole which rested on their shoulders. Pigs are also brought in from the country in boats, sometimes a distance of many miles, the baskets being piled one on top of the other in a way which cannot be very comfortable for the undermost pigs.

It has been a mystery to me, ever since I saw the first pair of chopsticks, how they could be made effective in conveying food to the mouth; but the mystery is solved here, for I find that almost every variety of food is served in bowls, and these bowls are held close to the mouth, and the sticks are used more for *poking* the food into the mouth than they are for lifting, as we do with the fork.

Rough rice is cleaned throughout the length and breadth of China, and indeed, I may say in Japan and the other great islands of the Pacific, by pounding it in a large wooden mortar with a pestle, which is operated by a lever worked with the feet. It is a slow and laborious process, not nearly so perfect in its results as the work of our rice-mills, yet immense quantities of rice are cleaned in this way.

Clothes are washed by dipping them into the water and then slapping them over rocks and stones. At first this seemed to me as if it must be bad for the clothes, but as yet I have detected no evidence of undue wear and tear in my own, and certainly both Chinese and Japanese laundrymen do their work well and cheaply —two cents per piece being the customary price in Japan, and three cents in China, this including large as well as small pieces.

Chinese kites are an institution; we happened to be in Canton just in the season when the greatest numbers of them are being flown. They are made in all sorts of fantastic shapes, figures of birds, insects, and men being represented, together with many fanciful designs which only a Chinaman could invent. During favorable weather one can see scores of these flying in every direction, some of them attaining (what seemed to me) a greater height than any I had ever before noticed.

The principal currency here, and indeed throughout China, are Mexican dollars; and a heavy, clumsy, inconvenient currency they are. If you wish to make any considerable purchase, you have to carry about with you a weight of money which is exceedingly inconvenient, and which makes one long for an equivalent in greenbacks. There are occasionally counterfeits among them, and to insure their genuineness and enable them to be traced from hand to hand, the Chinese have a way of stamping with a little steel punch or die the private mark of the person paying them out. By this practice the dollars gradually become so defaced that it is impossible to identify them, and so abraded that they are finally broken up into fragments, which serve as small change by weighing them, every Chinese dealer having a pair of tiny scales for this purpose.

The Chinese have also an original way of taking your measure for a suit of clothes. The measurer, who is usually the cutter, takes a long, thin tape of tough paper, goes through the usual motions, but instead of calling out the numbers and having them put down in a book, he simply nips off a small piece of the tape at each length, and these indications are to him as plain as figures would be to a European cutter. They are expert tailors, and work very cheaply. I had made to order in Hong-Kong, by a native tailor, a blue flannel suit for $9 that would have cost me from $35 to $40 in New York, and a white duck suit for $5.50 that would have cost me $20 to $25 in New York. I am convinced that this difference is not all in cheap materials and cheap labor, but that New York tailors must charge exorbitant profits. The fact is, Chinamen are very expert and skilful at anything. They can imitate anything for which you will give them a pattern, and indeed this imitative faculty is quite remarkable. They always follow the exact pattern; they are "realistic" in every sense of the word. It is an old story which many readers may have heard, but perhaps it may be new to some, that a gentleman wishing a dozen pairs of "nankeen" trowsers made, left a pair of old ones with a Chinese tailor as a pattern. This pair happened to have a patch on the place that usually gets the most wear. The goods were delivered to the gentleman punctually, according to agreement, but what was his dismay on examining them to find that every pair had a patch upon them in the same identical place as the pair which had been left as a pattern. In California I heard the story of a Chinese cook, whom the lady of the house desired to teach how to make an omelet. Breaking the eggs as usual, the third one which came to hand was not fresh, and consequently she threw it away. The Chinaman never required showing again; the omelets were always perfect, and were consequently frequently ordered. Happening into the kitchen one day, however, at the time the cook was preparing an omelet, she, to her surprise, observed him throw away an egg which was perfectly fresh. Investigating the matter, as a frugal housewife ought, she found that John Chinaman had been literally carrying out her example ever since the first showing, by throwing away every third egg that he broke, without any reference whatever to its quality. There are many other features in Chinese life which are novel and interesting, but in the limited space of this letter I am obliged to omit them. Suffice it to say that Americans in America see only the worst side of the Chinese, for those who emigrate, as is usual with all nations, are those of the poorer classes, who seek to better their condition. Perhaps after a time we may learn to treat the Chinese who come to America in a way that will make it an inducement for a better class to come—a class that in personal cleanliness, intelligence, ability, and enterprise, are not inferior to the average population in any part of the world.

SINGAPORE.

TROPICAL LIFE AND SCENERY—A VISIT TO PEPPER AND TAPIOCA PLANTATIONS, ETC., ETC.

From Hong-Kong to Singapore is a distance of nearly fifteen hundred miles, the course being nearly due south and covering something over twenty degrees of latitude. Arriving at Singapore, a glance at the foliage of the shrubs and trees shows that we are in a more tropical country than any we have yet visited. Cocoa-nut, betel-nut, and traveller's palm-trees are everywhere to be seen; bananas (or plantains, as they are called here), together with pineapples, grow by the way-side, and every wall and hedge is covered with a luxuriant growth of flowering vines, such as are seen nowhere except in the tropics. The palm-trees are exceedingly graceful, and, to a stranger, are quite the feature of the landscape; the "betel-nut palm" is very slender, and rises tall and straight seventy-five or one hundred feet, terminating with the usual tuft of long, graceful, fern-like leaves, and the bunch of nuts clustered among them. The natives, and also many Chinese, are continually chewing this nut, which stains their lips and gums of a reddish hue, and also colors their teeth very black, giving them anything but a prepossessing appearance. The "cocoa-nut palm" is very abundant and grows stronger than any other variety, although more crooked, and usually not so tall as the betel-palm; the leaves, which also grow only from the top, are long and graceful, and the fruit clusters in great abundance just at the base of the leaves. The "traveller's palm," however, is more picturesque than either of the two former varieties; the trunk is shorter, but from the top of the trunk its tall, graceful leaves shoot out in the shape of a "palm-leaf fan," or, as some persons have described it, like the rising sun. These leaves are deeply grooved, and at their base form quite a reservoir, where, when it rains, a supply of water is collected and retained for many days. In regions where water is scarce, travellers obtain a supply by puncturing these reservoirs; hence the name of "traveller's palm." A stranger is somewhat surprised to see the water follow the knife, pouring out of the puncture in a slender stream, quite reminding one of the "rock of Horeb."

Everything here constantly reminds me that I am in the tropics; but few of the houses have any glass in their windows, blinds answering the purpose of keeping out the sun and rain, and yet admitting as much as possible of the always-to-be-desired breeze. The hotels furnish no upper sheet or other covering for the bed, unless requested to do so, and, indeed, this is unnecessary where the thermometer ranges between eighty and ninety degrees throughout the year. Dusky bird-venders, with a long stick perched full of parrots of every hue, and stick peddlers, with their bundle of real malacca canes, everywhere greet you with "Buy a bird?" or "Buy a stick, master?" and in the shops, tigers' claws and bird-of-paradise skins are staple curiosities, of which nearly every traveller buys more or less.

Here also we met a new type of features, in the Malay race, and a stranger blending of nationalities even than at Hong-Kong. Malay boatmen and fishermen, Hindoo money-changers and shopkeepers, Bengalese washermen and hack-drivers, Parsee merchants, Portuguese clerks from Malacca, Chinese merchants, planters, and coolies, besides a representation of all the nations of Europe, make up a conglomerate population such as probably can be found in no other part of the world. Of these the Chinese are by far the most numerous, and their patient industry has made them a most important part of the population here. Indeed, it has passed into a proverb that "the Chinese are the backbone of the island." They own and cultivate more land than any other class, and pay more taxes; are quiet, orderly, industrious, and enterprising, and instead of carrying their bones back to China, as they do from California, they marry, raise families, and most of them are buried here the same as other people. Some of them have become naturalized British subjects, and one Chinese merchant, Mr. Whampoa, has been so benevolent and useful a citizen that the British Government has conferred upon him the Colonial Order of Knighthood. There is probably a larger percentage of the merchant and trading class here than in California, but this is due to the fact that the Chinese are so treated on the Pacific coast that there is no inducement for a well-to-do Chinaman to emigrate there, while here all are protected in their rights, both of person and property; and hence the result in their being permanent, useful, and respected citizens.

Pepper is one of the principal exports from Singapore, and the variety of this article produced in this section has always been more highly esteemed than that produced in Sumatra and other of the great Spice Islands. Desiring to learn as much as possible about the peculiarities of production of this, as well as other articles which enter into the trade with which I am connected, I arranged for a visit to a pepper-plantation. There are not many upon Singapore Island itself, the soil not being considered as rich and productive as that of the Malayan Peninsula, immediately opposite; but a number of Chinese planters have grown it successfully, and it was one of their plantations, owned by a Chinese planter named Tan-Oh-Hoon, at Sarengong, some nine miles from Singapore, that I visited. At a distance, a pepper-plantation somewhat resembles a hop-farm, the pepper-plant being a vine trained upon poles, much the same as hop-farmers train their vines in the United States. Unlike the hop-vine, however, the pepper-vine or plant has a strong, woody growth, and does not throw out long, slender tendrils, as does the hop-vine. Indeed, unless carefully tied and trained around supporting poles, it would, probably, in many instances, spread over the ground instead of climbing. It is propagated from cuttings, has a smooth, glossy leaf, and begins to bear when from two to three years old, after which, with proper cultivation, it lasts many years. The grains of pepper form on stems, much the same as currants, and are picked twice a year, for in this tropical latitude nearly all plants remain green the year round, and yield two or more crops. The first picking usually extends through November, December, and January. Then an interval of several months is allowed to elapse before the next picking takes place. That which is designed for black pepper is picked after the berries have attained a good size, but while they are yet green. They are usually picked in the cool of the evening, thrown upon a lattice-work of bamboo, which is placed over a furnace, the heat and smoke from which pass through the pepper and both dry and color it. (Both the leaf and fruit of the pepper plant also naturally turn black, if dried in the sun, when picked green.) This process is usually accomplished in one night, and the next day the stems are taken off the lattice-work, placed upon mats, and the berries detached from the stem by rubbing with the hands or treading with the feet. They are then sifted, to remove the dust and stems, and the dried berries or kernels are packed in bags to await shipment.

To make "white pepper" the stems are allowed to remain upon the vines until the berries are ripe, when they are of a red color and have considerable pulp around the inner kernel or seed. Immediately after picking they are thrown into shallow trenches or ditches, containing water, where they are allowed to soak ten or twelve days. By this time the pulp is much decayed, and the berries are then taken out and put into a strong bag, into which a coolie gets and treads vigorously with his feet to loosen the skin and pulp. This mass is then turned out upon sieves, and the seeds or kernels separated and put in the sun to dry. When dried the berries are of a grayish white color, but after being sold they not unfrequently undergo another bleaching by "chlorine," which improves their appearance at the expense of quality. The process by which white pepper is produced is much more tedious and expensive than in making black pepper, and the product is really not so good, the essential constituents of the spice being more abundant in the outer parts of the fruit than in the seed. Let any person take a sample of ground black pepper and ground white pepper, and use the two in the same manner; he will perceive that the latter has a bitterish taste and lacks the rich and spicy flavor of the former, and yet the demand for white pepper has largely increased during the last quarter of a century, notwithstanding the fact that the price has ranged from fifty to one hundred per cent. higher than for the black.

On my return from the pepper-plantation, I stopped at a large "pearl tapioca" manufactory. Here were some 2,000 acres in a plantation, owned by a Chinese planter named Tan-Ah-Seng. Tapioca itself is a tuber or bulb, from which springs a tender, woody shoot, attaining, at the age of sixteen months, when it is ready for harvest, a height of five or six feet, the only leaves being three or four at the top. The tubers or roots, from which the tapioca is made, are dug very much as potatoes are, and some of them very much resemble in appearance our American sweet potatoes; but the meat is whiter and contains large quantities of a starchy flour, which separates from the fibrous matter when ground, and it is this flour from which tapioca is made. The roots are first washed, and after having the outer skin removed, are ground up in a machine. A stream of water is turned upon the pulp, which carries the flour off into vats, where it settles. It remains in these vats twenty-four hours, and is then run off into large tubs, where it remains for about eight days, the water being changed each day, and thoroughly agitated, so as to mix with the flour. After the last water is drawn off it leaves a deposit of beautifully white flour, which is taken out in cakes and conveyed to the drying-house. Here it is broken up into small particles; indeed, I may say pulverized. A portion of it is then placed in a machine called a "yulong," which looks more like a small, canvas boat, suspended by strings from the ceiling at each end, than anything else, and by giving this a peculiar motion, which is half backward and forward and half rotary, the floury particles adhere to each other and are shaped into small, round balls, about the size of a No. 4 shot. The tapioca is then placed upon drying-pans, under which a steady and gentle heat is maintained for about half an hour, when it is sufficiently dry for packing and transportation. In fine weather it is sometimes dried in the sun, a process which usually occupies about a day to accomplish the result attained with the furnace in a half-hour. The tapioca flour can be made at will, either into small or large-sized "pearl" tapioca, or into "flake;" but the flake tapioca from this part of the globe does not possess as much gluten as that produced in Brazil, and, although beautifully white, is not as free from dust as the Brazilian tapioca.

TEA-GROWING IN JAVA.

I had occasionally heard of Java tea, but had no idea to what extent tea was cultivated in Java. I found on my arrival here, however, that there were annually produced from eight to ten million pounds, and I immediately became curious to see the method of culture and the quality and varieties produced. Through friends in Batavia I was kindly furnished with letters of introduction to Mr. E. J. Kirkhoven, who, in connection with his partner, Mr. Hohler, was represented to be an extensive tea-planter in Sinagar, a small place some sixty or seventy miles in the interior. We proceeded by rail from Batavia to Buitenzorg, some forty miles, and thence by two-wheeled spring-carts, each drawn by three tiny ponies, about the size of two months old colts, to Sinagar. Arriving there, we were most hospitably received by Mr. Kirkhoven, and not only had an excellent opportunity of seeing the process of tea-cultivation and manufacture, but also something of what a planter's life is like in the interior of Java. The estate extends over several square miles, and the area under tea-cultivation alone is upwards of 1,100 acres. There are, upon an average, about 6,000 plants to the acre, which, upon this area, would give between 600,000 and 700,000 plants. Some of these, however, are not in full bearing, owing to a severe blight which has affected the plants during the last year or two, making it necessary to prune them close to the ground, in order that they may produce fresh shoots; yet, even with this drawback, this grand estate will produce this year about 800,000 pounds, or 10,000 chests of 80 pounds, net, each. One great advantage of tea-culture in Java is that the picking and manufacture may be continued nearly the whole year through, while in Japan and China the severity of the climate limits the picking to three or four months. Labor is also much cheaper here than in China, although it is said that one Chinaman will do as much work as two Javanese. The average wages of adults in Japan and China is about 18 or 20 cents per day; here it is not more than half that sum, while that of women and children—by whom a large portion of the work is done—is paid for "by the piece" at even a less rate than this.

All the tea made here is black (Congou, Souchong, and a little Pekoe), and the culture and preparation are essentially the same as in China. The plants are grown at intervals of two feet, in rows, which are four feet apart; the spaces between are carefully kept free from weeds, and the earth loose and moist. There is also one feature which I did not see either in Japan or China, viz.: the digging of holes at short intervals between the rows, for the purpose of allowing the air to reach the subsoil, and to catch and hold the rain, so that it may gradually percolate through the soil, affording at all times sufficient moisture to the roots of the plants. The leaves, when picked, are first spread out on large, circular, shallow baskets, and exposed to the sun until wilted. They are then, for a few minutes, placed in firing-pans and stirred until thoroughly heated. They are next thrown on tables surrounded by operators, each of whom grasps a mass of the tea as large as he can hold in his hands and rolls it over and over, in order to curl the leaves and make them compact. They are then shaken out and again placed on the baskets in the sun for the balance of the day. When the sun goes down, the baskets, together with the tea which they hold, are placed in a drying-room, through which the heated air from a furnace is driven by a blower, which in ten hours completes the drying process, leaving the leaf much shrunken in size, and close, wiry, and black. It is a curious fact that at this time the leaf has scarcely any odor, and does not appear to have nearly as much taste as it has after it has lain a few days in bulk, when it acquires a marked fragrant odor, somewhat the same as new-mown hay, although nothing is used to scent it or otherwise add to its flavor. To some extent this is the case also in China and Japan, although the tea which I saw in those countries seemed to possess much more flavor immediately after firing than the Java leaf. In China it is also sometimes scented, in the manner previously described. At the time of picking, the different sizes of leaf are kept separate, and from these are made different kinds of tea, the smallest and tenderest leaf being made into Pekoe, the next size into Souchong, and the larger leaves into Congou. These teas, however, seemed to me to have a strong, peculiar flavor, much like the Assam teas, of which we occasionally get a shipment in America. After the completion of the curing process, the tea is packed in chests holding from 80 to 90 pounds net, and transported to Batavia, whence it is shipped to Holland; but some of it also goes to England, and, I believe, occasionally a small lot to the United States. Java tea has a handsome style of leaf, possesses good body, and is said to be an excellent tea for making the mixtures which are commonly sold in Holland and in England.

The residence, together with all the accessories of the life led by Mr. Kirkhoven, were to me very interesting, and I presume, constitute a fair specimen of the life led by a majority of the large planters in the interior of Java. These estates are generally very extensive, usually comprising many thousands of acres, the most eligible of which only are cultivated. The plantations of Messrs. Kirkhoven and Hohler cover about three square miles of ground, necessitating two establishments in different parts of this immense territory, with all the requisites for cultivating and curing the tea.

HALF WAY ROUND.

TROPICAL SCENERY—THE MOST BEAUTIFUL VIEW IN THE WORLD—BRITISH COLONIZATION POLICY, ETC.

I BELIEVE that all "globe trotters" give their friends at home a dose of lessons in geography and reflections at this period of their journey about their said friends being eight thousand miles beneath their feet, that noonday with them is midnight with the friends, etc.; but it was never clear to my mind whether the friends were on top or whether the travellers were; so I have concluded to spare the reader that part of my narrative, and merely state that I am on my way from Singapore to Ceylon; that we have just passed the port of Penang, on the Malayan Peninsula; are, therefore, a little more than half way round, and that we are now ploughing through the Indian Ocean, off the northerly end of Sumatra, as fast as steam and sails on the good steamer Tigre, of the French "Messageries," can carry us.

Penang, to most minds, is suggestive of nutmegs and other spices, but it also carries me back in memory to my school-boy days and the story of the youngster, who, on examination day, before the grave and spectacled trustees of a district school, spelled and defined the word rattan as follows: "R-a-t-t-a-n, rattan; a slender, fibrous wood which comes from Penang, Samarang, and Padang, and—is used by the school-master in this school *too-dang* often." I have always had a fellow-feeling for that boy, and respect him even now; besides, it taught me a lesson in geography, for, forget as I would the names of other places, Penang, Samarang, and Padang were always firmly fixed in my memory.

A sea-voyage is not considered the pleasantest and most entertaining thing in the world, especially if one is subject to sea-sickness; but I enjoy voyaging in these tropical seas, where all is so new and interesting to me. This morning I have been watching the shoals of tiny flying-fish as they rise from the water to escape the dolphins and other voracious monsters, and go skipping from wave to wave, sometimes for quite long distances; and last night we had a beautiful exhibition of phosphorescent light in the water, as it glided along the ship's side or curled upward from the screw astern. Nature is always providing beauties for those who have eyes to see and hearts to appreciate, and I feel myself fortunate in being able to find pleasure in her charms whether on land or sea.

I have enjoyed some most charming bits of tropical scenery, among them Buitenzorg, Java, which, as an entirety, is a most beautiful place; but the prospect from the Hotel Belle-vue is fairly entitled, I think, to the name of "*The most beautiful view in the world.*" The pretty river Tjedani runs just at the foot of the bluff upon which the hotel is built, and, with an abrupt turn, loses itself amid a mass of tropical foliage.

"Breadths of tropic shade and palms in cluster, knots of paradise."

The plain below is also covered with graceful cocoa-nut palms, and other tropical trees, and reaches away for several miles, gradually sloping upward until a belt of coffee and spice plantations is reached, and from these, for a background, there suddenly rises the grand volcanic peak of Mount Salak.

I shall never forget my last day at Buitenzorg: sitting upon the balcony during the closing hours of a tropical November afternoon, all nature seemed to be at rest; the slender palms, which are ever waving their restless leaves, were as still as silence itself, and the dragon-flies floated so lazily in the rays of the setting sun that I threw down my fan, so out of harmony was its motion with the spirit of the scene. Only the river, the ever running river, moved, and that seemed to have lost its ripples and glided where before it ran murmuring past. It seemed as if I could never tire of this scene; I sat and gazed at the shadows creeping slowly up the mountain-side until they reached the ragged crater at the top, and the halo of light suddenly faded. Then a purple mist enveloped the mountain; the deep ravines and fissures in its side, which before had been visible, faded away, and soon nothing was visible but the dim blue outline which long held its place amid the darkening shadows. I have enjoyed and left other places with regret, but I could not put aside the positive sorrow I felt at leaving Buitenzorg. The short stay in Java was so enjoyable that I much wish that my arrangements had been such that I might have devoted sufficient time to visit other parts of the island, which are said to be equal or superior in attractions to those which I visited.

Indeed, explorers tell us of a wealth of tropical scenery in all the great islands of the Malayan Archipelago, which is equalled nowhere upon the globe. Here are islands with an extent of territory which entitles them almost to the name of continent: Sumatra, more than 1,000 miles long; Java, 600; Borneo, 900, with a breadth almost as great; while Celebes and others of the Moluccas and Spice Islands are of a size and possess a soil and climate which would make them of great importance if situated anywhere else than in this vast and far distant Indian Ocean. Much of this great territory has not, as yet, even been visited by the explorer; not a ten-thousandth part has yet been cleared of jungle, and this small portion hardly scratched by the ploughshare. Yet its productions fill the ships and warehouses of all nations with the richest and most valuable products known in commerce.

All this great region is nominally in the possession of the Dutch; I say nominally, for it is only here and there that their authority is supreme and undisturbed, and the 25,000,000 of natives are controlled by probably less than the same number of thousands of white residents. Holland has a much more feeble hold upon her colonies than England has upon hers, and suppresses disturbances with so feeble and faltering a hand as to promise anything but permanency for her possessions in the East. The present war in Acheen, Sumatra, is a striking example of this. Here, a handful of natives, with no discipline or resources, have successfully defied the power of Holland for several years, and it presents a striking contrast with the manner in which England chastised the Abyssinians and suppressed the great rebellion in India.

Whatever may be said of Englishmen, it cannot be said that they are not good colonizers. In every English colony one finds good roads and good judicial and police regulations, insuring the safety of life and property, and descending into the minutest details of regulation upon which depend the comfort and convenience of Europeans. I could not but notice this in Hong-Kong, which was the first English colony I visited. Here was a large and sufficient force of native police; every chair or other public conveyance had its number, and the maximum scale of charges was prominently posted so that travellers need not be imposed upon. Each one of the vast number of boats in the harbor was also registered, licensed and numbered, and at night there stood at every landing-place an official who made a note of the number of every boat leaving the shore, together with the number of passengers carried and their destination, for it is said in by-gone times passengers would sometimes take a boat for a ship in the harbor, and never reach their destination. I also found the same regulations current at Singapore, where there are miles of macadamized roads so smooth that the small mountain ponies, which are chiefly used there, can easily draw a good-sized carriage, containing four persons, at a good rate of speed.

English policy in the East has been both aggressive and tenacious: first obtaining a hold, no matter how slender, and then holding on to it with a death-like grip. British dominion in the East has been greatly extended by enterprising Englishmen striking out for and exploring unknown regions, settling and perhaps planting there, and then claiming the protection of the British flag. In very many cases adventurous spirits have gone where they had no business to go, and assumed authority which they had no business to assume; yet if the natives resented this and these men suffered in life or property, a British gunboat was promptly upon the spot, and, if necessary, the whole power of this great nation was at hand to resent the "outrage upon the British flag;" generally the affair resulted in a British occupation, and new territory was added to the already immense possessions of the British in the East. However, perhaps Englishmen can retort by saying, with some truth, that our Indian policy has been a duplicate of that of Great Britain, and it may be that

"Through the ages one increasing purpose runs,"

and that the destiny of the aboriginal races, both in India and America, is to disappear before the onward march of European "civilization."

CEYLON.

CANOES AT POINT DE GALLE—COCOA-NUT TREES—FEMALE POLYGAMISTS.

The island of Ceylon, lying off the southern coast of India, is about two hundred miles long by one hundred broad. The first impressions that travellers usually get of this great island are derived from the little port of Point de Galle at its extreme southern end, which is the great port of call for all the steam lines to the east; and as you approach the island the thing that most attracts the traveller's attention is the surf, which breaks with great violence all along the coast. Galle Harbor itself is a little bandbox of a haven, rocky and somewhat dangerous of access, and not very secure after it has been reached. Immediately our steamer dropped anchor she was surrounded by a fleet of the queerest-shaped canoes I have ever seen. Imagine a log, eighteen inches to two feet in diameter, twenty-five or thirty feet long, tapered up to a point at the ends, and with a narrow slit, about eighteen inches wide, cut in it throughout nearly its whole length; through this slit the entire inside of the log is scooped out, leaving only a thin shell. Having no keel, this kind of a craft would, of course, very easily upset, were it not that this is provided against by having what is called an "outrigger," consisting of another smaller, solid log placed parallel with it and about ten feet off, connected with the canoe by two strong arms of wood, slightly curved above the water, and which are fastened so as to give them great rigidity—in effect, all the staunchness of a raft, but with clipper-ship sailing qualities. Above the slit in the canoe is built up a light weather-board, or rather water-board, to prevent the water dashing in during rough weather; and these crafts, carrying a large sail and manned by four or more natives, go through the water at a rate which, it is said, is equalled by no other class of sailing craft afloat. When there is a stiff breeze, in order to ballast them, they put a man out upon the outrigger, and when it blows heavily they put two men out, this living ballast clinging fast to lashings, and in their parlance it is called a "one-man" or "two-man" breeze. To a European, seeing them for the first time, they look precisely like a large and a small cigar, made with both ends tapered, placed parallel with each other in the water, connected by a couple of straws, and he will hardly believe that they are safe craft for him to venture in; but they are largely used as ferry-boats between the shipping and the shore, carrying trunks even, as well as passengers, and are said to be the best boats that can possibly be made for going through a heavy surf.

Point de Galle itself is a quaint old town, originally fortified by the Portuguese, from whom it was taken by the Dutch, and they, in turn, were dispossessed by the English about the beginning of the present century. It has but little commerce, the great bulk of the exports and imports of the island being made at the port of Colombo, which is about eighty miles along the coast to the northward. Between these two places communication is regularly maintained by steamers, and there is also a very excellent road along the coast, by which the distance between the two places is made by post-coach in nine or ten hours. This stage-coach ride proved one of the most enjoyable parts of my whole journey. The road, like most English roads, is smooth and level as a floor, and throughout nearly the whole distance is densely shaded by graceful cocoa-nut palms, which here grow in great abundance. In places the young trees are planted at regular intervals, and their leaves, arching upward in regular Gothic style, meet at the top in curved geometrical lines, and look exactly like the groined arches of a cathedral crypt. Throughout the whole distance the roar of the sea sounded in our ears, and occasional openings in the trees gave us glimpses of it, curling over in solid, green masses, and dashing its foam in concentric, circular rings, far up on the broad, sandy beach.

The cocoa-nut tree is the chief source of revenue and profit to the natives here, and, indeed, is a wonderful tree. From the nut large quantities of oil are made, and the milk contained in it is given to cattle. From the fibre of the thick outer husk, cordage is made, and also from it are manufactured vast quantities of "coir" yarn, from which is fabricated the cocoa-nut matting that is used extensively in America, and, indeed, all over the world. The outer shells of the nut and the wood itself are used for fuel, while the leaves furnish a thatch for the native dwellings. Thus every part of this wonderful tree is utilized. The process of oil-making is quite simple. The nuts are cut open, and the meat extracted and placed in the sun for a time until it shrinks and the oil begins to exude; it is then placed in a rude stone-mill, which is at the same time a sort of press. This is turned by bullock-power, and the oil is half-ground, half-pressed, and runs out through an aperture at the bottom into receptacles provided to receive it. This process is quite rude and primitive, and does not extract so large a percentage of the oil as the more perfect machinery does which has been established by Europeans in Colombo for the same purpose. I could hardly believe that by this improved process a quantity of oil equivalent to sixty-three per cent. of the entire weight of the nut is extracted. The oil is used here for burning in lamps and other purposes, but is principally sent to Europe, where it is utilized in the manufacture of soap, candles, etc., and portions of it are also refined and used in the manufacture of hair-oil and various toilet preparations.

The natives of Ceylon are a bright, intelligent-looking race, with an erect, manly carriage; are of a lighter color than most of the inhabitants of the Malayan Archipelago; and some of the women are positively beautiful. *En passant*, there is here a feature in polygamy different from any I have ever heard of—instead of a man having several wives, a woman here has several husbands. We heard of one case where one woman had married a family of six brothers, and it is a very common thing for a woman to have two or more husbands. So it seems that there is one part of the world, at least, where the female sex retaliates upon the doctrine and the disciples of Brigham Young.

Colombo is a city of considerable size, but it is the slowest and most deliberate place which it has been my fortune to visit. The cab-drivers are asleep two-thirds of the time, and, to match them, their horses seem to be all cripples. Still, there is a great deal of business done in Colombo, it being the shipping port for all the great coffee-plantations of the interior, the cinnamon-groves, and most of the cocoa-nut oil and coir-yarn manufactories of the island. As a merchant here said, "Our exports may be all enumerated under the head of C's—coffee, cinnamon, cocoa-nut, and coir," and when we reflect that they all come from Colombo, Ceylon, is it not a remarkable conjunction of C's?

COFFEE CULTURE—COFFEE IN THE EAST AS A BEVERAGE—LONG NAMES, ETC., ETC.

Ceylon coffee has always ranked high as regards quality, possessing a mild flavor somewhat similar to Java. Yet, strange to say, I did not have a good cup of coffee while in Ceylon, nor did the coffee I tasted in Java at all compare with that which we make in the United States. We frequently hear the quality of the coffee obtained at the railway eating-houses in the United States reviled by Americans; but at any of the stations along the lines of the New York Central, or the New York and New Haven roads, you can get a cup of coffee which is perfection itself compared with that which I found in Java or Ceylon, while the coffee which I have in my own house, when at home, is a nectar, the mere recollection of which in this far-distant country titillates my palate when I think of it. They may talk about the crudeness of American civilization in a gastronomic point of view, but in all my travels, I have never yet found a city, unless it be Vienna, where the quality of this universal beverage at all compares with that to be found in New York. I speak advisedly in this respect, although it may be egotistically; but on the principle that

"Who drives fat oxen should himself be fat,"

I believe that he who caters for others should be a judge of quality, and I have studied the conditions necessary for the production of good coffee as carefully as the true artist studies the effects necessary for the production of a perfect picture.

This is a great country for long names. I thought, when I arrived in Hong-Kong and read some of the names on the signs of the Parsee merchants there, that I had reached the limit in this respect; but I am now convinced that Ceylon can take the palm. If I should spell out and send you, detached from other matter, some of the names which I see here, you would certainly think that I was exaggerating; so I have cut from to-day's *Ceylon Times* an advertisement of an official sale.

FISCAL'S SALE.

No. 69,393.

IN THE DISTRICT COURT OF KANDY.

Kana Rana Obana Shoona Palaniappa Chetti........................ Plaintiff,

vs.

Periyakarpen Seruwokaran's Son Kali Muttu Kankani............ Defendant.

Notice is hereby given, that on SATURDAY, the 9th December, 1876, at one (1) o'clock P.M., will be SOLD BY PUBLIC AUCTION at the premises, the following property belonging to the Defendant in the above case:

All the Right Title and interest of the Defendant to and in the following Lands (subject, however, to the terms and conditions of the Planting Voucher No. 869, dated 9th June, 1871) to wit:—

1.—The Garden called Hapugahamulagawa Watta, about 12 acres in extent.

2.—The Garden called Elagaswatta *alias* Nawagahamulawatta, about one acre in extent, both situated at Dorakumbura in the Gampahasiyapattuwa of Matale South.

D. A. D'ALWIS,
For Deputy Fiscal.

Deputy Fiscal's Office,
Matale, 13th November, 1876.

This speaks for itself, and I think, as a phonetic curiosity, is worthy of publication.

SUNDRY SPICES.—THEIR GROWTH AND PREPARATION.

I have been much interested in observing the growth and manner of preparation of various kinds of spices, not separately affording sufficient material for an article, but which, grouped together, will furnish matter enough for one letter. Of these I will first mention cinnamon, which, in the shape in which it appears in commerce, is, of course, familiar to every grocer, but would hardly be distinguished from any other bush when seen growing in the field. Ceylon is the greatest centre of production for true cinnamon, but more of wild cinnamon, or cassia, is obtained from Malacca and along the coasts of Siam and Cochin-China. The cinnamon tree, if left to itself, sometimes attains the height of thirty to forty feet, and from twelve to eighteen inches in diameter; but, when cultivated, it is kept cut down close to the ground, and the fresh, new shoots only are allowed to grow, until they attain a height of from five to six feet, and are about half an inch in diameter. Some of the cinnamon-groves of Ceylon are very extensive, covering many hundred acres. They are originally planted in rows about six feet apart, and the plants are, perhaps, four feet distant from each other in the rows. The ground is usually well cultivated, being kept free from weeds and affording a chance for the plants to make a vigorous growth. When the shoots are three or four years old, they attain the size above-mentioned, and are usually free from branches until near the top. They are then cut close to the ground and the grayish, outside bark carefully scraped off. The inner bark, which is of a yellowish red color, is then ripped up longitudinally with a knife, and gradually loosened until it can be taken off. It is then spread in the sun to dry, when it curls up into the quill-like form in which it is known as the cinnamon of commerce. Some of the quills are smaller than others, and these are inserted within the larger ones, so as to make them as compact as possible. There are usually two crops gathered in Ceylon—one in April, the other in November, the first being much the larger of the two, and more easily gathered, owing to the sap being more abundant at that time, which allows the bark to be taken off with greater facility and despatch. The smell of the green cinnamon-bark is delightfully fragrant, but it varies greatly in quality, the younger and thinner pieces usually being much the best. The root of the cinnamon tree contains camphor, and the fruit, which is a sort of a nut, somewhat resembling an acorn, yields an acrid kind of oil called "cinnamon suet," which is also quite fragrant, and in Ceylon was formerly made into candles for the exclusive use of the nobility.

Cassia is prepared in the same manner as cinnamon, and is really a variety of that tree. There is much wild cassia gathered, however, and there is consequently a lack of the uniformity in thickness of bark and in perfection of preparation which we find in the Ceylon cinnamon, which brings a much higher price than cassia and, almost without exception, is sent to Europe. We occasionally get small parcels in America, but by far the larger portion of what is consumed in America under the name of cinnamon is really cassia.

NUTMEGS.

Nutmegs are grown more or less in all of the great Spice Islands of the Malayan Archipelago, and also on the Peninsula, Penang being one of the principal ports from which they are exported. The nutmeg-tree is a very beautiful one, growing in a compact conical shape to the height of thirty or forty feet. It has a dark, glossy leaf, and bears a profusion of fruit, which, however, on the tree, does not much resemble the nutmeg of commerce. In fact, when growing, it looks precisely like a black walnut, and the outer husk is of about the same thickness and consistency as that of the walnut. When the nut is ripe it cracks open and exposes the nut, growing closely around which is the fibrous mace. I had always supposed that the mace formed immediately next the kernel, which is the nutmeg of commerce, but on examining it closely, I found that the kernel was contained within a thin, hard shell, and it is around this shell that the mace forms. When the nuts are ripe they drop or are taken off the tree, and the mace at that time being of a bright scarlet color looks very beautiful; when it is separated and dried in the sun, however, it gradually assumes the brownish red or orange color which is familiar to all grocers. The nuts are also dried in the sun, and when this process is completed they are usually shipped to the place of export, where the outer shell is cracked, and the nuts taken out, and packed in casks or cases for shipment.

CLOVES.

Cloves grow on trees from twenty to thirty feet high, having a handsome pyramidal shape, with leaves that are large, glossy, and ever-green. It is a native of Malacca, but is now grown in nearly all of the Spice Islands of the Indian Ocean, the larger part of the crop coming from Amboyna, in the island of Ternate. Many years ago the Dutch undertook to control the production of this spice and to confine its growth to this island; they, therefore, destroyed the clove trees in the other Spice Islands, but the high prices which they demanded gradually led to its cultivation in territory outside of their jurisdiction, and they afterward abandoned that policy. Still most of the cloves now produced are grown in Dutch territory, and the high prices which have prevailed during the last year or two have been attributed partly to a failure in the crop in Ternate and partly to the Acheen war, which has considerably interfered with the supply usually derived from Sumatra. The cloves of commerce are not, as many suppose, the fruit of the clove tree, but are the *flower buds.* The ripe fruit in shape resembles a small olive; it is of a dark red color, with one or two cells containing as many seeds, and it is also aromatic to a certain extent, and sometimes appears in commerce in a dried state under the curious name of "mother of cloves." It is not nearly so pungent, however, as the flower stems. Indeed, the whole tree—leaves, bark, and wood—seems to be impregnated in some degree with the strong, distinctive clove flavor; but the flower buds are the principal commercial product of the tree. When first gathered, they are of reddish color, but in the drying process, which is generally partly done by wood fires and partly in the sun, they turn a deep brown color, as they are when they reach us in America. Although the tree grows wild to some extent, it is regularly cultivated in plantations, the plants being set some ten or fifteen feet apart and carefully pruned and cared for.

INDIA.

A BIRD'S-EYE VIEW—ITS EXTENT, POPULATION, PRODUCTIONS, GOVERNMENT, ETC.

One cannot see a great deal of India in three weeks, nor within the narrow limits of a letter can he describe all that he sees; but time is precious now-a-days, general ideas have sometimes to answer where a more thorough investigation of a subject would be desirable, and happy is he who can take the cream, and, discarding the water—"boil down," as it were, his ideas into the smallest possible compass.

"British India" extends from Cape Comorin, on the south, to the Himalayas, on the north, a distance of about eighteen hundred miles, and from the river Indus, on the west, to the Ganges, on the east, more than twelve hundred. In addition to this, it includes a considerable portion of Burmah and Siam (mentioned on the map under the head of "British Burmah") lying on the opposite side of the Bay of Bengal, and within this territory is situated the "Rangoon district," from which comes all our Rangoon rice. Within this total area are crowded over two hundred millions of people, and it is the production and consumption of this immense number of human beings that has constituted the largest and most remunerative item in the commerce of Great Britain for many years. Until we pause to think, it is hard to realize what "two hundred millions" means when applied to human beings—what their production and consumption may amount to.

A few figures in regard to rice culture, which I found among Government papers at Calcutta, served to widen my ideas in this respect. Speaking of but three districts, containing about sixty-five millions of inhabitants, the report stated that the annual consumption, exclusive of reserve stores, exports and quantities required for seed, was twelve and a quarter million tons, or twenty-seven billion four hundred and forty million pounds, a quantity equivalent to nearly one hundred and twenty-five million bags, or forty-five million tierces. I do not now remember the size of our Carolina rice crop, but I believe it was last year under eighty thousand tierces, or say about twenty thousand tons, against twelve and a quarter millions, and this, be it remembered, was only the consumption of less than one-third of the native population of India.

It is astonishing, however, how soon one becomes accustomed to figures, which, at first, perplex the understanding. When I first landed in India I could hardly believe the reports, which were then fast coming in, of the drowning of ten thousand natives by a tidal wave, which was raised in the Bay of Bengal and had swept over some of the coast islands. Later, however, after I had crossed India and seen the dense mass of population, I had no difficulty in comprehending and believing the official report of the loss of life, which had then reached the enormous number of two hundred and fifteen thousand. And yet this catastrophe, appalling as it was in magnitude, seemed to be quite overshadowed in the public mind by the famine which was at the time prevailing over a large portion of Southern India. Everywhere the railways were choked with rice and grain trains bound for that part of the country, and hundreds of vessels were employed in transporting rice from every point of supply in the East.

About two centuries ago, enterprising British merchants laid the foundations of British power in India, and shrewd old England, ever taking advantage of circumstances, has steadily pushed forward her boundaries, until now her possessions in the East have become, as they were recently termed by an English statesman, the "Greater Britain." Had she been as wise in the treatment of her American colonies, it is probable that they would not now have been an independent nation, but the injustice of George the Third lost her the choicest gem in her coronet. Perhaps, however, this circumstance had something to do with changing her colonial policy and strengthening her hold on her other possessions. It is a noteworthy fact, that while England was losing America she was gaining India, and the period immediately succeeding our war of the Revolution was the one in which she made the greatest progress there. Up to the mutiny in 1857 English interests in India were represented by the celebrated "East India Company," which, in a century and a half, had grown up from a comparatively small commercial enterprise to be a great government, maintaining an army of many thousand men, making laws, coining money, and exercising all the other principal attributes of sovereignty—a government which, in its relations to the English nation, was a sort of government within a government—an *imperium in imperio.* The controlling power was vested in a court, or board of directors, elected by the stockholders, and for a long time its affairs were ably and honestly managed, but after a time it became unwieldy, abuses set in, and after the mutiny it was thought that the interest of the entire nation in India had become so great, that it was better the country should come under the direct management of the Crown. This was done, and thus ended the greatest commercial venture the world has ever known.

The impression that a traveller gets of India in December is that by far the greater area is a dusty, arid, sterile waste; but this apparently unproductive soil is really very rich, and, when irrigated, produces, under even the careless cultivation of the natives, enormous crops of rice and various other grains; rape, lin, and other seeds; hemp, cotton, coffee, pepper, indigo, opium, sugar, tea, and many other products.

The Hindoo race or races are among the oldest of which we have any historical record, and the wealth and culture of ancient India was long the wonder of the Eastern world. It was not, however, until the invasion of Northern India by the Mahomedans and the establishment of the "Great Mogul" dynasty, that the attention of western nations was so strongly drawn to it; but the semi-barbarous magnificence of these remarkable rulers soon became proverbial throughout the civilized world. This was during the sixteenth and seventeenth centuries, after which their star gradually declined, and their power was finally broken by the warlike tribes of the Northwest. After that came a period of anarchy, the inhabitants of the different provinces constantly fighting among themselves for spoils and power, until finally, in the eighteenth century, British power began to make itself felt, and by dint of hard fighting and wise diplomacy it was steadily advanced, until it reached its present magnificent proportions. I say steadily advanced, for the mutiny in 1857 can hardly be called a serious check to the advancement of British power. It was promptly quelled, and the difficulty of communication during that episode has led to the construction of an extensive system of railways and telegraphs connecting all the principal parts of the empire, which have contributed, in a remarkable degree, to the subsequent prosperity of India, and renders any further opposition to British rule entirely hopeless. At present, the two hundred millions of natives are as completely under the control of the two hundred and fifty thousand British residents as Poland is under the power of Russia. Not that I would compare the English government of India with that of the Russian in Poland, for, in my opinion, it is far more mild, just, and equitable. Indeed, the strongest item in England's hold upon India is that she governs wisely and liberally, and the mass of the people know that they are much surer of peace and justice under the government of the English, than they would be under the despotic rule of their myriad of native chiefs. Of these there are nearly five hundred (whose jurisdiction is outside of the large district absolutely under British rule, and which may be esteemed British territory), of whose domain a recent report to Parliament speaks as follows:

"The native states of India form one of the most important and difficult sections of administration. Every state—and the number, including the smaller feudatories, exceeds four hundred and sixty—acknowledges the supremacy of the British Government; but, in other respects, their rights and obligations differ from each other. Some merely acknowledge our supremacy, like Nepaul; others also undertake to follow our advice and to govern their subjects with justice; others again pay tribute or provide for the maintenance of a contingent; some have power of life and death; others must refer all grave cases to English judges. Nearly all have, since the mutiny, received guarantees that their chiefs will be allowed to adopt successors on failure of heirs, and their continued existence has been thus secured. This measure represents a great change of policy, and is a return to that advocated by Lord Metcalf in 1837. The policy is now unalterably fixed by which existing native States will continue through the admitted right of adoption to maintain their positions as now admitted by treaty or agreement."

From this it will be seen that the present system of Indian government is quite complex, and requires a vast deal of attention to satisfactorily administer its affairs. Upward of forty thousand persons, many of them natives, are employed in the civil service, which is based upon that of England, the principal features of which are: 1st, competitive examinations in order to secure properly qualified persons; 2d, permanence in office, with a regular system of promotion for faithful service; 3d, a pension on retirement, in proportion to length of service. When we in America embody these features in *our* civil service, we will have honest and efficient management in our public service and tranquillity and prosperity in business affairs; but when men are turned out of office, no matter how faithfully they have served the country, to make room for the political henchmen of members of Congress, and an opportunity is afforded every four years for eighty thousand "outs" to try and oust eighty thousand "ins," we cannot expect either a satisfactory public service or a prosperous state of business. In 1876 England maintained in India an army of about sixty thousand Europeans, and one hundred and thirty thousand native or Sepoy troops, while the military force or retainers of the native chiefs numbered, all told, about three hundred and eighteen thousand. If these were a unit against British rule, England might have hard work to maintain her position—a fact that she well understands, and, therefore, carefully fosters the rivalries and jealousies of the rival chiefs, for which they are noted. These, in connection with the improved means of communication and the occupation of strategic points with white troops, makes her position, as before stated, almost impregnable.

In religious matters she does not interfere, and in this respect everybody is free to follow his own preferences. It is estimated that of the two hundred millions of population, about one hundred and sixty millions are Hindoos, forty millions Mahomedans, and about eight hundred and fifty thousand are Christians, of whom more than six hundred thousand are Catholics, resident principally in the south of India.

"Caste" is one of the prominent features in Hindoo life, and furnishes a most interesting study in itself. It is really a division of the population into several ranks, each of which is profaned by coming into contact with the others, or with Europeans; formerly infractions of many of the rules of caste were punished by death, but now, under English government, this practice has been abolished, and some of the rules have sunk into disuse. Still most of them are in force, with a power far greater than any rules of etiquette among Western nations, and violations are subject to an ostracism which is often fatal to business or social comfort and prosperity. The effect is to destroy enterprise and retard the progress of the whole country, for the great mass of the people feel that, no matter how hard they may try, they can never rise above the level in which they were born.

WAYSIDE SCENES, THOUGHTS AND FANCIES, IN INDIA.

From Colombo, Ceylon, across to Tuticorin, in Southern India, is only about one hundred and thirty miles, and landing here I received my first impressions of India. Southern India is quite unlike the Northern part, both in soil and productions, appearance and population; and although it is somewhat out of the beaten route of travel, my few days' stay there were most interesting and instructive. Here we find the population free from the character which has been impressed upon the population of Northern India by their Mahomedan conquerors of the Mogul era, and there are few or none professing the Mahomedan religion. Here, also, we find the old style of half-pyramidal, half-pagoda shaped Hindoo temples in their perfection, with their cars of Juggernaut and other paraphernalia, the former of which, however, under English rule, are rapidly falling into disuse. The natives are no longer permitted to sacrifice themselves under its wheels, which, in former times, was its most impressive feature. I travelled from Tuticorin to Madura and from Madura to Trichinopoly, a distance of over two hundred miles, by a narrow-gauge railroad (three feet three and one-third inches), very comfortably but very slowly. The road had just been opened, and things, as yet, were not working smoothly. At one water station the tank had proved leaky and was being repaired. In default of the usual facilities a hundred or more natives with earthen water-jars were set at work carrying water from a capacious well, or hole about twenty feet square and as many deep, from which the supply of water, when the tank was in order, was usually pumped. After waiting an hour or more in the cars, I became impatient at the delay, and taking my sun-hat and an umbrella, I went out in the broiling sun (19th of November), to prospect. I found the long train occupied, with the exception of our car, entirely by natives in third-class carriages, myself and two friends, with the engineer, being the only Europeans on the train. The native conductor was in vain trying to induce the lazy blacks to expedite their work, but without effect. I never saw such deliberate mortals in my life, although I could hardly blame them, for the temperature was over 100°, and much exertion, for a European at least, was neither comfortable nor safe. On consulting with the engineer, however, I found that the engine was steaming out the water faster than it was being put into the tender, and that something would have to be done or we would never get to Madura. There were plenty of men, but they were dawdling up and down the steps leading to the well, each one filling his own jar and occupying about half an hour in carrying it from the well to the engine. My first step was to promise them, through the conductor, three rupees, "backsheesh" (gift money), if they would submit to my orders; and then ranging them in line, I soon had a continuous stream of jars passing rapidly from hand to hand between the well and the engine. As soon as they caught the idea they entered into it with a will. Raising a strange, weird song or chorus, they gradually accelerated their motion until it grew into a positive enthusiasm, and no line of buckets at an American fire ever circulated faster than did those earthen water-jars at that station in Southern India. In ten minutes the reservoir of the tender was filled, and we were again *en route* for Madura, where we arrived at 9.30 P.M., hot, tired, and dusty.

At this place, as at many others in India, the only hotel is a "travellers' bungalow," which is a small, one-story house built by the English Government and placed in charge of a native, who is obliged to provide meals and other conveniences at a fixed tariff. The only furniture is a bedstead or two, with mattrasses, and generally two or three chairs, together with a table. Every traveller is supposed to provide his own bedding, soap, and towels. The same system is in vogue in Ceylon, and, as a curiosity, I append a scale of charges, which I copied from the tariff, which is posted up in every bungalow:

SCALE OF REST-HOUSE CHARGES.

Breakfast, with eggs, fowls, curry and rice, or equivalent	D 1 50
Dinner—Soup, ham, eggs, potatoes, fowl, curry and rice	1 50
Supper—Ham, eggs, potatoes, curry and rice	1 50
Room, exceeding two hours, not exceeding twenty-four hours	37½
Bedroom, with one bed, not exceeding twenty-four hours	50
Bedroom, with two beds or one double bed, not exceeding twenty-four hours	75
Bedroom, with three beds, not exceeding twenty-four hours	1 00
One sofa, without linen	37½
One sofa, with linen	50
Stable for one horse	50
Straw for one horse	25
Grass for one horse	12½
Carriages	12½
Oil for bedroom, per night	25
Cup of tea, with milk and sugar	25
Cup of coffee, with milk and sugar	25
Bottle of beer or porter, Bass or Allsopp, English bottled	75
Bottle of wine	2 00
Bottle of brandy	2 75
Bottle of soda-water	17
Bottle of lemonade	25
Pint bottle of beer or porter, Bass or Allsopp	50
Pint bottle of wine	1 25
Pint bottle of brandy	1 50
Brandy, per glass	25
Clean sheets and pillow-slips	37½
Cold bath, salt water or fresh	25
Hot bath	37½
For use of the rest-house utensils, per diem, irrespective of the number of individuals	50

Signed, JOHN MASON,
For Chairman P. R. C.

16th of October, 1875.

[NOTE.—A Ceylon dollar is only equivalent to fifty cents of our currency, so the above figures must be divided by two to obtain a correct idea of amounts.]

At the larger places, where there is a European population of any magnitude, hotels are being established and are gradually superseding "bungalows," but in the early days of India, when the white population was very sparse, and yet it was necessary to keep up certain lines of communication, with shelter and refreshment houses at regular distances, the bungalow was a necessity, and indeed the Government had to provide means of transportation, as well as entertainment, and the "dak," or post carriage, is still maintained in many parts of India, while these refreshment or post stations are commonly known as "dak bungalows." The word bungalow is a very common one, not only in India, but throughout the tropical countries of the East; where it originated I do not know, but, in India, it means a one-story house, generally constructed with very thick walls of masonry, and the roof thickly thatched with straw, projecting several feet on every side, forming a sort of porch or veranda to shade the entrances.

The natives of Southern India are tall in stature, of erect and graceful carriage, and, although quite black, having a European type of feature. Dressed in their flowing white robe and turban they present quite a picturesque appearance, and, as they stood gazing at our train as it went whirling by in the dusk of the evening, many of them were positively statuesque. The women are not in general as fine-looking as the men, and render themselves hideous by wearing immense rings in their noses, on these rings stringing all their available wealth in the shape of jewels and precious stones. In some instances I saw women who, in all other respects, bore every sign of poverty, thus wearing pearls which were worth many hundreds of dollars. To some extent also this practice of carrying their wealth about them in the shape of jewels prevails with the men; at Trichinopoly the station-master wore, as earrings, two solitaire diamonds which could not have been worth less than one thousand dollars each. This custom cannot be attributed entirely to personal vanity, but is largely due to the uncertainty of ownership which formerly attached to all forms of property which were not portable and which could not be concealed at a moment's notice.

I proceeded from Trichinopoly to Madras, between three and four hundred miles, through a rather unprepossessing country, and taking steamer from that port proceeded direct to Calcutta. Madras, formerly the most important European city in India, has made comparatively little progress during the past half century, and is now quite overshadowed in importance by both Calcutta and Bombay. Calcutta is situated on the River Hooghly —one of the mouths of the Ganges—a hundred or more miles from its outlet. At the entrance of the river the coast is flat and barren; but, further up, the banks are covered with cocoa-nut, palmyra, and other palms, from under which native mud-huts are everywhere peeping out. Boats loaded down by the head in a curious manner were crossing and passing up and down, and as we approached the city the most prominent feature for several miles were brick-kilns, impressing the beholder with the idea that very extensive building operations must be going on. I found, however, that they not only used brick for the purposes that we do, but that the bricks are again pulverized after burning and used for making mortar, there being no good natural sand for that purpose. There is also a large quantity of brick used for paving sidewalks, courts, etc.

The population of Calcutta, including both native and foreign, is estimated at about five hundred thousand. The European part of the city has wide, spacious streets and squares, ornamented by many statues and monuments, and, being the seat of the Anglo-Indian government, many fine public buildings are located here. Along the water-front are fine accommodations for shippers, and here one sees moored at all times a large fleet of steamers, besides numbers of the finest and largest class of clipper sailing vessels. Formerly the accommodations for shipping were quite insufficient and insecure; but some years ago, after great loss had been incurred from the visitation of a typhoon, the control of the harbor and other matters pertaining to shipping were transferred from the municipal authorities to a "Port and Harbor Commission," consisting of eminent merchants who were chiefly interested in having adequate facilities provided. Upon this commission was conferred the right to issue bonds for the construction of new accommodations, to collect all port and wharfage dues, and under its direction the present fine facilities were soon provided. Probably no port in the world now possesses more convenient and economical accommodations for shipping than does Calcutta, and this under great natural disadvantages. Across the river is the suburb of Howrah, which is the terminus of the East Indian Railway, which furnishes accommodation with Central, Northern, and Western India. The native part of Calcutta has wide streets, but they are lined with a dirty, tumbledown class of dwellings, not much better than the mud huts of the native villages.

Here, for the first time during my trip, the Oriental custom of the seclusion of women becomes prominent—women, excepting those of the lower classes, rarely being seen in the streets, and, when they venture from their houses being conveyed in carriages with closed blinds or in closed "palkahs." (The "palkah" is a sort of sedan-chair or box, resting upon poles, which is carried about on men's shoulders.)

Polygamy is practised here by the natives to a greater or less extent, and the women's apartments, which in Turkey are known as the seraglio or harem, are here known as the "zenara," and the same term also is in some instances applied to the occupants. A curious illustration of the extent to which this seclusion of women is carried is the advertisement of a lady photographer in Calcutta who announces herself as a "zenara photographer." Another curious feature in Indian life with which we first came prominently in contact at Calcutta is that of caste. One servant brings you food, but his hands would be utterly profaned if he were to take away the empty plate. One furnishes your room with water and towels, but another one has to be provided to carry away the slops. A Brahmin, eating at the same table with a European, or leaving his own country and crossing the sea, breaks his caste, and is ever after utterly ostracised for so doing. In Northern India we hired a carriage, and were surprised to see, besides the driver, an additional man accompanying us. We protested that we did not want more than one man, but the second fellow persisted in accompanying us, perching up behind and shouting at all who got in our way. When we alighted, he performed the services of a footman in opening the door, and, when we stopped to feed the horses, this man unharnessed and cared for them. On inquiry, we found that it would be beneath the caste of our driver to perform these services, and thus, two stalwart men had to be provided to perform the work of one. In many other ways these absurd customs of caste have the same effect; and, as before indicated, they serve to destroy all enterprise, for a person born in one caste can never rise to another.

The population is so dense, however, that labor is exceedingly plenty and cheap, and it has been surmised that many of the absurd rules of caste were designed and prescribed by the ancient

Brahmins to divide labor into many departments, thus furnishing employment for many hands. Labor is so cheap here that every family can, if they wish, have a dozen servants for a less sum than two cost in America. At the hotels in Calcutta each guest is provided with a servant as soon as he arrives, and we had hard work to explain to ours that we did not want them to accompany us up country. This class of servants are generally called "kitmaghars." Many of them are Mahomedans, and being exempt from the rules of caste, which so rigidly govern the Hindoos, they are the best servants in the world. They black your boots, brush your clothes, dust your room, arrange the mosquito netting, turn down the sheets ready for you to get into bed, and almost assist you to close your eyes. After you have retired, they spread their blanket on the floor in front of your door, and no one can cross the threshold without stepping over their body. This, at first, seems strange to an American, who is in the habit of doing everything for himself, but I soon became accustomed to it, and when I left India missed these little attentions almost as much, I fancy, as would one long resident there. People all take their servants with them when they travel, and a very low rate is provided for their transportation by the railroad companies, and for their board by the hotels.

One of the queer institutions of Calcutta is the "Great Eastern Hotel and Merchandise Company, Limited." As indicated by the name, the company carries on both a hotel and a merchandise business. The structure covers a large area, the first floor being occupied as a sort of general store or bazaar, in which one can find almost everything, either for the inner or outer man—or woman. I thought that I had seen a large variety in some of our American stores, but I certainly never saw such a jumble of dry-goods, both for male and female wear, millinery, carpets, boots and shoes, hats and caps, toys and notions, jewelry, groceries, provisions, and confectionery, as is collected in the warerooms of the "Great Eastern Hotel and Merchandise Company, Limited." The upper stories of this immense building are occupied as a hotel, and, as usual, when avocations of such a totally different character are mixed up with each other, it is not very well managed. Indeed, I have not seen a good hotel in India. Englishmen are not celebrated for keeping good hotels anywhere. The best English hotels are clean, and English servants, on an average, much better than those we have in America, but the table does not compare favorably with that of other countries. Speaking of service, it is probable that the good servants which are found in India are largely made so by the thorough drilling they receive at the hands of the English residents. An Englishman likes, and will have, good personal service if it can be obtained, and the Indian servants, in most cases, are carefully drilled, and are used to exacting masters. Indeed, in some cases they are treated in a very overbearing manner, a curious evidence of which is a notice that was posted up in the "Lord Lytton" hotel at Delhi, as follows: "Visitors will be good enough not to strike the hotel servants; any complaints made against them will be attended to."

At Calcutta I first saw the skins of animals used for holding water—the old water-skins of Scripture. Goat-skins are principally used for this purpose, the skin being stripped from the animal as far as the neck, where it is tied, as are also the legs. It is then sewed up tightly, and holds water without leaking. The streets are all watered here by men who carry the water in these skins slung over their shoulders, and spurt the water from a nozzle at the neck. In other parts of India they use the skins of young bullocks for the same purpose, but these being large, and containing a considerable quantity of water, are slung over the backs of other bullocks, like pack-saddles, one on each side, and in this way, in districts where water is scarce, it is sometimes conveyed long distances.

A feature of Calcutta, also, are the kites and crows; the latter are somewhat smaller than the American crow, and instead of being jet-black, the breast and back are of a greenish blue. They fairly swarm throughout the city, are apparently never molested by the inhabitants, and are the sauciest creatures imaginable, frequently flying in at windows and carrying off not only food, but other small articles which attract their attention. The kites, a species of hawk, a little larger than our American crow, are also very plentiful, and, together with the crows, act the part of scavengers; at times the whole firmament seems dotted with these birds flying overhead. Here and there also we see an enormous stork, known as the "adjutant bird," sitting or standing upon the roofs of the houses, and gazing with the utmost dignity at the scene below.

From Calcutta I crossed India by rail. The terminus of the East Indian Railway on the Howrah side of the Hooghly, with its many tracks, reminds one of the Pennsylvania road at Philadelphia. The ascent from the coast is very gradual, and there is much sameness in the landscape for several hundred miles. A novel feature, that I note as we fly along, is the telegraph poles, which are mostly made of iron, although here and there is a shaft of granite, which serves as an intermediate stretcher for the wires. The stations, many of them, are covered with the beautiful morning-glory creeper, which grows here in great luxuriance over trellised-walls and buildings, presenting a very beautiful appearance, and furnishing a grateful shade. Here and there I saw threshing-floors, a hard, smooth, circular piece of ground, upon which sheaves of unthreshed grain are thrown and cattle driven round and round upon it—the veritable old threshing-floors of Scripture—and I noticed that none of the cattle were muzzled, although it is not probable that the scriptural law, "Thou shalt not muzzle the ox," etc., is known and obeyed here. Everywhere also I saw irrigation-wells, from which oxen were raising, by means of a pulley and huge leathern bucket, water for irrigating the surrounding plain. In the south also I saw this being done by men, sometimes half a dozen at once being perched high in the air upon enormous well-sweeps, upon which they scrambled backward and forward, alternately raising and depressing the long end of the sweep, and raising the water by means of their weight acting on the sweep as a lever. It seems strange that they should not have utilized wind-power for this purpose, when windmills are so successfully used elsewhere.

I made my first stop at Benares, the holy city of the Hindoos. This is perhaps one of the most interesting points in India—a great city, situated on the banks of the Ganges, containing a large population, a majority of which, it is estimated, are pilgrims who are constantly coming from all parts of India to confess their sins before the celebrated gods, and to wash them away in the waters of the river, which are also esteemed sacred. Almost everything is worshipped here: idols, cattle, pigeons, monkeys, and the river itself. It is said that there are upward of two thousand five hundred temples in the city, including those of the Buddhists, Mahomedans, and the various sects of the Hindoos, the latter of which are completely filled with idols of all sorts and sizes, mostly springing, however, from the parent gods, Brahma, Vishnu, and Siva. One temple is devoted entirely to monkeys, of which we saw a hundred or more chasing each other over the walls and cutting up a variety of "monkey shines." In other temples and on the streets and "ghats" (steps leading down to the river) are quantities of cattle, which roam hither and thither at their own free will, feeding on the offerings of the pilgrims—which evidently keep them in the best possible condition—and leading what must be an ideal animal life; for, instead of bearing the burdens of the human race, and often coming to an untimely end to serve as food for them, they here lead a lazy, well-fed existence to the end of their days. Pigeons also, are esteemed sacred, and are provided for in the same way. Indeed, I believe, according to the Hindoo religion, all animal life is sacred, and certain it is that orthodox Hindoos subsist entirely upon a vegetable diet. There can hardly be a more picturesque scene than to take a boat and float down the Ganges, its upper banks lined with temples and the residences of the wealthier classes, and lower down with "ghats," or steps, where the people come down to bathe and drink. According to the Hindoo belief, the waters of the Ganges wash away all sins, and the banks of the river are constantly lined with people bathing and praying. In the early morning the women come, almost before it is light, timidly veiling their faces from the gaze of the passers-by, and after performing their ablutions retire to make room for others. In the winter-time it is not by any means comfortable, for in this latitude in India the climate is quite cold, and the morning we floated down the river it was freezing. Yet I saw crowds of men and women dipping themselves in the water, saying their prayers with chattering teeth, and carrying away their small brass vessels filled with the sacred water, which the pilgrims carry with them to their homes, even to the farthermost parts of India. One of the ghats is set apart for the burning of dead bodies, which is the disposition that the Hindoos make of their dead all over India, and here, after they are consumed, their ashes, or a portion of them, are thrown upon the bosom of the sacred river to float away to the Hindoo paradise, whither they believe its waters proceed; and ever after, at stated periods, wreaths of flowers are thrown into the river as offerings to the spirits of the departed dead. Here was an opportunity to see cremation practically illustrated, and, landing from the boat, I stood by while the ceremony proceeded. Some of the funeral pyres were just dying out, others were in full blaze, others were just being formed, the method of which is to first place several layers of dry wood in such a way that it will burn freely and at the same time afford a resting-place for the body, which is wrapped in several folds of cotton-cloth, and carefully laid upon its wooden bed; over it are again placed several layers of wood, and the torch is applied by the oldest surviving male of the family, the members of which stand by and watch the flames curling up through the pile. There does not seem to be much sentiment involved in this ceremony, and we saw no manifestation of emotion. Indeed, the hired attendants seemed to look at it in much the same business light that our sextons do, for, as the piles burned down and the bodies were partially consumed, they pounded them into the embers with long sticks in the most unfeeling way. I never realized the force of "Dust thou art, and unto dust shalt thou return" so forcibly as when I saw one of these calcined skulls crumble into ashes. But, after all, my impression was that this is a very sensible way to dispose of the dead, and my opinion of cremation is decidedly better than it was before.

From Benares I proceeded to Agra, one of the capitals of the Mogul emperors, and which, three hundred years ago, was said to be a beautiful city. Now the native city is composed of a collection of squalid, dirty mud-huts, while the European portion contains a considerable number of substantial private bungalows, together with a few tolerably good public buildings. In the suburbs, however, within a circle of five miles or more, are the structures which have made Agra, as well as the reign of the Mogul emperors, famons. Of these the "Taj Mahal," or Tomb of Banoo Begum, Sultana of the Emperor Shāh Jehān, is the most celebrated. It is a beautiful structure of white marble, constructed in an octagonal form, and occupying a square of one hundred and eighty feet upon a raised platform, also of white marble, four hundred feet square. At each corner of this platform is a graceful minaret, said to be two hundred feet high, while on the right and left of the platform, at a distance of perhaps three hundred feet, is constructed a mosque, apparently as outworks for the Taj, and constituting, in an architectural sense, a sort of frame for the central structure. This is certainly very beautiful, although it hardly justifies the enraptured descriptions which many travellers have written. The Italian workers in marble of the same era have produced work as fine, and the inlaid work is evidently after the Florentine school, probably executed under the tuition of Florentine masters. The central dome rises two hundred and sixty feet, and directly beneath this are situated the sarcophagi of Banoo Begum and her husband, Shāh Jehān. These are also white marble, and upon them are most elaborately carved texts from the Koran. They are also inlaid with malachite, topaz, jasper, garnet, cornelian, and other precious stones, in the Florentine style. The chamber directly below these contains the real sarcophagi, which hold the remains, and which are much plainer in execution than those above. The whole structure is more or less inlaid with colored marbles, and on the main floor there are a number of beautifully carved white-marble screens. It is said that the building of the entire structure occupied twenty thousand men for eighteen years. More extensive in its plan, and more massive than this, but not so beautiful, is the tomb of the Emperor Akbar, or Ukbur, the greatest of the Mogul dynasty. The enclosure in which it is built at Sikundra, several miles from the Taj, is surrounded with enormous walls four miles in extent, enclosing a perfect square, in the centre of which is constructed what is called a tomb. It is composed of four stories, or platforms, of red sandstone, supported by pillars of the same material, and on the top of these is built a fifth of white marble, which was originally covered by a dome, but is now open to the air. In the centre of this space is a marble sarcophagus containing the ashes of Akbar. The walls surrounding this story are filled with elaborately carved marble screens, but none of this work compares in fineness with that of the Taj. Within the walls of the fort, nearer the present city, are what remains of the palace, interesting as illustrating the life of Mogul royalty in those days, but containing little fine workmanship compared with the Taj.

"Fuhttepore Sikra," twenty-two miles west of Agra, also contains some fine illustrations of the architecture of the period. It was built by the Emperor Akbar as a sort of imperial suburb, was six miles in circumference, and enclosed by a high embrasured wall of red sandstone. This fortification, with its lofty Saracenic gate, still remains in a tolerable state of repair, but the elegant structures enclosed within this space are now in ruins.

A little more than one hundred miles to the northwest from Agra is Delhi, another capital of the Mogul empire, with a fort, palace, and other structures remaining, which give one a fuller idea of the magnificence of the Mogul dynasty than do those at Agra. It was here that the famous "Peacock Throne" was erected, in the construction of which Shāh Jehān is said to have expended six millions of pounds sterling, or thirty millions of dollars. The audience-chamber in which this was placed is a magnificent room, and bears the architect's inscription, which Moore has made familiar to all the world in "Lalla Rookh:" "If there be an elysium on earth, it is this." While one cannot but be impressed with the magnificence of the works of the Mogul emperors, yet it is probable that their wealth and power have been vastly over-estimated, and that the resources of their empire were largely expended in building magnificent tombs and palaces, while the material interests of the country were left to languish. The wealth that in most of the countries of the earth is now diffused among the people, was then concentrated in the hands of royalty and its favorites, while the people were miserably poor. Some chroniclers have stated that the Taj was built by forced labor, and that the laborers and artisans received only a scanty allowance of food in lieu of wages; that the mortality among them was very great, and a satirical couplet was composed at the time, to the effect that the memory of Banoo Begum ought to be green, for it was watered by the tears of thousands. Travellers in all ages have been apt to accept a single work or class of works as evidence of the civilization and progress of the age in which they were constructed, and then build up a framework of theory, which, although plausible, is often not well founded. Much "history" has been written in this way, and books of travel are full of high-flown writing and descriptions that will not bear analysis by dispassionate and impartial critics. It is so much easier to "soar" in describing an admirable work, than it is to quietly appreciate it and describe it in plain language. This is especially true of professional writers, who feel bound, perhaps, to make or keep a reputation for "fine writing," as well as to give an equivalent for the sums received for their articles. A magnificent glamour of romance has thus been thrown around oriental life which is as false as possible. Oriental life, as it has appeared to me, is founded upon ignorance, cruelty, and license. Luxury it may have for a few, but poverty, dirt, and misery are certainly the patrimony of the many.

Modern Delhi is the chief city of Northern India, possesses considerable commerce, and is a sort of entrepot between the northern and central provinces of India. At the time we were there it was just beginning to fill up with the visitors to the grand assemblage at which Queen Victoria was to be proclaimed Empress of India. Its streets exhibited a queer medley, locomotion being provided for with elephants, camels, horses, buffaloes, bullocks, and donkeys. Its bazaars were filled with the gorgeous shawls of Cashmere and the embroideries and jewelry for the manufacture of which Delhi is famous. Native artists, who copy photographs exquisitely upon ivory, abound, and jugglers, who perform marvellous tricks of conjuring, importune you to witness their exhibitions. The guide, or "valet de place," is also an institution that flourishes marvellously well in Delhi, and one who attached himself to our fortunes, was worthy of description. A sleek, oily little man, who glided rather than walked, and who exhibited marvellous testimonials as to the value of his services from former patrons. I have seen thrifty commissionaires both before and since, but I never saw one with such a talent for turning "an honest penny" as this fellow. Bishesh Arnath stands at the head of his profession in this respect. Of course we knew he was making his commission on every carriage we hired and on every purchase that we made, but it was not until we took an elephant ride, that we found out the full depth and breadth of Bishesh Arnath's capacity in this respect. Here we detected him actually stealing half the money which we gave him to purchase food for our elephants, leaving the poor brutes half starved and us wondering at their unamiability of temper. At first I was eager for his arrest and strongly resolved to make an example of him, but friends from Delhi, who had accompanied us on the excursion, took it quite as a matter of course, and advised us to pass it quietly by as a native characteristic. This we did, but when, at our departure, he came cringing for a certificate or recommendation, we in a manner "got square" with him by writing the following in his book, with which he was delighted, and left us, promising to show it to every American traveller with whom he came in contact:

"Bishesh Arnath has acted as guide for us in Delhi and vicinity for several days. He is a man after our own heart, and has acted with us on the principles which have guided us through life. He knows all the best shops, and understands 'addition, division, and silence.' In short, he belongs to our school of humanity, and we heartily recommend him to all who wish to deal with men of like progressive stamp.

(Signed)

———.

———.

Here we filled in the names of two most notorious public characters of America, one of whom is now in prison, it is to be hoped permanently, and the other, in the opinion of many people, deserves to be. In connection with the names, all Americans will quickly understand the character of Bishesh Arnath, and I hope that it may protect other travellers from his little schemes.

OUR TIGER HUNT.

Our tiger hunt, by the way, was not a success. Of course a visit to India without a tiger hunt would be Hamlet with the chief part left out, and when I arrived in India the most prominent feature of my slumbers were dreams of killing "man-eating" tigers by the score, and chief among my avocations during the day was the making of inquiries as to where this sport could be had in perfection. Through friends in Delhi I finally secured the necessary presentation to the Maharajah, or native ruler, of a neighboring province, to whom I am indebted for this experience.

In order to make it intelligible to your readers, I shall have to preface it with a little account of the habits of tigers and the different ways of hunting them. Native hunters, or "Shikaras," recognize, more or less, three kinds of tigers. One, the regular game-killing tiger, "*Lodhia bagh*," as he is called, is retired in his habits, living chiefly among the hills, retreating readily from man, and altogether a very harmless animal. He is a light-made beast, very active and enduring, and from this, as well as his shyness, difficult to bring to bay. The "cattle-lifter" is usually an older and heavier animal, called "*Oontia bagh*," from his faintly striped coat resembling the color of a camel, quite fleshy, and indisposed to severe exertion. In the cool season he follows the herds of cattle wherever they go to graze, or locates himself in some strong cover close to the water in the neighborhood, where the cattle are taken to drink and to graze on the greener herbage found by the side of streams. The third is the regular "man-eater," who, it appears, does not take naturally to this diet, but is usually driven to make a beginning by stress of circumstances, such as being an old tiger with worn-down teeth that require tenderer morsels than bullocks, or a tigress with cubs, that cannot conveniently carry a bullock long distances to her lair. Both of these causes frequently produce man-eaters, and once they have acquired a taste for human flesh nothing else satisfies them. There are also three ways of hunting them. One is to watch in a tree near a dead carcass which has been killed during the day, and to which the tiger usually returns after sundown to feed upon. Another way is to hunt them in their covers on a single elephant trained for this purpose, and this, with experienced hunters, is usually the most successful, but it is only undertaken during the hot weather. A third way is to beat them out of their midday retreat with a strong gang of natives, known as "beaters," supplied with drums, fireworks, etc., the sportsmen themselves being posted on elephants or other points of vantage at the likeliest spots ahead. The latter was the kind of an entertainment which was reserved for us.

Our party was most hospitably received by the Maharajah, who upon being informed that two of us were American gentlemen, who had come fifteen thousand miles to enjoy a tiger hunt, made immense preparations for a battue. The "Shikari," or professional hunter, of some of the villages in the neighborhood was summoned; his services, together with those of several hundred natives, commanded, and all the necessary preparations made. After a sumptuous repast we retired to our beds for the night, with visions of driving whole herds of tigers before us, and slaughtering them as we would rabbits at home. My hopes were so high and my imagination so excited by the novel situation that I must confess I was rather restless that night; but finally morning came, and with it the inspection of the preparations. Three elephants stood caparisoned with rude "howdahs," while a fourth bore the imposing trappings of the Maharajah; this was "for the two American gentlemen," upon whom the Maharajah was evidently determined to make an impression, while the others were occupied by the rest of the party, and, as we afterward discovered, were considered more secure and better adapted for the sport. We learned that a "shoulder-of-mutton" shaped piece of jungle, or bottom land, had been selected for the beat, and had already been surrounded by the natives who were to drive it, and after hastily partaking of a breakfast we mounted our elephants and set off for the neck, or locality where the river on one side and the high bluff on the other brought the jungle to a narrow point. Here we arrived at about ten o'clock, and the elephants were ranged in a V-shape, at distances of perhaps one hundred yards, extending completely across the neck. Here we waited for a long time without hearing any noise or manifestation of the beat, and we began to think that there had been some misunderstanding, and that, after all, we were to have no sport. Messengers were despatched to see what was the cause of the delay, and to try and expedite matters. Finally we began to hear a distant sound of "tom-toms," or native drums, together with an occasional shot. Then the "mahouts" (drivers) of our elephants drew more carefully into line, and all of us grew very attentive to the possibility of soon seeing a tiger. Nearer and nearer came the noise, until we could hear the shouts of the beaters and realize the fact that, whatever else they were doing, they were kicking up a most unearthly rumpus. The first live thing we saw was a pair of peafowl that came running by, but, of course, we disdained this game when larger sport was in prospect. Then came half a dozen "Sambars," or spotted deer, out of range for us, but quite near the elephant of one of our Delhi friends, who could not resist so fair a shot, and fired, knocking over one of them handsomely, and wounding another with a second shot from his breechloader before getting out of range. Whether or not this had anything to do with preventing our seeing any tigers I cannot say, but certain it is that these were all we saw in the way of game, and we were soon surrounded with the army of half-naked beaters upon whom had devolved the chief labor of the hunt. No other promising territory, the Shikari declared, was available, and therefore nothing remained but for us to make a present to the beaters and return to the Maharajah's palace, anathematizing the Shikari for not having found us a tiger, and indulging in some sceptical observations as to the existence of tigers in India anyway. The only satisfaction that we derived from the trip was a photograph of ourselves as we appeared on our elephant, when we returned, with our bloodthirsty firearms, which consisted of a double rifle and a cavalry carbine, displayed in full view. This was "a present" to us from the Maharajah's photographer as a souvenir of our trip, but we found that presents in this country were given with an expectation of more valuable ones in return, and our photographs, after all, proved rather costly. However, our welcome was cordial, our entertainment quite princely, and the trouble taken on our behalf by our Delhi friends something extraordinary; so we perhaps ought not to grumble, but we did come away somewhat under the impression that tiger hunting in India was a delusion, if not a snare, and that the number of the royal beasts in India had been grossly exaggerated.

Still, that they exist in considerable numbers is proved by a copy of the Government Blue Book, which I came across in Bombay, in which appears the following passage:

"One extraordinary feature of Indian life is the number of

human beings destroyed by wild beasts. Rewards are offered by the Government for the killing of these animals, but in some districts the loss of life is very great, and in others, where it is less excessive, the reason is given that cattle are very abundant, and afford more accessible food for carnivorous animals. In 1872-73 there were 2,334 deaths from snake-bites and wild beasts in the Bombay Presidency. The inhabitants of the border between jungle and cultivation are killed and eaten by tigers in such numbers as to require the immediate and serious attention of Government, both in India and in England. The following are a few out of many instances: A single tigress caused the destruction of 13 villages, and 250 square miles of country were thrown out of cultivation. Wild beasts frequently obstruct Government survey parties. In 1869 one tigress killed 127 persons and stopped a public road for many weeks. Man-eating tigers are causing a great loss of life along the whole range of the Nali-Mali forest. One is said to have destroyed more than 100 people. In Lower Bengal alone, in a period of six years, 13,401 people were killed by wild beasts. The Chief Commissioner of the Central Provinces, in his report, shows the following return of human beings killed by tigers:

In 1866-67	372
In 1867-68	289
In 1868-69	285
Total in three years	946

It appears that there are difficulties in the way of killing down these tigers; first, the superstition of the natives, who regard the man-eating tiger as a kind of incarnate and spiteful divinity, whom it is dangerous to offend; secondly, the failures of the Government rewards; thirdly, the desire of a few in India actually to preserve tigers as game, to be shot with the rifle as a matter of sport. Mr. Frank Buckland suggests an organized destruction of the tiger cubs in the breeding season, and the attraction of full-grown tigers to traps, pitfalls, and other devices, by means of a drug of valerian, of which tigers, which are only gigantic cats, are exceedingly fond."

So, after reading this report, I could not but again believe in the existence of tigers in India.

I had thought to remain in Delhi during the Imperial assemblage, but found that this would make too great an inroad upon my time, and I therefore was obliged to forego this spectacle—another disappointment.

Proceeding to Bombay by rail, I found it a bustling, business-like city, with even more imposing public buildings than those of Calcutta. From the Biculla side of the harbor it looks like a veritable city of palaces. Bombay is the home of vast numbers of the Parsee merchants, whose shrewdness and enterprise have made their name known throughout the commercial world. Speaking of names, they can "lay over" anything that I have seen or heard elsewhere, except, perhaps, Ceylon, a specimen of whose names I gave in a former letter. But I am not certain that Bombay, for irregular, right-angled jaw-breakers, does not even take the palm from Ceylon. I append herewith a couple of brief slips which I cut from one of the Bombay papers while there, and I can assure you that these are not exceptional, either in length or sonorousness:

"H. H. Tukhtsingjee, the young Thakore of Bhownuggur; Rawal Shri Hurrisingjee, a Chief of Sehore, and Mr. Gowreeshunker Oodeyshunker, one of the Joint Administrators of the State, leave Bhownuggur for Bombay, *en route* to Delhi, on the 5th inst."

"Sir Jamsetjee Jeejeebhoy, Bart., C.S.I., with his three sons, will leave for Delhi on Thursday next."

Comment is unnecessary.

I mentioned that Bombay was a bustling, busy city. It has been made so by the railway system of India and the Suez Canal. Twenty years ago Bombay was only a port of opium export and a way station on the overland route to India. After the mutiny the Government system of railroads was undertaken, and during our American war Bombay became the entrepot for the cotton trade of India, which has grown to be very large. On the completion of the Suez Canal many lines of steamers were established between Bombay and England, and within the last ten years the city has quite outrun Calcutta in the importance of its trade. The manufacturing of cotton goods for Indian consumption has been begun on a large scale, twenty or more factories of large capacity being now in full operation and strongly competing with Manchester, not only for the trade of Hindostan, but also for that of British Burmah, the Straits Settlements, and China. Indian cotton manufacturers say that there is a bright future before them, and, if this be true, taken in connection with the increased ability of American cotton manufacturers to compete with English cotton spinners for the rest of the markets of the world, I do not see what the latter are going to do. They certainly will have to open up Central Africa, and educate the negroes up to the necessity of wearing cotton breech-cloths, or the manufacturers of Manchester will have to go to the wall.

FROM BOMBAY TO EGYPT.

This part of my trip, for heat and discomfort, had the worst reputation of any. In China it was hot, but I was told: "Wait till you get to the Red Sea before you begin to complain." At Singapore and in Java I was told the same thing, and, while sweltering in Southern India, with the thermometer at upwards of 100° in the shade, I was consoled with the information that I "would find it much hotter on the Red Sea." So, when we sailed from Bombay, I got out my thinnest clothing, and prepared for a scorcher. From Bombay to Aden, the port of call and coaling station for most of the steamers plying between India and Europe, it is 1,664 miles, and from Aden to Suez, through the Red Sea, 1,308 miles; making a total of 2,972 miles. Seven days on the steamer Trinacria, of the Anchor Line, with delightful weather, and scarcely an incident except the occasional passing of ships and flights of flying-fish, brought us to Aden. The coast, as we approached this place, is the most sterile and forbidding that can be imagined; of volcanic origin, with scarcely a drop of rain falling throughout the whole year, not a blade of verdure is to be seen, and its successive mountains resemble more than anything else a series of gigantic ash-heaps. Aden itself has a pretty little harbor, but it is the dreariest place imaginable. Not a tree or a shrub is to be seen excepting a few little dwarfs in the yards of the Europeans who are compelled to reside here, and these have a stunted, sickly look, which tells plainly that their existence is not a natural one. The water for the use of the inhabitants of the place, and calling ships, is distilled from sea water, and sold at the rate of about two cents per gallon. There are traditions that rain formerly fell here in sufficient quantities, and ancient reservoirs still exist which were constructed for the purpose of holding the supply of water through the dry season. Now, however, it does not rain once in six months, and then only a few drops at a time; and yet, with all these drawbacks, the place has some commerce. Considerable quantities of Arabian coffee find their way from Mocha and other places along the Arabian and Berberian coasts to this point, and minor items, such as dates, figs, ostrich feathers and eggs, leopard skins, etc., are also dealt in here in a small way.

As soon as a steamer casts anchor she is boarded by half a dozen or more Arab ostrich feather venders, who, in their demands, are as much worse than Chatham Street Jews as the latter are worse than respectable dealers. Twenty, thirty, fifty rupees are demanded for a bunch of feathers, which they will sell at eight or ten if they cannot get more. It cannot be said that they are smart in this, for the asking of absurd prices at once places even the most verdant purchaser upon his guard, and leads to offers that are as much to the other extreme. Little Berber boys come off to the ship in the tiniest and lightest of wooden dug-out canoes, and dive for pennies which the passengers throw into the water for them, catching them ere they have a chance to sink to the bottom; for five or ten cents in silver they dive clean under the ship, coming up on the other side. It is an amusing thing to see three or four of these little chaps plunge from their canoes at the same instant after a coin, the nearest of them going down almost perpendicularly, with the white soles of their feet—the only spots of light color about them—moving like fishes' fins, and alone being visible. Those that are a little farther off go down like an arrow at an angle of perhaps forty-five degrees, meeting with the others at the bottom, and the strongest of them generally coming up with the coin. The reluctance with which the smaller ones competed when the larger ones were around led us to think that they did not always receive fair play, or, as a youngster on board of our ship remarked to his father: "I believe that big fellow hammers the little chaps under the water"—another illustration of the proverb that "might makes right," and that "Providence is on the side which has the heaviest artillery."

Down, or rather up the Red Sea, about one hundred and twenty miles from Aden, in the direction of Suez, is the little port of Mocha, which furnishes the trade name for most of the Arabian coffee, which is held in such high estimation in the markets of the world. As before noted, this coffee is now mostly sent coastwise to Aden, and reshipped from there upon passing steamers. Another example of fashion in trade is found here in the fact that Europe takes the larger beans, while the American demand is wholly for the smaller ones. So the coffee is carefully picked over, and only the small, uniform-sized beans, put up in a peculiar style, known to the trade as one-eighth, one-fourth, and one-half bales, are sent to the United States. This coffee by itself has a peculiarly sharp, almost acrid flavor, and when drunk alone will suit very few palates, it being much better when mixed with three parts of Java, or other mild coffee, to one of Mocha. I had always thought that the far-famed Turkish coffee was made exclusively from the Arabian berry; but, to my surprise, I found, when in Constantinople, this to be quite the reverse of true, most of the coffee used there coming from India and Ceylon.

But I am getting ahead of my story. Six days up the Red Sea brought us to Suez and the eastern entrance of the great canal of that name—the greatest commercial, if not the greatest engineering undertaking of modern times—an undertaking which has shortened the distance to India and points in the East from four to five thousand miles, and in six years has more than doubled the commercial steam fleet to Europe. I had no idea whatever of the magnitude of this trade until, in passing through the Red Sea, we met steamers almost hourly, sometimes three or four being in sight at the same time, and in looking over a copy of the London *Times* I found announcements of seventeen different lines of steamers passing through the Suez Canal to India and the East, some of these lines having weekly departures, and representing many millions of dollars capital. While most persons are, doubtless, familiar with the main facts in connection with this great work, a review of history is sometimes interesting, and I will give a few facts and figures in relation to it.

To Monsieur de Lesseps, the world is indebted both for the conception and execution of this work. Appointed French Consul in Egypt in 1831, after some years' residence in that country, M. de Lesseps became possessed with the idea of cutting a canal from the Mediterranean across the desert to the Red Sea, a distance of some eighty nautical, or about one hundred English miles. It was not till 1854, however, that the co-operation of the Egyptian Government was secured, and in November of that year the final concession was granted to M. de Lesseps. A company was formed, and a subscription to the stock opened in November, 1858. A large share of the subscriptions was reserved for English capitalists, but England stood aloof, and took no interest in the enterprise, although, if a success, the greatest benefit must inure to her. Twenty-five thousand French subscribers at once came forward, and these, with the aid of the Egyptian Government, insured the construction of the canal. The estimated cost of construction was at first twenty millions of dollars. The difficulties in the way gradually increased, until the estimated cost became forty millions of dollars, and, before the opening, the expenditure was seventy-five millions, and at this date has exceeded eighty millions, or about four times the original estimate, notwithstanding that the country through which the canal is constructed is peculiarly favorable for such a work, there being little or no rock-cutting, and the sand-hills in no place being more than forty feet high; while for about half the distance shallow lakes or lagoons could be utilized by merely dredging. An idea of the magnitude of the work, however, can be formed from the fact that, although prosecuted with the greatest energy, it took ten years to accomplish it. Besides the actual work on the canal, there was the commencement indispensable for the workmen; sheds and buildings for an army of men were necessary, and a supply of fresh water in the desert. To insure the latter, water was first carried from Zagazig through fifty miles of wilderness in skins on the backs of three thousand camels and donkeys, while two years later one thousand two hundred Egyptians opened a canal from Lake Maxima, which brought the waters of the Nile to Ismailia. During low water, however, in this river the supply failed, and finally, in 1864, the Viceroy of Egypt threw no fewer than eighty thousand men into the deepening and extension of the fresh water canal, so as to secure a supply at all stages of the Nile. At the cutting of the canal at El Guisar in 1862 and 1863, there were eighteen thousand laborers employed. For these tenements had to be erected, and a saw-mill was kept in constant operation. At one time there were thirteen thousand eight hundred barrows on the ground. At lake Timsah, one of the shallow bodies of water which were utilized in the construction of the canal, and on the banks of which the company's capital (Ismailia) now stands, there were two hundred and eighty-five dredging machines at work with a force equal to eighteen thousand horses, and consuming twelve thousand tons of coal per month. Port Said, the Mediterranean entrance to the canal is a creation of this work. In 1859, when the first spadeful of sand was turned for the canal, it did not exist; in 1861 it had two thousand inhabitants; in 1872, eight thousand six hundred, of whom four thousand two hundred were foreigners. A commodious harbor and basin for the accommodation of shipping has been created. Thirty-five miles of the canal are subject to sand-drifting, and sand barriers are erected somewhat similar to the snow fences along the line of our Pacific Railroad. The town of Suez, the Red Sea terminus of the canal, contains about thirteen thousand inhabitants, ten thousand of whom are Egyptians, Turks, and Arabs, and the balance principally Europeans. Extensive accommodation has also been here provided for shipping, and Suez is almost as much a creation of the canal as Port Said. The cost of the construction and maintenance of the canal has been so great that as yet it has not paid interest upon its cost; but the traffic through it is increasing so rapidly, that hopes are entertained of its soon doing so. Its importance to the world, however, is so great that no fears need ever be entertained that it will not be maintained in an efficient condition.

As an evidence of the great increase in its use, the following tables, showing the number of vessels and tonnage passing through the canal during the years from 1870 to and including 1879, will prove interesting:

YEAR.	Number of vessels.	Tons	YEAR.	Number of vessels.	Tons.
1870..........	486	435,911	1875.........	1,404	2,940,708
1871..........	765	761,467	1876.........	1,457	3,072,107
1872..........	1,082	1,439,169	1877 *	1,663	3,418,949
1873..........	1,173	2,085,072	1878.........	1,593	3,291,535
1874..........	1,264	2,423,672	1879.........	1,477	3,236,942

Navigation, by flags, through the Suez Canal for the year ending December 31, 1877.

Flag.	Number of vessels.	Tons.	Flag.	Number of vessels.	Tons.
British........	1,291	1,760,785	Egyptian.....	7	4,934
French	85	152,793	American	3	2,152
Dutch	63	88,198	Portuguese...	2	1.908
Austrian......	46	71,102	Belgian......	2	1,762
Italian	58	60,661	Swedish	3	1,696
German.......	41	40,501	Brazilian.....	1	555
Spanish.......	21	34,131	Turkish......	1	71
Danish........	5	15,728			
Norwegian....	12	13,577	Total.....	1,641	2,250,554

By this it will be seen that about 78 per cent., both in the number of ships and tonnage, are English, while the United States come in with a beggarly 3, against a total number of 1,641 vessels, and a tonnage of 2,152, against 2,250,554. The canal has become a necessity to great Britain, and a convenience to the whole world. That the English Government appreciates this is evident from the fact that during 1875 it purchased from the Khedive of Egypt 176,602 of his shares for $20,000,000. It is supposed that this was done in order that in any future opening up of the Eastern question, England might have a commercial claim to the great highway to India. M. de Lesseps, in a circular issued by him to the company after the purchase, while commenting somewhat bitterly on the opposition offered by Great Britain, as a nation, to

* The figures for the last three years have been supplied to bring the statement up to recent date.

the project at its commencement, says: "I therefore regard as a fortunate occurrence this powerful union which is about to be established between French and English capital for the purely industrial and necessarily pacific working of the great maritime canal."

As an indication of the importance of the canal to the tea trade, I may state that, in 1870, 711,000 pounds of tea passed through it for England; in 1871, 4,010,000 pounds; in 1872, 22,912,000 pounds; and now nearly the whole crop of both China and India tea destined for consumption in Europe, and a considerable portion of that used in the United States, passes through the canal.

If these statistics prove anything, they prove that an international ship canal through the Isthmus of Darien, connecting the Atlantic and Pacific oceans, must prove to be of the greatest possible benefit to the whole world, and also that the principal maritime nations of the earth would find it most profitable to their commercial interests to co-operate in the construction of such a work. Such a work would be too magnificent in its proportions to be undertaken by private enterprise, and it is doubtful if sufficient private capital could be mobilized to accomplish it; but by a co-operation of nations it would become a question of a few years, and, under a joint national ownership, it would be an important step in the march of progress, which will, in the near future, give us a universal system of weights and measures, and ultimately a universal language. These anticipations may be looked upon by some as the visions of an enthusiast, but the statesmen of the world are already looking forward to some of them as likely to be accomplished in the near future, and the construction of the Darien ship canal would be as important a step toward this commercial millennium as the arbitration between England and the United States for the settlement of the Alabama claims was toward the millennium outlined by Tennyson—

"Till the war-drum throbb'd no longer
And the battle-flags were furl'd
In the Parliament of man,
The Federation of the world."

EGYPT AND TURKEY.

Many travellers from India to Europe stop at Suez and make a short tour in Egypt for the purpose of seeing the Pyramids and other interesting antiquities of that wonderful country. This also our party did, and we were well repaid for our trouble. Cairo, the capital of Egypt, is situated about midway between Suez on the Red Sea and Alexandria on the Mediterranean; with both of which places there is rail communication. To reach Cairo from Suez, we pass through some fifty miles of sandy desert to Zagazig, which is situated on one of the branches of the Nile, which form the delta of that wonderful river; and from this place to Cairo it was one continuous garden, with a succession of rice, cotton, and sugar-cane fields, together with a variety of grains, and dotted here and there with beautiful orange groves. Just below Cairo the Nile spreads out like a fan, distributing its waters through numerous mouths into the Mediterranean at distances the extremes of which are one hundred and fifty miles apart. The whole space between these channels is annually overflowed, receiving a thin but fertile deposit of soil, which is brought down from the mountains of Africa by the overflowing waters; and immediately upon their subsiding there springs up a luxuriance of verdure which is probably equalled in no other country on the face of the globe.

Cairo is not only the seat of government, but also the emporium for the entire trade of the Upper Nile, which is of no mean dimensions. In her bazaars, are found the ivory, and ostrich plumes and eggs of Africa, the tapestries, carpets, and gems of Persia, quaint and curious antique arms and armors from Arabia, and a full assortment of European fabrics of every nature. A dependency of Turkey and under Turkish rule, it is Oriental in its prominent features, but there is also a blending of the ancient Egyptian and modern European which makes a rare and indeed unique type of civilization. One of the features which strike a stranger forcibly upon arriving here is that locomotion is largely performed upon donkeys. Diminutive creatures that a person would hardly think could carry the weight of a child may be seen trotting through the streets bearing a six-foot specimen of humanity, who to alight has only to put his legs down their full length and the donkey trots out from under him. Their braying resounds through the city at all hours of the day and night, and is about as musical as the filing of a saw-mill saw, and not very unlike it, although a friend of mine remarked when I made the comparison, that he thought it was an insult to the saw.

I had serious misgivings about bestriding one of these diminutive specimens of the animal kingdom, but in justice to the donkey species I must say that I never travelled more expeditiously and comfortably for the money. You extend your right foot over the little beast and draw up your legs, putting your feet into a pair of miniature stirrups; a driver (each donkey has its driver) trots after him on foot, and by dint of switching and punching keeps him up to the requisite degree of speed. One of these little animals will get over an astonishing amount of ground in a day, and, barring an occasional tendency to rub your legs against a wall or a passing camel, or to stumble and pitch you into a mud-puddle, this is by no means a bad method of locomotion. Indeed, it is far better and easier than riding upon either camels or elephants, which are much more pretentious members of the animal kingdom, and whose performances in this line have occasionally been greatly lauded. In Cairo, a common name for donkeys is "Bismarck," and upon inquiring the origin of this singular name, I found that during the Franco-Prussian war the many French residents of Cairo revenged themselves upon the German statesman by ordering a "Bismarck" whenever a donkey was required, and the Arab drivers, believing that this was a French name for the animal, finally came to adopt it as a common name. Whenever they saw a foreigner wanting a donkey they would greet him with the inquiry, "Want a Bismarck, master? *Bis*marck?" Some German officers, however, who were on a visit to the Pyramids about a year ago, thrashed some of the drivers, and since that time it is said that many of them have studied the law of nations, and now have an idea of the meaning of the word, and are cautious how they use it—particularly with persons having a German type of countenance.

Of course we went to see the Pyramids, for every one who

visits Egypt does that. Before I came here I never knew that there were more than three, but standing on the summit of the Pyramid of Cheops one can count a dozen or more, many of them of large size. Indeed, according to the best authorities, most of the principal rulers of ancient Egypt built a Pyramid to commemorate his reign, and receive his remains. The three Pyramids of Ghizeh, however, are the largest and most celebrated. They are situated in the desert, just on the border of the fertile lowlands of the Nile, some eight or ten miles from Cairo; the Pyramid of Cheops is the largest of the three; it is 445 feet high (formerly 479), and 767 feet square at the base, each of the four angles corresponding to the four points of the compass. They are composed of blocks of rather soft, somewhat chalky limestone, upon an average, perhaps, five or six feet long and three to four feet square; these are arranged in layers, each layer set back from the face of the one below it some three feet, and thus retreating, if I may use the phrase, in regular progression until they finally reach a point at the top—a solid, pyramidal mass of stone, containing so many tons that it almost defies arithmetical calculation to compute them; a mass so durable that they have stood here, according to the best authorities, some four thousand years, looking down upon the rise and fall of dynasties and empires, and indeed, witnessing the total wiping out of one of the greatest nations that ever existed, so thoroughly that its civilization and characteristics are still shrouded in mystery, and in many cases exist only in the conjectures of the learned men of the present day.

The point or apex is some twenty-five feet square, although the magnitude of the structure is such that, looking at it from the bottom, it appears to run up to a point, which chroniclers say it formerly did. Standing upon the summit, one gazes off upon the sand-hills of the desert on the one side, and the fertile valley of the Nile on the other, covered in January with a beautiful velvety green sward, across which, at a distance of ten miles, gleam the white walls of the mosques and minarets of Cairo. Here Napoleon Bonaparte addressed his troops on the eve of the battle of the Pyramids, telling them that forty centuries looked down upon their deeds that day, and from the summit he watched the tide of battle ebb and flow, which resulted in the defeat of the hitherto invincible Mamelukes. This little spot upon the summit of the Pyramid of Cheops has been trodden for centuries by the students and scientists of all nations. Every stone upon it is carved with the names of persons more or less known to the world, and probably no single spot on the face of the globe—not even the Holy Sepulchre in Jerusalem—has been visited, viewed, and studied with greater interest. Near the Pyramids of Ghizeh stands the Sphynx, one of the nine wonders of the world, and in Cairo the Government museum of sculptures, mummies, and other remains from the tombs of the ancient Egyptians, furnishes material for a most interesting study. The ruins of the Upper Nile, for which Cairo is the starting-point, are also most interesting, but I was obliged to content myself with a study of these from a distance.

From Cairo we proceeded to Alexandria, the chief seaport of Egypt, over a railroad built by George Stephenson, the rails of which are laid on iron sleepers, and which is said to be the smoothest running road in the world. The historical associations of Alexandria are most interesting to the tourist, but he looks in vain for the evidences of antiquity with which its history has filled his memory. Here the first light-house was constructed to guide mariners to a safe harbor—the "Pharos," and the fame of "Pharos light" has been handed down to all succeeding ages. The Alexandria of to-day is a bustling, modern city, with scarcely anything, excepting Pompey's Pillar and an Egyptian obelisk known as "Cleopatra's Needle," to testify to its greatness in bygone ages. As an evidence of an extensive business, however, I may mention that I counted twenty-six steamers lying at its wharves, most of which were busily engaged in taking in or discharging cargo, and there was besides to be seen a not insignificant fleet of sailing vessels.

From Alexandria we sailed for Constantinople by the way of Smyrna. The latter is the chief commercial city of Turkey in Asia, a curious old town with narrow, dirty streets, teeming with the smells that seem inseparable from Turkish cities. The streets are very narrow and are paved with large stone blocks which are terribly uneven, and make them almost impassable for carriages.

Almost everything is transported on the backs of donkeys and camels, which may be seen lumbering through the streets with huge panniers or pack-saddles swung on each side of them and filled with almost every conceivable kind of merchandise. It is a curious and not uninteresting sight for a stranger to see a long train of camels joined together with a rope leading from the nose of one to the saddle of the other, marching in single file through the narrow streets of Smyrna to the wharves, where one by one they are forced to kneel down and receive their burdens, with which they again start off under way to the desert. It is, indeed, a veritable meeting of the "ships of the desert," with the "white-winged birds of commerce." The chief exports of Smyrna are figs, cotton, and carpets, it being the place of manufacture for the celebrated Turkish carpets, which are, indeed, most beautiful and luxurious, and the carpet bazaars of Smyrna are a most seductive place to visit. In Smyrna the Turkish coffee-houses, which are so prominent a feature in Constantinople, are also largely patronized. All along the water front they are as thick as are drinking-saloons in West street, New York, and they seem to be filled at all hours with a motley crowd composed chiefly of Turks and Greeks, who are busily engaged in sipping their coffee and taking whiffs from the long, flexible stem of the *narghileh*, or Turkish pipe. Here our steamer took on board a thousand recruits for the Turkish army, Bashi-Bazouks, or irregular troops bound for Constantinople. They were mostly between twenty-five and thirty-five years of age; stout, athletic fellows, and generally quiet and good-natured; very different in appearance from what one might imagine the demons in human form who perpetrated the massacres in Bulgaria. Still it is difficult to say what these fellows might do when their blood was up, fighting under the inspiration of a religion which teaches that the most meritorious act a son of the Prophet can do is to kill "a dog of a Christian." Most of them were very devout in the observance of their religion; they were "told off" in squads to go forward and pray, and the forecastle deck, the only clear space on board was constantly occupied by half a dozen at a time, kneeling and mumbling their prayers, and making their genuflections or salaams toward Mecca. I fancied that in this devotion to their religion I found the reason for the acknowledged bravery of the Turks in connection with the Koran teaching that every one of the faithful who falls in battle is translated at once to Paradise, where he has any number of beautiful "houris" at disposal to wait upon him and gratify every passion. Is it any wonder that these men fight like demons for the defence or spread of their religion? In my opinion, it is by no means certain that Russia would get the best of a contest with Turkey at this time, at least until Turkey's resources had become exhausted, and hunger and disease had become Russian allies.

It is said, however, that the Turks have never expected to permanently remain in Europe, that they have always believed they would sooner or later be expelled, and for many years the Turks of Constantinople have buried most of their dead on the Asiatic side of the Bosphorus on that account.

Constantinople itself has the most beautiful situation that can be imagined either for commerce or residence, occupying the sloping sides of the Bosphorus—a salt water river, so to speak, connecting the Black Sea with the Sea of Marmora; it is fairly divided into two parts by the "Golden Horn," an inlet or bay which sweeps up between Pera and Constantinople proper, Pera being the residence of most of the foreign population and occupying about the same relation to Constantinople that Brooklyn does to New York.

Approaching the city from the Sea of Marmora, it presents a most beautiful appearance, its great mosques occupying the principal points of vantage, with their graceful minarets towering high in the air. Little steamers are darting here and there on their way to Scutari (the Asiatic side of the Bosphorus), or the various little villages along its shores; the light and graceful "caiques" (a species of row-boat) are plying hither and thither, and altogether, the scene is one long to be remembered. A walk through the city, however, dispels the illusion. The streets are narrow, crooked, and dirty, in many places fairly paved with mongrel dogs, which belong to nobody, and lie around under the feet of passers-by with the utmost unconcern, while in almost every quarter one is greeted with odors which are anything but pleasant. The Turkish and Circassian women that one sees, as a rule, are not pretty, and their costumes are ungraceful and enhance their natural ugliness. One looks in vain for the famed Circassian beauties, and Turkish society, so far as it is visible to the casual visitor to Constantinople, leaves anything but a favorable impression. The Turks, as a nation, are licentious, fanatical, cruel, and ignorant, and in my estimation, compare very unfavorably with any other nation pretending to civilization. How ignorant they are, may be inferred from an article in their new Constitution, recently promulgated, which, in providing for a legislative body, or House of Congress, specifies that in order to be eligible to membership, a Turk "must be able to read, and for a re-election must be able to read, and *so far as possible*, to write."

GREECE AND HER CURRANT CROP.

From Constantinople I went to Greece, with the double purpose of seeing the interesting antiquities of that country and investigating some matters connected with the trade in currants. I cannot say that the Isles of Greece, as they appear to the modern eye, fulfil the high expectations which one is apt to form from all that has been written about them in song and story; nor do the modern Greeks look very much as if they had descended from the heroes of Thermopylæ or those who fought with Marco Bozzaris. It is said, however, that the depressed condition of Greece to-day is due largely to the misrule of Turkey and the terrible struggles which the Greeks have had with that cruel and barbarous nation in the effort to obtain their independence. I was informed by an intelligent Greek gentleman that since the beginning of this century more than half a million of Greeks, the flower of Grecian manhood, had fallen in these struggles, besides large numbers of non-combatants who had been put to the sword by their cruel and barbarous opponents, who for many years crushed the Greeks by mere force of numbers, and perpetrated, when victorious, barbarities similar to those which have been recently enacted in Bulgaria, which have excited the indignation of the civilized world. More than half of Greek territory proper is still under Turkish rule, and its inhabitants, in common with the other Christians who constitute a majority of all the inhabitants of Turkey in Europe, barely succeed in existing under a government which, for oppression in taxation, and general tyranny, is not equalled elsewhere on the face of the globe.

Whatever the Greek islands may be in summer time, in winter they present a rocky, barren, unproductive appearance that is anything but pleasing. I looked in vain for the "eternal summer" which, according to Byron, "gilds them yet," and longed for access to a good-sized wood-pile or a well-filled coal-box to keep the temperature of my room up to a point where it would be comfortable. It seems, however, that these things are almost unknown in this country, and the people shiver through the cold weather, devoutly praying for the early return of that which is warm enough to make them comfortable. The only tree which grows in Greece to any considerable extent is the olive-tree, and the commercial product of this is too valuable to admit of its being freely used for firewood, while there is no native coal, and the people have very little money to buy that which is imported from other countries.

Athens is, of course, the most interesting place to visit, owing to its associations with the past. Indeed, it subsists principally upon these, for the surrounding country produces little that is exportable, and it has little or no commerce. It is said, however, to be gradually gaining in population; the modern part of the city is certainly well built and cleaner than any Eastern city I have visited. The great interest of the place centres in the Acropolis, with its noble old ruins, the sight of which must inevitably stimulate the appetite of the tourist for ancient history. Here one obtains a glimpse of the art which later, under the Romans, made Italy famous, and which makes her the most attractive field for the tourist, to this day.

The currant crop of Greece, the chief item of export, is raised in its westernmost islands and along the shores of the Gulf of Lepanto. Zante was formerly the most important depot for the export of this fruit, but of late years Patras has gradually been gaining in its exports, and is now the centre of this trade, without which Greece would scarcely have any commerce worth mentioning. England is the great market for currants, and English plum-puddings are the ultimate destination of by far the greater quantity. The story is told of a Greek lady who, in conversation with Sir Charles Napier, spoke of the English appetite for plum-pudding, and remarked: "We pray heaven your countrymen may never lose this taste, for in that event we should all starve." It is curious that the prosperity of any country should depend upon the production of such an unimportant item in the world's economy.

The Greek currant is really a species of grape, and a currant vineyard looks like any other vineyard, except that the vines are, perhaps, not quite so large, and are set and trimmed a little closer than in an ordinary vineyard. They are propagated from cuttings, which take from two to three years before beginning to bear, and it is five or six years from the time of planting before a vineyard arrives at full bearing, after which it lasts many years. The vines are set in rows four or five feet apart, and about the same distance from each other in the rows; while young they are supported by sticks driven into the ground, and are trimmed and trained on trellises, so as not to grow much above an even height. A curious feature of currant culture is that the vines are girdled each year, being cut entirely around and completely through the bark, at a distance of perhaps one foot from the ground. Such treatment would kill an ordinary plant, and, when this practice was begun, it was prophesied that it would have that effect in course of time; a result that, however, has not been experienced in practice. The object to be attained is to increase the size and quality of the fruit, which is undoubtedly accomplished. The theory, as explained to me, is that the sap rises through the centre of the woody stalk until it reaches the branches, leaves, and fruit, when it returns by the bark or the woody fibre nearest the bark. In its descending course, upon reaching the spot where the plant is girdled, its progress is stopped, and it is obliged to reascend and exhaust itself in the fruit. It is said that not only is the size of the fruit improved by this practice, but the amount of saccharine matter is also largely increased, which is considered a desideratum. The quality of the soil, however, has much to do with this, and different districts vary considerably in this respect. August and September are the months for gathering and curing. The bunches are picked and spread out to dry on little terraces of smoothly compacted earth, sloping toward the west, so as to get the full effect of the afternoon sun. They remain here six or eight days, according to the weather, when they become much dried and shrivelled; they are then stripped from the stems, and after a further exposure of two or three days, are sufficiently dried to be packed. They are then put into bags and transported to the nearest shipping point, where they are generally sold to the export merchants, and thrown into large piles in their warehouses, from which they are from time to time packed in barrels and shipped as required. Grocers who have seen how closely currants are packed in the barrel might think that it had been done by hydraulic pressure. In point of fact, however, it is done by men's feet. A man gets into an empty barrel, while another shovels in the currants, the first distributing them and treading them with his bare feet, pressing them and working them in very compactly, and gradually rising until the barrel is full. This certainly does not seem the cleanliest method in the world, but during my travels I have seen dirty operatives wading in the syrup from which the sugar is made, Chinamen treading tea into the chests with their feet, currants packed into barrels by the feet, and macaroni-dough kneaded with the feet; and I have finally been forced to accept the idea that the man who said "we were bound to eat our peck of dirt anyway" had a deep insight not only into human nature, but also into the various processes by which the food is prepared with which the human body is sustained and nourished. For myself, I prefer processes of manufacture which are less suggestive than those which I have mentioned, and so far as my influence in the trade extends, it will always be thrown in favor of cleanliness in the preparation of food products.

Of course the above-described methods of curing and preparing currants also leave a wide scope for care and cleanliness. Being dried on the ground, more or less stone and gritty matter is apt to become incorporated with the currants, varying, of course, with the nature of the drying-ground and the care exercised in their manipulation. This has a considerable influence upon the price, especially in the English market, where these matters are understood and appreciated better than in America. Indeed, until within the last two or three years, anything has been considered good enough to ship to America, and the orders which came from the United States for currants always contained limits as to price, but none whatever as to quality; of course, this resulted in all the poor goods going to the American market. Of late, however, the trade in the United States has been getting into other hands, wholesale grocers and distributing fruit merchants importing direct, where before a few speculative importing houses, which knew or cared little about the wants of the retail trade, controlled the entire business, and a much better and cleaner quality is now required for the American market than heretofore. We have yet, however, something to learn in regard to the *flavor* of the fruit. Some districts are greatly to be preferred in this respect. Their product contains a much larger percentage of saccharine matter, and the London houses, which have a first-class trade, will sometimes pay nearly double the price for favorite brands that they will for the ordinary run of goods.

The following statistics of the production of currants, together with the ruling prices, are interesting, as showing the course of trade:

In 1851 and previous years the production was large, and the average first-cost price about $25 per 1,000 pounds.

In 1852 a severe blight suddenly affected a portion of the currant district, the production fell to 13,584 tons, and the price rose to $62 per 1,000 pounds.

In 1853 the blight extended still further, affecting nearly the whole currant-producing territory; but 4,998 tons were produced, and prices ranged between $57 and $93 per 1,000 pounds, the lowest price being for the poorest quality.

In 1854 the production was 6,121 tons, and the range of prices $45 to $65.

In 1855 the production was 7,128 tons, and the range of prices $110 to $120, a great speculation having been inaugurated that year, which continued through the two subsequent years.

In 1856, having to a certain extent recovered from the blight, the production increased to 26,906 tons, but prices still kept up to from $70 to $85.

In 1857 the production was 23,327 tons, and the range of prices $70 to $100.

In 1858 the production had increased to 34,035 tons, which proved too heavy a load for the speculators to carry, and prices suddenly broke down to a range of $22 to $38 per 1,000 pounds.

	Production. Tons.	Prices.
1859	37,535	$27 00 to $55 00
1860	51,498	22 00 " 35 00
1861	43,365	20 00 " 50 00
1862	49,337	20 00 " 32 00
1863	57,830	21 00 " 33 00
1864	51,505	20 00 " 30 00
1865	51,440	22 00 " 40 00
1866	58,367	20 00 " 42 00
1867	65,146	16 00 " 40 00
1868	56,222	12 00 " 38 00

For the last eight years the prices have ranged between $25 and $50 per 1,000 pounds, and the production has been as follows: In 1869, 52,267 tons; 1870, 54,875 tons; 1871, 80,976 tons; 1872, 70,766 tons; 1873, 71,222 tons; 1874, 76,210 tons; 1875, 72,916 tons; 1876, 86,947 tons; 1877, 82,181 tons, being the largest crop ever known.

By these figures it will be seen that the fluctuations both in quantity and prices have been remarkable, and it is hard to draw any reliable conclusions from them.

The following figures of the shipments to the United States for the last ten years are also interesting, as showing the large increase in the consumption of this article: For the five years beginning with 1865, when our import duty was five cents per pound, the quantities are as follows: 1865, 1,411 tons; 1866, 2,637 tons; 1867, 2,182 tons; 1868, 2,808 tons; 1869, 1,143 tons. During 1870 and 1871 our duty was two and a half cents per pound, and the quantities as follows: 1870, 3,356 tons; 1871, 5,020 tons, a considerable portion of the shipments of that year being in anticipation of the reduction of duty to one cent per pound, which took place in 1872, in which year the importations were

4,458 tons; 1873, 6,280 tons; 1874, 6,129 tons; 1875, 8,857 tons. During the season of 1876, 7,353 tons; 1877, 5,912 tons.

The above are direct shipments, and do not include the considerable quantities which were first shipped from Greece to Trieste, and also to England, and from these points transshipped to the United States. These figures, however, show a steady and large increase under the stimulus of reduced duties, the year 1869 alone being an exception, due, no doubt, to the prices being very high, as also they were in 1872.

ITALY.

WAYSIDE SCENES, THOUGHTS, AND FANCIES IN ITALY.

From Corfu, in Greece, I crossed the Adriatic to Brindisi, in Italy, an important port in the time of the Roman Empire, but since the decline of Roman power a comparatively unimportant place until the completion of the Suez Canal, since which time it has been the Mediterranean port of call for many English steamers to the East, and possessing the best harbor on the East coast of the Italian peninsnla, it bids fair, in course of time, to again become a place of some importance. The old Roman citadel is still in existence here, in a fair state of preservation, and Roman architectural remains are abundant. Indeed, all along the coast the walls of fortifications and other buildings are abundant, and from the windows of the railway cars one occasionally catches a glimpse of a broken marble column, or other piece of ancient sculpture, built into the modern Italian walls.

Corfu, too, by the way, in the island of that name (one of the westernmost of the Greek Archipelago), deserves a word of description—a picturesque old town, with a harbor commanded by two citadels, built by the Venetians in their palmy days, when the whole East was tributary to Venice. A pleasant surrounding country, with orange and ancient olive-trees, and a charming climate, makes Corfu, in many respects, a very desirable place of residence, and in the winter it is quite a place of resort for tourists who desire to escape the rigors of a Northern winter. The olive-trees, by the way, remind me that I here met a combination of amazing stupidity in the person of one of the local guides. He was a pleasant amiable fellow, with the usual parrot-like lore which distinguishes many of his fraternity. An affirmative, or what a lawyer would call a leading question to these professional guides is sure to be met with a confirmative answer, and when this is mixed up with the information which they have acquired and make a business of relating to every new comer, with, perhaps, no idea whatever of its bearing, it becomes particularly entertaining. As an instance, our guide informed us that the old olive trees which we saw were there "since the time of the Venetians," from which everything in this old place seems to date. I asked him how long ago that was, which puzzled him very much, and he finally gave it up. I quizzingly suggested fifteen or eighteen years, and he returned an eager "yes," which showed how limited was his knowledge, and how eager he was to please. Thinking, perhaps, that he had not understood me, I put the question again in various forms, until I became fully satisfied that the fellow had no comprehension whatever of time.

In the older parts of the town of Corfu one can get a good idea of the domestic economy and methods of the primitive Greeks. All of the utensils are of the most antiquated pattern; wine and olive oil is carried about in goatskins similar to the water skins which I described in one of my letters from India. Down at the wharves, where I saw oil being poured into hogsheads for exportation, instead of lightering these casks off to the ships, which lie at anchor some distance from the shore, they simply roll them overboard and tow them off with a row-boat, oil being lighter than water. Olives and olive oil seem to be a chief article of commerce throughout this whole country. All the way up the eastern side of the Italian peninsula, for hundreds of miles, olive-groves are thickly planted, and their gnarled and twisted trunks give evidence of great age. Indeed, I think the olive-trees of Eastern Italy can take the palm for growing in the most fantastic forms and shapes. It is a common thing to see one side decayed so that it is more like a slab than a tree, and this thin, shrivelled, one-sided thing is filled with knots or rather knot-holes, so that it looks like a piece of perforated paper on a large scale, yet the tops seem to flourish and bear good crops. In one instance I saw where a tree had positively grown itself inside out; that is, had warped and twisted a large portion of the trunk so that what was originally the inside of the tree was now upon the outside, while the bark had exchanged places and was growing on the concave surface, with only a narrow slit to admit the light and air, and in numbers of instances the trees had grown themselves out of their original centre of gravity, taken a new start at right angles, wasted away until the substance of the wood in the trunk would no longer support the branches, and *stone columns* had been built to support them at the point where the large limbs began to branch off.

Many travellers from India to Europe disembark at Brindisi and make a short Italian tour, completing the rest of their journey by rail, and do a little sight-seeing in Italy. The railway along the eastern coast leads directly up to Venice, which, aside from Rome, is probably the most interesting and most frequented city of Italy. Founded soon after the fall of the Roman empire upon a number of small islands in a lagoon at the head of the Adriatic, it gradually prospered and developed until the necessity for a constitutional form of government was felt, and in the year 697 the first Doge, or President, was elected. For eight hundred years it continued to grow and prosper, notwithstanding occasional wars and reverses, and during the fifteenth century was the grand focus of the entire commerce of Europe, and indeed of the world. The city of Venice proper numbered 200,000 inhabitants, possessed 300 sea-going vessels with 8,000 sailors, and 3,000 smaller craft with 17,000 sailors, as well as a fleet of war-galleys manned by 11,000 men. In the sixteenth century the power of Venice, however, began to decline, and its commerce was gradually superseded by that of the Portuguese, in consequence of the discovery of the Cape of Good Hope route to India. Still for two hundred years longer Venice continued to exercise a considerable influence throughout Europe, but from this time forward her commerce practically ceased, and for the past two hundred years she has been chiefly interesting from the recollections of what she once was, and her peculiarities of situation and architecture. Situated on numerous islands with water communication between them, there are few or no streets, everything being conveyed by water. In all Venice there is hardly a conveyance other than boats, and the few streets are short, unimportant, and simply passage-ways for foot-passengers.

The principal business centre of the city is the Piazza San Marco, or Place of St. Mark, a space perhaps six hundred feet long by three hundred broad, around and near which are situated the public buildings and principal shops. At its eastern end is the celebrated church of St. Mark, to me the most interesting of the sights of Venice. It is an extensive and venerable old pile, covering, with its various parochial edifices, several acres. The church itself is a mass of rich marbles of various colors, interspersed with porphyry, alabaster, and other costly stones. The floor is paved in mosaic, with millions of fragments of the same material wrought in elaborate patterns, with here and there even more costly stones, such as jasper, amethyst, cornelian, and malachite interspersed. The walls and arches are covered with mosaic pictures, wrought with tiny cubes of many-colored glass, representing various scenes in sacred history, while the high altar is a mass of artistic work in gold, silver, and precious stones, a description of which alone would require a chapter, perhaps a volume. The smoke of the candles upon the altar and the incense burnt during the ceremonies of centuries, have darkened all this splendid work, and given the whole interior a dark, even dingy look, and it is only when the church is lighted up during festival times that it appears at its best. We were fortunate in witnessing one of these services, and when the long procession of white-robed priests, with their Cardinal, slowly made the circuit of the church, bearing gaily colored banners, around which the smoke of the burning incense curled in graceful clouds, I could not but think that the Roman Catholic Church knew best how to make an impression upon the mass of humanity which instinctively seeks some method of worshipping the Infinite. Whether the conditions under which I have seen St. Mark have anything to do with my impression or not I cannot say, but it seems to me the most interesting structure of the kind I have ever visited. St. Peter's, at Rome, is massively wonderful; the Cathedral of Milan is an incarnation of beauty; St. Sophia, at Constantinople, Notre Dame, of Paris, and Westminster Abbey, in London, all have their historical and architectural features of interest, but it remains for old San Marco to charm me into a brown study, and summon up visions of the past in which I lose myself. For a thousand years this old edifice has looked down upon the Piazza of St. Mark and the grand spectacles of which it has been the scene. A hundred Doges have worshipped before its altars, and generation after generation of proud Venetians has flourished and passed away while yet Venice was mistress of the world. These and kindred thoughts were passing through my mind during one of my visits to the old pile, when I witnessed an incident that I cannot forbear describing. A gentleman holding a little fair-haired girl upon his lap sat listening to the music. A decrepit old beggar-woman approached and stretching out her withered hand to the little girl asked for alms. The child in turn appealed to her father, who gave her some money which she laid in the old woman's hand. Just at that instant a ray of sunlight streamed down through an upper window, lighting up the group and falling full upon the face of the little girl, making it as radiant as that of an angel. The old woman stood for a moment looking steadfastly into the fair young face, and then suddenly seizing the child's hands, kissed them and hobbled away to the door as fast as her decrepit old limbs could carry her, never stopping to solicit other strangers who were near. The scene, in some of its features was remarkable and most impressive—the contrast between the little child just entering this life and the feeble old woman so near the end: the sunlight streaming in from the high window lighting up the scene and making the white smoke of the freshly burnt incense seem luminous and blue, and etherealizing even the very dust which floated in the air; while the blended music of the organ and men's strong voices, as they chanted a grand old anthem, went swelling up to the roof, and then, as if unable to find room, came echoing down on the farther side. I do not know that I can describe it in words, but I shall not soon forget the picture and its setting.

From Venice to Florence by rail over the mountain chain of the Apennines is a pleasant journey of some eight or nine hours over one of the most picturesque of routes. In a distance of thirty miles there is more costly railway engineering than I have ever before seen in the same space. Within this distance there are forty-five tunnels, and the spaces intervening between these are a succession of substantial stone bridges or heavy rock-cuttings, which must have cost an immense sum of money. Florence is a delightful little city, situated in the valley of the Arno, and containing treasures of art which are worthy of years of study. Another eight hours brings us to Rome, around which centre more associations of historical interest than belong to any other city on earth. The massive ruins which remain fill the beholder with wonder, and the beautiful specimens of the sculptor's art which still exist are so perfect that the sculptors of all the world come here to study, and seek in vain for inspirations which will equal them.

One good thing which the Popes of Rome have done is to expend the revenues of the Church for the past two centuries in purchasing and collecting within the walls of the Vatican a museum of art-treasures that is unequalled elsewhere in the world; it has cost untold sums, but the money might have been spent in a more foolish way—at any rate, it has made my stay in Rome a most enjoyable one. *En passant*, I happened to be in both Venice and Rome during the Carnival; I saw its beginning in the Piazza of St. Mark, and its ending on the Corso at Rome. During the month preceding Lent the Italians of all classes go in for a good time, and during the last ten days, are apparently beside themselves with merry-making. An opera has been named in honor of the Carnival of Venice, and the scenes on the Corso at Rome have been described by abler pens than mine each year for so long that the "memory of man runneth not back" to the beginning; so I will only mention the leading features. During the last few days the festivities are organized by the Carnival "Committee on Arrangements;" processions of maskers in fancy dresses take place every afternoon along the Corso (the principal business street), while every other day races between riderless horses take place. This is one of the principal features of the

Carnival; the pavement is covered with soft earth, and a half dozen or more fine horses without riders, saddles, or bridles, are turned loose at one end of a long street and spurred on by prickly balls, which are fastened by strings to a girth-strap, so that they will swing against the legs of the horse as he runs; they are urged at the top of their speed for a distance of a mile or more, the foremost at the goal receiving a prize of greater or less value. There is no barrier to separate the horses from the mass of people which line the street on either side, and when the horses run well together the space is too narrow and serious accidents occur. The many balconies along the Corso are gaily decorated during Carnival time, and are filled with spectators of the festivities, places frequently commanding a high rent. During the first three days of the festivities "comfit" throwing is largely indulged in, and the last night an illumination takes place, every person carrying a wax taper which he strives to keep alight, at the same time endeavoring to extinguish that of his next neighbor; this makes a deal of fun, and the effect of thousands of tapers gleaming from every point through the long street is very picturesque.

CITRON AND MACARONI.

Citron and macaroni are Italian products; therefore I trust the reader will take no exception to my coupling Italy—she of the sunny skies and the cradle of the arts—with the prosaic items above mentioned. People buy and use "Leghorn citron," and, when I came to Leghorn, I naturally expected to see it growing there, and post myself upon this article from beginning to end. But when I came to inquire for citron on the tree, it was nowhere to be found, and my visit to the manufactories developed the fact that the citron, a species of lemon, or the lemon, a species of citron, is chiefly grown in the islands of Sardinia and Corsica, where it is gathered, cut into halves, placed in salt, pickled, and shipped in casks to Leghorn, the principal point of preparation for use. As the citrons arrive in Leghorn, they look like very large lemons, with a tremendously thick rind, and very little substance inside of it. From the time they are cut they remain in the salt pickle, say thirty days, and are tough, leathery, bitter, and anything but agreeable to the taste. They are then placed in a huge boiler, wherein, for from one and a half to two hours, they are boiled tender. The seeds and pithy matter in the centre are then scooped out and thrown away, and the rind is put to soak in water slightly sweetened. This extracts a portion of the salt which it has received in the pickle, and imparts a slightly saccharine flavor. The next day it is taken out of the first solution and placed in a second; the next day in a third; the next in a fourth; the next in a fifth, and the next in a sixth; each of these solutions being a degree sweeter than the former, and by this time it has lost all the salt flavor and has become quite sweet. It is then boiled up for a short time in very heavy syrup, from whence it is taken out and placed in flat baskets, piled on racks in warm rooms, and left to dry and crystallize. Here it remains six or eight hours, when it is ready for packing, and is put up in the usual thin wooden boxes, in which shape it is familiar to all grocers. Here again, however, fashion in trade is exhibited; for the English market it is packed in half boxes, for the German market in quarters, and a portion of each style is sent to America. Lemon and orange peel is prepared and packed to a limited extent in the same way. In short, citron may be roughly described as the thick peel of a species of lemon, pickled to extract its bitter flavor and absorb the oil, boiled to make it tender, saturated with white sugar syrup to make it palatable, and in this shape it constitutes one of the ingredients of the plum puddings and wedding cakes of the world. So much for Leghorn and its citron.

Now for Naples and its macaroni. Naples is probably better known from its contiguity to Mount Vesuvius and Pompeii than from any other cause, but it deserves to be known for itself. Beautifully situated on a hillside, sloping up from the shores of a lovely bay—indeed, now that I recollect, Naples *is* celebrated for its beauty—with a climate probably as perfect as it is possible to find, and in the centre of a fertile district which grows wheat, wine, oils, and fruits in profusion, there are few places more favorably situated, either for commerce or residence, than Naples. A quaint old place it is, too, with its narrow streets and tall houses of six or seven stories, all of which seem to swarm with population to their very roofs. Flocks of goats, which pasture in the surrounding country, are driven backward and forward each night and morning through the streets, in order that they may be milked before the eyes of milk consumers, who are here evidently anti-adulterationists, and do not believe that water added to the natural product improves the quality. Here and there, in sheltered nooks, public writers may be seen, writing out epistles for those who are unable to write for themselves (and they comprise by far the larger portion of the community).

A hand-organ playing on every block explains to an American where all the hand-organ players in America come from, and various other novel sights and sounds greet one at every turn. Beautiful shops for the sale of tortoise-shell, lava, and coral abound, for Naples is the great depot for these articles; and glove manufactories, where are manufactured most of the cheaper brands of "Paris kid gloves," are everywhere to be seen. The streets are paved with large blocks of lava from Vesuvius, which just around the point of the bay, some eight or ten miles off, rears its massive cone several thousand feet high, and from the crater at the top continually sends forth a column of steam and smoke, which is very suggestive of the mass of fire beneath. On the other side, at the foot of the mountain, lies Pompeii, with its streets and houses just as they were 1,800 years ago, when they were covered twenty feet deep with a mass of stones and ashes from Vesuvius. It has gradually been excavated during the last century, until now nearly the whole city is uncovered and exposed to view. The remains which have been found furnish material for a most interesting study of the habits of the people of that day and generation. In the museum at Naples are preserved the charred remains of fruits and nuts, and an assortment of different grains and vegetables, of the same varieties and species as are used to this day; even loaves of bread, which still perfectly preserve their form, are here to be seen. A bottle is also exhibited containing olive oil in a tolerable state of preservation, besides an immense assortment of household utensils, works of art, etc.

But I find I am describing everything in and around Naples excepting the manufacture of macaroni, the process of which is as follows: The hardest and flintiest varieties of wheat are selected, first washed, and then thoroughly dried in the sun. This wheat is then coarsely ground and run through an immense revolving sieve to separate the starch from the bran and flinty portions. It is then successively passed through a series of six hand-sieves, each a little finer than that preceding, for the purpose of separating the flinty portion from the bran. This apparently simple process requires considerable skill and a certain knack, which it takes time to acquire. The motion which is given to the sieves by the sifters is half rotary and half up and down, with an indescribable side motion, which I can only characterize as "boomerang," for it throws the mass which is being sifted in an opposite direction to that taken by the sieve. Every few minutes each sifter pauses and skims off the bran which has worked to the top and centre of the sieve, and after these various manipulations there remains a clean, flinty farina, known as *semolina*. This is then mixed with warm water into a stiff dough, and this dough is thoroughly kneaded by means of a long prism-like, hard-wood lever, so adjusted that the spring of the timber may be utilized in alternately raising and depressing it upon the mass of dough, which is thus pressed and kneaded into the required consistency. It is rather amusing to see two or three men sitting on the end of this lever and bobbing up and down, so as to throw their weight at one instant on the lever, bringing it down into the dough and then allowing it to spring up again, in order that it may be brought down in a new place. After this kneading lever has been passed over a mass of dough the latter resembles a huge cake of chocolate, or rather a cake of maple-sugar, which has been run into the mold known as "chocolate style." After it has been thus mixed and kneaded for about one hour, the dough is put into presses with perforated bottoms, and pressure being applied, it comes out through these holes in the shape known to us as macaroni. At this stage of the process it is, of course, soft and flexible, and in order to keep the various little strings of dough from sticking together, it is constantly fanned by a boy, in order that the current of air thus made may slightly dry the outside of the strings and prevent them from sticking together. It is then cut off and hung on racks or frames made of bamboo, to dry. As it hangs on the frames the different pieces are of unequal length, and a boy passes rapidly over them, wringing off the longer ends so as to make them uniform in that respect. The drying has to be done in the shade and in a place not exposed to the wind, as, if dried too quickly, or if the slender pieces were blown against one another, they would be apt to break. When sufficiently dry, it is removed from the frames and packed in boxes, such as are familiar to all grocers.

The different sizes are made by changing the movable bottoms of the press and employing different sized perforations. I also forgot to say that each of these perforated holes has a core or centre around which the dough has to pass, and this produces the hollow which is a characteristic of macaroni. The reason for this arrangement is, if the macaroni were made solid, it would take very long to dry when hung upon racks, and, also, when dried, it would be very difficult to cook it without a great deal of boiling, and impossible to do so uniformly. So important is this considered, and so defective do the Italians regard the product if not thus perforated, that a proverb has arisen in Italy to the effect that "a foolish person is like macaroni without any hole in it."

Vermicelli is made from the same material and in the same way as macaroni, except that it is not hollow, it being so small that it is neither practicable nor necessary to make it so.

The *cooking* of macaroni in Naples is a feature which also deserves description. I here, for the first time, understood why Italians are so fond of this dish, and why it has never attained a very large consumption in America. It is because they know how to cook it so as to make it palatable, while we do not. A majority of American cooks put a quantity of macaroni in cold water and let it half soak, half boil for an indefinite time, until it is a watery, doughy mass. Then they throw some soft cheese crumbs on top of it, put it in a dish, place it in an oven and bake it until the top is thoroughly crusted and tough. As a contrast to this, the Neapolitans place the macaroni in boiling water, boil it for twelve to fifteen minutes, when it is tender but yet slightly elastic, and there is no danger of one piece sticking to another. The water is then poured off, and if to be served "au gratin," a little *hard, dry* cheese is *grated* and not only sprinkled over it, but thoroughly mixed through it, so that the flavor of the cheese is to be found at the bottom as well as at the top of the dish, and a lump of butter or a trifle of fine salad oil is also added, together with a little salt. It is then placed in the oven, baked for a moment, until a slight film forms on top of the dish; then a trifle more cheese is grated upon the surface "for looks," and it is replaced in the oven and baked quickly for a few minutes until the top has a rich, brown appearance, and it is then ready for the table. The way in which Neapolitans, however, oftener prepare their macaroni—and which I greatly prefer—is that known as *à la Neapolitaine*. It is boiled in the same manner as above described, but instead of serving with cheese, a rich sauce composed of the gravy or juices of meat is mixed with it, and it is then slightly browned in an oven as above. Instead of gravy or juices they sometimes use a tomato sauce in the same manner, and sometimes a combination of the two is employed. To my taste, either of the above makes a most agreeable dish, far superior to that prepared with cheese. If Americans will try macaroni *à la Neapolitaine*, I think the consumption of this palatable and wholesome article of food will be largely increased.

A GLIMPSE AT SPAIN IN 1877.

From Marseilles I went to Barcelona by sea, and found it a considerable city, possessing large manufacturing industries, and, indeed, much more business-like in appearance than anything I had expected to see in Spain. From Barcelona I proceeded by rail to Valencia, passing through Tarragona and a number of other inconsiderable places along the coast. Valencia, as most readers know, is a port of considerable importance for the export of oranges, and for many miles before reaching the city the railway passes through a series of orange groves, which are most beautiful. At this time (March) the trees were covered with ripe fruit, and occasionally also the ground beneath, where they had fallen. Indeed, they seemed so plentiful that in many places they were hardly considered worth gathering. I need not touch upon the journey from Valencia to Malaga, or my impressions of that place, as they are embodied in my description of raisins. From Malaga

I proceeded to Cadiz by way of Gibraltar, stopping at that famous place long enough to visit the fortifications which have such a world-wide reputation. I must confess that I was somewhat disappointed in these, as I had formed an idea that it was an almost wholly inaccessible rock rising abruptly from the water and bristling with cannon at every point. In point of fact, it is nothing of the kind; a narrow, flat neck of land runs out from the Spanish coast, ending in a promontory or knob of higher ground, and, while one side of it is exceedingly rocky and precipitous, the other is quite accessible, has considerable soil and vegetation, and upon this side has sprung up a small city of, perhaps, 15,000 or 20,000 inhabitants, whose chief business consists in supplying the wants of shipping, as well as of the garrison and the families of the officers who reside there; like all English colonies, it has good roads and pleasant gardens. There has also been quite a trade done from this place in smuggling goods into Spain, principally tobacco, but under the recent treaty agreements with England, Gibraltar is no longer a free port, and a heavy English duty is imposed upon tobacco landed here, much to the chagrin of the adventurers who made a living by evading the Spanish revenue. The galleries cut into the rock on the precipitous side, which have so long been considered a wonder of the world, are really very extensive and curious, although they are not esteemed so formidable in modern warfare as the recently constructed batteries lower down along the water-front. It is upon these that the attention of the British Government has been directed of late years, and here is where the heaviest guns are mounted. These are not, perhaps, more than fifty to one hundred feet above the water, while those in the galleries are far up upon the cliffs, at various altitudes ranging from eight hundred to twelve hundred feet. The most important of the rock-cut galleries were constructed by the British in the beginning of this century, but certain of them date back to a much earlier period, some even having been constructed, it is said, by the Moors during their occupation of Spain. The neck of land connecting Gibraltar proper with the main land is jointly occupied by British and Spanish troops, with a neutral ground, perhaps half a mile wide, between them. The Straits which here separate Europe from Africa look, perhaps, five or six miles wide, although at their narrowest part—between Europa Point and Cape Ceuta—the distance is really fifteen miles.

From Gibraltar to Cadiz is about eighty miles, or say eight hours' run by the little coasting steamers which ply regularly between Malaga and Cadiz, calling at Gibraltar. The city of Cadiz, viewed from the sea, presents a more striking and picturesque appearance than any city that I have seen, not even excepting Constantinople. Being situated upon a low neck of land projecting out into the sea, it seems to rise abruptly from the water, and the tall, white houses, with their many cupolas, interspersed here and there with a gilded dome, present a dazzling appearance that one does not soon forget. On landing, the illusion is dispelled, however, as there is a sameness about the appearance of all the streets, and little or nothing to see. Being situated at the mouth of the Guadalquivir, Cadiz possesses a considerable import and export trade, and commercially is one of the most important cities in Spain.

From Cadiz to Seville by rail, via Jerez, is a pleasant railway ride of a few hours, and Seville, I think, is quite the most attractive of the Spanish cities I have visited. Most of the streets are wide and clean, and the public buildings many and imposing. The old Moorish palace, or "Alcazar," is being restored in a way which gives one a better idea of Moorish architecture even than the Alhambra at Granada, and the cathedral at Seville is one of the finest in Spain.

Speaking of cathedrals, one finds them here most imposing structures, even in the poorest towns. They are of such magnificent proportions and appointments that one cannot help thinking that the people have been impoverished for the purpose of building them. It is quite evident that the priestly element is a controlling power in Spain. Everywhere one goes, crosses are seen on all sorts of buildings, both public and private, and at street-corners the images of saints are almost as frequent as are the street-lamps. I was informed by a resident of Valencia that the census of some of the principal districts showed one priest to every thirty-two inhabitants, and, while it would be, perhaps, unfair to say that all the troubles which Spain has experienced are due to priestly influence, yet it cannot be denied that the priests are a great incubus, and have materially assisted to keep Spain back in the march of progress which the civilized nations of the world have been making during the present century. It is but a few months since the influence of the church prevented the adoption of a system of public education in Spain, and only a few days ago four hundred Spanish Protestants, who had met for worship in a back street in Cadiz to listen to a sermon from their pastor, were turned out of doors by armed policemen and the service prohibited. It seems that, according to an article of the Spanish Constitution, such gatherings are illegal; this article forbids every "public display of heretical teaching." "Protestants are not allowed to make their places of worship known by any public placards;" they are "prohibited from worshipping with open doors," and they "may not sing or pray so loud as to be heard in the streets." So wide are the powers of repression given by this article, that it would enable the police to seize any copy of the Protestant bible which may be exposed for sale, or any literary work the clergy may think calculated to injure the national faith. This, perhaps, is hard for an American to believe, but, when in Madrid, I saw a notice for the sale of indulgences publicly posted on the entrance-doors of a church, together with a notice to the effect that all the indulgences were to be obtained there which were for sale at a rival church down the street. The state of affairs in Spain to-day is another illustration of how ignorance and intolerance go hand in hand, and it is evident that the opposition to public instruction on the part of the Spanish clergy arises from a fear that they would not be able to so absolutely control an intelligent population as an ignorant one. Spain has a glorious climate, a fertile soil on which can be grown almost every product of both temperate and tropical climes; is most favorably situated, when geographically considered, for commercial purposes, and yet she is behind all the other principal nations of the earth. Educated Spaniards are chivalrous and hospitable, and second to none in ability and intelligence, but the mass of the people are sadly ignorant, and, of course, correspondingly fanatical and cruel.

In Valencia I saw placards announcing cock-fights, "under the auspices of the society for promoting the culture of game fowls," and in all the principal cities everybody seemed to be anticipating a great deal of pleasure from the bull fights which were to take place on the occasion of the King's visit, then near at hand. At first I thought I should like to see what "the national amusement" was like, but after conversing with an English friend who had recently witnessed one, I altered my mind; the successive disembowelling of a dozen horses is not a sight that the average American appreciates, and this, with the ultimate slaughtering of the bull, with a little more than the usual risk to the butcher, is all there is of it. It is to be hoped that, with the onward march of intelligence and civilization, such spectacles will soon cease to be esteemed amusements, even in Spain.

The Spaniards are a handsome race, the women especially so, and their natural beauty is much enhanced by the graceful mantilla or head-dress which is almost universally worn. I think I never saw so many beautiful women in the same space of time as I did during the month I was in Spain.

Spanish architecture is peculiar, the houses being usually built around a square, open court, which is planted with dwarf trees and often beautifully ornamented with flowers; the door or passage-way to the street is usually closed with only an elaborately wrought open iron-work door, if I may be allowed the expression, which admits a current of air, and, at the same time, affords passers-by a glimpse of charming interiors, and windows with similar guards are almost always left open to admit the air. Walls are usually brilliantly whitewashed, which imparts a dazzling whiteness to everything that is extremely trying to the eyes, and makes a Spanish city often look cleaner than it smells.

Spanish currency is "a delusion and a snare," at least to a stranger; nominally the unit of value is the "real" (about five cents), but *really* there is no such coin, and the stranger has to make his way among a bewildering maze of "cuartos," "pesetas," "duros," etc., which strongly try both his temper and his mathematical abilities.

In Spain everybody smokes, even the ladies "taking a hand" at it, and it is no uncommon thing to see a pretty woman, after dinner, pull out a cigarette and request a light from her next neighbor; in railway cars, diligences (stage-coaches), etc., it is not even considered necessary to ask ladies if they object, and, indeed, the practice may be said to be universal. Tobacco is a government monopoly, and (including cigars and cigarettes) is manufactured at immense government factories, the one at Seville alone employing about four thousand persons, principally women; plug tobaccos are, however, purchased by the government from our Richmond manufacturers.

RAISIN CULTURE AND PREPARATION FOR MARKET.

"Valencia" raisins are grown within a small territory near Cape San Antonio, on the eastern coast of Spain, and of which Denia is the shipping point. They take their name, however, from Valencia, a somewhat larger place, about thirty or forty miles to the North. The grapes are the same variety of muscatel as that from which the "Malaga" raisins are produced, and when ripe, are white or semi-transparent; they grow in large bunches, similar to the "Almeria" grapes, which are exported green to America, but possess less water than the Almeria, and more saccharine matter; and they also have more of the muscatel flavor. The Valencia district, being so much farther north, they cannot rely upon the necessary length and intensity of sunshine to cure the grapes in Malaga style, and therefore a different mode is adopted.

When first picked they are put into a wire basket and dipped in a solution of boiling lye (in Spanish, *lejia*), for the purpose of slightly cracking or shrivelling the skin, which allows the moisture in the grape to dry out faster, but this also permits the saccharine matter to exude slightly, which accounts for the fact that Valencia are somewhat more sticky than the Malaga raisins. They are then spread upon mats made of reeds, called *canistos*, and these are placed on a piece of level ground known as the *secadero*, or drying-place, where they are spread out during the daytime, and at night put together in piles of ten mats and covered to shield them from rain or dew. In this way the raisins are dried in from five to seven days, when they are put in baskets, conveyed to Denia and sold to the shipping merchants there. These baskets are made of grass, and the tare will average about four and a half per cent. of the total weight of the package, but a curious custom of the trade is to allow nothing for the tare, and, therefore, merchants have to calculate the price that they pay accordingly. This custom originated many years ago, and has been continued down to the present time. The merchant also has to lose, in a great degree, the weight of the stems, for, although a portion of the raisins drop off the stems in the process of handling and drying, yet many of them remain, and they have to be stripped from the stems at the shipping ports, where they are packed in boxes containing just twenty-eight pounds net, or a quarter of an English hundredweight. By far the larger portion of the Valencia crop goes to England, but the demand for Valencia raisins has been rapidly growing in the United States and Canada, until, in 1875, 533,224 boxes out of a total crop of 1,580,000 were consumed in the United States. Out of the crop of 1876, however, a larger proportion went to England, owing to the fact that prices in Malaga were much lower than in Denia, and shipments of Valencia raisins to the English market realized better prices than those which were sent to the United States. The average production for the last three years has been about a million and a half of boxes, but within ten years has fluctuated between 800,000 and 1,600,000.

"Malaga" raisins are produced within a limited territory in the neighborhood of Malaga, some two or three miles farther south, and principally along the coast of the Mediterranean. A raisin vineyard looks like any other vineyard, except, perhaps, that the vines are pruned closer to the ground, and, consequently, produce less foliage than those in some other countries. Many varieties of grape will not bear this close pruning, but the vine which bears the raisin grape has sufficient vitality to throw out shoots which bear fruit the same season, and the younger a shoot will bear the more perfect the fruit it produces. There are few or no trees in the raisin district, except orange and olive trees, and these, of course, are cultivated. The first impression of an American seeing this country in March, as I did, is that the whole of it would not be worth a thousand dollars. I have seen no country, except, perhaps, the Greek islands, that compares with it in a sterile and forbidding appearance. A range of mountains, the "Sierra Nevada," runs along the coast at a distance of some ten or fifteen miles, and from these jut out a series of spurs or foot-hills, upon which the raisin crop is grown. They are "all up and down," and, indeed, I believe are only available for the cultivation of the grape. The grapes begin to ripen about the first of August, and, as soon as picked, are conveyed to the drying-places, which here are called *toldos*. These are probably one hundred feet long by twenty feet broad, paved with clean gravel stones, and sloping toward the west in order to have the full effect of the afternoon sun. They are surrounded by a low wall, for the purpose of allowing this space to be covered at night, which is usually done with boards, but sometimes with canvas. Several of these places are usually ranged side by side. The grapes generally remain here for twelve or fifteen days, according to the weather, being turned from time to time so as to expose all parts of the bunch to the sun, and, when dry, are packed in boxes such as are familiar to us in the United States. The boxes are manufactured at large mills in Malaga, and, together with the white paper for packing, are furnished by the merchants to the farmers, who, after filling them, ship them again to the merchants in Malaga.

This brings me to the consideration of the weight of raisins in the box. This is absolutely within the control of the merchants in Malaga, and, in turn, within that of the dealers of the United States. "Those rascally Spanish farmers" pack neither more nor less quantity than what they are ordered to do, and, as above mentioned, the question of having a uniform weight of raisins packed in the boxes is wholly within the hands of the dealers in the United States. It simply requires concert of action and a demand on the part of the Spanish merchants and American dealers that all raisins shall be packed so and so, and it will be done. A large raisin shipper in Malaga remarked to me that when the dealers in New York kicked up a row about the matter two years ago, the shippers in Malaga came together and resolved that they would not ship under ten kilos, or twenty-two and a half pounds. This was adhered to until certain importing merchants in New York sent out explicit orders for boxes of less weight than those, and they either had to fill the orders at the weights named or lose the business. Of course it is to the interest of these importing merchants to continue this practice, for, as long as the duty is two and a half cents per pound, *and they only pay duty on actual weight*, they make two and a half cents on every pound of raisins short in a box, and supposing they only make five cents on every box upon a cargo of thirty thousand boxes, it amounts to the nice little sum of $1,500. While it is both desirable and feasible to have a uniform quantity packed in the boxes, a still greater reform, which is within the power of the dealers in the United States (and one which would insure the continued practice of packing a uniform quantity in a box), is the inauguration of the practice of buying as well as selling all raisins by weight. I do not believe that the retail merchants of the United States are so unmindful of their own interests as to desire to continue the practice of buying an uncertain quantity of raisins "by the box," when they can buy a certain quantity "by the pound," nor that they are so foolish as to wish to continue figuring their margin of profit on an uncertain basis. It only remains for them to manifest to the wholesale houses with whom they trade their wish to buy their raisins by *weight*. The wholesale merchants in turn will then combine and force the importing fruit houses, who are alone to blame, into the practice of selling by weight.

I forgot to state that loose muscatels were originally those raisins which fell from the stems during the process of drying, or were clipped off from the fuller bunches in order that all parts of the bunch might be exposed to the sun. These at first were sold for a lower price, but as they were usually large, fine fruit, they became very popular, and now fashion in trade is again exemplified by growers positively having to strip from the stems a considerable quantity of fine fruit in order to fill the orders for "loose muscatels." I also forgot to mention that the experiment of drying raisins by artificial heat is being tried here, two dryers, somewhat on the Alden process, being already in use, and the results thus far are quite encouraging.

After the raisins are received from the farmers by the shipping houses in Malaga, they are placed in warehouses and every box is overhauled, each layer being turned and inspected and on all the better qualities the papers changed, sometimes very ex-

25

pensive lithographed ones being used for packing the finer fruit. The system of advances to growers is also quite general, many farmers being under contract not to sell their crop to any other than certain shippers, but on the other hand there is always a certain amount of stock awaiting sale in Malaga, and shipping merchants can, by going through this stock, purchase different qualities to fill orders as received. Unlike the Valencia crop, the Malaga raisins are mostly shipped to the United States, as will be seen by the following table, showing the total crop and shipments for the last four years:

	Season 1876-77.	Season 1875-76.	Season 1874-75.	Season 1873-74.
United States..............	1,311,966	856,277	956,318	1,220,277
Other countries............	947,034	671,223	479,682	746,723
Total..................	2,259,000	1,527,500	1,436,000	1,967,000

Most of the best fruit still goes to London (from whence originated the term "London Layers"), but the term "American fruit," which formerly here meant refuse of the market, has begun to lose its original significance, and the United States now takes a much larger quantity of fine fruit than formerly.

Different houses make up slightly different statistics of exports, and the official figures of the United States Consul make quite a different showing from that of any of the statistics which I have seen. This, however, is perhaps inevitable, as the different mercantile houses are not fond of telling their business to each other, and the records which they make up are in many cases estimated.

OLIVES AND OLIVE OIL.

But few Americans have an idea of the magnitude of the business done in these items, or of the vast extent of country over which the cultivation of the olive tree extends. In coming from the East Indies I first saw the olive-tree growing in Greece, although I believe that it flourishes in Asia Minor and also throughout a considerable portion of Syria and Palestine. Throughout nearly the whole of Italy the olive is a chief crop, and in Spain I saw hundreds of thousands of acres covered with this beautiful tree. It is also grown to a considerable extent in the South of France, and indeed, it may be said that from Turkey in Asia to Spain, over a strip of country two thousand miles long and three or four hundred miles wide, it is almost the only tree that flourishes. In general size and appearance it is somewhat like an apple tree, and an olive grove seen at a distance looks like an apple orchard. More close, however, the appearance is different. The leaf is long and slender, somewhat like a willow leaf, and the branches, although not quite so slender and bending as those of the willow, are much more so than those of the apple tree. The color of the leaf is a grayish green, especially on the under side, and when a breeze is blowing, the leaves turn upward like those of a poplar tree, making one side of the tree appear quite different in color from the other. The trunks of the older trees have a strange propensity to grow into fantastic shapes, and they appear to be constantly decaying in parts, but this decay is replaced by new growth. They are carefully and closely pruned, and it is quite common both in Italy and Spain to see all the limbs of an old tree cut away in order to produce a young and fresh growth, upon which the fruit is much finer than that grown on the older branches. Raised from the seed, it takes about five or six years before the trees begin to bear, and about twenty years before they arrive at maturity and produce a full crop; after this, however, they last for hundreds of years.

Table olives are pickled while green, and are placed at once in a brine, or lye, usually made of salt water and wood ashes. In about eight days they are ready for use, but may be kept in the brine an indefinite time without injury. Sometimes the brine is changed, however, two or three times, each time being made a little weaker.

The olives destined for producing oil are allowed to remain on the tree until they are ripe, at which time they are of a dark purple color, and the meat quite soft and pulpy. These usually drop off the trees of their own accord, and being picked up, are carried to the press-house, where they are placed together in piles and allowed to remain from ten to twenty days. This softens them still more, and they are then ground under heavy stone rollers until thoroughly crushed. Small portions of this pulpy matter are then placed in envelopes of coarse bagging, which are laid up in piles under a screw-press, and the screw being brought down, the oil and juice exude and run down in a purple stream into a reservoir beneath. The oil being lightest, rises to the top, and is drawn off into receptacles provided for it. After the first pressure the envelopes are taken from the press, moistened with hot water, again placed under the press and squeezed until no more oil can be extracted, but the oil obtained from this last pressure is kept separate, and is not esteemed so highly as that first extracted. The oil as it runs from the press is necessarily quite crude, containing much sediment; different countries, and different districts, even, producing oil of different flavor and quality. It is usually refined by the manufacturer by straining it through layers of cotton cloth, and also in some places by means of charcoal filters.

But little has been done, however, either in Italy or Spain, the great oil-producing countries, in the way of completing the refining process and packing the oil in bottles for foreign consumption. It is usually shipped in large casks to Marseilles and Bordeaux, where refining and packing is a large business, amounting in Bordeaux to probably 150,000 to 200,000 cases of fine oil per year. I could obtain no statistics of the exports from Marseilles, but it is probable that the quantity exceeds that sent from Bordeaux; the quality, however, does not stand as high, owing to the fact that the Marseilles manufacturers have always endeavored to furnish a low-priced article, while those at Bordeaux sought chiefly to deal in the better qualities. Hence the fact that the Bordeaux brands are much more highly esteemed in America than those which come from Marseilles. Probably three-fourths of all the olive oil bottled in Bordeaux comes from Italy, while about one-fourth is produced in France. Little or none comes from Spain, notwithstanding the vast quantity produced there. Where it all goes is a mystery, but large quantities are consumed in Spain, where it is used for burning, cooking, and even lubricating purposes, besides quite supplanting butter as a table article. Indeed, in all oil-producing countries, butter, as an article of table consumption, is of quite secondary importance. This at first, to an American, seems quite singular, but one soon becomes accustomed to olive oil, and as fond of it as the natives themselves. I do not know why it is that Americans generally consume so little of it, unless it be that they are so dosed with castor and cod-liver oils for medicine that the very name of oil becomes disagreeable to them. Certainly the vegetable product, olive oil, compares favorably in cleanliness and healthfulness with the animal product, butter, and the dislike which some people entertain for it is wholly the result of education.

As above stated, the bottlers in Bordeaux buy the oil in large casks in a partly refined condition, and complete the process, which requires considerable experience and great care. Different bottlers produce oil of slightly different flavor, by blending the products of different sections of country, and considerable scope is afforded in this direction. As a rule, the French oil is most highly esteemed, but some of the finer Italian oils (from Tuscany) are probably as good as any in the world. The term "Virgin Oil," however, is applied exclusively to the finest quality of French production.

The green olives put up for table use by the Bordeaux bottlers are of several different varieties. The large Spanish olives, known to us as "Queen Olives," are known to the trade as "Gordalles." These, by the way, are quite a distinct variety from the other olives grown in Spain, known as "Manzanillas," which are used for making oil, the "Gordalles" having much more meat but less oil. The smaller olives put up in Bordeaux are principally of French growth, and are known as "Ammelleaux" and "Verdalles." The "Verdalles" have a strong, full flavor, and are much used for sauces, to be served with meats, while the "Ammelleaux" have a little more oil and less flavor. There is also a third variety, known as "Picholles," similar to the "Ammelleaux" in character, but larger and longer. "Olives farcies" are, as most grocers know, olives stuffed with either anchovies or capers. As a rule, the American trade prefers the "Queen Olives," on account of their size and fine appearance; but in Europe the smaller olives are quite generally preferred on account of their flavor and the finer texture of the meat.

The season for making oil lasts about six months, say from

October to April, varying somewhat in different countries. That made during the first two months is not as good as the quality produced later, being green in color, and so cloudy ("louche," in the vernacular of the trade), that no amount of refining can make it brilliant. And this quality also becomes rancid quicker than the finer oil. As a rule, the more thoroughly oil is refined and the less trace of fruity sediment there is left in it, the better it will keep. Oil should never be exposed to the heat or sun, and consequently the show window of a grocery store is about as bad a place to keep it in as can be found. Manufacturers find that it keeps best in a cool, dry place, and the larger the quantity together in bulk, the better. Large earthen jars are used to some extent for this purpose, and the larger manufacturers and dealers frequently dig huge cisterns in the ground, known as "Piles," which are carefully cemented and then filled with oil, some of them holding many thousands of gallons.

There are doubtless many other points connected with this subject which would be interesting if I could think of them, but I have just jotted down, in a somewhat disjointed way, all that have occurred to me as I wrote. It was said of Horace Greeley that his first contributions for the press, although crude, were attractive, because of their freshness and vigor, and I am therefore emboldened to send what I am well aware is a crude production, relying upon my grocer's eyes having seen, and my pen having recorded, what may be of interest to the members of the guild.

SHERRY—ITS MANUFACTURE, TREATMENT, AND CHARACTERISTICS.

If there is one thing more than another which has surprised me during my present trip, it has been to find how woefully ignorant I was of the whys and the wherefores connected with many of the different staples in which I have been dealing for years, and in regard to which I had professed to be an oracle, giving advice and affording information which I now find, in most instances, I was not qualified to give. Indeed, I think, as a rule, the average grocer knows less about the origin of the goods in which he deals than almost any other class of merchants. Perhaps this is due to the fact that grocers handle a great variety of articles from many different countries, and, besides, are usually self-made men, who have been deeply absorbed in the struggle for a livelihood, and have had their noses kept, as it were, so close to the business grindstone that they have never had much chance to investigate the pedigree of the articles in which they deal. A trip around the world, such as I have taken, teaches a man something about these things, and also geography, toleration, and his own unimportance in the great planet we live on. I have learnt something during my trip in all of these respects, and I trust that in the future I shall be not only a better merchant, but also a better citizen than before.

One of the things in which I had professed to be somewhat of a connoisseur was sherry wine, but, when I came to Spain, I found nearly everything about it new and interesting. Jerez, or Xeres, from whence the name sherry is derived, the great centre of this trade, is situated about thirty miles in the interior from Cadiz, the shipping port, and here, within a limited district, perhaps ten miles square, of hilly, rolling country, are grown the grapes from which the true sherry is made. I say true sherry, because a very large quantity of wine is yearly put upon the market, which is grown, not only in other districts in Spain, but is also manipulated into sherry at Hamburg from common German wines, and at Cette, in France, from the common white wines of that country. Some coloring, sweetening and flavoring matter, together with a little alcohol, added to the light wines of these countries, makes a tolerable imitation of the poorer qualities of Jerez wines, and vast quantities of this stuff are yearly put upon the English market, a considerable proportion also finding its way to America. Some very good wines are grown in other districts in Spain, which find their way to Jerez, and are sold as wines of Jerez growth. Some of these are excellent wines, perhaps equal, or superior in quality, to some of those grown within the Jerez district, for there is a considerable difference in the wines grown in Jerez proper. As a rule, the wine produced on the plains in the immediate vicinity of the town is of quite ordinary quality, while that grown upon the outlying hills, which have a white, chalky soil, known as "albariza," is of the finest quality. When the grapes are ripe they are picked and conveyed in panniers, slung upon the backs of mules, to the press-house, where they are thrown into large wooden vats, known as "lagares," eight or ten feet square and about two feet deep, slightly raised above the ground.

After being slightly sprinkled with gypsum to prevent excessive fermentation of the juice, they are here trodden with the feet. When sufficiently crushed they are shovelled to one side and a fresh layer of grapes is spread over the bottom of the "lagare" and again trodden until crushed, this being continued until a sufficient quantity has been accumulated to put under the press. Here they are built up in a compact mass, somewhat the same as pomace at a cider-mill, and a flat wooden slab being placed on the top, the screw is brought down with sufficient pressure to express the juice. This treading and pressing of the grapes is generally done at night, the vintage being a very busy time, usually lasting altogether a little more than two weeks. After most of the juice has been expelled from the grapes, the stalks are separated from the pressed grapes and the skins again subjected to a severe hydraulic pressure; but the product of this pressure is kept separate from that first expressed, and is usually distilled into spirits. The grape-skins are also sometimes distilled direct and the refuse used for fertilizing purposes.

The juice of the grape, or new wine, called "mosto," yielded by the first pressure, is first strained and then put into ordinary butts or casks holding about one hundred and eighteen gallons, but only filled to perhaps three-fourths of their capacity. This is so as to afford room for fermentation. The casks are then sent to the "bodegas," or wine-cellars in Jerez or the outlying towns nearest the vineyard, where the bungs are loosened and the wine is left to ferment. These are really not cellars, but immense one-story warehouses built upon a level with the ground and covered with a substantial roof of earthen tiles; each "bodega" has four or more aisles, along each of which is ranged a double row of casks, usually three tiers high. Some of these "bodegas" are of immense size, holding as many as five or six thousand casks. In February or March succeeding the vintage, the fermented wine is drawn from its lees into new casks and more or less grape spirit usually added to it; it now enters upon a period of development in which different samples of wine from the same vineyard will turn out to be of a totally different character, in the vernacular of the "bodega" being known as "palmas," "palos cortados," and the inferior wines as "entre finos" or middling fine, "bastos," rough or coarse, "redondos," round, and "abocados," mild. These latter are also often described as "single, double, and triple rayas," which grades are indicated by one, two, or three lines chalked upon the butts, these lines representing respectively first, second, and third quality. While it is possible to note a different character in the different butts of wines immediately after they are racked from the lees, yet it cannot be classified with any degree of certainty until after the third year. Those which are classed as "palmas" usually develop in the course of time into "amontillado," which, as most grocers know, is a pale, dry wine, possessing a sort of etherous flavor. The "palos cortados" in course of time become "olorosos," and are smoother, fuller, and richer in flavor than the "amontillados," and usually darker in color.

The development and ageing of the finer Jerez wines is usually carried on by a system of blending known as "soleras," which in brief consists of drawing off a portion from each cask of the older wines and replacing this with the same quantity of newer wine of similar character, which soon assimilates with and becomes as good as the older wine; in short, the old wine "eats up" the new. In this system of building up their stocks lies the chief profit of the bodega proprietors, and it enables them to maintain, for an indefinite period, uniform types of wines, upon which many of them have made a reputation and a fortune. It is only the finer wines, however, that are known as "solera" wines, by far the larger quantity shipped from Jerez being simply wines of various character from three to six years old, blended so as to fairly represent the character of wine ordered. These are frequently branded "Oloroso," "Amontillado," etc., in compliance with instructions received with the orders, but are in no way entitled to these designations, which, of course, are given them to make them *sell;* it is the old story of strong competition, with consequent misrepresentation, and the only sure guide a purchaser of sherry has, is to deal only with houses that know their business thoroughly, and have a reputation for honesty and reliability.

The range of prices here is extraordinary: one of the largest shippers in Jerez assured me that during the past season he had shipped wine ranging from £16 sterling up to £200 per butt of 118 gallons, the greater part of his business ranging, however, between £30 and £60 per butt.

All sherry is more or less sweetened before shipment by the admixture of a little "dulce" or sweet wine, which is made from a different variety of grape—the *Pedro Jimenez*—which is cultivated for this purpose. While some dealers both in England and the United States pretend to sell *natural* dry sherry, I venture the assertion that they either misrepresent or are mistaken; the finest solera wines—and I tasted some valued at £300 sterling per butt and upward—are naturally so dry that they are unpalatable even to those who are fond of the "driest" wine; and two shippers told me that although they frequently received orders for dry natural wine—the driest they had—their experience in having wines rejected for this cause had taught them that a slight blend of dulce was necessary to insure satisfaction to their customers.

A large portion of the sherry shipped from Jerez is also colored. This is done by adding a trifle of "vino de color," a very dark, heavy wine made by boiling unfermented "must" down to one-fifth of its original volume, producing a heavy, brown, bitterish syrup ("arope" or "arrope"), which is again diluted with new wine to a somewhat thinner consistency, after which it is stored away in butts to attain age before being used to deepen the color of the paler wines as above stated. Natural sherry, as seen in the Jerez bodegas, is quite a different article from that commonly sold; it is (with the exception of the old wines, which gradually acquire color from the cask) nearly as white as a Rhine wine; and, although possessing a more aromatic flavor, is equally dry.

I suppose that a description of the titillations of my palate by the rare old vintages of Jerez would scarcely be sufficiently interesting to the reader to justify my describing them in extenso. I have endeavored rather to give facts of interest to the trade than to touch upon the points which are usually most prominent in a tourist's mind, namely, his own personal sensations and experiences. I will briefly state, however, that I tasted vintages here that were three times my own age, and I must confess that my veneration for them is less now than before I tasted them. I believe that a vintage is like a human being; it requires a certain amount of time to mature, after which it begins to deteriorate. There is much humbug about very old wines. The finest wine I tasted in Jerez was an Oloroso, only about ten years old.

FRANCE.

WAYSIDE SCENES, THOUGHTS, AND FANCIES.

The moment you cross the frontier from Spain to France you begin to realize that you are in a different country. The first station in France on the international route between Madrid and Bordeaux is Hendaye, where we change from the Spanish to the French train, and the contrast is something remarkable. The railway carriages are newer, brighter, and cleaner; the refreshments served in the "buffet" quite unexceptionable; and the inspector of tickets when performing his duty greets you with a pleasant "Billets, Monsieur, s'il vous plait!" and after checking them returns them with a bow and a polite "Merci, Monsieur!" all very different from the treatment received at the hands of the Spanish officials just across the frontier. Our train, too, after it starts for Bordeaux, makes double the average speed that the Spanish trains have made, and altogether an American begins to feel that he is in a civilized country again.

Bordeaux is a commercial city in which it is quite evident to a stranger, from the large lots of goods which are constantly being moved, a heavy business is transacted; but the wholesale merchants seem to take things quite easily, going to their offices between eight and nine o'clock, and after working for two or three hours, then adjourning for "breakfast," which is here a hearty meal, equivalent to the mid-day dinner of the American people, and to this they usually devote a couple of hours. After this some of them visit the cafés, where more or less business is transacted over coffee and cigars, or perhaps a glass of absinthe or other liqueur. Dominoes and cards are sometimes brought into play here to while away another couple of hours until "'Change" time, when everybody doing a wholesale business goes "on 'Change." Here, for about an hour, business is transacted and information acquired, after which some proceed to their offices to finish correspondence, while others go to their homes, the usual dinner hour being about seven o'clock. While there are hard working exceptions to this rule, the above description fairly represents the life of an average wholesale merchant in France, but the retailers have a much harder time, their shops being kept open on an average as many hours as those of retail dealers in our country, and the men not only work themselves, but their wives and children work also. Indeed female labor in France is quite a feature. Most of the sales in retail shops of every branch of trade are made by women, and, to their credit be it said, they are, as a rule, much more industrious, energetic, and frugal than the men. In short, they are every way more self-helpful than women are in America, and it would be much better for the United States if shopkeepers generally could receive the same efficient aid from their wives and daughters that French shopkeepers do. I was much impressed with this thought on reading, a few days since, a letter from a grocer in Virginia, who remarked that his wife, in his absence, took charge of the store, and could sell and put up a bill of goods and say "thank you, sir," in as acceptable a manner to a customer as any salesman could.

It is conceded here, in France, that but for the savings of the women belonging to the lower and middle classes the milliards of the Prussian war indemnity would not have been paid so promptly as they were. And this can be readily understood when we estimate what the earnings of say 5,000,000 women are for a single year. At two francs a day for 300 days in the year only, each person would earn 600 francs, or $120, making the aggregate earnings of 5,000,000 women equal to $600,000,000 annually. Whether there is a greater or less number of laboring women than this I cannot say, but in a population of 38,000,000 this would seem not an unreasonable proportion; and certain it is that nearly every female of the lower and middle classes in France earns her bread with the labor of her hands. Among the peasantry in the rural districts the women work habitually in the field; in the towns and cities they pursue avocations in which women are usually employed in this country, besides monopolizing, to a great extent, many of the branches for which, in this country, we rely entirely upon men's labor. I would commend to the thoughtful consideration of grocers, and other small dealers who at present find it hard to get along and pay clerk hire and other expenses, whether or not they cannot get their wives and daughters to occasionally "look after the store," and thereby save the expense of an extra hand. I have not now in my mind the larger class of stores, where there is heavy work and constant occupation for two or three men, but allude more particularly to the smaller class of shopkeepers, whose business is not large, and to whom it is an important matter to keep expenses down to the lowest possible point. Are there not many such to whom a woman's assistance in looking after the interests of the store at odd times would make the difference between success and failure?

In the agricultural districts of our own country, where much butter is made under the old dairy system, farmers' wives probably work harder than do the women in the agricultural districts of France, notwithstanding there is much field work done here by women; but in other farming districts the women have comparatively easy times, and certainly the shopkeepers in America do not receive nearly the same amount of help from the women of their families as those of France do; but pardon me for this long digression on the subject of women's work. I do not mean in any way to insinuate that women in America are less willing to work than those of France, nor do I suggest that able-bodied male loafers should rest while women toil; I simply call attention to the fact that the customs of the two countries differ somewhat in this respect, and that the intelligent labor of women may be utilized to a considerable extent by grocers as well as by other shopkeepers.

From Bordeaux to Paris is a distance of three hundred and sixty miles, yet it took us but nine hours by the mail train to make this, including stops—not a bad rate of speed for even our fastest trains in America—and considering that we made one stop of thirty minutes for "breakfast," and three or four others of from five to ten minutes each, our average rate of speed could not have been far from fifty miles an hour. This is perhaps one of the most beautiful sections of this beautiful country. As we pass out of Bordeaux, for many miles the road is lined with vineyards. Further on we get into a magnificent grain-growing country, which continues all the way to Paris. Throughout this country there is but little timber, making fuel scarce; every tree is carefully trimmed, and the little branches bound together to make faggots, which are used with a degree of frugality quite at variance with the lavish use of wood in the United States. All through this section one sees the magnificent Norman horses, working in the fields, sometimes five or six of them harnessed tandem and drawing clumsy plows through the stiff soil. This is one of the items which impress the traveller as being very different from what is to be seen in Italy and Spain, where the same work is done, in Italy by oxen, and in Spain by insignificant looking mules.

Paris is a world in itself. The largest city in the world with but one exception; the most beautiful without any exception. Though situated in the interior, a great commercial city, manufacturing an endless variety of articles which, owing to their high value, are in a measure independent of cheap transportation, upon which the prosperity of other commercial cities depends. The following are some of its novel features: Long boulevards or avenues, with tall, mansard-roofed houses built to a uniform line, the upper stories of which are occupied as dwellings, while the ground-floors are fitted up with gorgeous shops; whole streets of dressmakers and tailors, with here and there a jeweler's or fancy goods store sandwiched among them. In the principal streets one sees more foreigners than natives; most of the shop doors and windows display the sign, "English spoken," and a queer American eagle, looking like a phœnix rising from its ashes, and dotted all over with stripes and stars, is also frequently depicted in the most brilliant colors to attract Americans, of whom there is always a liberal sprinkling to be found here. The cleanest streets with the smoothest of pavements; delightful parks in the suburbs for excursions; every amusement that thought or fashion can suggest; treasures of art rivalling those of Italy, and attractions in literature and science, music and the drama, such as are found nowhere else in the world, bring together at this point persons from all parts, who have the time and money to gratify their respective tastes.

In short, Paris is a city of pleasure, toward which all the pleasure-seekers of the world gravitate. Here one finds more politeness and culture, more wit and wisdom, more vice and virtue (perhaps) than in any other place on the face of the globe.

PARISIAN PECULIARITIES—HORSEMEAT AS FOOD—VISIT TO A "BOUCHERIE DE CHEVAL."

The French people are original in more ways than one. Pioneers in many of the walks of science and art, they are absolutely pre-eminent in that of alimentation, and the variety of things which they utilize as articles of food is something surprising. Dealing largely in food products, I naturally take an interest in and endeavor to be an authority upon articles in this line. So when my eye met the following article in *Galignani*, I forthwith determined to investigate its truth; if possible, visit an abattoir and see what kind of horses were utilized in the way described, and test the "nourishing" properties of horse-meat by personal experience:

HIPPOPHAGY.

"The Committee for Propagating the Use of Horseflesh as an Article of Human Food has issued the following notice: 'The prevalence of cattle disease in different countries of the Continent having determined the British Government to prohibit the importation of oxen, cows, and sheep into England, we think the public may be usefully reminded of the fact that the employment of horse-meat as an article of food has for some years made rapid progress in France. Thus, at Paris, the first butcher's establishment for that aliment having been opened in 1866, already in the following year 2,152 horses, mules, and asses had been killed for consumption; and the number rose gradually to 2,658 in 1869; 5,732 in 1872; 6,865 in 1875; and 8.693 horses, 643 asses, and 35 mules in 1876; the number of butchers' establishments for this article of food being fifty-eight on December 31st last. From Paris the use of horseflesh has spread rapidly to all the chief towns of France, and veterinary surgeons are appointed by the government to examine horses in the same way as cattle. The price of such meat is materially lower, notwithstanding the fact that it is most nourishing.

At Paris, a special committee exists, composed of philanthropists whose aim is to extend the use of this new article of food. The founder of this committee, M. Decroix, has placed at its disposal the sum of 1,100 francs and a medal of honor, to be awarded to the person who first opens and carries on an establishment in London for the sale of horse-meat. (For information address Mr. George Fleming, Veterinary Surgeon, Brompton Barracks, Chatham; or M. Decroix, 5 Rue Saint Benoît, Paris.)'"

One rainy day I set out upon this mission. My first move was to call upon M. Decroix, 5 Rue Saint Benoît, but that gentleman was absent from home—at the veterinary office of the Mounted Garde de Paris, I was told—and to the veterinary office I proceeded in search of him. Here I was again disappointed, however, in seeing M. Decroix, but a gentlemanly assistant in the office, in answer to my inquiries, kindly furnished me with the address of one of the largest horse-meat butchers, for whose office I at once started.

M. Tétard,
Boucherie de Cheval,
Rue de Paris 133,
Pantin,

was the address, and before I got there I had it vividly impressed upon me that Paris is a great city. Mile after mile we rolled along, every now and then turning into a long boulevard, which I thought must certainly be the last one. Scanning the retail butchers' shops that we passed, I occasionally saw the sign "Boucherie de Cheval" displayed, with an array of meat that looked, however, very like that ordinarily sold. Finally we reached the Rue de Paris, and following it until we reached the "chemin-de-fer de ceinture" (circular railway around the city), we passed this, also the inner line of fortifications, and I found myself at No. 133. Here, however, I only found the residence of Monsieur Tétard, the abattoir was a mile further on; this mile, however was soon traversed, and presently a long, low structure came in sight, upon which was painted "achat du cheval pour alimentation" (horses bought for food). The proprietor was absent, but, presenting my card to the person in charge, I was shown the abattoir, which was like any other establishment of the kind, except that in one corner was piled an enormous pyramid of horse-shoes of all shapes and sizes. But little meat was visible, the business of the day being principally transacted in the early morning, and the meat sold to the retail shops I had seen on my way out of the city. What I did see, however, looked very like the usual fore and hind quarters of beef—perhaps a little leaner. I was more desirous, however, of seeing what the horses looked like before being killed, and on expressing a desire to visit the stables, I was at once shown them. Here were some thirty or forty horses awaiting their fate; some of them very nice-looking ones, and some rather "hard specimens of horse-flesh." Judicious pumping of my cicerone drew out the following facts: That the horses purchased for this purpose were all of them, in one way or another, unfitted for further work; most of them were disabled by some form of accident; some had contracted diseases of the feet, and a few were debarred from further service by old age. I asked if these were not very tough? "Yes," answered the cicerone, "but they do very well for sausages." The prices paid for horses at the abattoir range from 50 to 150 francs ($10 to $30), according to size, weight, and condition, with occasionally, perhaps, extremes both lower and higher. The meat is subject to a rigid inspection by the official inspector before being marketed, but I did not learn that there was any inspection of the animals before slaughtering. This would seem also to be necessary, as some forms of disease might then be detected that would not be apparent in the meat. On an average eighteen horses per day are slaughtered at this establishment, with now and then a few asses and mules. The superintendent, with much pride, brought out for our inspection a photograph of some beasts which were exhibited at the last Paris Exhibition, and for which he received a prize "over all competitors." Speaking of competitors, there is competition even in this line, and there are several other horse-abattoirs, although that of M. Tétard is the largest. As above stated, eighteen animals per day is the average of his establishment, or say between five and six thousand per year. On the way back we stopped at one of the retail shops we had noticed coming out. Here, on the usual racks of a butcher's shop, were displayed chops, steaks, and roasting-pieces, while through a partly open door, leading to the rear of the building, I caught a glimpse of a steam-engine driving a number of sausage-meat choppers. I asked to inspect them, but was not allowed, from which I inferred that they were working up some of the ancient animals which my cicerone at the abattoir had remarked "did well enough for sausages." I bought a steak, paying therefor about fifteen cents per pound, and taking it home had it prepared as one of the entrées for that night's dinner. It was a little tough, but very good flavored meat, hardly to be distinguished either in looks or taste from an ordinary beefsteak. I do not, however, go into ecstacies over horse-meat as do some enthusiastic Frenchmen here. There can be no doubt that there are, especially in and near all large cities, many horses disabled for work that could be utilized as food, and that a considerable supply of good and cheap meat could thus be provided. To most people in this country, however, the idea of eating horse-flesh is repugnant, and it will doubtless be some time before American or English people adopt this practice to any extent. My observations in Paris led me to believe that horse-meat is mostly consumed by the poorer classes, and that the principal incentive is not its superior nourishing properties, as some enthusiasts have claimed for it, but its lower price. Our German sausage manufacturers have occasionally been accused of utilizing stray canines to increase their stock of "luscious bolognas," and here they have a material at hand which, both in quantity and quality, is preferable. I charge nothing for the suggestion.

BORDEAUX WINES—A DESCRIPTION OF THE MÉDOC DISTRICT—OFFICIAL CLASSIFICATION OF CELEBRATED VINEYARDS—A VISIT TO CHÂTEAU LAFITE, ETC.

The district where most of the wines which are exported from Bordeaux are grown is not a very extensive one, and is situated in the "Département" of the Gironde, in the southwest of France, principally within a circle of thirty or forty miles from the city. The city of Bordeaux is situated on the river Garonne, which combines with the Dordogne to form the river Gironde, some few miles below the city. The principal district for the production of red wines is situated on the south side of the Gironde, between Bordeaux and the sea, and is known as the "Médoc District." It is here that all of the celebrated vineyards are situated which have made Bordeaux wines famous all over the world. The district of Médoc is divided up into "communes," or townships, the principal of which are Pauillac, Saint-Julien, Margaux, and Saint-Estephe, although there are a dozen or more others which yield large quantities of good wines, but which are not as well known as those which I have enumerated. These "communes," or townships, furnish a general name for all the wine grown within their boundaries, but here and there are situated celebrated vineyards, the proprietors of which have erected fine châteaux, named, in some cases, after the districts in which they are situated, and in others after the family by whom they are owned. Thus, in the Margaux commune is situated the Château Margaux; in the Pauillac commune the Château Latour, and the celebrated Château Lafite; in the Saint-Julien commune, Château Léoville, Larose, and others, and in each of these communes are a considerable number of other vineyards less celebrated.

The quality of the products of all these vineyards is well known, and they are classed by the Bordeaux Chamber of Commerce as first, second, third, fourth, and fifth crûs, or qualities. The word "crû" is also somewhat indiscriminately used in the trade to designate the chief vineyards, as will be seen by the following list, copied from the official classification of the Chamber of Commerce of Bordeaux:

RED WINES.

Premiers Crûs (First Quality).

Crûs.	Communes.	Proprietors.
Château Lafite	Pauillac	Rothschild heirs.
Château Margaux	Margaux	Aguado.
Château Latour	Pauillac	de Beaumont. de Courtivron. de Flers.
Château Haut Brion	Pessac	Eugene Larrieu.

Deuxièmes Crûs (Second Quality).

Mouton	Pauillac	Baron Jas. de Rothschild.
Rauzan { Segla Gassies	Margaux	Durand. Rhone Péreire.

Crûs.	Communes.	Proprietors.
Léoville	St. Julien	Marquis de Las Cazes. A. Lalande & Erlanger. Barton.
Vivens Durfort	Margaux	de Lamar & Richier.
Gruaud Laroze	St. Julien	de Bethmann & Fauro. Baron Sarget.
Lascombe	Margaux	Chaix d'Est Ange.
Brane	Cantenac	Berger Brothers & Roy.
Pichon	Pauillac	Vicomtesse de Lavaur. Bne de Pichon Longueville. Contesse de Lalande.
Ducru Beaucaillou	St. Julien	Nath. Johnston.
Cos Destournel	St. Estephe	de Erraza.
Montrose	St. Estephe	Mathieu Dollfus.

Troisièmes Crûs (*Third Quality*).

Kirwan	Cantenac	C. Godard.
Château d'Issan	Cantenac	G. Roy.
Lagrange	St. Julien	Comptesse Duchatel.
Langoa	St. Julien	Barton.
Giscours	Labarde	J. P. Pescatore.
St. Exupery	Margaux	Core, de Boissac, Bernos.
Boyd	Cantenac	A. Lalande.
Palmer	Cantenac	Emile Péreire.
La Lagune	Ludon	Piston heirs.
Desmirail	Margaux	Sipierre.
Dubignon	Margaux	——
Calon	St. Estephe	Lestapis heirs.
Ferriere	Margaux	Vve J. Ferrieres.
Becker	Margaux	Sznadjerski.

Quatrièmes Crûs (*Fourth Quality*).

St. Pierre	St. Julien	Bontemps Dubary. de Luetkens.
Talbot	St. Julien	Marquis d'Aux.
Duluc Aine	St. Julien	Heirs of Du Luc Aine.
Milon Duhart	Pauillac	Casteja.
Bouget Lassale	Cantenac	C. Godard.
Pouget	Cantenac	de Chavaille.
Càrnet	St. Laurent	de Luetkens.
Rochet	St. Estephe	Vve Lafon de Camarsac.
Château de Beychevelle	St. Julien	P. F. Guestier, Jr.
Le Prieure	Cantenac	Mme. Rosset.
Thermes	Margaux	Oscar Sollberg.

Cinquièmes Crûs (Fifth Quality).

Crûs.	Communes.	Proprietors.
Canet	Pauillac	Cruse.
Batailley	Pauillac	Halphen.
Grand Puy	Pauillac	Mme. Vve. Lacoste and Vte. de Saint Legier.
Artigues Arnaud	Pauillac	Bne. Duroy de Suduiraut.
Lynch	Pauillac	Cayrou.
Lynch Moussas	Pauillac	Vasquez.
Dauzac	Labarde	Nath. Johnston.
Mouton Darmailhac	Pauillac	De Ferrand.
Le Tertre	Arsac	Koenigsvarter.
Haut Bages	Pauillac	Vve. Liberal.
Pedescleaux	Pauillac	Vve. Pedescleaux.
Coutenceau	St. Laurent	Vve. Brun Devez.
Camensac	St. Laurent	Popp.
Cos Labory	St. Estephe	Louis Peychaud.
Clerc Milon	Pauillac	Clerc heirs.
Croizet Bages	Pauillac	Calvé Julien.
Château de Cantemerle	Macau	Mme. d'Abadie.

WHITE WINES.

Premier Crû Superiéur (First Class, Superior Quality).

Yquem	Sauternes	de Lur Saluces (Bertrand).

Premiers Crûs (First Quality).

La Tour Blanche	Bommes	Merman & Maitre.
Peyraguey	Bommes	Cte Duchatel.
Vigneau	Bommes	de Pontac.
Suduiraut	Preignac	Guillot Frères.
Coutet	Barsac	de Lur Saluces (Bertrand).
Climens	Barsac	Ribet.
Bayle	Sauternes	Bernard.
Rieusec	Sauternes	Maye.
Rabeaud	Bommes	Drouillet de Ségalas.

Deuxièmes Crûs (Second Quality).

Mirat	Barsac	Vve. Moller.
Doisy	Barsac	Debans.
Pexoto	Bommes	Ribet.
D'Arche	Sauternes	Lafaurie, Jr., & Co.
Filhot	Sauternes	de Lur Saluces (Bertrand).
Broustet, Nérac	Barsac	Capdeville.
Caillou	Barsac	Saraute.
Suau	Barsac	Mme. Vve. Paris.
Malle	Preignac	de Lur Saluces (Henri).
Romer	Preignac	de la Myre Mory.
Lamothe	Sauternes	Massieux, and others.

By this it will be seen that of red wines there are only four vineyards, viz., Château Lafite, Château Margaux, Château Latour, and Château Haut Brion, in the first class, eleven in the second class, fourteen in the third class, eleven in the fourth class, and seventeen in the fifth class. Of the white wines, which are mostly grown a few miles above Bordeaux, on the river Garonne, there are only two divisions made in this classification, namely, premier and deuxième (first and second), but the celebrated Château Yquem is given a special class by itself, "Premier Crû Superiéur," that is, of the first class, superior quality. The principal townships, or "communes," producing white wines are Barsac, Preignac, Bommes and Sauternes, in the latter of which is situated Château Yquem, and the name of this township (Sauternes) has become so well known in connection with the production of white wines that in some markets it is quite indiscriminately applied to all white wines of French growth.

When in Bordeaux I made an excursion to the Médoc district, and being furnished with letters to the custodian of Château Lafite, which now belongs to the Rothschild family, I had the pleasure of inspecting the vineyards and cellars of this renowned château. Leaving Bordeaux by the "Chemin-de-fer du Médoc," we stopped at Blanquefort, Margaux, Saint-Julien, and finally arrived at Pauillac, a distance of thirty miles. Most of the country through which we passed was of a rolling character and covered with vines as far as the eye could reach. Taking a carriage at the station, a drive of a mile or more brought us to the château, a picturesque old structure, situated on a slight eminence, and commanding a fine view of the surrounding country. It not being the season of the vintage, we of course could not see the actual process of crushing and pressing the grape, but all the paraphernalia for this work were inspected, and we then proceeded to look at the various vintages which were stored in the cellars of the château. Perhaps I should here state that the quality of the wine produced by this celebrated vineyard is so well known that it is sold in advance, excepting the portion which is reserved by the proprietors for the cellars of the château. The bulk of the crop is seldom kept on the premises more than two seasons, by which time the fermentation is completed, and the wines are in a condition to be sent to the cellars of the purchasers in Bordeaux. The last two vintages, those of 1875 and 1876, were still on the premises, and, as a matter of curiosity, I tasted them. They were simply curious as showing what a very fine wine is in its earlier stages, as of course, they were as yet not fit for drinking.

The private cellars of the château, however, contained a collection of vintages, enough to throw a lover of Bordeaux wines into raptures. Here were collected vintages of every year from 1810 to the present time, nearly all of which were in bottle. Here one could walk for a mile or more, up one aisle and down another, flanked on either side with regular tiers of bottles containing wine, some of which was simply priceless, and of a character unique in its way. Not only are specimens of the products of the Lafite vineyard preserved here, but also those of other well known vineyards for comparison, all of which are systematically arranged, according to the various dates of production. After educating our palates we left the cellars, took a hasty glance at the soil immediately surrounding the château, picked up some of the white, flinty pebbles as souvenirs of our visit, and then, jumping into a carriage, were fortunate enough, by quick driving, to be just in time for the return train for Bordeaux, reaching the hotel in time for dinner, and delighted at being able to make the trip within the short time at command.

A MODEL ENGLISH GROCERY-STORE.

ARRANGEMENT OF STOCK, DRESSING OF WINDOWS, ETC.

In whatever line of business a man may be engaged, the shops in that line are always of interest to him: the publisher can always see a book-store quicker than any other; a manufacturer of furniture finds something to interest him in the show-windows of dealers in that branch, and I can vouch for the fact that, however carelessly I may pass by other shops, the well-dressed windows of a grocery-store always detain me long enough to take a critical glance at the arrangement and the prices which may be ticketed.

The French are eminently tasty in the arrangement of their modistes' show-rooms and windows, and dealers in fancy goods, jewelry, etc., also excel in their display and decorations; all sorts of small packages are put up in the neatest manner, but I do not think the French grocers keep up to the standard established by their brethren in other lines. While there are some handsome grocery-stores, the majority of them are small, and there is a dingy look and an air of confusion about them which does not speak well for their arrangement. The English grocery-stores, or "shops," as they are called, are larger and better arranged; show-windows are utilized to the fullest extent for display; coarse and uncleanly goods are kept out of sight, while shelf and all small package goods which have attractive labels, are arranged with a neatness and a precision which gives a cheerful look to the whole store. Taken altogether, I believe that English retail grocers are more thoroughly educated and drilled, and know their business better than those of any other country.

When in London I had an opportunity to inspect the arrangement and business system of Messrs. Leverett & Frye, leading retail grocers in London. Beginning with one store at Greenwich, in the suburbs of London, they have steadily increased their business until now they have thirteen, and every new one that is added contains in its arrangement some improvements which experience has suggested. Of those I visited, the most perfectly arranged was No. 119 Gloucester road, Regent's Park, a small corner store, but with every inch of space so well utilized that as full an assortment was kept here as in any of the larger stores. Two large show-windows were most tastefully dressed, one with canned goods and other neatly labelled packages, the other with the bottled wines of Messrs. W. & A. Gilbey, the great wine importers of London, for whom Messrs. Leverett & Frye are local agents. Only bottled wines and liquors are kept, thus avoiding the trouble, waste, and expense of breaking packages. A feature of the window-dressing was different-colored tissue-paper, cut into thin, grassy strips, and these crumpled up and laid as a garnishment between each layer of cans or bottles, gave a very pretty effect of color, and made as much of an improvement in the looks of the windows as a few green sprigs of parsley make in the looks of dishes of fish and meat when brought upon the table. This is a little thing, costs but a trifle, and if the grocer will try the experiment he will be surprised at the improved effect. In this store, also, the show-windows were shut off from the rest of the store inside by glass-doors, so that the goods placed in the windows might be protected from the dust and dirt. Along one side and at the rear of the store extend the counters, which are of mahogany, and the shelves are faced with a narrow strip of the same wood, highly polished, making them look as if they were all mahogany also. The most prominent thing behind the main counter, against the wall, are the tea-boxes, which outside are of wood, handsomely decorated and labelled, but lifting the half lid reveals a tin box the size of a chest of tea; this is to retain the flavor of the tea and prevent it absorbing that of the wood, and as the wooden fronts of the boxes are arranged to slide out, the tin box can be taken to another part of the store to be filled and then replaced in position. I forgot to state that the tea-boxes are twenty-four inches square and raised about eight inches from the floor, this space being occupied by a row of drawers, which are used for various articles. Above the tea boxes begin a row of shelves eleven inches deep; the first is also eleven inches high, and occupied with small shelf goods; then one nine inches high, where various colored papers, cut to convenient sizes and printed with the firm's name and address, are ready for use. Above this is a space of twenty-four inches, which is utilized for cans of green tea, cocoa, etc., and above this is a twenty-one inch space, which is filled with canned and other small shelf goods in great variety. Above these is the cornice, which projects over the shelves six inches, being about eighteen inches wide, and on the top of the cornice are placed cans of biscuits, and other light goods. The above describes the arrangement behind the main counter, which extends, perhaps, two-thirds the length of the store; then comes a break for a passage-way, and beyond extends a similar counter, behind which, instead of shelves, are arranged a "chest of drawers," if this expression may be allowed to describe a series of drawers, rising one above the other, something like the arrangement I have seen in many country drug-stores in the United States. In these are kept the various articles which are sold in bulk in small quantities. Under the counters are arranged, also, a series of large drawers, in which are kept sugar, roasted coffee, currants, raisins, and various farinaceous goods, the coffee-drawers being tin-lined for the purpose of preserving the flavor, and only a week's supply is furnished at a time. Every morning enough coffee of the different grades is ground for the day's supply, and kept in closed tin-canisters. A day's supply of sugar is also kept, put up in convenient-sized packages, ready for immediate delivery. Before the fruit is put into the drawers, the currants, prunes, and Valencia raisins are cleaned or "dressed;" this is done, with currants, by breaking them up, sifting them in a sieve with a square mesh about five to the inch, which lets the dirt and pieces of stems go through, and then they are sprinkled with a dressing composed of one part of molasses or syrup to say two parts of water, and shaken and rubbed about until they look clean and bright. With raisins (except bunch fruit for dessert) the same process is used, except that the meshes of the sieve are an inch long and a quarter of an inch apart—a screen rather than a sieve. Old fruit will sometimes be candied and wormy, but this process removes the worms, renovates it, and renders it fit for use. The rear of the store is occupied by hams and the coarser kinds of goods. No butter and cheese is handled by grocers here, the sale of those articles being a distinct business, and transacted exclusively by the "cheesemongers," who are quite an important class, much more so than in the United States. The English are very large consumers of cheese, no meal being considered complete without cheese with bread and butter being served as a closing course; and while they fondly cherish the illusion that England produces the best cheese in the world, by far the larger portion of their best "Cheshire" comes from the United States. But to resume my description of the arrangement of the store. A liberal floor space is kept clear for the use of customers, but along the wall opposite the counter are arranged various goods, which show well, including a few lemons, oranges, nuts, and other dessert articles. Along a portion of the front of the counter also is suspended a shallow glass-covered rack, in which is a small assortment of "fruits glacés" and choice confectionery, which is kept fresh by frequent renewals, and by the door is a "biscuit rack," in which cans of choice dessert crackers, covered with glass, are shown to the best advantage by tipping them forward, so that a person entering the store can hardly fail to see them, and, at the same time they are accessible for weighing out as wanted.

Every inch of the room "down-stairs" is utilized for storage of surplus stock, empty packages, etc., including the sugar-cutting machine, the only thing about the place which I thought inferior to our American way of doing things. The hard sugar is bought in the usual concave loaves, and cut up by hand into square lumps for the table; but our American "cut loaf," which is now being exported in liberal quantities to the English market, will soon cure them of doing business in that way.

Messrs. Leverett & Frye do business for cash over the counter or one week's credit, credit customers being furnished with a book for convenience sake, and called upon each day at their residences by a clerk, who takes and delivers their orders. Every Monday he brings back with him the amount of the previous week's account, or no more orders are filled. Deliveries are made mostly with small hand-carts, although horses and wagons are used to some extent. Mr. Leverett attends principally to the buying, and Mr. Frye to the selling and executive part of the business, visiting all the different stores daily and taking a weekly statement of business done from each one. Stock is taken every six months, and a thorough system of book-keeping shows the result of the business of each store, and also the aggregate business of the firm. It is difficult to find efficient superintendents, but they are paid by an interest in the profits, and where results are not satisfactory a change is made. A catalogue and price list is issued uniform at all their different stores, and based upon the same scale of prices as charged at the civil service co-operative stores. Messrs. Leverett & Frye have no difficulty in competing with these societies, although many small grocers who do not apply the same principles feel the competition seriously. These principles are: Buying and selling for ready money, or very close to it, local convenience of stores, free collection of orders, and delivery of goods. They estimate their gross profit at 14 to 15 per cent.

THE SALT DISTRICT OF CHESHIRE.

ENGLISH SALT, HOW IT IS MADE—DOWN IN A SALT MINE—THE DIFFERENT STRATA AND QUALITIES OF ROCK SALT IN THE CHESHIRE DISTRICT.

Leaving Liverpool by the London and North Western Railway, a ride of twenty miles brought me to the little station of Hartford, where I left the train and took a carriage for a drive through the salt district. Before reaching Hartford, however, we passed several pretty rural villages, and also the great chemical manufacturing town of Widnes. Here are situated the great works of Muspratt & Co., Golding, Davis & Co., Gossage & Co., and many others whose brands are familiar to American manufacturers and dealers, all for the manufacture of soda ash, carbonate and caustic soda, etc., and the town of Widnes, now containing several thousand inhabitants, has been created solely by this industry. Here also is situated the great bridge of the London and North Western Railway over the river Mersey, one of the engineering wonders of the age. But to return to the subject of salt. I entered a carriage at Hartford, and proceeding by an old road, dating back to the Roman period (in fact part of the old Roman highway from Chester to York), I soon reached Delamere Park, a portion of the landed estate of Lord Delamere. Here, turning off from the main road, I passed through the park, and on by a charming English back country road, skirted by picturesque straw-thatched vine-clad cottages, to the little village of Over. Here I began to see the tall brick chimneys of the salt works, and, driving down to Winsford Bridge, perhaps half a mile further, I was in close proximity to a perfect forest of these, all belching forth clouds of heavy black smoke, which fairly obscures the sun, and at all times fills the air with the black floating particles thrown off by the bituminous coal—imagine a black snow-storm on a gentle and light scale, and you have an idea of the atmosphere. This smoke is so dense and constant that it almost ruins vegetation, even the foliage of large trees being affected, so that it looks as if a blight had passed over them, withering the leaves and blackening the branches. A salt district is perhaps the most uninviting of localities, for, in addition to the blighting effect which the smoke has upon the verdure, all the houses have a dilapidated, tumble-down appearance, caused by the sinking of the earth where the salt beneath has dissolved, and has been pumped up in the shape of brine. Quite a number of ponds and small lakes have been formed in Cheshire from the earth sinking, and the depression thus formed gradually filling up with surface-drainage. These ponds and lakes are here known as "flashes." I was now in the Winsford upper section of the Cheshire Salt district, covering an extent of perhaps two and one-half square miles, and near me were the works of Verdins, Deakin, Falk, Evans, the Amalgamated Company, and a host of others. From here to the lower end of the salt district, known as Northwich, it is four or five miles, and the Northwich district comprises an area of perhaps two square miles. Between these two sub-districts are several little villages or hamlets. In the Northwich district there are situated a large number of works, among which are those of the British Company, Worthington, Ashton, and Higgin, besides a number of salt mines. Before proceeding to describe the usual process of salt-making, perhaps I ought to state what a salt mine is. In both Winsford and Northwich there are found two layers or strata of solid salt-rock, and it is supposed that these extend under a great part of the county of Cheshire. The first, or upper stratum, is found at a depth of one hundred and eighty to two hundred feet below the surface, and is about ninety feet thick. Then comes a layer of rock, three hundred and fifty to four hundred feet, when the second, or lower stratum of salt-rock is reached; this is about twice the thickness of the upper stratum, and of better quality, being cleaner and freer from impurities. The quality of the salt-rock in the same stratum also varies much, and, as a rule, the best is found at the bottom of the stratum. In opening a salt mine, a shaft is sunk until rock-salt of a satisfactory quality is reached, and then it is worked the same as a coal mine. But to give an idea of what "down in a salt mine" is, I must describe my experience. Stepping into a bucket specially prepared for visitors, the signal was given, the engine reversed, and we were lowered, or rather dropped, at a rate which gave me a rather uncomfortable, "all-gone" feeling in the region of my stomach, but in a few seconds the speed slackened, and our guide pointed out the location of the first stratum, as we slowly passed it. The speed again increased, and in a few more seconds we were at the lower stratum; but, to my surprise, instead of finding lofty chambers the entire thickness of the stratum, as I had imagined, I found only a thickness of from twelve to fifteen feet, taken out from the very bottom. From the shaft, tramways led off in every direction, and little platform cars, on which were hoisting buckets ready filled with large lumps of salt, were being drawn by horses to the shaft. Following one of these galleries, I soon found myself where the miners were at work. The salt-rock is about as hard as anthracite coal, and is worked by being blasted in the same way. Regular pillars of salt (considerably larger than Lot's wife, I fancy) are left as supports for the roof, but the salt is so solid and homogeneous that there is less danger than with coal, and these pillars are less frequent than in any coal mine I have ever visited. The air in this salt mine was also much better, being pure, dry, and cool. Here were acres and acres of cool, pure-aired galleries, which, if they could be utilized for storage by the brewers of Germany and America, or the champagne manufacturers of France, would be worth fortunes.

Ascending again to the surface, I witnessed the treatment of the salt-rock. Much of this is shipped as it is when raised from the mine, direct to Denmark, Norway, and Sweden (whose customs tariffs discriminate against refined salt), where it is refined for use. Some is crushed as soon as raised from the mine, and used in its natural state for agricultural and manufacturing purposes, and more is refined and used in various ways. The best, and by far the greater quantity of salt manufactured in the Cheshire salt districts, however, is made by pumping up the water which has come in contact with the salt strata, in many places dissolving the rock and becoming strongly impregnated with saline matter. In this way most of the earthy and insoluble matter remains below ground, and the salt manufactured turns out pure and white. As may be inferred from the above description of differences in the quality of the rock-salt, the quality of the brine also differs, that from the lower stratum being generally the best. It is pumped by steam-power into reservoirs, for the double purpose of allowing it to settle, and to have a supply in case of the pump breaking down. From thence it is run into iron evaporating pans, perhaps twenty by twenty-five feet and eighteen inches high; under these runs a furnace flue, and in about three hours the brine begins to boil; in twelve hours much salt has precipitated, and about five tons is usually taken out of each pan. This is done with a "sieve spade" (a shovel with a perforated bottom). The wet salt is thrown into conical moulds, left to drain one hour, and then taken to the drying room, where it remains five or six days in a temperature of 180° to 190°; thence to the breaking room, where it is broken up fine, and packed for shipment.

In witnessing this apparently simple process, I was tempted to say, "Well, anybody can do that," but on closer examination I found that some of the processes required as much care, skill, and experience as almost any other branch of business, and that quality of production depended, first, on the quality of the brine; second, on improved appliances and utensils; and, third, on the experience, skill, and care devoted to the business. For instance, the Ashton and Higgin Works are the only ones using iron floors for drying rooms, which, although more expensive than brick, dry more quickly, uniformly, and cleanly. They also use a different form of mould from the others, and Higgin's Works stand pre-eminent in one important feature, namely, having a set of pans for giving the brine a preliminary heating and treatment which precipitates all sediment and impurities before running it into the evaporating pans. Indeed, every part of the Higgin Works bears evidence of the care and cleanliness bestowed upon their product; every mould of salt is carefully scraped before breaking, to remove any soot or dirt which may have settled upon it; the sacks are the best that can be procured, and many similar items, small and unimportant in themselves, are carefully looked after, and doubtless in the aggregate have something to do with the popularity of this brand. The Higgin Works are owned by Thomas Higgin & Co., and the Ashton by a Mr. McDowell. The largest manufacturers in the Cheshire salt districts are the Messrs. Verdin, and, probably, Deakins' Works come next. The district has cheap transportation to Liverpool by canal and river (the Mersey), and without this the salt deposits of Cheshire would be of little value, for salt, being a heavy article of low value, will not bear high rates of transportation. Cheap coal and labor are also necessary to make salt cheaply, and in this, as well as in the quality of the brine, the Cheshire salt district is specially favored. Liverpool, doubtless, owes much of its prosperity to the salt of Cheshire, which furnishes return cargoes to a large portion of the ships bringing cargoes to Liverpool; indeed, I am told that salt is sometimes taken as ballast for nothing. The principal markets for English salt are the United States and India, but it goes, in greater or less quantities, all over the world.

THE END.

www.ingramcontent.com/pod-product-compliance
Lightning Source LLC
Chambersburg PA
CBHW031957300426
44117CB00008B/795
* 9 7 8 3 3 3 7 1 4 6 9 6 2 *